The Day Care Ritual Abuse Moral Panic

The Day Care Ritual Abuse Moral Panic

Mary de Young

McFarland & Company, Inc., Publishers
Jefferson, North Carolina, and London

LIBRARY OF CONGRESS CATALOGUING-IN-PUBLICATION DATA

De Young, Mary, 1949–
    The day care ritual abuse moral panic / Mary de Young.
      p.   cm.
    Includes bibliographical references and index.

    ISBN 0-7864-1830-0 (softcover : 50# alkaline paper) ∞

    1. Child sexual abuse. 2. Ritual abuse. 3. Day care centers.
I. Title.
    HV6570.D4   2004
    302'.17—dc22   2003026999

British Library cataloguing data are available

Cover illustration ©2004 Photodisc

Manufactured in the United States of America

McFarland & Company, Inc., Publishers
  Box 611, Jefferson, North Carolina 28640
    www.mcfarlandpub.com

In loving memory of my parents,
Ken and Doris

Acknowledgments

This book was a long time—a *very* long time—in the making. I have racked up more debts that I can ever repay or, for that matter, even remember. In the decade that it took to acquire information on the day care ritual abuse cases for this book, I have benefited from the kind and patient assistance of more librarians than, were I so inclined, I could throw books at; court clerks who cheerfully rummaged in dank basements for old and dusty files; social service and mental health professionals and attorneys who earnestly racked their brains to remember details I felt, for some reason, I just had to know; and providers, parents and former preschool enrollees who, in response to questions, relived the worst moments of their lives. I am grateful to all of them.

I am blessed with a cadre of good friends and family members who are always ready, willing and able to relieve the tedium of research and writing with social activities and a good laugh or two. For keeping things in balance, I thank them. I would also like to thank my colleagues in both the Sociology Department and the Dean of Social Sciences Office of Grand Valley State University, without whom this book would have been finished a year earlier.

Finally, I would like to thank my parents, Ken and Doris, to whose memory this book is dedicated. When I got bored and restless as a kid, they would say in unison, "Go read something"; when I got confused and puzzled about how things worked and why things happened, they would say in unison, "Go figure it out"; and when I was bothered by unfairness and injustice, they would say in unison, "Then go do something about it." Occasionally those exhortations felt like rejection, but now, older and wiser, I appreciate what very good advice it was. Thanks, Dad and Mom.

Contents

List of Tables

Preface

It was Easter Sunday, 1964, in the tatty English seaside resort of Clacton-on-Sea. The weather was bone-chillingly cold, dreary and very wet, the kind of weather, as one pundit put it, that has provided the world's most colonizing impulse. Hundreds of bored youth roamed the streets in search of distraction that was conveniently provided by a rumor that local bartenders would no longer serve them. As the rumor spread, so did the agitation. A few shop windows were smashed, a few beach huts tipped over, and scuffles broke out between the two factions of youth milling about the town on that holiday weekend: the middle class, Beatles-crazed, fashion-conscious Mods, and the working class, politically reactionary, and quite proudly delinquency-prone Rockers.

West Side Story on the English coast? Even without the Leonard Bernstein score, the two-day altercation between the Mods and the Rockers, so named by the press, had a certain theatricality. Over £500 in damage was done to property, nearly 100 were arrested. But the real drama was created by the media in the days following the incident. Local papers featured breathless first-person accounts of shopkeepers who had "survived" the "mob violence." The national press, with headlines like "Day of Terror," and "Wild Ones Invade Seaside," carried editorials urging the government to take immediate and aggressive action to quell youth violence, and quoted experts of various stripes who opined that there was indeed much to be feared from the ranks of morally bankrupt youth.

Richly resonant with the strains of Western culture—post-war ennui, deepening schisms between socioeconomic classes, clashes between generations, shifts in social values, the weakening of familial and institutional authority, expanding sexual freedom—the Clacton-on-Sea episode was widely reported by the world press. The *New York Times* featured a front page article headlined "Rival Teen-Age Gangs Terrorize British Seaside Resort," accompanied by a grainy photograph of Mods and Rockers, in an apparent moment of rapprochement, jeering at approaching police officers.

Other incidents of "youth hooliganism," as it came to be called, occurred in other English seaside resorts during the rainy spring and summer of 1964 while the British public was debating its causes and cures. Moral deterioration, liberal child-rearing and growing affluence were indicted in heated public discussion, political debates and pastoral discourses; corporal punishment, national service, stiff fines and hard labor were proposed as remedies. Legislation was hurriedly passed to give police the authority to ride suspicious youth out of town before trouble started, to increase legal penalties for malicious damage, and to empower local organizations and citizen groups to defend their communities.

Enter Stanley Cohen, a University of London doctoral student in search of a dissertation topic. While public and political attention drifted to other displays of youth hooliganism and rebellion during the tumultuous 1960's—hippies, drug-takers, dropouts, delinquents, football rowdies—Cohen was exercising his sociological imagination about the Clacton-on-Sea episode that, in his eyes, had triggered this new and pernicious demonization of English youth. What struck him about that episode was not the altercation, which was minor, but the immoderate reactions to it. Hostile, volatile, repressive and often irrational, those reactions, in his assessment, had all the hallmarks of a moral panic.

In his 1972 book *Folk Devils and Moral Panics: The Creation of the Mods and Rockers,* a reworking of the doctoral dissertation he finally wrote, Cohen describes a moral panic in these terms:

> Societies appear to be subject, every now and then, to periods of moral panic. A condition, episode, person or group of persons emerges to become defined as a threat to societal values and interests; its nature is presented in a stylized and stereotypical fashion by the mass media; the moral boundaries are manned by editors, bishops, politicians and other right-thinking people; socially accredited experts pronounce their diagnoses and solutions; ways of coping are evolved (or more often) resorted to; the condition then disappears, submerges or deteriorates and becomes more visible. Sometimes the subject of the panic is quite novel and at other times it is something which has been in existence long enough, but suddenly appears in the limelight. Sometimes the panic passes over and is forgotten, except in folklore and collective memory; at other times it has more serious and long-lasting repercussions and might produce such changes as those in legal and social policy or even in the way society conceives of itself [p 1].

The term "moral panic" has the unfortunate tendency to conjure up images of folks frantically fending off more demons than hell can hold, but Cohen asks that it be appreciated in its sociological sense, a request that over the years has served sociologists well. The concept has been used as a tool for analyzing, among other things, both religious and political witch-hunts, temperance movements and drug panics, anti-pornography and censorship campaigns, law and order crusades and public health battles, all of which have the effect of defining and defending the moral boundaries of society, establishing moral authority, tightening moral regulation, and creating moral certainties in an age of what seems to be moral decline.

In the 30 years since the publication of Cohen's book, the term "moral panic" has been facilely appropriated by media pundits, social commentators, and the public at-large, and its casual use has divested it of much of its sociological relevance. And that is really a shame. It is a robust term, and the theory that surrounds and supports it, although a tad faded and frayed, still has a great deal of explanatory and analytical power.

This book is an attempt to reclaim the term and make-over moral panic theory through the process of using it to analyze the day care ritual abuse moral panic of the 1980's. During that decade, a hundred or more day care centers and preschools around the country were investigated for what many believed was a new, or at least newly discovered, sex crime—ritual abuse. Now, ritual abuse is a remarkably protean term, as this book explains; it seems to be different things in different cases, and to different people. In the early years of the moral panic, the word "satanic" was appended to it, but that adjective fell out of favor after repeated failed attempts to prove the providers accused of it were, in fact, devil worshippers or satanic cultists. Even stripped of the adjective, the term retains its devilish connotation. It describes acts of sexual, emotional and physical abuse conducted as part of, or in conjunction with, such ghastly ceremonies and rituals as infant sacrifice, blood-drinking and cannibalism.

The folk devils in this moral panic are day care providers. How they came to be folk devils in the first place is elaborated upon in the book through the lens of moral panic theory, but the important point here is that the term "provider" is, itself, a somewhat protean term in this book. Not all of the accused who are discussed were directly involved in the daily care of young children; some were spouses of providers who had occasional interactions with the children, others were friends of providers who stopped by for a visit every now and then, or custodians who swept the halls the children ran through. What might forgive this rather economic use of the term "provider" is that the various roles the accused play are evidence of how the moral panic was contained within a specific locus—the local day care center—and of how it spread within it. Both the containment and the spread are matters of considerable concern to this book.

Stanley Cohen's somewhat literary description of a moral panic sets out elements for analysis: a perceived threat, the identification of a folk devil responsible for the threat, a rapid buildup of public concern, a response from officials, resulting social change. But as this book explains, the best analysis of just those elements would render only an incomplete and unsatisfying explanation of the day care ritual abuse moral panic. To really appreciate it for the fascinating slice of cultural history it really is, more than just this skeletal list of elements has to be considered. So this book examines how the threat of ritual abuse was discursively constructed out of the anxieties and social stresses of the era, by whom, and why; how the persuasiveness of this discourse recruited others into the belief that ritual abuse is a real and exigent threat, despite the repeated failure to find evidence to corroborate it; how they acted on that belief and with what consequences. It looks critically at the role of one particular interest group—called, in this book, the child-savers to denote both its eclectic composition and its shared concern—and treats its members as cultural intermediaries, of a sort, and examines new roles minted during the moral panic. It examines the mass media, communities, professional organizations, systems of social control, and a whole host of different social audiences as they responded or contributed to the moral panic. And the book analyzes the way that images of those critical to the panic—the children, the providers, and the child-savers—were massaged and manipulated to achieve both ideological and material ends, as well as how culturally significant signs and symbols were used and abused to further those ends.

The list of elements of a moral panic derived from Cohen's description misleads in another way: it suggests that moral panics proceed in a logical, step-by-step fashion over time. The day care ritual abuse moral panic did not. Instead, it ricocheted around during the decade, bouncing in fits and starts from one place to another. The simple act of narrating it imposes an order that the day care ritual abuse moral panic never really had. Between the lines of this book lurks the chaos and confusion that narration could not capture.

The children who were the alleged victims of day care ritual abuse are never named in this book, even if they were in the media—they are entitled to their privacy. Accused providers and child-savers are, however, and although this is, of course, a book about who people are and what they say and do, it is not intended to be read as a work of investigative journalism or an exposé. It is, in keeping with the tradition set out by Stanley Cohen, a sociological treatise to be read most satisfactorily with a fully exercised sociological imagination that appreciates the existence of a reciprocal relationship between social structure and human behavior, values and beliefs; the past and the present; the private and the public; and the real and the imagined.

1

Scenes from the Zeitgeist

Hundreds of young children, all past or current enrollees in the McMartin Preschool in Manhattan Beach, California, accuse their provider of sexually abusing them during "naked games" in subterranean tunnels beneath the center. An expert witness explains to an Austin, Texas, jury that the defendant in a sexual abuse trial is using hand signals to cue a recantation from the child who is testifying against him. In Edenton, North Carolina, an award-winning documentarian reveals the tangled skein of rumors about devil worship and infant sacrifice that led to the arrests of seven local citizens. And in the mill town of Rochdale, England, a common-law couple living on a rundown estate demand the return of their children, snatched by social workers in a dawn raid and taken into care.

How are these fantastic and far-flung vignettes related? Certainly not by place. Like many beach towns in southern California, Manhattan Beach often is described in terms of "miles from"—three short miles from the airport, nineteen miles from downtown Los Angeles and, in its easy-going pace, a million miles from Austin. That "Best City for Business in North America," in turn, is not even linked by a direct flight to Edenton. The two places have nothing in common. Austin is as spirited as Edenton is somnolent, as anxious to prove itself as Edenton is content to luxuriate in its esteem as "The South's Prettiest Small Town." And none of these places is linked to Rochdale where a fabled history is an enchanting distraction from the gritty working class environs.

Nor are these vignettes linked by person. Peggy McMartin Buckey, the preschool teacher, was a bespectacled matron with a penchant for colorful muumuus and flashy jewelry. The expert witness, psychologist Dr. J. Randy Noblitt, is more interested in the mind than in appearances and is unshakeable in his conviction that an evil menace is stalking the world's children. Ofra Bikel, the documentarian, believes in evil too, but the banal kind that comes from the best intentions of misguided and myopic people. And the common-law couple, never publicly identified, find in the answer to the well-worn riddle, "What's the difference between

5

a Rottweiler and a social worker?" the reason for their plight: "With a Rottweiler you have at least half a chance of getting your kids back."

If these vignettes are not linked by person or place, they are by time, or at least a stretch of time near the end of the millennium. The 1980s had its share of social problems and economic crises, threats to established institutions, and challenges to comforting ideologies and dearly held values. To paraphrase novelist Angela Carter, the *fin* came a little early that *siècle*. American society expressed its millenarian anxiety in strong opinions, nostalgic desires, crippling fears and irrational moral panics. It is one of those moral panics, in fact—this one about the ritual abuse of young children in day care—that most solidly links these vignettes.

It Must Be Real After All

So just what is this thing called ritual abuse? To date, there still is no consensus definition of it, no agreement as to what it comprises or, for that matter, what comprises it (Gallagher, 2000; Jones, 1991; Lloyd, 1992). No material evidence has ever been found to substantiate cases of it or to confirm theories about it (Lanning, 1991; LaFontaine, 1998; Medway, 2001). After a decade's worth of controversial day care cases in the United States and a smattering of similar cases in sundry settings around the world, more than a little question remains as to whether ritual abuse exists at all outside of late modern culture's Gothic imagination.

Ah, but it certainly has its proselytizers. And since it is discourse, that is, both written and spoken statements that designate, label, typify, organize thinking, and direct action (Foucault, 1977), that narrate this moral panic, what these social workers, mental health clinicians, survivor support groups, religious fundamentalists, feminists and law enforcement officers say and write is worth listening to. They agree the "abuse" of ritual abuse is sexual in nature: young children, they say, are fondled, fellated, raped or sodomized, and all manner of frighteningly sharp objects are inserted into every orifice (Gould, 1992; Hudson, 1991). The "ritual" of ritual abuse, they also agree, is carried out in satanic or satanic-like ceremonies that involve acts of cannibalism, blood-drinking and infant sacrifice (Hill & Goodwin, 1989), live burials and forced impregnations (Young, Sachs, Braun, & Watkins, 1991), and confinement inside animal carcasses and upside-down hangings that parody the crucifixion (VOICES in Action, 1991).

One rhetorician claims that the ritual abuse of children can be traced to prehistory and is depicted in Paleolithic cave drawings (DeMause,

1994). Others variously trace it to 4th century satanic cults (Hill & Goodwin, 1989), medieval witch covens (Feldman, 1995), African religions (Noblitt & Perskin, 1995), Freemasonry, Mormonism, occultism and paganism (Kent, 1993), and even to a Faustian bargain between an Hasidic Jew and his Nazi captors (Hammond, 1992).

And the consequences of these ghoulish acts for the children? A veritable grab bag of maleficent sequelae is posited, from somatic complaints, social withdrawal and sexual problems (Kelley, 1989), hyperactivity, eating disorders and multiple personalities (Cozolino, 1989), self-hypnosis, self-mutilation and dissociation (Valente, 1992), body image dissatisfaction and post-traumatic stress disorder (Kelly & Ben-Mier,1993), to aversion to the color black, preoccupations with ghosts and goblins, and fascination with passing gas (Gould, 1992).

Ritually abused children, some say, have a guarded prognosis. Others go on to insist that their future is made all the more terrible by the way in which their free will is contravened. The horrific rituals not only assault their young bodies but numb their minds, brainwashing them to respond in the most self-destructive ways to the most innocuous stimuli. A stuffed animal, for example, can trigger self-mutilation, a simple phrase like "I love you" can incite a suicide attempt, or a hand signal can cue the appearance of an uncooperative alternate personality (Gould & Graham-Costin, 1994; Young, 1992).

Ritual abusers, they say, are satanists who lurk behind the friendly façade of the neighborhood day care provider. They are aided and abetted by "physicians, psychiatrists, psychotherapists, principals and teachers, pallbearers and morticians, public workers, police, politicians and judges, priests and clergies of all religions" who procure the children, destroy the evidence, thwart discovery and silence disclosure (Braun, 1988). This cabal of satanists is organized into local, regional, district and national cells (Braun, 1988). Perhaps it is also internationally organized through the auspices of the Central Intelligence Agency, the military, the Mafia, the World Bank, and the captains of industry and head honchos of the entertainment business—satanists all, and all of them bent on taking over the world by "creating an army of Manchurian candidates" out of ritually abused children; "tens of thousands of robots who will do prostitution, do child pornography, smuggle drugs, engage in international arms smuggling, do snuff films, all sorts of very lucrative things" that will advance the new satanic world order (Hammond,1992).

If they are satanists, then they have company. There are, depending on who is doing the counting, anywhere from 500 to 8,000 satanic cults across the United States, claiming anywhere from 100,000 to over a million devotees (Brennan, 1989; Schwarz & Empey, 1988). The cults ritually abuse over 10,000 children every year, ritually sacrifice another

50,000, and follow a calendar that has over a 100 ritual days (Larson, 1989; Ryder, 1992). If they cannot get children from day care centers, they kidnap them, or procure them from orphanages, hospital maternity wards, abortion clinics and computer bulletin boards (Michaelson, 1989). Or they breed them. The satanists are said by some to impregnate their young captives only to sacrifice their newborn infants, and in rituals that are the epitome of evil, drink their blood and eat their flesh (Sachs, 19980; Stratford, 1988).

Or, perhaps, ritual abusers are not really quintessentially evil after all. Perhaps they have only identified with evil as a consequence of their own "childhood abuse, sexual repression, or some other humiliation" (Finkelhor & Williams,1988, pp. 63–64). Perhaps they only use the trappings of satanism to terrorize their young victims and assure their silence (Schumacher & Carlson, 1999). Maybe they are really nothing more than dabblers, psychopaths looking for the *frisson* of excitement that frolicking with evil affords (Feldman, 1995).

About one thing, however, the rhetoricians speak as one. Ritual abuse is a "serious problem to us as a nation" (Gould, 1995, p. 34), in fact, "the most serious threat to children and to society that we must face in our lifetime" (Summit, 1990, p. 39).

Well, if not serious, it is at least an interesting threat. It is a threat constructed by discourse, its contradictions and discrepancies made unimportant by the urgency of its appeal. It is a threat that begs explanation, a call to which social workers, mental health clinicians, survivor support groups, religious fundamentalists, feminists and law enforcement officers have hastily responded, creating by doing so the kind of explanation that social critic Frederic Crewes (1995) would describe as "a bewildering but handsomely ecumenical palimpsest of accommodative gestures" (p. 23). It is a threat reified by repetition in seminars, conferences, professional journals, the mass media and courtroom testimony, and by its resonance with the fears and anxieties of 1980s America. It is a threat repellant to criticism. After all, if ritual abuse has the innocent victims and the evil perpetrators, the horrific sequelae and the deep historic roots that so many say it has, then it must be written and talked about. If it poses an exigent threat to children and to society like so many claim it does, then it must be acted against. So, by the same imperative, after all is said and done, it *must* be real after all.

So real had ritual abuse become during the 1980s that it fueled a virulent moral panic that targeted day care centers in major cities and small towns across the United States. Over a hundred centers were investigated and scores of providers were arrested and put on trial. From the witness stand their accusers, the three and four years olds once entrusted to their care, described horrific acts of sexual abuse, ghastly ceremonies and bizarre rituals. Despite the absence of compelling corroborative evidence, many providers were convicted and to the cheers and jeers of their deeply divided communities were sentenced to what often were draconian prison terms, only to have their convictions quietly overturned years later. Of those child-savers[1] who interviewed the children, testified on their behalf in court, consulted with and trained colleagues in the detection and treatment of ritual abuse, spoke at conferences in the United States and abroad, and acted as media mouthpieces, some survived that tumultuous decade with reputations intact; others fared not nearly as well. And the young accusers, now adolescents or even young adults, these days credit either their unerring memory or their macabre imagination for their recollections of childhood ritual abuse.

THE CULTURAL CAULDRON

Every moral panic has its start in social stresses and strains, and there were plenty of those roiling about in the cultural cauldron of the 1980s. Double digit inflation, 15 percent mortgage interest rates, a bloated federal budget deficit and the highest unemployment rate in forty years threw the country into a recession at the decade's start. The stock market rebounded eventually, finishing above 2,000 for the first time ever, but the same "voodoo economics" that was credited for the turnaround was vilified only months later when the market plummeted 508 points on Black Monday, that dark day when the word "Depression" was anxiously bandied about for the first time in half a century.

The "Evil Empire" that was the Soviet Union loomed large and menacing in cultural imagination. While the government proposed spending $500 billion to create a defense shield of lasers, swarmjets, particle beams and plasmoids to protect citizens from Soviet nuclear warhead missiles, those same citizens, in a curious act of synchronicity, made "The Empire Strikes Back" one of the top grossing films of the decade.

There was an assassination attempt on the President of the United States, not by a communist sympathizer, but by a homegrown madman. And there were assaults on democracy, itself, by those sworn to uphold it. Lies were told, laws broken, people killed, arms traded for hostages, and for much of the 1980s the terms "ABSCAM" and "Iran-Contra Affair" were synonymous with the disgrace of government.

Others fell from grace, too. Televangelist Oral Roberts said he was being held hostage by the God he worshipped until his followers contributed $8 million to his ministry. Jim and Tammy Faye Bakker turned religion into tragicomedy, and Jimmy Swaggart turned sanctimony into hypocrisy. Born-again Christians were called out to vote *en masse* and were rewarded with the election of a President who pronounced that religion and politics "are necessarily related." The Moral Majority set out a political and social agenda to win the hearts and minds of the body politic, unfazed by the occasional bumper-sticker that read, "The Moral Majority Is Neither."

From the very start of that decade, Americans grappled mightily with the moral quandaries posed by the social, political and economic issues of the day. A 1980 public opinion poll[2] found that 60 percent of respondents believed that pornography leads to the moral breakdown of society; 73 percent agreed that homosexuality is always morally wrong; 59 percent said Communism is the most immoral form of government; and 66 percent had more confidence in their churches and synagogues than they did in the military, big business, the Congress or the United States Supreme Court. And in another curious act of synchronicity, the 1980 American Book Award was given to *Sophie's Choice*, that quintessential tale of moral relativism.

The madding crowd had its say, too. Over that decade African-Americans declared the criminal justice system unjust, the poor declared federal cuts in welfare unscrupulous, citizen groups declared medical research using human fetuses unethical, and educators declared the banning and burning of "objectionable" books unconscionable. The same year the Prayer Rally for Jesus drew a quarter of a million people to the nation's capitol, the National Organization for Women marched for passage of the Equal Rights Amendment. It died aborning, just three states shy of ratification in 1982, the same year that the number of day care centers had increased 233 percent from just five years before in response to the needs of women with young children who were flooding the work force.

The personal computer graced desks in offices and homes. Americans wore acid washed jeans and shoulder pads while they surfed the net and became citizens of a new global electronic village that grew up around it. They learned a language of abbreviations like DOS, URL, RAM and ROM, and sneaked epigrams like "Let me process that" and "I'm on sensory overload" into everyday speech.

Americans just said no to drugs and wondered who shot J.R. They played with Rubick's Cubes and Cabbage Patch Dolls and listened to the musical pabulum of ABBA and Kenny Rogers, and they watched the world unfold before them on a new television station called CNN.

There they saw the Berlin Wall fall, the Challenger space shuttle explode, and tanks immobilized by student protestors in Tiananmen Square. They watched in awe as the "Evil Empire" lost its luster in uprisings in faraway places like Hungary, Bulgaria and Poland, and in admiration as American troops invaded Grenada and later Panama. They heard about a virus called HIV and a disease called AIDS and refused to believe that in this scientifically advanced decade there could ever be anything so medieval as an epidemic. On other channels they watched Oprah, Phil, Sally Jesse and Geraldo and listened to perfect strangers tell their most intimate secrets to millions of other perfect strangers.

Some of those secrets were about child abuse. Reported cases doubled from the previous decade and a once secret, shameful thing called sexual abuse became the most public of commodities. Celebrities revealed childhood histories of it, made-for-television movies featured it, survivors wrote tell-all autobiographies about it, and a new group of experts on it seemed to emerge out of nowhere. Social workers, mental health clinicians, advocates and survivors claimed expertise, and Americans heeded their call to resurrect and resolve the traumas of their own childhood by spending as much as $10 billion for counseling each year of that decade.

"*Repose Taboo'd by Anxiety*"

About this trip down memory lane, many sociologists would respond, "So what?" Every decade has its strains and stresses, its scarlet threads of scandal and tragedy that sometime make previous decades seem idyllic in comparison. The very process of modernization, after all, increases risk and the awareness of it (Beck, 1992; Giddens, 1991). The issue is not so much that there are deep and complicated social strains and stresses, but that simpler, more accessible "master symbols" come to stand in proxy for them (Hunt, 1999). When these master symbols then are discursively linked by interest groups, the social anxiety each generates is amplified, and the need to do something, and quickly, to address the threat seems all the more exigent (Hall, Critcher, Jefferson, Clarke, & Roberts, 1978). So the first step in understanding the day care ritual abuse moral panic is pulling out of the roiling cultural cauldron of the 1980s these master symbols. There are three of particular importance: the vulnerable child, the menacing devil, and the psychological trauma model—a troika of secular, sacred and theoretic master symbols of the decade.

The Secular: The Vulnerable Child. During the tumultuous 1980s the master symbol of the vulnerable child stood in proxy for the discomfiting changes occurring in the family and in the traditional gender roles that sustain it. As a foundational social institution the family always has been a weathervane, of sorts, for social change. Consequently, every generation recreates family patterns as it reacts to, accommodates or resists the deeper and more complex social, political, economic and ideological forces of the era that impinge upon it. Each shift in family pattern, in turn, recreates a cultural image of childhood and of the embodied children who occupy it (Christensen, 2000), of threats to their safety and well-being (Best, 1990), as well as an aching nostalgia for what always is remembered as better childhoods of the past (Jenks, 1996).

The baby-boom generation that came into its own in the 1980s created its own unique family patterns. More liberal in its attitudes and values than its parent generation, it had higher rates of cohabitation, divorce and out-of-wedlock births; more economically strained, it had later marriages, more dual income marriages, fewer children and more critical decisions about their care than its parent generation (Waite, 2000).

It is from the collision between the latter two family patterns—dual income marriages and child care—that the master symbol of the vulnerable child emerged. The economic strains of the 1980s that made participation in the market economy a necessity for most families, and the ideological force of feminism that made it an increasingly attractive alternative to unpaid housework, combined in that decade to put more and more women with young children into the work force. At the decade's start a record 45 percent of them were working outside of the home; at its end, that figured increased to 54 percent (Hofferth & Phillips, 1991).

The question of what to do about the daily care of its young children vexed the baby-boom generation. Despite the rapid proliferation of day care in private homes and church basements, quality, licensed and regulated day care was difficult to find. Deep cuts in federal funding that over half of the public day care centers had received just a few years before had closed down many of them, leaving those that remained with high enrollment fees, too many enrollees and, because of low wages and even lower occupational prestige, too few qualified providers and high staff turn-over (Phillips, Howe, & Whitbrook, 1991). Trapped between necessity and contingency, working parents more often settled for, rather than chose, available day care and reluctantly began transforming the almost sacred convenantal duty of caring for their children into businesslike contractual relations with day care providers (Bromley & Busching, 1989).

Most working parents, especially mothers, did so with more than a little anxiety and considered day care centers a change for the worse from the stay-at-home care of their parents' generation (Hutchison, 1991). Their anxiety was heightened by widely circulated neighborhood gossip about toddlers in soiled diapers forlornly waiting for the attention of indifferent providers in overcrowded centers, and by parents' magazine exposes with provocative titles like, "'Mommy, Don't Leave Me Here!' The Day Care Parents Don't See" (Fallows, 1985), "Do Working Mothers Cheat Their Kids?" (Brown, 1985), and "Can You Work and Have a Happy, Healthy Child?" (Mittenthal, 1985).

The same questions were being asked by social scientists and pedagogues who actively debated the emotional, social, intellectual and moral consequences for children of extended stay in day care. For every thrust there was a parry: studies that found more deleterious effects of day care than salutary were countered by those that with the same confidence found just the opposite (Belsky, 1980; Etaugh, 1981; Zaslow, 1991). Although not of one mind as to the consequences of day care, the experts agreed that the development of young children would be perhaps irreparably compromised by the absence of nurture and love, regardless of the context.

Sensitive to the rising social anxiety about vulnerable children in day care, many centers packaged themselves as a home-away-from-home, using educational toys to stimulate the mind, play-ground equipment to develop the body, community excursions to heighten social awareness and, only when needed, just the right touch of discipline to correct behavior. But no day care center could ever guarantee that a child would be nurtured and loved. It was this reality—that the affectivity necessary for healthy development is non-negotiable—that only heightened social anxiety about vulnerable children.

The Sacred: The Menacing Devil. The process of "unnaming evil" began centuries ago (Delbanco, 1995, p. 4), but it may have ended in the 1980s. Rationalized, psychologized, internationalized, secularized, satirized and trivialized, by that decade the old and resonant idea of evil had been stripped of its denotative dignity and no longer boldly marked the moral contours of late-modern American society.

In the apocalyptic vision of a burgeoning group of conservative Christians, there was plenty of evidence of America's imminent moral collapse. As religious scholar Robert Fuller (1995, p. 173) points out, from the perspective of the New Christian Right:

> Twentieth century American culture had evolved in ways that have proved to be a nightmare for the nation's premillennial population. The "baby-boom" generation has been raised in an era that glamorizes all that dare to call traditional religious values into question. Humanistic psychologies have made self-actualization the goal of human existence. Existential philosophies have boosted the virtue of self-gratification over communal commitment. The media have glorified promiscuous sexuality. The advertising and film industries have made both alcohol and drugs seem sophisticated. Rock music has voiced defiance of authority and glorified unreflective spontaneity and impulse-driven behavior. The feminist movement has undermined traditional authority structure and stripped males of their once unrivaled access to the sources of social power.

To regain its moral bearings American society needed a strong sense of evil, and the new Christian Right provided it in the form of its ancient and familiar personification, the devil. This revivified devil, upon whom the disconcerting social strains and stresses of late-modernity could be blamed, and against whom an end-times battle for hearts and souls would be waged, became another of the master symbols of the1980s.

This was a peculiarly secularized personification of the devil, and therefore appealing as a master symbol to believers and unbelievers alike (Woodman, 1997). Not only was he cavorting in the social and political affairs of the nation, according to the New Christian Right, but he was finding mischief within the American family. What better evidence of that dalliance was there then the disconcerting changes in the family in the face of the forces of modernization, humanism and secularism? If the devil aimed to triumph, the New Christian Right insisted, he would do so by breaking the spine of that most foundational of social institutions, the family, leaving its children vulnerable to his influence (Robison, 1980).

So it was the New Christian Right, more socially attentive and polit- ically active than any religious movement before it (Hadden & Shupe, 1981), that first discursively linked two of the master symbols of the decade—vulnerable children and a menacing devil—and, in doing so, heightened social anxiety about both. That anxiety gave impetus and legitimacy to the New Christian Right's agenda to protect children from the influence of the devil. Divorce, dual income marriages and day care were seen as evidence of his handiwork and were the favored targets of righteous indignation, but so were abortion, feminism, the teaching of evolution, the Constitutional ban on school prayer, homosexuality, drug use, pornography and sex, each stamped a "pro-child" issue and then discursively linked to end-times eschatology (Jorstad, 1987; Lorentzen, 1980; Wilcox, DeBell, & Sigelman, 1999).

To get this message across, the New Christian Right relied on a vast infrastructure of churches, prayer groups, bookstores, radio and televi- sion programs. By mid-decade there were over a thousand religious radio stations, three Christian television networks and twenty-two religious television stations, reaching an audience of over sixty million Americans each day (Mackenzie, 1987). At that same point in time, the number of religious bookstores had doubled from the previous decade, selling over $600 million in books, for nearly one-third of the commercial book mar- ket (Edmondson, 1988).

In the eyes of the New Christian Right, the devil was a formidable foe. But "to discover the devil—in a sense both literal and metaphoric," writes John Demos (1982) in whose work on the 17th century witch-hunts can be found striking parallels to the 20th century ritual abuse moral panic, "involves the naming, locating, the making tangible of what hith- erto seemed obscure" (pp. 129–130). The exhortations of the New Chris- tian Right may have created a master symbol in the form of a revivified devil, but it left to dark imaginings the demonology of his worship. The task of making the obscure tangible was assumed by the authors of popular Christian books, the self-proclaimed former satanists now born again, and the devout law enforcement officers who carved out careers in a new specialty called "occult crimes" that included everything from cemetery desecrations, to cattle mutilations, to serial murders (Hertenstein & Trott, 1993; Hicks, 1991; Passantino & Passantino, 1992).

These crusaders created a wholly factitious demonology that incautiously mixed folkloric and popular culture images of devil worship, satanism, witchcraft, paganism and occultism with the apocalyptic images of evil from the teachings of the New Christian Right (Ellis, 2000). Replete with descriptions of rituals, roles, rules, holidays, signs and symbols, this demonology transformed satanism, its term for all things devilish or occult, into a real and exigent threat to vulnerable children and to society-at-large.

Public opinion polls, those barometers of "the mob's fear," as pundit H.L. Mencken once wrote, reveal the social anxiety embodied within the master symbol of the menacing devil. Of those questioned in national polls in the mid–1980s, 68 percent believed the devil was real, 60 percent felt that devil worship was a very serious or somewhat serious problem in American society, and 55 percent opined that the threat posed by this problem had significantly increased over the previous five years.

The Theoretic: The Psychological Trauma Model. In contemporary culture, psychological trauma is both a clinical syndrome and a trope. The syndrome first was set out in the form of the diagnosis of Post-Traumatic Stress Disorder in the 1980 edition of the *Diagnostic and Statistical Manual of Mental Disorders*, the nosologic bible of mental health clinicians. Its appearance was due to the concerted efforts of a cadre of clinicians and Vietnam War veterans to introduce something akin to war neurosis into official nomenclature (Lembcke, 1998). With its symptoms of intrusive memories and distressful dreams of the traumatic event, sleep disturbance, difficulties in concentration, numbed responsiveness to the world and constricted affect, the diagnosis was well suited for the "crazy Vietnam vet" that by 1980 had become a disturbing American archetype (Young, 1995, p. 108).

Psychological trauma is also a trope. The 1980s, filled as it was with pervasive fears about the future, a creeping sense of ontological insecurity, a welling anxiety about real and imagined risks and threats plaguing collective well-being, found in psychological trauma a perfect trope for "account[ing] for a world that seems increasingly out of control" (Farrell, 1998, p. 2). As such, the very idea of psychological trauma was appropriated, used, manipulated, reinforced and rewarded by any number of interest groups organized around their own sense of injury and injustice. As a result, the diagnosis of Post-Traumatic Stress Disorder was generously extended to survivors and witnesses of traumatic stressors other than war, such as crime, natural or technological catastrophes, accidents, and even political oppression, ethnic cleansings, homelessness, poverty and racism (Marsella, Friedman, & Spain, 1996). But it was feminists who first appreciated its relevance for victims of the gender war on the domestic front and who discursively linked the master symbol of the psychological trauma model with that of vulnerable children by turning their attention to sexual abuse.

Forging that discursive link proved a daunting challenge to feminists. Sexual abuse, more than any other kind of traumatic event, has been subject to the social processes of silencing and denial, even by those whose vocation it is to repair the wounded psyche. Consider Sigmund Freud— feminists certainly did. The father of psychoanalysis cast aside his own insight that child sexual abuse was the cause of his female patients' hysteria for a less plausible, but more palatable, theory that it was really little girls' repression of forbidden sexual desires for their fathers that was the origin of hysteria (Masson, 1984). Eager to not repeat the "Freudian error," as this theoretical sleight-of-hand came to be known, feminists worked to create a culture of belief to work against the historic culture of denial.

This new culture of belief invited a spate of autobiographic accounts written by women who refused to stay silent about their traumatic experiences of child sexual abuse. With chilling titles like *Father's Days* (Brady, 1979), *Daddy's Girl* (Allen, 1980), and *I Never Told Anyone* (Bass & Thornton, 1983), these mass-marketed books turned up the volume of public discourse about sexual abuse. That those who read them still struggled with the impulse to silence and deny is illustrated by one critic's devastatingly *ad feminen* review of *Kiss Daddy Goodnight* (Armstrong, 1978), the first and arguably the best, of the survivor autobiographies: "[I]t will put you off any kind of sex for a while. I don't mean that incest should not be discussed. I just don't think it should be wallowed in for the sake of titillation" (Sokolov, 1978, p. 20).

Sexual abuse indeed was wallowed in during the 1980s. Dramatized in made-for-television movies, discussed *ad nauseam* on television talk shows, confessed by celebrities, featured in hundreds of magazine articles, child sexual abuse not so much influenced social consciousness as changed it (Beckett, 1996; Champagne, 1998). And as if that were not enough, its new cultural profile produced "a staggering array of clinicians and counselors and therapists and researchers and authorities and experts, all with their careers sighted on one aspect or another" of the psychological trauma of child sexual abuse (Armstrong, 1994, p. 77).

In all of the cultural cacophony over sexual abuse during that decade, there was another leitmotif that problematized the discursive link between the master symbol of the psychological trauma model and that of vulnerable children: the belief that children are as reluctant to talk about the trauma of sexual abuse as mental health clinicians are to hear about it. This belief was reified in an influential paper by psychiatrist Roland Summit (1983) who would go on to become the ideologue-in-chief of the day care ritual abuse moral panic. Summit, who had little clinical experience with either psychological trauma or children, nonetheless discursively linked the two with the concept of the "child sexual abuse accommodation syndrome." The syndrome consists of a cluster of five "categories," two of which—secrecy and helplessness—define basic childhood vulnerability to sexual abuse, with the other three—entrapment and accommodation, delayed and unconvincing disclosures, and retraction—sequentially contingent upon sexual abuse.

Summit asserts that for children the traumatic experience of sexual abuse is only exacerbated by the disbelief and denial of mental health clinicians. Children, he insists, "never ask and never tell" (p. 181) about sexual abuse, suffering for a lifetime for their silence with a panoply of traumatic symptoms, including "domestic martyrdom, splitting of reality, altered consciousness, hysterical phenomena, delinquency, sociopathy, projection of rage, even self-mutilation" (p. 186). The silence of children makes it incumbent upon mental health clinicians to discover the sexual abuse, but in doing so they must struggle with their own incredulity. Summit offers some bromides to assist in that struggle: the more "illogical and incredible" (p. 183) the child's disclosure, the more likely it is true; if a child errs in detail it is on the side of underestimating the duration and frequency of the sexual abuse; whatever a child discloses about sexual abuse likely will be retracted later; and a child "never fabricates" (p. 191) the explicit details of the sexual abuse.

The article, which circulated among mental health clinicians for several years before it was published and was required reading in a national training program on sexual abuse, is impressionistic rather than empirical in nature. Despite Summit's warning that the child sexual abuse accommodation syndrome "should not be viewed as a procrustean bed which defines and dictates a narrow perception of something as complex as sexual abuse" (p. 180), a "procrustean bed" is exactly what it became. By linking the master symbol of the psychological trauma model with that of vulnerable children, it defined into existence a uniform reaction of children to the trauma of sexual abuse and its disclosure, and it dictated a non-negotiable role for mental health clinicians as interrogators and advocates. Although the article was written to battle incredulity, "the rigid ideology which lay behind it meant that in too many cases an attitude of systematic disbelief was replaced not by an open-minded willingness to investigate, but by a kind of systematic credulity" (Webster, 1998, p. 37).

Endlessly repeated and referenced, the child sexual abuse accommodation syndrome linked two of the master symbols of the 1980s: the vulnerable child and the psychological trauma model. It entered into the recursive domains of the professional literature on child sexual abuse, the testimony of expert witnesses in criminal trials, the workshops and trainings that were all the rage during that decade, and the "labyrinthine rumor/communication networks" (Putnam, 1991, p. 178) that connected child-savers across the country. "Believe the Children" became the banner of that decade, and those who marched under it were of a single mind that no allegation of sexual abuse was unbelievable, no retraction or denial was acceptable, and no hesitation could not be breached by a caring, yet persistent, interrogator.

THE STORY ALWAYS OLD AND ALWAYS NEW

It might be tactical at this point to repeat the assertion that the "master symbols" that came to stand in proxy for the deeper and more complex social strains and stresses of the 1980s provide an entrée for an analysis of the day care ritual abuse moral panic. The vulnerable child is one of those master symbols; it typifies the disconcerting changes occurring in the family and in the traditional gender roles that gird it. The menacing devil is another. As a master symbol it personifies the presence of evil and its creeping influence on political and social affairs. The psychological trauma model is the third of the troika of master symbols of the 1980s. It signifies both the real and imagined threats to collective well-being and the individual psychological vulnerability to them.

Each of these master symbols generates its own social anxiety. The process of discursively linking them, however, creates a narrative—a coherent and plausible story about the traumatic consequences of satanic threats to vulnerable children. Some narratives are just plausible enough to set off short-lived collective responses that have neither the virulence nor the volatility to meet the sociological definition of a moral panic. Other narratives, though, are so compelling, so deeply resonant with cultural fears and anxieties, so historically familiar, that they can incite a moral panic. The 1980s saw a smattering of the first, and one startling and provocative example of the latter.

Satanic Panics

Sociologist Jeffrey Victor (1993) uses the term "satanic panics" to describe the evanescent collective reactions to the just plausible enough narratives that result from attempts to discursively link the three master symbols of the 1980s. One of those satanic panics had to do with rock music, always the perfect patsy of conservatives and traditionalists. At the start of the decade the New Christian Right launched a fresh attack on it. It claimed that subliminal messages like "my sweet Satan" that supposedly were back-masked into the music (Arzana, 1983), as well as the debauched lyrics of heavy metal groups in all their Gothic finery, were luring vulnerable children into the traumatizing black hole of satanism. New Christian Right crusader and Jesuit priest Vincent Miceli (1981, p. 230) narrates the traumatic consequences for vulnerable children of listening to the devil's wild rhythms: "The result is that today millions of youth will 'groove' with rock music, but tomorrow they will be passively submissive to the cadences of some demagogue behind whose tyranny will be the controlling power of the puppet masters, Satan and all the forces of hell."

The narrative about a *civitas diaboli* of vulnerable, traumatically brainwashed children goose-stepping to the command of the devil was just plausible enough to enjoin other interest groups into a short-lived satanic panic over rock and heavy metal music. Anxious parents demanded a lyric rating system to warn of violent, sexual or occult content; law enforcement officers urged their colleagues to search for links between demonic music and occult crimes (Simandl, 1997); local news media guilelessly reported untested claims about back-masking and brainwashing as scientific fact (Richardson, 1991); and mental health clinicians developed therapies to rescue children from the psychologically traumatizing consequences of cavorting with the devil (Moriarty, 1990; Wheeler, Wood, & Hatch, 1988).

Despite this coalition of interest groups, the satanic panic over rock and heavy metal music was short-lived, its just plausible enough narrative unable to withstand the nostalgic reminiscences of older generations whose own taste for swing, jazz and the blues tolled, for some given to lamentation, society's imminent collapse. The satanic panic peaked with a couple of high profile and spectacularly unsuccessful civil suits against musicians by grieving parents who claimed their children had been urged into suicide by the back-masked messages or the demonic lyrics of their favorite groups.[3]

Another transitory satanic panic had to do with fantasy role-playing games, particularly "Dungeons and Dragons" in which players assume roles loosely based on medieval folklore and then strategize their way through the geography of the imagination, populated by hazards and foes of their own creation. The most publicly visible campaign against fantasy-role playing games was led by a distraught parent whose son, obsessed with "Dungeons and Dragons," had hanged himself.[4] But once again it was the New Christian Right that created the just plausible enough narrative about vulnerable children, the devil and psychological trauma to instigate a collective reaction. One of its crusader forges the discursive links between these master symbols in the following way: "'Dungeons and Dragons' is not a game but a teaching on demonology, witchcraft, voodoo, murder, rape, blasphemy, suicide, assassination, sex perversion, homosexuality, prostitution, Satan worship, gambling, Jungian psychology, barbarism, cannibalism, sadism, desecration, demon summoning, necromantics and divination" (Robie, 1991, p. 54).

With a provenance like that, the game was bound to evoke ire, even alarm. As in the satanic panic over rock and heavy metal music, the New Christian Right found allies in other interest groups. Parents' groups lobbied to have the game banned from schools and taken off store shelves; law enforcement officers warned about its link to occult crimes; local media sensationalized cases of suicide or antisocial behavior by young players; and mental health clinicians hastily prepared and disseminated checklists of symptoms of satanic dabbling that included not only playing fantasy role-playing games, but changes in diet, periods of fatigue, self-mutilation and a preference for wearing black (Hicks, 1991). Like the satanic panic over rock and heavy metal music, this one's just plausible enough narrative was unable to withstand vigorous cross-examination in civil suits against fantasy role-playing games manufacturers, or the challenges posed by a modest body of scholarly research that concludes, "involvement in fantasy role-playing games seems unrelated to the allegedly more maleficent outcomes of gaming claimed by crusading groups" (Martin & Fine, 1991, p. 220).

The final example also neatly illustrates what happens when the master symbols of vulnerable children, the devil and the psychological trauma model are discursively linked by a just plausible enough narrative to prompt a collective reaction. Victor (1991) traces a rumor about predatory satanic cults that spread across small town American where the economic cycle of the 1980s left more bust than boom, and traditional moral values in desperate need of revitalization.

The Jamestown, New York version of the rumor is an interesting case study. There, community suspicion about an emerging punk subculture of disenfranchised local youth turned into fears of satanism when a nationally syndicated television talk show featured a segment on punks who had descended into the psychological black hole of devil-worship. Fretful parents met with local law enforcement officers and mental health clinicians who, in the argot of their respective profession, validated the link, as did local fundamentalist churches that sermonized on the evils of devil worship and sponsored self-proclaimed experts to address the community (Victor, 1993).

As the rumor roiled, it cohered into a narrative that discursively linked the master symbols of that decade: the disenfranchised punks were brainwashed members of a satanic cult that was bent on kidnapping and sacrificing a local blonde, blue-eyed, young virgin. The narrative was just plausible enough for the good people of Jamestown to start seeing evidence of its truth. They began reporting dozens of bizarre incidents, from glimpsing dead animals hanging from lampposts, to overhearing punk youth invoking the devil.

On Friday the 13th, the rumored day of the sacrifice, community anxiety spiraled into collective action. Young children were kept out of school, armed local citizens patrolled the streets, property was damaged and the lives of punk youth were threatened. No blonde, blue-eyed virgin was kidnapped, though, and none was sacrificed. In the anti-climactic days that followed, this rumor quietly left town and took up temporary residence somewhere else.

These and other satanic panics of the 1980s were evanescent, if only because their just plausible enough narratives could not withstand disconfirmation. But there was one other narrative that could, this in the form of a best-seller that serves as a historical marker for the start of the day care ritual abuse moral panic.

Michelle Remembers ... Something

One last vignette: Michelle Smith, 27 years old, lies on the couch in the office of her psychiatrist, recovering one memory after another of fourteen months of childhood horror as a captive of a satanic cult that boasted her own mother as a devotee. The long-repressed memories of the pseudonymous Michelle were published in 1980 as *Michelle Remembers* (Smith & Pazder, 1980), a best-seller that not only discursively links the master symbols of that decade—vulnerable children, the menacing devil and the psychological trauma model—but does so in an archetypal moral drama that so deeply resonated with cultural fears and anxieties that it incited the day care ritual abuse moral panic.

Emotional complications from a miscarriage, compounded by unresolved grief over rejection, abandonment and death, brought Michelle to Lawrence Pazder, a British Columbia psychiatrist who had helped her years before when minor fears and dark thoughts about death vexed her university years as a psychology major. Although sessions with Pazder ameliorated her considerable distress, she remained convinced that there was "something important" (p. 14), yet inaccessible to her conscious mind, that she yet had to deal with. Her memories of that important thing came slowly, eased into consciousness by Pazder's soothing reassurance that she was not mad and would not die for having them. In sessions lasting as long as six hours, punctuated by screams that gave chills to the psychiatrists with whom Pazder shared an office suite, Michelle remembered being hung upside-down as a child and twirled in dizzying circles by a black-robed man named Malachi,[5] and having colored sticks dipped in liquid from a silver goblet inserted in every orifice of her body while beautiful black-robed women chanted and danced around her.

Pazder, who had a diploma in tropical medicine and had practiced in West Africa in the early 1960s, found her story eerily familiar. He was well-versed in African lore about "leopard children" confined in cages and ritually tortured by black magic cults. Although he did not share his own recollection with Michelle, the memories she recovered over the next three months began to cohere with his and a story formed about an innocent child at the mercy of evil cultists, forced to rely on her own pluck to survive until someone came to her rescue.

Michelle was reluctant to tell Pazder, a staunch Catholic, that she believed her captors were witches, but Pazder was quick to do her one better: he believed they were satanists. Indeed, in the memories she recovered next, her evil captors became satanists, members of a well-organized and nefarious cult that included her own mother as a devotee. She recalled her mother putting the body of a woman she had killed into a car with her and then Malachi driving them to a secluded spot, exiting the car, and pushing it over an embankment where it crashed and burst into flames. Trapped in the burning car with the corpse of the woman—"The face was all mashed up... . It has a broken neck and the face is turned around backward!" (p. 62)—five year old Michelle clawed her way out of the wreckage and into the arms of the mysterious Malachi who told the police she had caused the accident by putting her hands over his eyes while he was driving.

The nurse who cared for her in the hospital made no such criminations. She, too, was a member of the satanic cult and she was to become Michelle's primary tormentor. It was the nurse who surreptitiously spirited Michelle from the hospital to a spooky Victorian house in need of repair and locked her in the basement without food or drink. When she escaped and ran to her mother, it was the nurse to whom her mother returned her. It was the nurse who brought her to a cemetery and forced her to stand in an empty grave, tricked her into defecating on a crucifix and Bible, injected her with stupefying drugs, made her consume the flesh of a dead person, and brought a statue of the devil alive by daubing it with blood from an amputated finger. It was the nurse who also laid Michelle on a cold slab while satanists danced and chanted, and then pulled a bloody dead baby from beneath the terrified child's legs in some obscene parody of birth.

But Michelle's spirit, her "powerful goodness" (p. 129) as Pazder refers to it, was not to be undermined by her satanic tormentors. Sensing, rather than knowing, it was all things Christian to which they were opposed, she grabbed the crucifix she had secreted from the hospital room and held it high, throwing a roomful of satanists into a frenzy before Malachi grabbed it and "drove the base of the cross down upon the body of the baby" (p. 138) she still believed she had given birth to. During another satanic ritual, this one involving young children who exuded the innocence she already had lost, Michelle was confined with snakes and decaying parts of a baby's body inside an effigy of the devil. Desperate to save the children from a fate like her own, she "gathered [the snakes] up by the handfuls and pushed them through the effigy's eyes... . And the decaying pieces of the baby. She shoved them out of the mouth of the image" (p. 167). Screaming, she burst out of the effigy and "grabbed a snake and, before she could think about what she was doing, put it in her mouth and ran around the room, dangling it from her teeth" (p. 169), scaring the children into fleeing.

Whatever reluctance, and it does not appear to be much, that Michelle had about believing it was a satanic cult that had held her captive was resolved by Pazder's assertion that the Church of Satan is a "worldwide organization, actually older than the Christian Church" (pp. 127–128) and active in the Pacific Northwest. To bolster her spiritual defenses during the harrowing months of memory recovery, he brought her to be baptized by a local priest. In the corner of the church, Michelle noticed a wooden bench incised with what appeared to be satanic symbols. At a loss to explain how the bench had come to be in the church in the first place, the priest offered to douse it with holy water and burn it. The photographs Pazder took of the burning seemed to the three of them to show a glowing spectral presence at the edge of the fire, a presence they took to be that of the Virgin Mary and her child, Jesus.

The Virgin Mary played a central role in the recovered memories of an 81 day Black Mass that Michelle then related, interestingly enough in rhyme, to the credulous Pazder. "The time is ripe, the time is near,/The time of the Beast, the time of the year,/The time to come, the time to begin,/The time to spread, to thrive, to win" (p. 310). During this "Feast of the Beast," Michelle was subjected to electric shocks, the forceful extraction of teeth, and the surgical implantation of horns to her head and a tail to her spine. In her agony and terror, she called out to the Virgin Mary for intercession. Ma Mére obliged and released Michelle from the clutches of the satanists and into the open arms of her satanic mother, with the reassurance that "you don't have to be what she is" (p. 316).

With the imprimatur of the Bishop of Victoria, British Columbia, *Michelle Remembers* was published in the United States in 1980, and in England a year later. This "Shockingly true story of the ultimate evil—

a child's possession by the Devil," as the mass-marketed paperback's cover proclaims, reached a wide and diverse audience before it even appeared in bookstores. *People Weekly* published a thoroughly gullible article on the account (MacMurran, 1980), as did the tabloid *The National Enquirer,* while the popular Canadian magazine, *Maclean's,* took a more jaundiced view of Smith and Pazder's claims (Grescoe, 1980). The latter article features a photograph of the two of them lying on the psychiatrist's couch in an embrace; meant to show the comfort they provided each other after a draining session of memory recovery, it easily could be mistaken by the casual browser for a portrait of post-coital bliss.

Michelle Remembers was a publishing success, earning Smith and Pazder, now married to each other, a $342,000 advance, enviable royalties, and the immediate status of "experts" in this horrific form of child abuse that Pazder, in a 1981 meeting of the American Psychiatric Association, was the first to call "ritual abuse." The two traveled across North America giving radio interviews, appearing on television talk shows, training law enforcement officers, addressing child abuse conferences, and consulting on the suspected cases of day care ritual abuse that began cropping up like pernicious weeds in the wake of the publication of the book.[6]

Ironically, the popularity of the book is, itself, a testimony of sorts to the kind of survival in the face of adversity it purports to document. Michelle's story has been completely debunked (Allen & Midwinter, 1990; Nathan & Snedeker, 1995). There is no record of her prolonged hospitalization, no newspaper or police report on the staged car crash that supposedly resulted in the death of a woman; there is no corroboration of any of the story's details by her teachers, former classmates, neighbors, pediatrician, or her father and two sisters, never even mentioned in the story, who have publicly branded her a fantasist. There are, however, photographs of Michelle Proby, her *nom de famille,* in the St. Margaret's Elementary School yearbook, chubby-cheeked and smiling, taken about the same time she remembers being confined by satanists in the dank basement of an abandoned house.

Pazder's credibility is also in question. All criticisms of his therapeutic skills and professional ethics aside, his unwavering belief in African black magic cults and leopard children is more sophistical than not. Cultural anthropologist J.S. LaFontaine (1998) relegates such beliefs to the rumors that ran rampant among anxious white missionaries in Africa during the early 1960s, and questions the facile use of such legends to corroborate his patient's story. Soon after the publication of the book, Pazder was forced to withdraw his assertion that the Church of Satan was responsible for Michelle's ritual abuse when the San Francisco, California–based Church, founded by Anton LaVey, a colorful impresario with a flair for the dramatic a decade *after* Michelle's remembered encounter with satanists, sued him for libel (Hicks, 1991).

This archetypal moral drama, so deeply resonant with the burgeoning fears and anxieties of late-modern American society, and so fully believable because of it, inspired a genre of equally specious autobiographical accounts.[7] Functioning as both narrative and meta-narrative, this genre "tells a story, explains that story, and draws moral conclusions simultaneously" (Ingebretsen, 2001, p. 34). With its preoccupations with diabolical cults, monastic institutions, subterranean spaces, live burials and secret rooms, double lives, possession, rape, madness and death, this genre of literature lent clinical authority to the accounts of young children during the day care ritual abuse moral panic.

MAKE A MORAL OF THE DEVIL

Michelle Remembers discursively links the master symbols of the vulnerable child, the menacing devil and the psychological trauma model that stood in proxy for the deeper and more complex social strains and stresses of late-modern society. But just as master symbols stand for the "real problems" that are the cause of a moral panic, a master narrative is needed to incite one. *Michelle Remembers* provided that narrative in the form of an archetypally familiar plot, and the new and disturbing notion of "ritual abuse."

All that was needed for a moral panic was some kind of spark that would "link ethereal sentiment to focused action" (Adler, 1996, p. 262). That spark was lit in 1983 at a day care center in southern California with the whispered words of a two-and-a-half year old enrollee in the McMartin Preschool.

2

The Devil Goes
to Day Care

Hardly the dark satanic mill of cultural imagination, the McMartin Preschool occupied a small, pale green L-shaped building on the main boulevard of the southern California town of Manhattan Beach where, if the tourist brochure were to be believed, residents enjoy " small town living, friendly neighbors, and community spirit." Founded in 1956 by Virginia Steely McMartin whose devoutly religious, teetotaler husband had left her for a younger woman a decade before, the preschool had a certain cachet among local residents and a six month waiting list.

The McMartin Preschool was a family enterprise in 1983. Virginia McMartin, then 75 years old and confined to a wheelchair with crippling arthritis, was its titular head. A no-nonsense matron with an encyclopedic knowledge of baseball, she pointed with pride to the preschool's record of glowing state inspection reports, as well as to the community's Rose and Scroll Award presented to her for her contribution to its children and families. The day-to-day administration of the preschool was left to her 55 year old daughter, Peggy McMartin Buckey, a garrulous former dancer and social gadfly. It was her husband, Charles, who had built the whimsical child-sized wooden animals that dotted the preschool yard that also featured a wooden car, a jungle gym, a fort and a playhouse *sans* doors. Peggy's daughter, Peggy Ann, 28, occasionally taught at the preschool when she could take time from her job as a teacher for the hearing impaired in the Anaheim Union public schools. Her 25 year old son Raymond, a lanky, lantern-jawed college dropout also taught at the preschool, attracted to this traditionally defined "women's work" by the opportunity to work with children, whom he considered "more honest than adults" (Timnick, June 26, 1990. p. B-1). Virginian McMartin had recruited the rest of the staff from her local Christian Science church. Betty Raidor, an Olympic swim team alternate in her youth, was 64; Mary Ann Jackson, a published poet, was 56; and Babette Spitler, a former social worker, was 36 with two young children of her own (Arnold & Decker, 1984).

The "grand life" that Virginia McMartin had written about in a thirteen page autobiography began to unravel in the spring of 1983 when Judy Johnson, recently separated from her husband, drinking heavily, and raising their two young sons alone, left her two-and-a-half year old in the yard of the preschool. Taking pity on the woebegone child whose name they found on a slip of paper in his pocket, the providers took him in. Over the next few months, he attended the McMartin Preschool fourteen times (Sauer, 1993).

In August, Judy Johnson called the local police to accuse Raymond Buckey of molesting her son. The boy had come from the preschool with a reddened anus and had spent the night restless and whiny, finally responding to his mother's relentless questioning by saying the Buckey had taken his temperature rectally. Assuming the "thermometer" her son described actually was Buckey's penis, she concluded that he had been sodomized by the only male provider at the preschool (Nathan & Snedeker, 1995).

The medical exam conducted the next day was inconclusive for sodomy, however, and the boy disclosed nothing to an investigating detective. But the matter was far from over. Johnson began calling other parents of the preschool enrollees, asking them to question their children. None confirmed the stories her son allegedly was telling her—the stories about sexual abuse, bondage and nude photographs that she was passing on to the police in almost daily telephone calls. The police, in turn, requested another medical exam of her son. This one was conducted by an inexperienced intern who, convinced by the allegations Johnson made on her silent son's behalf, diagnosed anal penetration and referred mother and son to a local counseling center.

The ensuing police investigation was deeply unsettling for Buckey whose reputation as a loner and ne'er-do-well was quite well known to the parents of the preschool enrollees. After searching the home he lived in with his parents, Buckey was arrested and then quietly released for lack of evidence. Persisting in their investigation, however, the police sent the following letter to two hundred families of children currently or previously enrolled at the preschool:

> Please question your child to see if he or she has been a witness to any crime or if he or she has been a victim. Our investigation indicates that possible criminal acts include oral sex, fondling of genitals, buttocks or chest areas and sodomy, possibly committed under the pretense of "taking the child's temperature." Also, photos may have been taken of the children without their clothing. Any information from your child regarding having ever observed Ray Buckey to leave a classroom alone with a child during any nap period, of if they have ever observed Ray Buckey tie up a child, is important. Please complete the enclosed information

form and return it to this department in the enclosed stamped envelope as soon as possible [cited in Hicks, 1991, p. 189].

Although the letter also admonished parents not to discuss the investigation with anyone, the same "small town living, friendly neighbors, and community spirit" that made Manhattan Beach a nice place to live also quickly made it a vipers nest of rumors. Parents not only questioned their own children, but interrogated each other during chance meetings in local stores and in frantic late night telephone calls. Only a few children disclosed anything, but some who did embellished the accounts of Judy Johnson who ventriloquially was still speaking for her silent son. While Johnson told police her son disclosed that Buckey had inserted air tubes in his anus, killed a dog, took him home to have oral sex with a stranger, wore clown and minister costumes, and chopped living rabbits into pieces, other children now talked about naked games and sexual abuse of all kinds not only by Buckey, but his grandmother, mother, sister, and the other three providers.

By the fall of 1983 the laid back seaside community of Manhattan Beach was in turmoil. Taking the opportunity to get some political mileage out of the uproar in a county that had cited child abuse as one of its most pressing issues, District Attorney Robert Philibosian assigned one of his assistants, Jean Matusinka, to oversee the case. She, in turn, introduced the anxious parents to the Children's Institute International, a non-profit child abuse diagnostic and treatment facility, where video-taped interviews would be conducted by experts in order to reduce both the number of interviews and interviewers the children would have to encounter.

The expert who would assume the responsibility for conducting most of the interviews was social worker Kee MacFarlane, a former grants reviewer for the National Center for Child Abuse and Neglect. With Jean Matusinka and psychiatrist Roland Summit, she was part of a group discussing the sexual abuse of young children and was eager to test the received wisdom that only persistent and leading questions would break through the "child sexual abuse accommodation syndrome," the interrogative effects of that style of interview softened through the use of hand puppets. MacFarlane had stumbled upon the technique of using hand puppets a year or so before she even became involved in the McMartin Preschool case. "I was talking to a preschooler who was holding a puppet in her hand," she recalls, "and she refused to answer a question. I said, 'Maybe the puppet would like to answer!' And it worked" (Carlson, 1984, p. 79).

It certainly did. By the time she and her colleagues were finished, over 350 of the 400 children interviewed, at a cost to the state of $455 for each interview and medical examination, had made allegations against one or more of the McMartin providers (Nathan & Snedeker, 1995, p. 83).

The puppets hardly deserve all the credit. It was in interviews that led, begged, bribed, cajoled, shamed and intimidated that the allegations came forth. A few examples illustrate this critical point. Consider this interview in which the interviewer, *sans* puppet this time, leads a child to imagine a scenario rife with new details the child had not previously disclosed (Garven, Wood, Malpass, & Shaw, 1998, p. 348):

> INTERVIEWER: Ray and Miss Peggy? Did Miss Peggy take her clothes off?
> CHILD: Yeah.
> INTERVIEWER: I bet she looked funny, didn't she? Did she have big boobs?
> Child: Yeah.
> INTERVIEWER: Yeah, and did they swing around?
> CHILD: Yeah.

In some interviews, children were lavishly praised for confirming the interviewer's bias. Take as an example the approval heaped on one child who, after a series of suggestive questions, finally agreed with the interviewer that a provider had photographed the children while they were naked: " Can I pat you on the head...? Look at what a good help you can be. You're going to help all these little children because you're so smart" (Garven, Wood, Malpass, & Shaw, 1998, p. 349). Yet as facilely as praise was proffered, so was shame, as the following exchange about the "Naked Movie Star Game"[1] that some of the children described as a pretense for taking pornographic pictures of them illustrates (Wexler, 1990, pp. 148–149):

> INTERVIEWER: I thought that was a naked game.
> CHILD: Not exactly.
> INTERVIEWER: Did somebody take their clothes off?
> CHILD: When I was there no one was naked.
> INTERVIEWER: We want to make sure you're not scared to tell.
> CHILD: I'm not scared.
> INTERVIEWER: Some of the kids were told they might be killed. It was a trick. All right Mr. Alligator [the puppet the child is using], are you going to be stupid, or are you smart and can tell. Some think you're smart.
> CHILD: I'll be smart.
> INTERVIEWER: Mr. Monkey [a puppet the child had used earlier] is chicken. He can't remember the naked games, but you know the naked movie star game. Is your memory too bad?
> CHILD: I haven't seen the naked movie star game.
> INTERVIEWER: You must be dumb!
> CHILD: I don't remember.

In a different tactic, some children were badgered not only in making an allegation, but in providing perceptual detail. In this interview a PacMan puppet is used to intimidate an eight year old in describing ejaculate (Gorney, May 18, 1988, p. D1):

> INTERVIEWER: Here's a hard question I don't know if you know the answer to. We'll see how smart you are, PacMan. Did you ever see anything come out of Mr. Ray's weiner? Do you remember that?
> CHILD: [No response]
> INTERVIEWER: Can you remember back that far? We'll see how ... how good your brain is working today, PacMan. [Child moves puppet around.]. Is that a yes? [Child nods the puppet]. Well, you're smart. Now, let's see if we can figure out what it was. I wonder if you can point to something of what color it was. [Child tries to pick up the pointer with the PacMan's mouth.]. Let me get your pen here [puts pointer in PacMan's mouth].
> CHILD: It was...
> INTERVIEWER: Let's see what color is that. [Child uses the PacMan's hand to point to the PacMan puppet.]. Oh, you're pointing to yourself. That must be yellow. [Child nods puppet yes.]. You're smart to point to yourself. What did it feel like? Was it like water? Or something else?
> CHILD: Um, what?
> INTERVIEWER: The stuff that came out. Let me try. I'll try a different question on you. We'll try to figure out what that stuff tastes like. We're going to try and figure out if it tastes good.
> CHILD: He never did that to me, I don't think.
> INTERVIEWER: Oh, well, PacMan, would you know what it tastes like? Would you think it tastes like candy, sort of trying...
> CHILD: I think it would taste like yucky ants.
> INTERVIEWER: Yucky ants. Whoa. That would be kind of yucky. I don't think it would taste like ... you don't think it would taste like strawberries or anything good?
> CHILD: No.
> INTERVIEWER: Oh. Think it would so ... do you think that would be sticky, like sticky, yucky ants?
> CHILD: A little.

Part of the grist for these interviews most certainly came from Judy Johnson who, Cassandra-like, was warning interviewers of what they would hear if only they could work through their own incredulity and listen as well as she was to her own son. In telephone calls and letters Johnson claimed the McMartin providers had stapled his eyes shut, stabbed scissors in his tongue, buried him in a coffin without air holes, and forced him to drink blood. She said he described black candles, witch costumes, Raymond Buckey flying through the air, animal sacrifices, and his providers chopping off a baby's head and burning the brains (Nathan & Snedeker, 1995, pp. 84–85). The claims *du jour* of Judy Johnson were the main topic of discussion in the regularly held meetings between worried parents, the district attorney, the police and the interviewing social workers Gorney, May 17, 1988).

"Imagination Bodies Forth"

A six minute television news story during "sweeps week" in February 1984 gave credence to what was still rumor, suspicion and innuendo. "More than sixty children, some of them as young as two years of age ... have now told authorities that he or she has been keeping a grotesque secret of being sexually abused and made to appear in pornographic films while in the preschool's care, and of having been forced to witness the mutilation and killing of animals to scare the kids into staying silent," intoned KABC reporter Wayne Satz. " The allegations are being taken very seriously" (Shaw, 1990, January 19, p. A-1).

They were indeed, especially by the local media. Although KABC led the pack with its own brand of gonzo journalism, the pillow talk between the romantically involved reporter Satz and social worker Mac-Farlane the source of its increasingly horrific exclusives (Shaw, 1990, January 20, p. A-1), other local news stations breathlessly contributed to the hysterical pitch. Journalistic skepticism was replaced with credulity, critical thinking with mushy emotionality, and objectivity with an ardent belief that the McMartin providers were guilty and could not be proved innocent.

Even the venerable *Los Angeles Times* could not rise above criticism. In a Pulitzer Prize winning series, reporter David Shaw castigates his own newspaper for minimizing or ignoring completely stories that would have called into question the allegations against the McMartin providers, and for pandering to the growing community hysteria (Shaw, January 20, 1990). Indeed, in the sort of shadow-play that was the McMartin case, seven other local day care centers came under suspicion. The *Los Angeles Times* published one story after another about their closings after some McMartin enrollees alleged they were swapped for children there for the purposes of pornography and prostitution. The newspaper, in fact, featured eight separate stories about one center, the Peninsula Montessori, but never reported its reopening when police declined to file charges against the providers, until its owner complained to the editor (Shaw, January 22, 1990).

In this milieu of surmises, conjectures and rumors, the seven McMartin providers were indicted by a grand jury in March 1984 on 115 counts of child molestation and one count of conspiracy. A few weeks later an additional 208 counts were added, and they were promptly arrested. In a press conference, Assistant District Attorney Lael Rubin, newly appointed to the case, confidently announced that the preschool was a front for child pornography and that " enormous quantities of photographs" of the children were circulating through the dark and slimy underbelly of American society[2] ("Preschool Investigated," 1984, p. A-1). Social worker MacFarlane agreed. In testimony before the U.S. House of Representatives, she described the McMartin Preschool as linked to an "organized operation of child predators, whose operation is designed to prevent detection, and is well insulated against legal intervention ... [and that] may have greater financial, legal, and community resources than any of the agencies trying to uncover them" (U.S. House of Representatives, 1984, p. 86). This touch of conspiracy thickened the plot, but the role of the devil as *agent provocateur* was not introduced until later that year.

Enter Lawrence Pazder. Since the publication of *Michelle Remembers*, he had been traveling across North America, talking to mental health clinicians and law enforcement officers about satanic threats to children. Pazder's notion of ritual abuse, the term he had coined in 1981 to label the childhood memories of his erstwhile patient, Michelle, was going through a curiously accommodating transmutation. Michelle had never remembered sexual abuse by her satanic captors, thus Pazder's original definition of ritual abuse as "repeated physical, emotional, mental and spiritual assaults" that are carried out through the "systematic use of symbols, ceremonies, and machinations designed and orchestrated to attain malevolent effects" (cited in Kahaner, 1998, pp. 200–201), did not include it. Sensing the *Zeitgeist*, perhaps, Pazder now tagged "sexual" to his list of ritually abusive assaults and told the timorous parents, social workers, law enforcement officers and district attorneys he met with that the McMartin Preschool case was at the center of an international satanic conspiracy.

In the linguistic economy of the moral panic the McMartin case soon would spark, ritual abuse became synonymous with sexual abuse— but not with the "ordinary" kind of sexual abuse that occurs within families. With its ceremonial trappings, costumes and rites, ritual abuse was something altogether different. It was the ultimate evil that came to seize the pinnacle of the hierarchy of child abuse the ensuing moral panic would create. And if the child victims of what soon would become just prosaic child abuse are thoroughly traumatized by the experience, then what could be expected for ritually abused children? That vexing question prompted everyone involved in the McMartin Preschool case to look for symptoms, and in their urgency, to mistake normal developmentally-based behaviors, quirky idiosyncrasies, and even the iatrogenic effects of intimidating interviews for sequelae of ritual abuse (see Table 1). In this

TABLE 1
Signs and Symptoms of Ritual Abuse
(Gould, 1988)

Sexual Problems
Age-inappropriate sexual knowledge
Fear of touch
Excessive masturbation
Sexually provocative behavior
Vaginal or anal pain
Relaxed anal sphincter, enlarged
   vaginal opening
Venereal disease
   Toileting/Bathroom problems
Bathroom avoidance, toileting acci-
   dents
Preoccupation with cleanliness
Preoccupation with urine and feces
Ingestion of urine or feces
   Problems Associated
   with Supernatural
Fear of ghosts, monsters, witches,
   devils
Preoccupation with wands, spirits,
   magic potions, curses, crucifixes
Odd songs and chants
Preoccupation with occult symbols
Fear of attending church
   Problems Associated
   with Confinement
Fear of closets and other small spaces
Fear of being tied up, ties up others
   Problems Associated with Death
Fear of dying, preoccupation with
   death
   Problems Associated with Doctors
Fear of doctors
Fear of injections, blood tests
Fear of removing clothes
   Problems Associated with Colors
Fear of colors red and black
Preoccupation with color black

Eating Problems
Refusal to eat red or brown food
Fear that food is poisoned
Bingeing, gorging, vomiting, anorexia
   Emotional Problems
Rapid mood swings
Resistance to authority
Hyperactivity, poor attention span
Anxiety
Poor self-esteem
Withdrawal
Regression and babyish speech
Flat affect
Nightmares, night terrors
Learning disorders
   Family Problems
Fear of death of parents, siblings, pets
Separation anxiety
Avoidance of physical contact
Threatens or attacks parents, siblings,
   Play and Peer Problems
Destroys toys
Death, mutilation, confinement
   themes in play
Inability to engage in fantasy play
   Other Fears and Strange Beliefs
Imaginary friends
Fear of police, strangers, bad people
Fear of violent films
Fear of aggressive animals
Fear of cemeteries, mortuaries,
   churches
Fear of something foreign inside body,
   e.g. bomb, devil's heart

nascent moral panic, the widely circulated "symptom lists" transformed messy subjectivity into embodied and interpretable texts (Epstein, 1995). The symptoms now could be used to tell the story any silent or denying child was simply too "accommodating" to tell.

There is reason to believe that those involved in the McMartin case were familiar with the notion of ritual abuse before meeting Pazder. The topic had been discussed by the social workers and mental health clinicians who were meeting about the sexual abuse of young children (Nathan & Snedeker, 1995), and a local Catholic church had brought in an expert on satanism who addressed the Manhattan Beach community. But after that meeting with Pazder, ritual abuse colonized their imagination. All of the interrogators, including the parents, began asking the children different kinds of questions, sometimes using devil puppets as props, and comparing answers against checklists of satanic rituals, roles, ceremonies and holidays put together by New Christian Right crusaders. With the "ultimate evil" of ritual abuse as the rudder of their imagination, anything the children revealed was deemed plausible.

In the face of relentless grilling with this new demonic twist, the young children soon figured out that "round, unvarnish'd tales" were not what their interrogators wanted to hear. So they told other tales—"tales about the ritualistic ingestion of feces, urine, blood, semen and human flesh; the disinterment and mutilation of corpses; the sacrifices of infants; and the orgies with their day care providers costumed as devils and witches, in the classrooms, in tunnels under the center, and in car washes, airplanes, mansions, cemeteries, hotels, ranches, gourmet food stores, local gyms, churches, and hot air balloons" (de Young, 1997, p. 21). And they eventually named not only the seven McMartin providers as their ritual abusers, but their soccer coaches, babysitters, neighbors, and even their own parents, as well as local businesspeople, the mayor's wife, news reporters covering the story, television and film stars, and players on the Anaheim Angels baseball team (Nathan & Snedeker, 1995).

Ceremonies of Fear, Ceremonies of Restoration

Over the three years between the arrests of the McMartin providers and the criminal trial, another 100 children were interviewed and 150 adults were questioned, 50 of whom were considered serious suspects. Searches were conducted in 82 locations including the Wind Cave National Park in South Dakota where Raymond and his sister Peggy Ann Buckey were believed to have buried caches of pornographic photographs of the McMartin Preschool enrollees. Dozens of cars and motorcycles were searched as were 21 private residences and one farm where Raymond was alleged to have clubbed a horse to death in front of terrified children. Photograph line-ups were held, bank records were seized, laboratory tests were conducted on blankets found at the center and on the underwear of the complaining children, and thousands of pornographic films and photographs, confiscated by police in unrelated cases, were viewed for glimpses of McMartin Preschool enrollees (Eberle & Eberle, 1993, p. 42). The cliché aside, the community of Manhattan Beach was gripped by fear, chilled by a pervasive feeling that "something had happened [there], something dreadful and massive and utterly new ... but nobody in town could prove exactly what it was" (Gorney, May 17, 1988, p. D1).

These intense public emotions were given social approbation through "ceremonies of fear" that made "spectacles out of punishment and rituals out of shame" (Ingebretsen, 2001, p. 20). Ceremonies like these are intimately linked with a moral panic. They both express the public fear the moral panic is generating, and fuel its volatility as it grows and spreads.

The McMartin Preschool, the "Nightmare Nursery" as it was christened in an early national tabloid magazine story (Green, 1984), was the object of more than one ceremony of fear in the three critical years between the arrests of the providers and the start of the criminal trial. It was firebombed soon after it was closed, what windows remained were pelted with eggs and the walls spray painted with the words, " Ray Will Die." An epitaph in red added later simply said, " Dead." Its grounds were dug up by a cadre of parents searching for a labyrinth of tunnels leading to a subterranean secret room some of their children described, then by an archaeological firm hired by the district attorney and then once more by the parents, this time under the direction of their own privately hired archaeologist.[3]

As the years wore on, the parents lost faith in the legal system that was moving at a snail's pace, in their religion that often provided only cold comfort for their misery, in their children's pediatricians for not picking up the ritual abuse that they, themselves, had missed, and in the media that exploited their distress (McCord, 1993a). Some took matters into their own hands. They spent evenings and weekends driving through the streets of Manhattan Beach looking for the places their children said they had been taken to be ritually abused, tailing suspicious people, searching for the odd scrap of evidence that would deliver the *coup de grace* against the providers. They came up against unfriendly law enforcement officers, rapacious lawyers, persistent reporters and the occasional detractor, and while many of the parents lost all faith in a fair and just world, their conviction that their children had been ritually abused by satanic providers only increased (McCord, 1993a).

And it increased in the community as well. The rumors about devil worship were reified during the preliminary hearing of the seven providers that began in June 1984 and lasted eighteen months—the longest hearing of its kind in the history of the United States. Thirteen children testified. In the face of blistering cross-examination by seven separate defense attorneys, some stood firm in their accounts of excursions to cemeteries where their providers hacked up dead bodies, to a house where a basement full of roaring lions terrified them, and to a church where black-robed strangers danced around the altar. Some wavered, though, and a few contradicted themselves completely after days on the witness stand (Waters & Timnick, 1985).

In the end, the judge bound over all seven of the providers to stand trial on 135 counts of child molestation and conspiracy. Days later, newly elected District Attorney Ira Reiner dropped all of the charges against five of the providers, characterizing them as "incredibly weak." Peggy McMartin Buckey and her son Raymond were left to stand trial on 99 counts of molestation and one count of conspiracy.

A telephone survey revealed just how hot for certainty the community was about this case. Conducted by Duke University researchers, it found that 98 percent of the respondents believed Raymond Buckey was "definitely or probably guilty" of the charges against him, 93 percent believed the same about Peggy McMartin Buckey, 80 percent were sure the five other providers also were guilty, and 80 percent had no doubt that the providers had engaged in the acts of ritual abuse the children had described in the preliminary hearing (Fukurai, Butler, & Krooth, 1994).

The feeling that "something dreadful, massive and utterly new" had happened in Manhattan Beach tightly bonded the community and found social approval in ceremonies of fear. The five recently released providers were shamed by whispered death threats in late night telephone calls and by public shunning. When Peggy McMartin Buckey made bail after twenty-two months of pretrial detention, she was verbally and physically assaulted on the streets of Manhattan Beach; between her release and the trial, she moved herself and her elderly mother, Virginia, a half a dozen times.

Yet, to treat the community as if it were of one mind about the McMartin Preschool case would be a mistake. Not everyone was recruited by the discourse of this fomenting moral panic, and those who were not also made their feelings known through ceremonies of restoration (Schur, 1980) that made public spectacles out of attempts to restore the social honor of the folk devils the providers had become. "The Friends of the McMartin Preschool Defendants," for example, placed full-page ads in southern California newspapers condemning the case as a witch hunt and comparing the soporific seaside community of Manhattan Beach to the small-minded Puritan village of 17th century Salem, Massachusetts.

The providers, themselves, set out publicly to elevate their own status (de Young, 2000a). Before they were indicted they were law-abiding, financially stable, active in their churches and community, well-regarded and respected. They had a great deal of cultural capital to lose in this moral panic, and a great deal to spend in restoring their social honor. So they gave interviews to the media and appeared on syndicated radio and television talk shows. In each of these ceremonies of restoration they discursively situated their identities, telling the deeply suspicious public who they really are, how they became that way, and what the public can expect of them in the future. Virginia McMartin's attempt to "set the record straight" in a *People Weekly* interview just two months after her indictment (Green, 1984) is an interesting example of just this kind of identity politics. In it, the matriarch gives a breezy account of her life, emphasizing her happy childhood, loving family, deep religious faith, uncompromising work ethic, and unconditional love of children. By discursively linking her own identity with the dearly held values and interests of the larger community, indeed, of larger soceity, she actively resisted attempts to marginalize her, and challenged any attempt to demonize her.

Courts were the settings of other ceremonies of restoration. In their effort to restore their social honor the McMartin providers initiated a flurry of civil suits and countersuits. Peggy McMartin Buckey, for example, sued the local police for false arrest and libel just months after she was dragged handcuffed from her home by the police, only to collapse in a dead faint in front of awaiting television cameras. Raymond Buckey sued social worker Kee MacFarlane and the Children's Institute International contending they violated his civil rights by conspiring to fabricate evidence against him (Savage, 1990). The five providers whose charges had been dismissed sued reporter Wayne Satz and television KABC for "creating rather than reporting the news," and then joined the Buckey's in a suit against the preschool's liability insurance carriers for refusing to pay all of their defense costs (McGraw, 1990). Virginia McMartin even took on the parent of one of her alleged victims. When Bob Currie[4] appeared on a nationally syndicated television talk show and branded her a "satanic ritual abuser," she sued him for slander—and won. The judge awarded her only $1 in damage, but she claimed a pyrrhic victory. " I got what I wanted—the truth to come out," she told a press conference. " I don't care one snip about the money. I just wanted him to shut-up" (McGraw, 1991, p. B-1).

While the providers who were the folk devils in this moral panic had the most to gain by elevating their status, the social honor of the children also was in need of restoration. In the eyes of the majority they had been robbed of innocence, that quintessential quality of childhood over which adults in late-modern society tend to wax nostalgic (Jenks, 1996). To restore it, the community securely wrapped them in its protective embrace. They were the guests of honor at public rallies featuring television and film stars, the topics of Sunday sermons and classroom discussions, the subjects of conversations on the golf course and in the grocery store, the reasons for the pink and yellow ribbons tied around trees and lampposts (Hubler, 1990). And they were the sum and substance of the ubiquitous bumper stickers and window signs that read, " Believe the Children."

"Believe the Children" was not just the mantra oft-repeated to invoke the social honor of the accusing children, but a political banner under which some of their parents came together to form the Believe the Children Organization, a clearinghouse for ritual abuse information and advocacy center. Through its efforts, the state of California passed legislation that allowed for closed-circuit television testimony of children in some criminal cases. Although it did not apply to legal proceedings already under way, including the McMartin Preschool case, the law heralded a wave of legislation that created special testimonial opportunities for children in the day care ritual abuse cases that kept cropping up as the moral panic triggered by the McMartin Preschool case spread across the country.

But by July 1987 it all came down to a question of final belief. The criminal trial of Peggy McMartin Buckey and her son Raymond on 100 counts of child molestation and conspiracy opened in a packed Los Angeles courtroom.

"Sad Eye'd Justice"

"This is a case about trust and betrayal of trust," Assistant District Attorney Lael Rubin asserted. " This is not a case about trust. This is a case about victims," defense attorney Dean Gits countered. "You must decide who are the victims."

The opening statements of the prosecution and the defense in the case of *People v. Buckey* were prologue to a twenty-eight month long argument about "narrators, genre and tone, finally about interpretation" (Kincaid, 1998, p. 210). More candidly put, the longest and at $15 million the most expensive criminal trial in American history was, in so many ways, a literary argument over the master narrative of ritual abuse.

Consider, first, the narrators—the children who ended up testifying in the criminal trial. The prosecution insisted that anything these fourteen children said about ritual abuse must be taken as truth; any discrepancy, contradiction or retraction must be seen as a consequence of their "accommodation" to the abuse and therefore as validation of the truth of their testimony. Because children cannot imagine what they have not experienced, the prosecution argued, their testimony requires no interpretation. The defense disagreed. It asserted that anything the children said about ritual abuse must be taken as what they believe to be the truth; any discrepancy, contradiction or retraction must be seen as an invalidation of the truth of their testimony. Because children can be naively led to believe they actually have experienced something they never have, the defense argued, their testimony requires careful interpretation. In this trial, then, "the prosecution's child cannot author, the defense's child cannot interpret" (Kincaid, 1998, p. 211) the master narrative of ritual abuse.

As a result, much of the direct and cross-examination of the children took the form of trying to disentangle authorship from interpretation, a process so incessant, so verbose, that jurors in this, the largest and most horrific mass molestation case in United States history, had to be admonished more than once by the judge for dozing off (Eberle & Eberle, 1993). One by one the children left the witness stand dazed and confused after days of relentless questions about what they remembered, what they imagined, what they were told, when and by whom.

If the testifying children faulted in reciting the ritual abuse master narrative, its Gothic genre was revived by other witnesses. There were the parents, distraught and angry, their testimony full of the "textual leaps, deflections, fissures, silences and absences" that characterize Gothic discourse (Ingebretsen, 2001, p. 37). One parent testified that all of her inchoate worries about her two children—her daughter's bladder infection, her son's pallor—finally made sense when she was told they had been ritually abused; another broke down on the stand, unable to reconcile her deep religious faith with her deeper need for vengeance; another still, defiantly mimetic, spoke for her child whom she described as too traumatized to speak for herself.

If, indeed, Gothic discourse also is characterized by absences, gaps to be filled by the imagination, then the silence that attended the absence of testimony from Judy Johnson and her son is especially noteworthy. Seven months before the trial began, Judy Johnson was found dead in her home. The woman whose allegations started the case, whose psychiatric history including a recent period of hospitalization and a diagnosis of paranoid schizophrenia was withheld from the defense by the prosecution,[5] drank herself to death over the Christmas holiday (Chambers, 1987). The jury would never hear from the woman whose passions spun the plot of the ritual abuse narrative, nor from her then seven year old son whom the presiding judge had declared testimonially incompetent.

The tone of the ritual abuse master narrative was set by the heated exchange between counsel and a parade of expert witnesses whose claims of fidelity to scientific truth were both hotly disputed and defended. Whatever lingering notion that "expert status and knowledge are statically encoded in pre-given qualifications and judicial ruling" (Matoesian, 1999, p. 492) should have evaporated into thin air during this trial. In the matter of *People v. Buckey,* the "science" of child abuse, more particularly of ritual abuse, took a backstage role to the on-going construction, negotiation and deconstruction of expert identity.

In that process, Kee MacFarlane did not fare particularly well. In the years since she interviewed the McMartin Preschool enrollees, her identity as an expert in day care ritual abuse had been buffed and shined by invited speeches at national and international conferences, guest appearances on syndicated television talk shows, and consultative roles in other cases. That expert identity was subject to enthusiastic deconstruction by defense counsel, however, in this trial. Revealed to be unlicensed and essentially untrained in interviewing children, the social worker attempted to regain her expert footing by standing firm in her belief that the interviews she conducted with the children elicited the truth about ritual abuse at the hands of Peggy McMartin Buckey and her son, Raymond.

The appeal to belief, not to science, left the social worker's expert identity even more vulnerable to deconstruction. Segments from interview transcripts were read to the jury and videotaped interviews, grainy and sometimes garbled, were played in their entirety. To every inquiry as to whether this question from the interview or that segment from the videotape was, in fact, evidence of leading the children into confirming the ritual abuse master narrative that she, herself, had scripted, MacFarlane countered that she believed her techniques enabled the children to tell the truth. This semiotic gridlock over the authorship of the ritual abuse master narrative went on for five unrelenting weeks.

In courtroom dramaturgy, the present and the past unfold simultaneously. Peggy McMartin Buckey, testifying on her own behalf, discursively managed the inherent tension of that simultaneous unfolding with terse, one word answers to the questions put to her by her defense attorney in direct examination. "Did you ever molest those children?" he inquired. "No," she responded. "Did you ever transport any of the children off the school grounds for the purpose of engaging in satanic acts at a church?" he asked. To that, she simply replied, "Never" (Timnick, May 17, 1989). In denying any wrongdoing, she emphatically situated herself in the present, communicating to the overflow audience that the charges of the past, the truth be told, had absolutely nothing to do with her.

But the normally loquacious McMartin Buckey reverted to character when cross-examined by the prosecution. She ardently defended herself and her son against any suggestion that that either of them had behaved inappropriately with children. She angrily bantered with Assistant District Attorney Lael Rubin, ridiculing the charges against her as a pack of lies, and her label as a ritual abuser as preposterous. Only nature, itself, could steal her thunder: the morning after her last day of testimony an earthquake shook the courthouse and forced its immediate evacuation (Timnick, May 17, 1989).

Six years after the first whispered allegation was made against him, two years after the start of his trial, Raymond Buckey took the witness stand in his own defense. Reticent and awkward, he too rejected each charge against him in single word denials that revealed little about him as a person. In fact, of all of the McMartin providers it was Raymond about whom the least was really known; held incommunicado in jail for five years, he had little of his fellow providers' opportunities to try to restore social honor. Now on the witness stand, he challenged his most ardent detractors to reconcile his attentive and polite mien with their long-held image of him as a sadistic ritual abuser.

Worried that Buckey might successfully pass, that is, conceal his true self from the judge and jury, Assistant District attorney Lael Rubin set out in cross-examination to strip his putative identity as a decent, conforming person, more victim than victimizer. Buckey's diffident façade cracked and he responded testily, at first, then angrily to her questions (Timnick, July 29, 1989). She stripped away his pretenses to being just an average, everyday person by securing his admission of a past drinking problem, a lack of motivation to finish college and pursue a career, an antipathy towards wearing underwear, an interest in soft-core adult pornography and a belief that pyramids, like the steel-framed one over his bed and the wire one he sometimes wore as a hat, had healing powers. In the end, the blistering cross-examination revealed that what really lurked behind his carefully managed presentation of self was more stereotypical than authentic—an eccentrically trendy southern Californian with enough family money to drift through life until he came across a vocation he really fancied.

On November 2, 1989 the case of *People v. Buckey* went to the jury. Over the twenty-eight months of the trial 124 witnesses had testified, over 900 pieces of evidence had been introduced, 64,000 pages of transcript had accumulated, and 100 charges had been whittled down to 65 when parents had a change of mind and refused to let their children testify (Fukurai, Butler, & Krooth,1994).

On January 18, 1990, the jury returned the verdicts. It acquitted Peggy McMartin Buckey of all of the charges against her, and Raymond Buckey of 29 of the 52 charges against him. The jury had deadlocked on the remaining 13 charges. In the hurry-to-get-it-over pace of an anticlimax,

Buckey was retried on 8 of the strongest remaining charges. Once again the jury deadlocked and with the words "All right, that's it," the judge dismissed all charges against Raymond Buckey.

THE END OF THE BEGINNING

At their start, moral panics generate a centrifugal force, spinning emotions, reactions and beliefs to the margin, readying professionals and the public alike for the voracious moral consumerism that will follow. At their end, they bring about social and institutional change, on some occasions or, more often, devolve into folklore.

The McMartin Preschool case marks both the beginning and the near-end of the day care ritual abuse moral panic. When it began, no one could get enough of it. The ritual abuse narrative "made sense" because it discursively linked the master symbols of that decade, personified the inchoate fears and anxieties of that time, and clarified moral positions. But by 1990, almost everyone had supped their fill of horror. The ritual abuse narrative had lost most of its Gothic appeal.

The beginning and the ending of a moral panic are always interesting, but it is what happened between the two—the scores of other day care ritual abuse cases the McMartin Preschool case triggered—that reveal the most about its volatility, perniciousness, and its extravagant irrationality.

3

Enter the Child-Savers

A moral panic germinates in the stresses and strains of the historic moment, but it is interest groups that give it life. By talking and writing about the identified threat, and directing and taking action against it, interest groups play a critical role in determining the trajectory, diffusion, outcomes and duration of a moral panic.

Not surprisingly, scholars of moral panics have a keen interest in interest groups. They dice them up according to their origin (Goode & Ben-Yehua, 1994), location *vis-à-vis* the policy-making arena (Best, 1990), and motives (Jenkins, 1992). They chop them according to their type of rhetoric (de Young, 1996a, Hawdon, 2001), style of leadership (Duyvendak, 1995), and strategies for singling out folk devils (Cross, 1998; O'Donnell, 1999).

The interest group that gave life to the day care ritual abuse moral panic in the years betwixt and between the McMartin Preschool case makes a mess of such tidy classification schemes and, in doing so, divests them of much of their explanatory power. The members of this loosely congealed interest groups—social workers, mental health clinicians, law enforcement officers, sexual abuse survivors, advocates, feminists, New Christian Rightists, parents and, arguably, even the children, them-selves—have little in common. Some are just ordinary folks, others are mid-level professionals, others still are academics and scholars; some have power or easy access to it, most others do not; some are morally motivated, others materially, and others still ideologically inspired. And although their allegiance to each other proved rather fickle over the course of the moral panic, these strange bedfellows joined in a quixotic quest to prove day care ritual abuse real.

That said, the child-savers, as this interest group can be called, deserve a closer look. From the start of the moral panic to its end, this interest group had one primary goal: to discursively construct the threat of day care ritual abuse.

DISCURSIVE CONSTRUCTION OF RITUAL ABUSE

The widely publicized McMartin Preschool case set out the ritual abuse master narrative, but for ritual abuse to be imagined as both a real and exigent threat, it had to be constantly reiterated.

Extremes Meet

In the years between the start of the McMartin Preschool case and its end, those most intimately involved in it took to the national conference, lecture, consultation and expert testimony circuit to give a discursive existence to the "perfectly hidden evil" of day care ritual abuse (Summit, 1994a, p. 339). So persuasive was their rhetoric that they ideologically recruited others who, in turn, went on to find cases of day care ritual abuse in their own communities and then trained others still to do the same in their communities. Rather like the parlor game of "six degrees of separation," most new recruits to the child-savers interest group can trace their interest in ritual abuse to this small cadre of moral entrepreneurs.

Consider the role of psychiatrist Roland Summit. As early as 1984, and just a few weeks after social worker Kee MacFarlane added a *soupçon* of conspiracy to the McMartin Preschool case in her testimony before a sub-committee of the U.S. House of Representatives, Summit urged the National Symposium on Child Abuse conferees to consider themselves privileged to hear the horrible secrets of ritually abused children (Nathan & Snedeker, 1995, p. 91). A year later, he and parents of some of the alleged McMartin Preschool victims testified before the Meese Commission on Pornography, and urged that privilege be transformed into practice by the creation of a national task force to examine the link between day care ritual abuse and child pornography production and distribution (U.S. Department of Justice, 1986). The testimonies of Summit and the parents resonated so well with the *Zeitgeist* that they became the prime movers and shakers in the creation of new legislation that facilitated the investigation and prosecution of day care ritual abuse cases.

In all of his appearances, Summit wore his *idée fixe* on his sleeve. Having already laid the foundation for believing anything children said with his "child sexual abuse accommodation syndrome," he now set about extending it to the more improbable stories of day care ritual abuse. Summit's message was not based on child development theories and research, therefore it rarely invited questions about children's developmentally-based ability to be truthful or to resist suggestion. Rather, it was all about belief. By elevating belief over empiricism, he exhorted audiences to abandon critical thinking and healthy skepticism[1] and, in doing so, encouraged a kind of moon-eyed gullibility.

A sample of his comments at various ritual abuse conferences that were all the rage during the 1980s illustrates this point. At one, he urged his audience to believe that lack of evidence is really evidence of ritual abuse by insisting that the inability to prove a satanic conspiracy is behind the day care cases is due to the conspirators' skills in "creating paralyzing, calculated confusion and mind control" of their young victims (Summit, 1987). In another, he admonished mental health clinicians to believe that conspiring law enforcement officers may hide evidence of day care ritual abuse to protect satanic providers. "Any investigation that you might prompt on behalf of your client needs to be channeled as much as possible to trusted individuals," he asserted, although he hastily expressed regret for the comment when confronted on camera by a skeptical documentarian (cited in Earl, 1995, p. 124). And in another venue, he urged conferees to believe the ritual abuse allegations made by mentally unstable individuals like Judy Johnson whose fantasies fueled the McMartin Preschool case, because they are able to discern what those with logical and analytical minds simply cannot—a conspiracy of evil. "Eccentric, alienated, unsocialized and paranoid personality types are needed to ferret out allegations," he explained. "It takes somebody paranoid to continue to express suspicion" (Summit, 1989).

Summit's own credulity, expressed in his oft-repeated credo, "If I hadn't believed it, I wouldn't have seen it" (Summit, 1994b), stamped as true every fanciful conjecture about ritual abuse. In a 1985 conference in a southern California county where what many believed was a community-based ritual abuse case was rapidly imploding,[2] the lead investigator told the audience that the discovery of pesticide-tainted watermelons and a colony of killer bees was evidence of a local satanic conspiracy. Summit, a panelist, agreed and went on to warn that those who thought differently very well may be "agents from the other side" (cited in Nathan, 1987, p. 29).

By the mid–1980s, some adult patients diagnosed with multiple personality disorder, arguably the most severe of the psychological manifestations of Post-Traumatic Stress Disorder, also were remembering "agents from the other side." During what often were grueling sessions of recovered memory therapy, they were recalling childhood histories of ritual abuse, not in day care centers, of course, since they were few and far between when these adult patients were children in the 1940s and 1950s, but at the hands of cultists who often included their parents and family members (Goodman, 1997). An informal survey conducted at the International Conference on Multiple Personality/Dissociative States reveals that 25 percent of the multiple personality patients being treated by conference participants were recovering memories of horrific acts of childhood ritual abuse (Braun & Gray, 1987).

Their narratives more closely resembled that of the tragedian Michelle in the best seller, *Michelle Remembers,* than the day care ritual abuse master narrative created in the McMartin Preschool case, but Summit facilely linked the two. In a 1987 presentation he told his audience that "[The children's] descriptions of ritual cult practice came out of nowhere in their backgrounds, and the stories are told to adults—parents or therapists—with no background or knowledge of ritual cults. And they match rather perfectly the descriptions of adults who have survived these things" (Summit, 1987).

This link had a crucial consequence for the ritual abuse moral panic. It provided entrée to a new group of moral entrepreneurs: psychiatrists and clinical psychologists doing recovered memory therapy with adults diagnosed with multiple personality disorder. Vested with "clinical authority" (Stone, 1992), this second wave of claims-makers forged a more scientific, and therefore a less obviously moralistic and ideological, link between the master symbols of the decade—the vulnerable child, the menacing devil, and the psychological trauma model—thus keeping the ritual abuse controversy alive well past the early 1990s when the devil left the last day care center.

Second Wave. Two of these second wave claims-makers deserve special attention. Well known and widely quoted, their exhortations about childhood ritual abuse, entirely derived from their recovered memory work with adults diagnosed with what then was termed multiple personality disorder, were uncritically added to the endlessly reproduced "stuff," *i.e.,* photocopied handouts of indicator and symptom lists, satanic holidays, roles and rituals, that circulated through the child-saver interest group.

Psychiatrist Bennett Braun is one of those claims-makers. His high profile as founder of the International Society for the Study of Multiple Personality and Dissociation, and clinical director of the Dissociative Disorders Clinic at Rush Presbyterian-St. Luke's Hospital in Chicago, Illinois, always guaranteed an attentive audience. But it was less the messenger than the message that secures Braun's place in the day care ritual abuse moral panic: his discourse resonated so remarkably well with the decade's social anxieties, fears and yearnings that were the "real problems" that generated the moral panic in the first place.

A 1988 conference presentation, as an example, very well could serve as a primer for that decade. In it, he analogized satanic cults to communist cells, an analogy deeply resonant with unease about the "Evil Empire" the Soviet Union was in 1980s cultural imagination. "We are working with a national-international type of organization," he told conferees, "that's got a structure somewhat similar to the communist cell structure, where it goes from local small groups to local councils, regional councils, district councils, national councils, and they have meetings at different times." He then went on to tell an audience that surely must have shared the populace's distrust of government and big business, that shadowy satanists have infiltrated the Central Intelligence Agency and the Federal Bureau of Investigation, AT&T, Hallmark Greeting Cards, FTD Florists and, in a bit of a reach here, were sending coded messages to each other via tote board figures during the nationally televised Jerry Lewis Muscular Dystrophy Telethon. Further pumping the conspiratorial imagination, he then provided his audience with his "Rule of P's," a handy guide to the identification of professions most likely to harbor satanists: providers of day care, physicians, psychiatrists, psychotherapists, principals and teachers, pallbearers (morticians), public workers, police, politicians and judges, priests and clergies of all religions, and public officials.

As if all of this were a plausible subplot, Braun's discourse was facilely grafted on to the day care ritual abuse master narrative by the child-saver interest group. A new factoid[3] began circulating that profession determines the role a satanist plays in the cult. A day care provider, for example, will be responsible for procuring children for ritual abuse, a mortician for disposing bodies of the sacrificed infants, a police officer for stymieing the criminal investigation (Lundberg-Love, 1988; Michaelson, 1989; Ryder, 1992).

D. Corydon Hammond is the other second wave claims-maker of note. On the faculty of the University of Utah Medical School, former president of the American Society for Clinical Hypnosis and recipient of its Presidential Award of Merit, he is lauded by one reviewer of his text, *Handbook of Hypnotic Suggestions and Metaphors* (1990), as a "master clinician of unusual breadth and talent who has become one of the giants in the field of clinical hypnosis." His discourse on ritual abuse also reveals he is a master late-modernist who views the self as on-going narrative rather than stable entity, and treats narrative knowledge as superior to scientific knowledge (Giddens, 1991).

From his hypnotherapy sessions with adults diagnosed with multiple personality disorder, Hammond claims to have uncovered the "whole story" of ritual abuse. It goes like this. Near the end of World War II, American intelligence agents initiated Project Monarch, a top secret initiative to bring Nazi scientists to the United States. The agents contacted a small group of scientists who had conducted mind control experiments in the concentration camps. In that group was a young man who was neither scientist nor Nazi. Greenbaum, the only moniker Hammond knows him by, was a Hasidic Jew who had struck a Faustian bargain with his captors: in exchange for being spared the gas chamber, he would teach them the secrets of the occult philosophy of the Cabala and assist them in mind control experiments. By the way, Hammond hastily adds, these Nazis were also satanists. Because Cabala mysticism already had been integrated into satanism by Aleister Crowley, the 19th century occultist, magician and impresario who, as the self-proclaimed "field marshal to the devil" would have reveled in Hammond's assertion that he is also the "father of contemporary satanism," these satanic Nazi scientists were more than a little eager to learn what young Greenbaum could teach them.

Once in the United States, and after earning a medical degree under the name of Green, Greenbaum took over for his Nazi collaborators and conducted mind control experiments in military hospitals and base schools. Many of his early subjects were children. Although designed to contribute to the intelligence community's knowledge about mind control, the experiments also cleverly and covertly brainwashed the child subjects into satanism. According to Hammond, it is this postwar generation of children, all grown, some successful, some powerful, a few just toiling away as local day care providers, that fills the ranks of an international cabal of satanists, run by the Illuminati Council of which Dr. Green, himself, is titular head.

Hammond (1992) goes on to delineate the intricate layers of satanic brainwashing that produce the programmed alters of the multiple personalities that fill his office. Alpha is general programming, Beta is sexual, Delta produces killer alters that carry out the satanic sacrifices, and so on. He then instructs his audience, the first computer literate generation, on the use of erasure codes that wipe out these programs and their backups. "When you give the code and ask what the patient is experiencing," he advises, "they will describe computers whirring, things erasing and things exploding and vaporizing."

While the word "brainwashing" already had found its way into the day care ritual abuse master narrative, it was only in its colloquial, even euphemistic sense, until Hammond's assertions gave it scientific credibility. Then child-savers made the word central to their discourse with references to mind control, programming and triggers. One hand-out, widely circulated among child-savers and even sent to parents of children allegedly ritually abused in day care, borrows liberally from both Hammond and Braun, and states:

> Brainwashing, often in conjunction with drugs, is sophisticated hypnosis which involves the associative pairing of induced pain/terror + the cult message + the trigger cues. Trigger cues are planted in the unconscious and are too numerous to list. They are later used by the cult to control the survivor without his or her conscious awareness (visual symbols on

greeting cards, flower colors and arrangements, common hand gestures, verbal phrases, body postures, facial movements). Brainwashing is an integral part of ritual abuse and cult indoctrination and also serves to create amnesia for cult information such as names, places, etc., thus protecting cult secrecy [VOICES in Action, n.d.].

Dissociation and multiple personality disorder, the alleged sequelae of brainwashing, simply were added to the widely disseminated symptom lists. Already part of the vocabulary of the master symbol of the psychological trauma model, their inclusion enhanced the clinical authority of the lists even while it diminished any optimism that children would ever fully recover from day care ritual abuse.

Ritual Abuse for Rent. The disparate themes of discourse on ritual abuse—children and adults, intact and repressed memories, day care centers and cults, intuition and science, the past and the present—are woven together into a single narrative in a 1989 video titled, "Ritual Abuse: A Professional Overview" (Cavalcade Productions, 1989), one of many training films available for rent to interested parties.[4] This one deserves a look because it features child-savers Roland Summit and psychologist Catherine Gould, the author of a widely disseminated symptom list; second-wavers Braun and Hammond, as well as Roberta Sachs, a psychologist in the Dissociative Disorders Clinic run by Braun; Walter Young and Richard Kluft, both experts on multiple personality disorder; and Jean Goodwin, psychiatrist and aspirant historian. While there is little dialogue between them, the monologue of each is curiously accommodating to the others' opinions, as the following excerpts illustrate, and the half-hour film in its totality rather artfully spins a Gothic plot that appeals to child-savers and second-wave claims-makers, alike:

> GOULD: [The day care reports] include lots of sexual abuse, drugging of the children, pornographic pictures being taken, threats to the child and to the child's family, animal killings and blood rituals and even human sacrifice including the child being forced to perpetrate in that sacrifice, which of course is probably the most damaging aspect of the abuse itself. But I think that one of the most difficult aspects of abuse in out-of-home day care to cope with is that the fact that we're finding that you can abuse a hundred children ritualistically with all the overlay of terror and brainwashing that's been discussed, and pretty much a hundred children will keep the secret of their abuse until there's some kind of intervention.
>
> HAMMOND: Some of the children may retract a story at some point because, for example, they've seen people killed.... After all the senses have been broken down in every conceivable way with electric shocks, with drugs, with fatigue, with lack of food they can be conditioned to do things on cue. And very strongly brainwashed.
>
> KLUFT: You hear a kid who's obviously hurting saying something that probably just couldn't be, and you say well, I guess it couldn't be. Actually,

that account that couldn't be is a tell-tale sign of something that was so overwhelming that the child could not retain it and could not process it in the normal sequential way.

YOUNG: It's not uncommon for an adult to suddenly recollect events which were occurring when they were small that had been completely held in a state of amnesia. During the course of treatment they began to recover and report events of a satanic type and these can be such things as having adults participate in human and animal sacrifice even as young as three years of age.

SACHS: Patients that I have dealt with who remained in the cult and became active perpetrators and became leaders of the cult, when they began to discover what they have done at an adult level there is really very little desire to live. They lose all reason for going on. It's a very difficult treatment issue to work with because it's a reality. Whether they've been programmed or brainwashed or whatever, the truth is they have participated in blatant murder.

HAMMOND: What we're talking about here goes beyond child abuse or beyond the brainwashing of Patty Hearst or Korean War veterans. We're talking about people—in some cases who are coming to us as patients— who were raised in satanic cults from the time they were born. Often cults that have come over from Europe, that have roots in the SS, in death-camp squads in some cases. These are children who tell us stories about being deprived of sleep all night, of then being required to work at manual labor exhaustingly all day long without any food or water. When they reach a point of utter fatigue they may then watch other people tortured. Perhaps a finger might be cut off and hung around their neck on a chain or a string as a symbol to them that they had better be obedient. They may be given drugs.

BRAUN: What you're trained to do is to self destruct if you should remember too much.

GOODWIN: [There are] historical accounts of satanic cults. There was a monk who lived from about 300 AD to about 400 AD who in his youth before he became a monk, he later ended up as a bishop, entered briefly one of these cults, the Sybionite Cult it was called at the time and described, and this was back now over 1500 years ago, he was describing nocturnal feasts, chants, infant sacrifice, cannibalism, ritual use of excrement and various body excretions in a way that's very similar to some of the fragments and material I've heard from patients.

SUMMIT: Around the country there are great numbers of centers that have been identified, most of them investigated, most of them confirmed by at least one agency, some fifty centers in my experience where this kind of complaint has been made by dozens to hundreds of children in each case.

It is a Gothic plot like this, with all of the familiar conventions—sinister perpetrators, innocent victims and heroic rescuers; astonishing horror; silence, amnesia, dissociation and splitting; the ontogeny of evil, and the recapitulation of the past in the present, the child in the adult—that "made sense" of the disparate discourses on ritual abuse and, in doing so, enlarged and emboldened the ritual abuse master narrative.

Extremes Meet Again. The dramatic rise and fall of Braun and Hammond as second wave claims-makers is detailed elsewhere,[5] but their influence on the day care ritual abuse moral panic should not be underestimated. Neither should Summit's. He consulted on many of the day care ritual abuse cases during the 1980s and provided expert testimony in several trials, always seizing the opportunity to weave the particulars of his "child sexual abuse accommodation syndrome" into his testimony.

In the kind of triumph of ideology over science that is the very essence of this moral panic, Summit successfully traded on his role as ideologue-in-chief in other, more popular, arenas as well. He often was interviewed by the press and for news and parents' magazines and frequently guested on the syndicated talk show circuit. And it was Summit who consulted on the filming of the made-for-television movie, *Do You Know the Muffin Man?* (Cates, 1989) that brought day care ritual abuse into the living rooms of people across the country, and that raised the specter of ritual abuse in a number of day care cases where, at first, only sexual abuse had been suspected.

"Today's Guests Include..." Conferences, seminars and training films were not the only pulpits from which child-savers delivered their homily about the devil in day care. Television news format shows provided the opportunity to reach a larger and more diverse audience. A May 1985 segment of *20/20* titled, "The Devil Worshipers," was the first of the tabloid news shows to bring ritual abuse into the living rooms of tens of millions of people across the country. Viewers were warned at the start by host Hugh Downs that the segment would reveal "perverse, hideous acts that defy belief." It did indeed. The audience heard about human sacrifices, cannibalism, animal mutilations, grave robberies, missing children and child pornography, and saw flashes of Gothic images on the screen accompanied by a Wagnerian operatic score.

The "experts" who mediated the tension between these hideous acts and audience incredulity illustrate the ecumenical makeup of the early child-savers interest group. There were "cult cops" Dale Griffis and Sandi Gallant, former satanic high priest Mike Warnke, and psychiatrist Lawrence Pazder, in role and in words facilely linking the master symbols of the decade by urging the audience to believe that vulnerable children were being menaced by the devil with horrific psychological consequences. What the audience did not know, in fact could not know, is just how ephemeral the status of expert really is in a moral panic, how insubstantial it is before the winds of cultural change. By decade's end, Griffis would become the object of ridicule, Gallant would renounce her belief in ritual abuse (Carlson & O'Sullivan, 1989), Warnke would be exposed as fraud (Hertenstein & Trott, 1993), and Pazder would be thoroughly discredited (Allen & Midwinter, 1990).

And then there was Geraldo Rivera's 1988 special, *Devil Worship: Exposing Satan's Underground,* a two hour primetime "documentary." Sharing the dais were "cult cops," heavy metal musicians and fans, Believe the Children representatives, satanists, repentant satanists and Catholic priests, convicted murderers, farmers with mutilated cattle, a prosecuting attorney and a state legislator, and women who recently had recovered childhood memories of ritual abuse. The special, an extravagant mix of myth, folklore, paganism, occultism and pure nonsense, all conveyed with the kind of "linguistic flatulence" (Ingebretsen, 2001, p. 59) that all too often is mistaken for passionate expertise, garnered the largest viewing audience in television history.

Child-savers also guested on nationally syndicated television talk shows that in late-modern American society "have replaced the confessional of old as places where tales of sexual suffering, secrecy, shame and surviving are told" (de Young, 1996c, p. 111). There they served as cultural intermediaries of sorts, stamping as credible and believable the horrible tales of little children and the gruesome recovered memories of adults with the imprimatur of an expert.[6]

Cult Cops

In 1987 R. Jerry Simandl, a 20 year veteran of the Chicago Police Department, gave a talk to 150 law enforcement officers, child protection workers and prosecutors in St. Paul, Minnesota. The topic: satanic crime. "It's not a pleasant topic," he warned his audience, "but I believe it's going to be the crime of the 1990s." Since it had already been the crime of the 1980s, it was not too difficult to convince his rapt audience that his accounts of ritual abuse, infant sacrifice and devil-worship in day care centers were real. "It was terrifying," a conferee told a reporter. "It was chilling and overwhelming. You don't want to admit this is going on." But belief that it is going on permeated the audience. "It reminded me of when we first heard about gangs and everybody thought it was blown out of proportion and it wouldn't happen here. Now it's a way of life here" explained another conferee. "But with these cults it can be more dangerous because you're dealing with smarter, more educated, more sophisticated people. I think it's going to be a real problem" ("Satanism Growing Worry," 1987, p. 45).

So did Simadl and other "cult cops" recruited to the child-savers interest group. In law enforcement seminars across the country, they disseminated ritual abuse symptom lists and handouts of satanic symbols, holidays and rituals. Often sharing the dais with mental health clinicians, parents of ritually abused children, adult survivors and clergy, they incorporated the jargon of psychological trauma and the exhortations of the New

Christian Right into their treatises on investigation, evidence gathering and interrogation. Armed with props and a convincing polyglot script, the "cult cops" became admired and enviable figures in the law enforcement profession. As criminal justice analyst Robert Hicks (1991, pp. 33–34) observes:

> Now cult cops appear everywhere: officers attend a few cult seminars, return to their departments, and organize portfolios of Satanalia so that they themselves can give seminars to teachers, parents, and enforcers; they join informal networks of other cult cops, then parade their own consciousness-raising seminars by inventing a *mise-en-scène* replete with Black Mass artifacts, books adorned with garish pentagrams, and resurrected photographs of Anton LaVey's 1966–67 Church of Satan featuring nude women as altars…. Vague on causal relationships and ambiguous on the investigative value of seminars, cult cops leap logical problems in favor of *tableaux vivants,* featuring priests and cult survivors with lurid tales backed by slides of graffiti, dead animals, and occult bookstores.

Despite the staging and the borrowing of language, or perhaps because of them, "cult cops" were influential figures in the child-savers interest group. Familiar with the criminal justice system, they often were called upon to prepare children and their parents for the rigors of day care ritual abuse investigations and the demands of court testimony. They lobbied state legislators for the passage of ritual abuse laws, and served on state task forces on ritual crime. And in doing all of this, they redefined the often discredited role of law enforcement officer by becoming community liaisons, child advocates, lay therapists, and moral arbiters (Hicks, 1991).

PASSIONATE PARENTS

Another key player in the child-savers interest group was an organization that parlayed a credo into a title and a mission: Believe the Children. The history of the organization is testimony to the democratization of expertise in this moral panic. In 1986 some of the parents who had taken on the lonely role of parent-advocate in the McMartin Preschool case were invited to share the dais with social workers and mental health clinicians at the 1st National Conference on Child Victimization. The parents' presentations were poignant and their call to action persuasive. Realizing the strength in numbers and in organization, the presenting parents allied with each other as well as with interested audience members from all over the country to form the organization, Believe the Children.

From its inception the organization grew quickly from an informal support and information exchange network into a national clearinghouse, referral, advocacy and support center on all matters having to do with ritual abuse. With some of the day care ritual abuse moral panic's most visible moral entrepreneurs on its board of directors, the organization was cloaked with credibility, and it went on to play an instrumental role in many of the day care ritual abuse cases that followed its formation, sending parents, investigators and prosecuting attorneys lists of indicators and symptoms, recommending consultants and expert witnesses who would testify on the children's behalf, and stacking courtroom audiences with advocates sporting large lapel buttons pronouncing its credo.

Long after the devil left the last day care center, the Believe the Children organization maintained a web site that was at the center of cyberspace discourse on ritual abuse. Although the organization folded in the mid–1990s, its list of "successful ritual abuse prosecutions," factually inaccurate and horribly out-of-date, remains on the web as a last gasp warning that ritual abuse was real and a nostalgic reminder that ordinary people banded together to eradicate it.[7]

"*List, List, o List!*" The Believe the Children organization was not the only purveyor of the ritual abuse symptom list that assisted parents and professionals in the onerous task of identifying child victims. There were many lists circulating during the decade of the day care ritual abuse moral panic, and as inventories they were remarkably dissimilar. With what only could have been carefree abandon, list-makers added unique symptoms they came across in particular cases or heard about in conferences, and deleted others that were inconsistent with what they saw or heard, or were in their opinion, just plain improbable.

Social worker Pamela Hudson's (1991) quasi-empirical study of 11 ritual abuse cases is a fascinating example of list-making. Her telephone survey of the parents in these cases finds there is only one "exceptional symptom" that clearly differentiates ritual abuse from ordinary sexual abuse—"sudden eating disorder," a sequela, she insists, of the forced cannibalistic consumption of the flesh of sacrificed infants (p. 7).

While one exceptional symptom should a short symptom list make, Hudson adds a few culturally familiar post-traumatic symptoms like fear and anxiety to round out the inventory. But the critical point here is why sudden eating disorder is on this list at all. According to her own data, this exceptional symptom was not even reported in 2 of the 11 cases she surveyed and was only inferred in another case based on a parent's report that a child had "poor eating habits." Further, Hudson never reveals how many children were allegedly ritually abused in each of the 11 cases, and what proportion of that number actually experienced this symptom. So, presumably, the sudden eating disorder of a single child in a multi-victim case is reason enough to elevate it to the status of an exceptional symptom. To add further madness to the method, Hudson insisted a controversial British sexual abuse case was really a ritual abuse case. Although the children allegedly victimized in it did talk about consuming the flesh of sacrificed infants, none of them ever reported having experienced this exceptional symptom (LaFontaine, 1998).

The various lists not only do match each other, but they have little correspondence with the very few controlled studies conducted on the sequelae of ritual abuse. The disparity between two such lists, one put together by the Believe the Children organization and disseminated to parents in many of the other day care ritual abuse cases, and the other circulated by the advocacy group VOICES in Action, is evident in Table 2. What is also evident, though, is the disparity between either and both of these lists and the findings of a controlled study that compares the sequelae of children allegedly ritually abused in a day care case, with those of children sexually abused in a different day care case, as well as with children with no documented history of abuse of any kind.

The spread of the ritual abuse moral panic from the United States to Canada, Europe and Australasia, about which more will be said later, followed the trail of these various symptoms lists as they circulated among international child-savers at conferences and seminars. Cultural anthropologist J.S. LaFontaine (1998) discusses the role the lists in all of their iterations played in case-finding in England, Scotland and Wales, and journalist Lynley Hood (2001) examines how one symptom list influenced the parents in New Zealand's infamous Christchurch Civic Creche case to come to the conclusion that their denying children really had been ritually abused after all.

"THE READINESS IS ALL"

It actually may be difficult to overestimate the role that conferences, seminars, training sessions and symptom lists play in the spread of the day care ritual abuse moral panic. A survey of 2,136 clinical psychologists, psychiatrists and social workers who had dealt with at least one alleged case of ritual abuse reveals they "had a very high rate of attending lectures, seminars or workshops concerned with ritualistic crime or ritualistic child abuse" (Goodman, 1997, p. 62). Another survey of 433 mental health clinicians practicing in San Diego, California finds that respondents are more likely to identify ritual abuse in their practices if they previously had attended trainings and workshops on the subject (Buckey & Dalehouse, 1992).

Regardless of the profession of conferees, ritual abuse conferences

TABLE 2

Ritual Abuse Sequelae in Children: Contrast and Comparisons Between Symptom Lists

Believe the Children (n.d.)	*VOICES in Action (n.d)*	*Kelley (1989)*
		Social withdrawal
		Somatic complaints
Marks and bruises	Brands, scars, burns	
Aggressive behavior		Behavior problems
Fixation on urine, feces	Body function fixation	
Toileting problems	Toileting problems	
Preoccupation with death	Preoccupation with death	
Overreaction to sight of blood		
Preoccupation with magic		
Sings odd songs and chants	Recitation of chants	
Writes backwards		
Fear of bathrooms and water		
Fear of something foreign inside the body, *e.g.* bomb	Fear of cherry bomb implanted in body	
	Low self-esteem	
	Rapid mood changes	
	Night terrors	
	Suicidal ideation	
	Childhood amnesia	
	High I.Q.	
	God-phobia	
	Bi-polar thinking	
	Multiple personalities	
	Dissociation	
	Guilt	
	Depression	Depression
	Anger	
	Hate	
	Excessive masturbation	Sexual problems
	Desensitization to pain	
	Preoccupation with number 6 and its multiples	
	Excessive fears	Excessive fears
	Eating disorders	

serve as bully pulpits for believers, according to cultural anthropologist Sherill Mulhern (1992) who attended 14 of them as a participant observer. She identifies the proselytizing techniques that create a "belief filter" through which all manner of pseudoscientific, folkloric and quasi-religious materials on ritual abuse, put together by child-savers, are filtered. First, "bits" of primary source materials, such as a photograph of satanic graffiti or a drawing by an alleged ritual abuse survivor, are extracted from their discrete contexts and then discursively linked together as if they relate to each other and, in doing so, substantiate some factual scenario. The weakness of the link between these "bits" is then masked by emotion-rousing testimonies of alleged survivors of ritual abuse and/or their parents and loved ones. Group participation and discussion techniques are used next to marginalize any skeptics and to encourage group-think. In the process, the conferees become thoroughly socialized into "belief-aligned" words, such as "survivor" as substitutes for more cumbersome terms like "alleged survivor" that more accurately reflect the specious evidence. Secure now in their belief that ritual abuse is real, the conferees are primed to act as if it is. They are, in essence, new recruits to the child-saver interest group.

Unpunctured Discourse

Although eclectically constituted and motivated, the child-savers interest group discursively constructed the threat of day care ritual abuse and mobilized action against it. The discourse was often inconsistent, inaccurate, and at times lavishly irrational, but despite that, or perhaps because of it, it was also powerfully persuasive. Those who were swayed by the message were both ideologically and materially recruited, that is, they came to think and to act in ways that spread the day care ritual abuse moral panic across the country.

Over the decade betwixt and between the beginning and the end of the McMartin Preschool case, the child-savers interest group lost much of its cohesion and a great deal of its influence. But by the time it fell apart completely, it had recreated the ritual abuse master narrative in a hundred or so day care centers across the country, and had coaxed its repetition from the mouths of thousands of young children.

4

Betwixt and Between

In 1983 the "Just Say No" to drugs campaign was launched; in 1990 drug abuse was epidemic. In 1983 the United States invaded Granada, the world's second largest nutmeg producer, to wrest the island from the control of communist Cuba; in 1990 the United States was on the verge of war with Iraq to wrest Kuwait, the world's largest oil producer, from its control. The Moral Majority, all that was right in 1983, was gone in 1990; sexual abuse, all that was wrong in 1983, was battered by a backlash in 1990. And the McMartin Preschool ritual abuse case, the "Crime of the Century" in 1983, was satirized in 1990. A comic in the role of reporter in a *Saturday Night Live* sketch pointed to a picture of Peggy McMartin Buckey, Bible in one hand and handkerchief in the other, wiping tears from her eyes when her "not guilty" verdict was read. "Peggy McMartin Buckey," he funereally droned, "caught in the act of molesting her eye." The audience roared with laughter.

A great deal happened between the beginning of the McMartin Preschool ritual abuse case and its end: old enemies gave way to new, razor toothed ideologies lost their bite, fads faded, and tragedy became farce. What also happened between those two dates was a moral panic, with the child-savers at the vanguard, that targeted a hundred or so day care centers in large cities and small towns across the United States, and transformed scores of providers into folk devils. A closer look at a sample of 22 of those cases (Table 3), some more notorious than others, provides the entrée for the analysis of that moral panic.

"Passions Spin the Plot"

Each of the 22 sample cases unimaginatively plagiarizes the Gothic plot of the McMartin Preschool case. Each, for example, has the familiar *dramatis personae*—a child who says something suggestive of sexual abuse, a worried parent or two, earnest social workers or mental health clinicians, dedicated law enforcement officers, an upstanding prosecutor, all of whom, over time, work that vague comment into an allegation of ritual abuse.

TABLE 3
Sample of 22 American Day Care
Ritual Abuse Cases

Day Care Center	Year	Location	Accused
Manhattan Ranch	1984	Manhattan Beach, CA	Michael Ruby
Country Walk	1984	Miami, FL	Frank Fuster, Iliana Fuster
Jubilation	1984	Ft. Bragg, CA	Barbara Orr, Sharon Orr
Small World	1984	Niles, MI	Richard Barkman
Fells Acres	1984	Malden, MA	Violet Amirault, Cheryl LeFave, Gerald Amirault
Georgian Hills	1984	Memphis, TN	Frances Ballard, Betty Stimpson, Jeff Stimpson, Paul Shell
Rogers Park	1984	Chicago, IL	Deloartic Parks
Craig's Country	1985	Clarksville, MD	Sandra Craig, Jamal Craig
Wee Care	1985	Maplewood, NJ	M. Kelly Michaels
Felix's	1985	Carson City, NV	Martha Felix, Francisco Ontiveros
Mother Goose	1985	Winslow, ME	Reginald Huard
East Valley	1985	El Paso, TX	Michelle Noble, Gayle Dove
Cora's Day Care	1986	Sequim, WA	Cora Priest, Ralph Priest
Presidio	1986	San Francisco, CA	Gary Hambright, Michael Aquino, Lilith Aquino
Gallup Day Care	1987	Roseburg, OR	Edward Gallup, Mary Lou Gallup, Edward "Chip" Gallup, Jr., Charlotte Steidl
Glendale Montessori	1987	Stuart, FL	James Toward, Brenda Williams
Miss Polly's	1988	Smithfield, NC	Patrick Figured, Sonja Hill
Old Cutler	1989	Miami, FL	Bobby Fijnje
Breezy Point	1989	Langhorne, PA	"Mrs. Janet B.," "Mrs. Lois S."
Faith Chapel	1989	San Diego, CA	Dale Akiki
Little Rascals	1989	Edenton, NC	Robert Kelly, Betsy Kelly, Dawn Wilson, Shelley Stone, Darlene Harris, Robin Byrum, W. Scott Privott
Fran's Day Care	1991	Austin, TX	Fran Keller, Dan Keller, Janise White, Raul Quintero, Douglas Perry

Consider the Georgian Hills case as illustrative, if not just plain typical, of the sample cases. Here, a four year old told her mother who was bathing her that she "hurt down there," referring to her genital area. Her mother questioned her as to why and the child eventually said that Frances Ballard, her day care provider, had sexually abused her. Understandably upset, her mother discussed this disclosure with some of the other parents who had children enrolled in the Baptist Church–affiliated center; when they questioned their own children, three more claimed they, too, had been sexually abused by Ballard. Several months later, and after an intensive police investigation, the prosecuting attorney called a press conference to announce that over 19 children had been identified as victims, although some were too young to testify and were not named in the indictment. All of the complaining children were referred to local mental health clinicians under contract with the county to conduct "disclosure interviews" that would solicit additional information needed to prosecute Ballard. Over the next several months, the children began telling their interviewers about satanic rituals that included animal sacrifices, baptisms in the name of the devil, and confinement in cages.

Some of the children in the Georgian Hills case also claimed Ballard gave them "movie star hairdo's" every morning, then strapped them into a helicopter to fly them to the mountains where she filmed them having sex with her and with each other (Berry, 1987). Kudos just have to be given to children like these who resist the pressure to parrot the ritual abuse master narrative and, in doing so, exercise their creative imaginations. The 22 sample cases are filled with this type of serendipitous, even anarchic, allegation. A child in the Manhattan Ranch case, for example, insisted he had been ritually abused in a pink haunted house (Feldman, 1984), while children in the Cora's Day Care case said their abuse had taken place in a pink polka-dot silo ("Bizarre Rights," 1986). A child in the Miss Polly's Day Care case said he had been forced to eat a feces covered banana (*North Carolina v. Figured*, 1993); a child in the Roger's Park case claimed she had been forced to eat the body of a baby cooked in the basement boiler by the center's janitor (Emmerman & Taylor, April 21, 1985); a child in the Fells Acres case said she had been raped with a lobster (*Commonwealth v. Amirault*, 1989); and a couple of children in the Little Rascals case insisted they had been bound with ropes and used as bait in shark-infested waters (Durkin, 1991).

Even the most credulous of interviewers was likely to either dismiss these fanciful allegations out-of-hand, or rationalize them as drug-induced hallucinations or distorted post-traumatic memories. But to paraphrase poet T.S. Eliot, between the idea and the reality falls the shadow. The dread that comes with not knowing for certain if ritual abuse is real, yet expecting it is, is a feature of every one of the 22 sample cases. In all of those cases, everyone suspended in the shadow between not knowing and knowing exchanged "improvised news" in an effort to deal with the dreadful uncertainty. The Small World case that began with a child's claim that Richard Barkman, a provider and husband of the center's owner, had forced her to perform fellatio, is illustrative. During the ensuing investigation, 50 more children said they, too, had been sexually abused by Barkman, and some went on to describe rituals that included orgies with robed and hooded adults. Anxious parents in this small rural community met weekly, sometimes with the social workers and mental health clinicians interviewing their children and other times with the law enforcement officers investigating the case and the prosecutor who would later try it, to exchange observations, fears and speculations, the "improvised news" that in the constant saying and repeating comes to be mistaken for cold, hard reality (Lengel, 1985).

There is one case in the sample, though, in which parents refused to entertain the very idea of ritual abuse, and their unwillingness led to a most unusual outcome in this pernicious moral panic. The Breezy Point case began typically enough, with a four year old telling her mother who was quizzing her about the "good touch/bad touch" lesson she had had that day in day care, that her provider had rubbed "cinnamon cream" into her vagina. The child later said that her two best friends also had been digitally penetrated by their provider and her 68 year old aide (Rubenstein, 1990).

What at first blush appeared to be a sexual abuse case transmogrified into a ritual abuse case when the parents of the three children, who themselves were good friends, settled down one October evening to watch the CBS Sunday Night Movie, *Do You Know the Muffin Man?* Loosely based on the McMartin Preschool case, the lurid tale of the ritual abuse of children in a black mass conducted by their satanic day care providers, ended with curiously contradictory messages flashed on the screen: "This story is fictional," the first read, followed immediately by, "Talk to your children. And listen." So the parents did. And over time they heard accounts remarkably similar to the fictional ones depicted in the film. Convinced that ritual abuse had happened, they attempted to recruit other parents with children enrolled in the exclusive center into their belief, but failed. Some of those other parents, in fact, filed harassment charges in an effort to stop the late-night telephone calls and the so-glad-I-ran-into-you conversations in the grocery store and on the church steps. The more certain the complaining parents became that ritual abuse had occurred, the more evangelical they were in their attempt to recruit others to their belief, the more they were marginalized by the other parents and the community. And the case fell apart. No criminal charges were ever filed (Conroy, 1991).

In a few of the sample cases, *à la* the McMartin Preschool case, official missives meant to sort idea from reality only darkened the shadow between the two. A couple of examples illustrate how good intentions can go awry. When a four year old told her pediatrician that her vaginal sores had been caused by Reginald Huard, the husband of her provider and co-owner of the Mother Goose Nursery School, an investigation immediately began. Huard was asked for the names and addresses of all of the children enrolled in the center. The next day, the Department of Human Services sent letters to parents informing them that a complaint had been filed and urging them to bring their children to Department social workers for interviews. The letter closed with the ominous warning that any parent who refused to do so, "would be putting your child at risk by continuing your child in the Mother Goose Nursery School program" (Riddle, 1988, p. 43). Only one other child was identified as a victim during the investigation that followed, but it was she who told a story reminiscent of *Michelle Remembers,* about confinement in a gold cage and threats with live snakes. Even in military patois, the letter sent to parents in the Presidio Army Base Child Development Center case had the same darkening effect. After a three year old told his mother that his provider Gary Hambright, a civilian employee and ordained Southern Baptist minister, had fondled his penis, the Army formed a strategy group to investigate. It sent a letter to 242 parents whose children were enrolled in the center. "The Commander, Presidio of San Francisco, has been apprised of a single incident of alleged child sexual abuse," it read. "We have no reason to believe that other children have been victimized" (Goldston, 1988, p. 14).

The Army may have had no reason, but the letter it sent gave parents plenty. As the investigation proceeded at a snail's pace, and more and more children accused both Hambright and Lt. Col. Michael Aquino of sexual abuse in rituals that involved the consumption of urine, feces and blood, a core group of parents sent a letter of its own to the other parents with children enrolled in the center. "We feel you should know that there are now 37 children identified by authorities as suspected victims," it read. "We are very concerned that there may be more children affected and in need of help, yet remain unidentified" (Goldston, July 24, 1988, p. 14). The letter prompted parents to accelerate their interrogation of their children, and bring them in for repeated medical exams and interviews by military and civilian investigators. Within several months, another 33 children were identified as victims.

A different kind of case-finding occurred in the shadows between idea and reality in some of the other cases in the sample. The ritual abuse "symptom lists," those ever-growing, ever-changing catalogs of horror, were disseminated to parents and among social workers and mental health clinicians. In the Fells Acres case, for example, 80 parents received a list in a meeting with police and state social workers just a few days after Gerald "Tooky" Amirault was arrested for touching the genitals of a boy enrolled in the family-owned day care center. Disseminated along with the list came this warning from one of the social workers present: "God forbid any of you should show support for the accused. Your children may never forgive you" (Sennott, 1995, p. 1). The list and the warning had the desired effect. Soon, dozens of children were telling stories about magic rooms and rapes with purple wands. Now, nearly 20 years later, and after the most complex legal machinations of any of the day care ritual abuse cases, the Fells Acres case is no closer to resolution than it was when it began on that warm September day in 1984.

OF CHARACTER AND CHARACTERS

The passions that spin the ritual abuse plot rancorously split the communities where the day care cases occurred, pitting neighbor against neighbor, child against adult and sometimes, sadly, child against child. In every case in the sample, passion built character, transforming otherwise loving parents into ferocious advocates for the children. In other cases, passion built characters, transforming otherwise uncredentialed advocates into ferocious pretenders to expertise.

The Country Walk case exemplifies the influence of the newly minted role of parent-advocate in the ritual abuse moral panic. In 1984, Country Walk was an upscale neighborhood of 600 homes selling for an average of $49.76/square foot (Adams, 1996) when that world of "butterflies and blueberry skies," as the promotional brochure so poetically describes it, was haunted by the specter of ritual abuse. The case began like so many of the others in the sample with a statement by a three year old. Running naked out of the bathroom, he asked his mother to kiss his body, adding that "Iliana kisses all the babies' bodies." Worried that something inappropriate had happened at the babysitting service, his mother talked to a friend who, in turn, confided in a friend well-placed in the prosecutor's office. He conducted a record check and discovered that Cuban immigrant Frank Fuster, who ran the unlicensed babysitting service out of the home he shared with his 17 year old Honduran wife, Iliana, had a criminal record for child molestation. As the news traveled through the close-knit community, worried parents took their children for interviews with Joseph and Laurie Braga, child advocates who shared an unpaid position in the prosecutor's office as "special interviewers." Although every child initially denied having been abused, through repeated and intensive interviews they began to parrot the ritual abuse master narrative. They talked about prayers to the devil, animal sacrifices, cannibalism and posing for pornography, and by summer 1984, certain they had "another McMartin" on their hands, the parents were in an uproar (Nathan, 1993).

Over 300 of them met with former United Sates Attorney General Janet Reno who was then the county prosecutor, two state legislators, representatives from the offices of a United States senator and the Governor of Florida, and the Bragas at the Country Walk Community Center.

Out of that cacophonous meeting one parent, a Miami police sergeant, emerged as model for the new role of parent-advocate, and it was she who would go on to speak for the parents and the children in this controversial case. Standing before the meeting, she read a petition she had drafted: "We, the undersigned residents of Country Walk Development and other communities of Dade County, request an immediate investigation by the state attorney as to why a day care center was allowed to be operated in Country Walk by a convicted felon on probation for lewd and lascivious acts on a child" (Balmaseda, 1984, p. 1C).

In this new role, she was the only parent invited by prosecutor Reno to appear before the grand jury, the first parent to file a civil suit against the Fusters (Ynclan, September 12, 1984), and the spokesperson for all of the parents before the Governor's commission on child abuse in day care (Ynclan, September 16, 1984). And she spoke for all of the children. She was the only parent interviewed by the media about the impact the release of the videotaped interviews conducted by the Bragas would have on the children (Daughtery, 1984), the reaction of the children to the delay in Fuster's trial (Daughtery, June 8, 1985), the reasons why the pretrial interrogation of the children should not be restricted (Daughtery, July 17, 1985), and the psychological boost the revocation of Fuster's probation would have on the children (Ducassi, 1985). A decade after the case began, she was the only parent interviewed for a reaction to Fuster's petition for a new trial on the grounds that leading and suggestive interviews had elicited both false stories from the children and a false confession from his wife (Dewar, 1994). Nearly two decades after the case began, she was the only parent whose opinion was solicited for the PBS *Frontline* documentary, "Did Daddy Do It?" that reexamined the Fuster case (2002).

Most parents find this new role of advocate daunting. And it is. In assuming the role of speaking for other parents and, most importantly, for all of the horrifically victimized children made invisible by the protective shield of confidentiality, they also assume the responsibility of fixing both emotional tone and moral judgment into daily news and social exchange. In this role, they sometimes are factually inaccurate, grammatically incorrect, and even clumsily inarticulate, but the public always seems to accept that language is only supplemental—it is their fear, sorrow, outrage and condemnation that make the impression—and that vivifies the moral panic.

There are different discursive expectations, however, when uncredentialed advocates assume the role of expert on ritual abuse. From them, the public expects "a sober use of language commensurate with high moral purpose" (Ingebretsen, 2001, p. 59), but what it more often gets is a linguistic plundering of Gothic images, metaphors and tropes that in the short run whips up the fervor of the moral panic, but in the long run contributes to its ignominious end. The 22 sample cases are peopled with these pretenders, from the self-appointed expert who used her considerable physical and social capital to convince others that children really had been ritually abused in the Faith Chapel day care center (Granberry, November 29, 1993); to the self-anointed expert who took over the interviewing of the children in the Rogers Park case and was later found to have doctored his credentials (Emmerman & Taylor, April 19, 1985); to the self-opinionated expert who met with parents in the Presidio case and then used her radio talk show to promote an elaborate conspiracy theory implicating satanists, the military, Nazis and the CIA (Millegan, 2000).

The most illustrative example of a pretender to expertise on a case, though, occurs in that curiously anomalous Breezy Point case. After three sets of parents who suspected their children had been sexually abused at the exclusive center sat down to watch the CBS movie, *Do You Know the Muffin Man?* they became convinced their children had been ritually abused. Their conviction fell on deaf ears, however; law enforcement officers refused to pursue their demand for a vigorous investigation, so they contacted the Believe the Children organization and asked it to recommend a consultant and investigator. The organization endorsed ritual abuse expert James Stillwell, founder and president of the National Agency Against the Organized Exploitation of Children, a 300-employee advocacy group based in Silver Springs, Maryland (Conroy, 1991).

His investigation quickly confirmed their worst fears. He discovered that the accused provider, her aide, and the owners of the center were devotees of the Satanic Worship Church, and were members of the same satanic coven as the McMartin Preschool providers. Their mission, he concluded, was to use ritual abuse to indoctrinate children into satanism. And the evidence of satanism, according to Stillwell, was everywhere his expert eye could see. What looked to the inexpert investigator to be just a popular Cabbage Patch doll sitting on a classroom counter was really a satanic totem. What sounded to the inexpert investigator to be just a simple, silly song sung by the children in a promotional video was really a satanic message. Incidentally, it went like this: "I have a little puppy/he has a stubby tail/he isn't very chubby/he's skinny as a rail./He'll always be a puppy,/he'll never be a hound,/they'll sell him at the butcher shop/for twenty cents a pound./Bow wow-wow-wow-wow-wow-wow/Hot dog!" (Rubenstein, 1990, p. 64). And what appeared to the inexpert investigator to be just a promotional video with the children dressed in bathing suits on an ersatz Hawaiian set with construction paper crescent moons and stars, is really a piece of satanic pornography. "The person behind the video camera is a pedophile," he told the parents. "On the tape you can see all their little heinies and all their little vaginas" (Conroy, 1991, p. 139).

As advocate-*cum*-expert, Stillwell did not hesitate to publicly pronounce the Breezy Point case another day care ritual abuse case. The pronouncement stunned the already deeply divided community and deepened the schism between those who believed something must have happened at the center, and those who did not. In that dark shadow between the idea of ritual abuse and the reality, the complaining parents and the mental health clinicians already involved in the case redoubled their efforts to get to the bottom of it. And over the next several months, the children's stories started conforming nicely with the ritual abuse master narrative. They talked about participating in orgies with their providers, drinking urine and eating feces, taking stupefying drugs, and participating in human sacrifices.

In the whirling passions of the moment, the police investigation that had found no convincing evidence that the children had been sexually abused, now aggressively set out to determine if they had been ritually abused. No evidence to corroborate the allegations was ever found; a great deal to contradict them was. But it was the investigation of advocate-turned-expert Stillwell conducted by the Office of the District Attorney that is of most interest here. It uncovered that he was a former refrigerator repairer with no credentials or training who, after a prolonged period of unemployment, started what was really only a one-person operation run out of a post office box. At the time his expert eye was seeing the ritual abuse no one else could, he was on probation for transporting a gun in his vehicle. In that case, he had staked out the home of a young runaway, and when his behavior aroused suspicion, the police were called. They arrested him and confiscated from his van a police scanner, a camera and lights, a handgun, and an Uzi semiautomatic machine gun (Conroy, 1991).

With the parents already marginalized for their zealous beliefs in ritual abuse, and their expert thoroughly discredited, Bucks County District Attorney Alan Rubenstein called a press conference and announced he would not prefer charges against the provider and her aide (Conroy, 1991). "The greatest hoax in the history of my commonwealth" as he would later describe the case, was officially over ("100 Protest," 1997).

Twice Told Tales

Even all of this rather frenetic activity to prove ritual abuse real would be for naught if the ritual abuse master narrative could not be recreated by child-savers in interactions with the children. To further that goal, a leading and suggestive style of interviewing, rooted in the quasi-theory of the "child sexual abuse accommodation syndrome" and the shibboleth of "believe the children," became all the rage in the decade after the McMartin Preschool case began. Often preserved on audiotape or videotape, the interviews offer a fascinating illustration of why "twice told tales" are told in the first place, and how they, too, gave discursive life to the day care ritual abuse moral panic.

Developmental psychologists Stephen Ceci and Maggie Bruck (1995) identify the features of these types of interviews that exemplify "the potential for error and misinterpretation when scientific knowledge and common sense are banished in the forensic arena" (p. ix). They focus on stereotype induction, repeated interviewing, coercion, peer pressure and emotional tone, but foundational to all of these interviewing errors is confirmatory bias, that is, the pursuit of a line of questioning aimed at soliciting responses that confirm the interviewer's belief, and the concomitant avoidance of a line of questioning that may solicit responses that disconfirm that belief.

The interview conducted by a tag team of therapist and law enforcement officer in the Felix Day Care case illustrates this foundational mistake. In this case, a child told her mother that she had hated going to the day care center Martha Felix ran out of her Carson City, Nevada home with the occasional assistance of her nephew, Francisco Ontiveros. Asked repeatedly by her mother if something sexual had happened to her there, the child finally replied that Ontiveros had molested her. Her mother called the police. Anticipating "another McMartin," the police referred parents with children in Felix's care to local mental health clinicians for interviews. Over the course of the next several months, 19 children accused Felix and Ontiveros of sexual abuse and described confinement in closets, forced ingestion of gasoline and dog urine, and participation in human sacrifices. One child, a six year old, had since moved with her family to northern California where she was interviewed by family counselor Patricia Bay who had been apprised by the Carson City police of the ritual abuse allegations. One of those interviews, conducted with Detective Sgt. Harry Bishop, illustrates the relentless pursuit of the ritual abuse master narrative (*Felix v. State*, 1993).

> BISHOP: (T)hink about this real careful. Did anybody touch you when you were at Martha's in a place you didn't like?
> CHILD: No
> BISHOP: Would you tell me today if somebody did?
> CHILD: Can't remember, it's too far back.
> BISHOP: If someone would have touched you in a place you didn't like would you tell me about it? Would you?
> CHILD: Yes, but I, but that never happened to me.
> BAY: Where would be a place that someone shouldn't touch you? Can you show me on this [anatomically correct] doll? What do you call that?

CHILD: I don't know.
BAY: What would you call this area right here? What do you do with that part of the body?
CHILD: Go potty.
BAY: Right. Did anybody ever try to touch you there?
CHILD: No
BAY: Did you ever see anybody get touched there?
CHILD: No
BISHOP: Did anybody ever take pictures while you were at Martha's?
CHILD: No.
BISHOP: Did you ever see anybody get put in closets to get punished?
CHILD: No.
BISHOP: Are there some things that you just don't want to talk about?

In a pretrial hearing to determine the testimonial competency of the child, Bay defended her suggestive and leading interview style on the basis that it was necessary to coax the child into disclosure. In expert testimony at the hearing, psychiatrist Roland Summit agreed, adding, "The assumption that children can be moved into believing that they have experienced a complex and traumatic set of circumstance because of leading questions or repeated interviews or the suggestions from important people, that's not well established in any empiric data or data" (*Felix v. State*, 1993).

Summit's conclusion is arguable: even if a child is not led to *believe* that ritual abuse occurred, he or she certainly can be led to *say* that it did. But it is not just relentless questioning that reveals the confirmatory bias of the interviewer. In the Fells Acres case, graduate student Susan Kelley, with *Sesame Street* puppets Bert and Ernie literally on hand, pleads with a four year old to confirm her bias that she was ritually abused (Shallit, 1995, pp. 14–15):

KELLEY: Did anybody touch you on your bum?
CHILD: Nobody. Nobody didn't do it.
KELLEY: Oh, you don't think anybody touched the children on their bum?
CHILD: No
KELLEY: What should I do if they touch the children?
CHILD: [No answer]
KELLEY: What should I do if they did?
CHILD: Nobody didn't do it!
KELLEY: Don't you want to help me? Ernie [puppet] would be so happy if you tell me.... Did anybody ever touch that part of you?
CHILD: No.
KELLEY: Would you tell me if they did?
CHILD: No, I don't want to,
KELLEY: You don't want to tell me?
CHILD: No.
KELLEY: You can help me. Oh, come on, please tell Ernie. Please tell me, please tell me, so we can help you. Please? Mommy would be so happy

if you would help us; so would Bert [puppet]. Please tell me. Tell Bert [puppet]. Okay, you tell Ernie [puppet]. You whisper it to Ernie. Susan's going to cover her face, and you whisper it to Ernie. All right. Who touched you there?
CHILD: Okay
KELLEY: Okay?
CHILD: My teacher.

Any relief about this confirmatory statement was short-lived, however. The teacher the child finally named actually was a provider at the new day care center she was sent to after her parents removed her from Fells Acres upon the arrest of the Amirault family on a total of 52 counts of sexual abuse, some of it committed in a "magic room" where Gerald "Tooky" Amirault, dressed as a clown, raped them and his mother Violet and sister Cheryl LeFave were said to have sacrificed infants.

Another feature of these day care interview is stereotype induction. Here, the interviewer reveals his or her own bias by suggesting to the child that the accused provider is bad, sick or evil. While an interviewer may passionately defend this technique as a way of empathetically connecting with a child, Ceci and Bruck's (1995) empirical studies find that it actually reduces the accuracy of a child's disclosure and, even more disconcertingly, prompts the child to spontaneously elaborate on the stereotype.

The Supreme Court of New Jersey recognized this interview contamination technique when it affirmed the Appellate Court's decision to reverse the convictions of provider Kelly Michaels on 115 counts of sexual abuse and child endangerment in the Wee Care ritual abuse case. In reviewing the interviews, the Court noted that "throughout the record, the element of 'vilification' appears. Fifteen of the 34 children were told, at one time or another, that Kelly [Michaels] was in jail because she had done bad things to children; the children were encouraged to keep Kelly in jail," as the following interview illustrates (*State v. Michaels*, 1994):

INTERVIEWER: It would be okay to tell me the truth if she did try to bother you just so that you can show me how she might just try to hurt these other kids. 'Cause the more we know, the longer she will stay in jail. You understand...? What were some of the other stories that she used to scare the kids? That they wouldn't tell anybody. Did she tell them she would hurt their parents or something? Do you know if she said that?
CHILD: Yeah
INTERVIEWER: You know that's not true.... The police put her in jail. Because she was hurting you, you know. That's why I really need your help.... And you will be helping to keep her in jail longer so that she doesn't hurt anybody else.
CHILD: It's scaring me.
INTERVIEWER: That's okay. Believe me, she's not going to be coming out of jail. She's not going to be hurting you guys anymore...

CHILD: I didn't get hurt.
INTERVIEWER: No, maybe you didn't; maybe you fought her off. Maybe you really didn't hurt then. Maybe you saw your other friends getting hurt and you didn't like it very much, you know.

Well, maybe, but only if the solipsism of the "child sexual abuse accommodation syndrome" replaces critical thinking and common sense. According to it, denial really means affirmation. The necessity of getting to affirmation compelled many of the interviewers in the day care cases to subject children, often as young as three and four, to multiple interviews until the children finally affirmed that ritual abuse occurred and then shaped their stories to conform to the ritual abuse master narrative. The six year old in the Felix case, for example, had 98 interview sessions with family counselor Bay who then testified in the preliminary hearing that the child would be irreparably psychologically traumatized if she told her story one more time in court (*Felix v. State*, 1993). In the Craig's Country Day Care case in which Sandra Craig and her son Jamal were accused of photographing the children in their care in sex acts, inserting thumbtacks and screwdrivers into their vaginas and rectums, confining them in cages and burying them alive in the woods, one denying child was interviewed 27 times, another 54 times, another over 60 times before she finally affirmed the interviewer's belief that ritual abuse had occurred at the sprawling "children's country club" in the woods (*Craig v. Maryland*, 1988). The Little Rascals case serves as a good reminder that parents also are part of the child-savers interest group and have as much, in fact probably more, of a vested interest in "getting to the truth" than any of their professional associates. The role of parents as interviewers and re-interviewers often is overlooked simply because they are not usually inclined to audiotape, videotape or transcribe their interactions with their own children.[1] But from the witness stand, one mother describes how her repeated questioning of her three year old son finally confirmed that he, too, had been abused by Bob Kelly, one of seven defendants in the most controversial case in North Carolina history (*State v. Kelly*, 1991–1992):

> MOTHER: First time I questioned him, we were laying on my bed and I was just, you know, "Do you like Mr. Bob...?" "Has Mr. Bob ever done anything bad to you...?"And as we were talking I got more specific with him. I asked him, "Has Mr. Bob ever touched your hiney?" "Has he ever put his finger in your hiney...?"
> ATTORNEY: Was that only time you questioned him?
> MOTHER: No, it went on...
> ATTORNEY: Now tell me how it developed that you began to get statements from him that raised a question in your mind about sexual abuse.
> MOTHER: [My son] was being questioned a lot from that first time on,

quite often. And then that last week then it was probably a few hours every day thing.... I got a response from him. Um, he told me that Mr. Bob had put his penis in his mouth and peed on him...

ATTORNEY: How did he come up with those kinds of statements?

MOTHER: Because I asked him ... he had been hearing it at least once a week since I first started questioning him and then that last week he was hearing it every day.

In their empirical research on repeated interviewing, Ceci and Bruck (1995) find that while children do remember more with each additional interview, their reports also become more inaccurate over time. Simply put, they recall both more accurate *and* inaccurate details with each successive interview. Further, repeated interviews signal the interviewers' bias to the children, cueing them on how to answer in a way that pleases their interrogators.

As if defying their allegiance to the child-savers interest group, some of the interrogators are downright mean-spirited, so bent upon having their bias confirmed that they coerce the very children they are trying to help. The husband and wife team of Laurie and Joseph Braga, whose commitment to child-saving led them to eschew a salary for interviewing the children in the Country Walk case, was not above resorting to coercion when other techniques failed. In this interrogation of the six year old son of accused provider Frank Fuster, the Bragas tell him he had tested positive for gonorrhea of the throat[2] and therefore had not been truthful in previous interviews when he denied having been forced to have oral sex with his father (*Fuster v. Singletary,* 1997):

JOSEPH BRAGA: Did they tell you not to tell anybody that you had gonorrhea?

CHILD: Gonorrhea...? I didn't know that.

JOSEPH BRAGA: But you know now?

CHILD: [Inaudible]...

JOSEPH BRAGA: Let's go back to talking. I said to you earlier that I know you are not telling me the truth because you said that no one put their penis in your mouth but yet you had the test; the test said you had gonorrhea. If you have gonorrhea, someone put their penis—

CHILD: I don't remember, maybe they did. I don't remember...

JOSEPH BRAGA: You said you don't remember anybody putting their penis in your mouth? Do you think it was your father?

CHILD: I don't know who did it...

LAURIE BRAGA: Let's suppose that it did, okay" Because the doctor said it did, even though you don't remember who did, who might have done that to you. Do you have any idea, even if you don't remember?

CHILD: I think maybe my dad and someone else.

Consider also this interview excerpt from the Georgian Hills Baptist Church day care center case in which a determined social worker attempts to coerce a child into reciting the ritual abuse master narrative and naming Frances Ballard as his abuser (Carlson & O'Sullivan, 1989, p. 198).

> SOCIAL WORKER: What's Miss Frances doing while children are in the other room?
> CHILD: I don't know.
> SOCIAL WORKER: Come here ... I want to talk to you a second. [Boy's name] you do know. Look at me. Look at me. You know about the secret. But see, it's not a secret any more, because [another child] told us about it and [another child] told us about it, and your parents want you to tell us.... You can be a very good boy and tell us about it.
> CHILD: I don't know.
> SOCIAL WORKER: Yes, you do.

Peer pressure is another form of coercion. While more has to be understood about its effects on young children, the few empirical studies that have been conducted find that children will give inaccurate, sometimes completely false, accounts in order to fit in with a real or even imagined group of peers conjured up by interviewers (Ceci & Bruck, 1995). Consider this interview by Lou Fonolleras, an investigator in the Institutional Abuse Unit of the Department of Youth and Family Services, who did most of the interviews in the Wee Care case (Hentoff, 1992, p. 22):

> FONOLLERAS: We've gotten a lot of other kids to help us since I last saw you.
> CHILD: No, I don't have to...
> FONOLLERAS: We talked to a few more of your buddies. We talked to everybody now. And everyone told us about the nap room, the bathroom stuff, and the music room stuff, and the choir stuff, and the peanut butter stuff, and everything. Nothing surprises me anymore.

But what should have surprised Fonolleras and the interviewers in the other day care ritual abuse cases is not only the initial insistence of most of the interviewed children that they had not been abused, but their naive strategies of resistance and their sometimes touching attempts to negotiate their identities as "good," that is, truthful, children during the interviews. In the interview just cited, Fonolleras goes on to interrogate the child about what provider Kelly Michaels did to him; to each question the child responds, "I forgot," a mildly defiant answer his interviewer simply will not accept:

> FONOLLERAS: Tell me now. What did Kelly put in your hiney?
> CHILD: I'll try to remember.
> FONOLLERAS: What did she put in your hiney?

CHILD: The fork? [Becomes very distressed].
FONOLLERAS: I thought you were going to help me?
CHILD: It's all lies!

Another child in the Wee Care case was interviewed by Eileen Treacy, a state appointed interviewer. During trial, she defended her leading and suggestive interview methods with an impassioned reference to the child sexual abuse accommodation syndrome. The Appellate Court was not impressed. In a ruling that reversed the convictions of provider Kelly Michaels it states: "[Treacy's] testimony constitutes nothing less than substantive evidence of guilt, albeit Treacy's opinion thereof. This constituted error because syndrome evidence is not probative of sexual abuse. The syndrome assumes the presence of sexual abuse and only seeks to explain the child's reaction to it" (*State v.Michaels*, 1993). Treacy's assumption about sexual abuse, and the child's strategies to resist it, are illustrated in this interview (Ceci & Bruck, 1995, p. 118):

> TREACY: Did Kelly ask the kids to look at her private parts, or to kiss her private parts?
> CHILD: She made me. She made me, but I couldn't do it. So I didn't even really do it. I didn't do it.
> TREACY: Did it smell good?
> CHILD: Shhhh.
> TREACY: Did it taste good? Did it taste like chocolate?
> CHILD: Ha, ha. No, I didn't even do it.
> TREACY: You Wee Care kids are so scared of her.
> CHILD: I wasn't. I'm not even...
> TREACY: But while you were there, were you real scared?
> CHILD: I don't know.
> TREACY: What was so frightening about her; what was so scary about her?
> CHILD: I don't know. Why don't you ask her?
> TREACY: Did she drink the pee-pee?
> CHILD: Please, that just sounds crazy. I don't remember about that. Really don't.

In an effort to build rapport with the children, many of the interviewers in the day care ritual abuse cases went to great lengths to be warm and supportive. They effusively thanked the children for their cooperation, heartily congratulated them on giving the "right" answer, and rewarded them with candy, ice cream and junior police badges. Keeping in mind that many of the children in these cases were only three or four years old, and talking to strangers in unfamiliar settings, this kind of reassurance and encouragement, at first blush, seems laudable. But it also creates reliability risks. By selectively reinforcing certain responses, it not only shapes children's answers but increases their frequency. Empirical studies demonstrate that when interviewers are overly supportive, like this law enforcement officer in the Wee Care case, children tend to offer as many inaccurate as accurate details (Ceci & Bruck, 1995, p. 145):

> INTERVIEWER: Do you want to sit on my lap? Come here. I am so proud of you. I love big girls like you that tell me what happened. That aren't afraid and I can protect you…. Because that is my job to protect cute, little beautiful little girls, God bless you, just like you. Okay. You got such pretty eyes. You're going to grow up to be a beautiful young lady. I'm jealous I'm too old for you.

"DOUBTFUL AT BEST"

In the 22 sample day care cases, hundreds of children were interviewed by hundreds of different child-savers, including social workers, mental health clinicians, advocates, law enforcement officers and attorneys. It goes without saying that some of those children were simply too young, too confused, too frightened, perhaps, to answer their interviewers candidly and truthfully; it also goes without saying that some of their interviewers were too eager, too anxious, too incompetent, even, to ask questions carefully and objectively. That said, though, it is vital to emphasize that the cited interviews are more typical than not of those conducted with the children in the day care ritual abuse cases.

In an *amicus curiae* brief submitted to the Appellate Court of New Jersey by developmental psychologists Stephen Ceci and Maggie Bruck on behalf of 46 members of the Committee of Concerned Social Scientists, the leading and suggestive interviews conducted in the Wee Care case are cited as reasons to question the reliability of the children's testimony. The Committee saved its most excoriating comments not for the children, however, but for the child-savers who interviewed them (Bruck & Ceci, 1995, p. 40):

> It is difficult to believe that adults charged with the care and protection of young children would be allowed to use the vocabulary that they used in these interviews, that they would be allowed to interact with the children in such sexually explicit ways, or that they would be allowed to bully and frighten their child witnesses in such a shocking manner. No amount of evidence that sexual abuse had actually occurred could ever justify the use of these techniques especially with three and four year old children. Above and beyond the great stress, intimidation and embarrassment that many of the children so obviously suffered during the interviews, we are deeply concerned about the long-lasting harmful effects of persuading children that they have been horribly sexually and physically abused, when in fact there may have been no abuse until the interviews began.

Ceci and Bruck's outrage was not limited to the Wee Care case. In looking at other day care ritual abuse cases, they conclude that "the rash of allegations of these children emerged as a result of highly biased interviews.... [T]he persistent biased interviews created a situation in which we will never know what happened to these children. The interviewers' methods have rendered their testimony doubtful, at best" (1995, p. 297).

Doubtful, yes. But until the day care ritual abuse moral panic ran out of steam, the words of children, formed in conversational partnership with their interrogators, made ritual abuse real. And the providers once entrusted with their care were transformed by those words into the moral panic's folk devils.

5

Demonizing Defiant Folk Devils

Folk devils. The term so nicely resonates with medieval notions of *maleficia,* the evil-doings of seemingly ordinary folk who are slyly wreaking havoc on the social and moral order. Indeed, there is an enticingly sinister air about those targeted in the moral panics that first caught the eye of scholars after the publications of Stanley Cohen's (1972/2002) seminal work. There were the coarse women of the witch hunts (Ben-Ye-huda, 1980), the volatile underclass racial minorities of the street crime scares (Hall *et al.,* 1978), the antisocial youth of the drug panics (Goode, 1990), all different, odd, strange, before they "emerged," to use Cohen's careful word, as the folk devils of moral panics.

More recent scholarship, though, is less seduced by the sinister air than by the social atmosphere from which folk devils emerge. It takes as a given that each society at each historical moment redefines its own centrality and then pushes to the margins those who by age, gender, sexuality or religion, as examples, are not part of the current dominant group (Cullen & Pretes, 2000). In this view, those who are targeted as folk devils of moral panics have a liminal status; they occupy the margins of society as the geography of the imagination envisages them. These are the anomic youth of the school shooting panic (Burns & Crawford, 1999), the sexually nonconformist teenage mothers in the illegitimacy scares (Blaikie, 1995), and the purveyors of television trash and sleaze in the media censorship campaigns (Trevener, 2000), all already outsiders, outcasts, pariahs, before they "emerged," to use Cohen's word again, as folk devils in moral panics.

The day care ritual abuse moral panic, though, calls for another way to understand the emergence of folk devils, as well as their demonization. The accused providers, after all, were neither sinister in air nor outsiders in station. They were, for the most part, well-liked and well-integrated into their communities before they ever were accused of gruesome acts of ritual abuse. They were not situated at the margins of late-modern United States society, but in socially acceptable roles at its center.

And they certainly are not "of a type," in any sociological sense of that phrase. A closer look at the 51 accused providers in the sample of 22 day care cases confirms that observation. The accused are of both genders, in fact, just as likely to be women as men. The oldest were, to paraphrase the poets, "feeling their touch of earthly years": Reginald Huard, who once had run for the state senate, was 60; both Edward Gallup and Violet Amirault, who died of cancer in 1997; were 61; Cora Priest was 62; and "Mrs. Lois S.," the perennial community volunteer, was 68. The youngest were mere adolescents: Iliana Fuster was 17, as was high school athlete Michael Ruby; Jamal Craig was 16; and Bobby Fijnje was only 14 years old when he was rumored to be the head of an international cartel of satanic child pornographers. While most of the accused are white, Paul Shell, Jamal Craig and his mother Sandra are African-American; Martha Felix, Francisco Ontiveros, Raul Quintero and the Fusters are Hispanic. Among the accused were three men of the cloth and one of the cape, and a priestess: Gary Hambright, who died of AIDS in 1990, was an ordained Southern Baptist minister, as is Paul Shell; Edward Gallup is a former Church of the Nazarene pastor; Michael Aquino is a satanic priest who founded the Temple of Set, a satanic church dedicated to freeing its followers from the tyranny of the Judeo-Christian doctrine the other three men so ardently embraced, and his wife, Lilith, is a priestess in the Temple's Order of the Vampyre. The vocations and avocations of the accused varied as well. Jeff Stimpson was a law student when he was accused of ritual abuse; Kelly Michaels was an aspiring actress; Sonja Hill was a divorcee having an affair with Patrick Figured; Michelle Noble was a housewife who took the minimum wage job of day care provider at the East Valley YMCA because she enjoyed children; Dale Akiki is developmentally delayed with an IQ in the 70s; Ralph Priest battled debilitating bouts of mental illness. A few of the providers, like Martha Felix and Cora Priest, ran mom-and-pop day care centers from their homes, barely making ends meet; others, like James Toward and Sandra Craig, parlayed the care of young children into lucrative enterprises.

What this case of characters does have in common is a role. And it is the concept of role that offers an entrée to the third way of looking at the emergence of folk devils. In the *Zeitgeist* of the 1980s the role of day care provider lost much, although of necessity, not all, of its "social honor," as the sociologist Max Weber would have put it (Gerth & Mills, 1958). The shifts in economic, social and moral stratification of that decade transformed the much needed service of day care into a necessary evil, and those in the provider role into the embodiment of the conflict between the traditional family and the market economy. Far from sinister, far from marginalized, the role of day care provider nonetheless was made visible and problematic by its loss of social honor, and those who carried it out were left vulnerable to the vagaries of social discourse.

Demonizing the Folk Devil

The word "demonize" certainly has a nice fit with the term "folk devils," but it is not just for its semantic suitability that it is of importance when considering the day care providers in the 22 sample cases. The folk devils of any moral panic always are "victims of metonymy and metaphor, prey to sloppy habits of public thinking, linguistic failure and a narrative rush to closure that is tantamount to an act of direct prejudice" (Ingebretsen, 2001, p. 52). But to emerge as the folk devils of the ritual abuse moral panic, providers had to be talked about and perceived not just as odd or strange, outsiders or outcasts, but as evil. More directly put, they quite literally had to be demonized.

The process of demonization required situating the personal identities of the providers in the discursive web that linked the master symbols of that decade. They had to be seen as agents of a menacing devil, sexually preying on innocent children, and indifferent to, or perhaps even delighted in, the psychological trauma they inflicted. While some of the discursive strategies for doing just that—fear-mongering, biographical gerrymandering and rumor—were the same for the males in the sample as for the females, demonization actually was an interestingly gendered process.

"HOW AGREES THE DEVIL AND THEE?"

During the 1980s there was no louder voice about the master symbol of psychological trauma than that of feminists. In the feminist view, the sexual abuse of children is as much, if not more, a political act as a psychological one. Unlike physical abuse, most sexual abusers are male, most victims female, and the striking gender asymmetry begged analysis of, and action against, the oppressive patriarchal power relations underpinning it.

Patriarchy, feminists argued, sanctions males to sexually abuse, provides them the opportunities to do so, empowers them to cover it up and silence their victims, and to successfully defend themselves from social and legal sanctions when they cannot. Patriarchy is, as feminist writer and incest survivor Louse Armstrong (1994) so provocatively puts it, the "cradle of sexual politics."

Rocking that cradle in the decade of the 1980s were feminist scholars, clinicians and activists whose critique of gendered power relations both inside and outside the family profoundly influenced the child-savers interest group. The received wisdom that all males are potential sexual abusers and that those who work with, or around, young children are particularly suspect, quickened the imagination and rather expediently caught the males in the sample in the discursive web ensnared between two of the master symbols of the decade: vulnerable children and psychological trauma. The process of demonization, though, required that web also be tangled around the third master symbol of the menacing devil.

Sexual abuse, after all, is not ritual abuse. The fondling and oral-genital contact that are the preferred acts of sexual abuse almost pale in comparison to the rape and sodomy that supposedly are the preferred acts of ritual abuse. The idiosyncratic practices to heighten the abusers' arousal in sexual abuse almost fade to insignificance in contrast to the infant sacrifices, blood-drinking and cannibalism that are the alleged rituals of ritual abuse. And the bribes, coercions and manipulations that keep sexual abuse secret simply cannot hold a candle to the death threats, brainwashing, forced drug ingestion and induction of multiple personalities that are said to guarantee the silence of ritually abused children. In the moral economy of the 1980s, sexual abuse was horrible, shameful—but ritual abuse was evil. And evil acts require evil actors.

Aided and abetted by the media and the popular culture, whose role in the post–McMartin Preschool cases deserves a close look, the child-savers set about to discursively stake the 24 males in the sample to the third master symbol of the decade—the menacing devil—in an effort to transform them from suspected sexual abusers into certain ritual abusers. The truth be told, they failed more often than not. And the very fact that they did had an interesting impact on the moral panic.

A Confession Good for the Soul—But Not for the Reputation. The child-savers savored an early success, though, that increased their confidence that ritual abuse was a real threat to children in day care, and that primed the larger culture for ensuing cases. That success came in the person of Frank Fuster, the perfect fly to be entrapped in the discursive web. A bit of a lothario, Fuster had fathered his first child at the age of 14 and had married three times, the last to Iliana who was less than half his age. Charismatic, controlling, crafty, he was the embodiment of *machismo*, the Latinized version of patriarchy that was just beginning to arouse the acrimony of the larger culture. He came on to the scene already firmly ensnared in the discursive web spun between the master symbols of the vulnerable child and psychological trauma: he had not only spent time in prison for killing a man in an act that in today's parlance would be referred to as "road rage," but he was on probation for sexually molesting a nine year old girl[1] when he was accused of ritually abusing children in the unlicensed babysitting service his wife Iliana ran out of their home. It was Iliana, in fact, who confirmed the rumors that "another McMartin" had occurred under the leafy palms in the upscale neighborhood of Country Walk. Her confession offers an interesting glimpse into the demonization of Frank Fuster.

Iliana also was charged in the Country Walk case, but after considerable inside politicking her case was severed from her husband's so that they would be tried separately (Nathan, 1993). Without evidence to corroborate the horrific stories of filmed and photographed sex games, animal sacrifices and prayers to the devil, the prosecution needed an adult witness. Iliana fit the bill. To accuse her husband of ritual abuse, though, was tantamount to confession, since the children had named both of them. Thus, the strategy for her defense was for her to admit she was a ritual abuser, but only because she, a mere 17 year old, was a victim of her husband's demonic rage and under his Svengali-like control.

Held in isolation in jail, she was subjected to 30 to 40 sessions with the two psychologists hired by her attorney to help her remember the details of the ritual abuse. During "relaxation and visualization" exercises, described rather glibly by one of those psychologists, Michael Rappaport, as exercises in "reverse brainwashing" (Nathan, 1993, p. 6), a stubbornly resistant Iliana finally accused her husband of physically and sexually abusing her, and then confessed that both of them had ritually abused the children in their care, including Fuster's six year old son from a previous marriage. With then Dade County District Attorney Janet Reno present, she talked about how Fuster had scared the children with a snake, and then tried to make it wriggle into her vagina; how he had tied her up in the garage, beat her, and then covered her with feces while the children watched; how he drugged her and then fellated his six year old son ("Did Daddy Do It?" 2002).

That the confession linked all three master symbols of the decade and, in so doing, disputed any devil-born doubt that ritual abuse was real, was evident in an editorial written by the *Miami Herald* staff upon Fuster's conviction on 14 charges of sexual abuse and his sentence to 165 years in prison (*Herald* Staff, 1985, p. 22A):

> Few criminals in South Florida history have deserved a genuinely lifelong prison sentence more than Frank Fuster Escalona. The man lurked at his Country Walk Babysitting Service like a venomous spider that has built a web to bring his victims near. He practiced gross sexual acts on small children entrusted by their parents to his care. He violated them systemically and over time, as a life style, not as a momentary aberration.... If these horrors had to be visited upon these tiny innocents, then

the maximum positive results have been realized. Laws have been changed, victims comforted, parents emboldened, prosecutors strengthened, public consciousness raised. And the monster Fuster is destined to spend the remainder of his unnatural life deservedly caged.

The *Miami Herald*'s Gothic prose was echoed in the book, *Unspeakable Acts* (Hollingsworth, 1986), a nearly 600-page account of the Country Walk case penned by a former television news assignment editor who became a "consultant" to interviewers Joseph and Laurie Braga and a "full-time advocate" for the Justice for Sexually Abused Children group the parents had formed (Nathan, 1993). The book popularized the Country Walk case, which was being touted by child-savers as the case that proved day care ritual abuse real. And in prose that plundered Gothic folklore, it thoroughly demonized Fuster.

The author, who had never interviewed him because she did not think she "could stand to be in the same room with him" has him tell "his own story" in the lengthy segments of trial transcripts she presents in the book (Voboril, 1986, p. 1C). That the transcripts are often paraphrased and edited is never mentioned, but it is the author's descriptive asides that vivify the popular cultural image of the ritual abuser. Fuster is described as a person whose "humanity [was] gradually replaced by a hollow darkness" (p. 210), as an atavist, of sorts, who "functioned according to two primitive and unbridled instincts: self-gratification and survival" (p. 210), and as a "Rev. Jim Jones in the making, an aborted replica of the man whose pious wife had helped him poison nearly a thousand men, women, and (mostly) children in the jungles of Guyana" (p. 239). His heavy accent is likened to that of a "vampire in a low budget horror film" (p. 380), and his swarthy Latin appearance to that of Dracula (p. 521).

If the book *Unspeakable Acts* failed, for some reason, to conjure up an image of a ritual abuser, the film by the same name does. Aired as an ABC made-for-television movie in January 1990, ironically just days before the jury acquitted the Buckeys in the McMartin Preschool case that triggered the day care ritual abuse moral panic, the movie had all the requisite Gothic conventions: innocent children screaming in the night, ferociously protective parents, virtuous professionals and, of course, an evil abuser lurking behind the thin façade of normalcy. In an unusually insightful review for a magazine that panders to populist tastes, *People Weekly* panned the movie, calling it "harsh and sanctimonious," and a "grim, somber and unremittingly bruising viewing experience that stirs up a lot of moral anxiety without creating any dramatic tension" (Hiltbrand, 1990, p. 9).

What the review overlooks, though, is the fact that it is moral anxiety that fuels a moral panic. The moral panic is not about a person, like Fuster or Raymond Buckey or, for that matter, any of the others who were accused during the 1980s, but about the people, groups and institutions that defined their own moral identity in reaction to them. In asking questions like, "What kind of person would do this to a child"; "What kind of evils that we could never anticipate, let alone imagine, threaten our social and moral order"; and "How do we protect our children and, in doing so, secure our future?" society seeks its moral compass. If satisfactory answers are elusive, then moral anxiety grows and finds another arena—another day care center, in this case—to attach itself to. Childsavers may insist that Country Walk is the case that proves ritual abuse real (Almond, 1993), but the frangible confession of Iliana provided few answers if any to these and other anxious questions—especially when she retracted it, and in doing so de-demonized Frank Fuster.

After serving less than half of the 10 year sentence she received in exchange for her confession and being deported to her native Honduras, Iliana retracted her confession. In a 1994 deposition taken by attorney Arthur Cohen, she described the process of "reverse brainwashing" her visiting psychologists had used to lead her to believe that both she and Fuster indeed were ritual abusers. The process, as she described it, bears an eerie resemblance to the one that led the Country Walk children to believe they were ritual abuse victims in the first place (*Statement of Iliana Flores*, 1994):

> COHEN: Did you believe at the time that the truth was that nothing happened in the house?
> ILIANA: Yes. Yes. Hmmm. I, you know, I ... because I kept saying that I was innocent, but nobody would listen to me. And they [visiting psychologists] said I was suffering from a blackout, and that those things had happened because the kids said it, and the kids don't lie. And they said that it happened, so it must have happened...
> COHEN: All right.... Do you recall when they would start these sessions? What would they say to you?
> ILIANA: I remember just that I will calm down, and I just wanted to get it over with because, you know, they told me this happened, this happened, this happened. And I break down and say no, no, no, it didn't happen. And then they would tell me that yes, I have to accept it, I have to confront it. So they were long sessions and tiring.... And I would go to bed, and I don't know why, but I would dream about the same things the kids were saying and the same things they were telling me. So I came back, and the first question was, so what did you dream about last night? Did you have any bad dreams, or did you not? If I had bad dreams I had to tell them about my bad dreams in detail. And they did tell me, you see, you remembering. And I say, no, it cannot be because I have still no memory; I just have bad dreams. And they say that that was the way of me remembering.... And they said that I was remembering, and then after remembering I was going to feel better. And that

> I needed to help the children, and the only way to help them is remembering and backing their word up. I have to backup their word.

The retraction was entered into the record as part of Fuster's motion for a new trial. But this was 1994. Fuster, in fact, was one of only a small number of convicted providers who remained in prison, and those who had a stake in the case and the ideological miasma surrounding it, were determined to keep him there. So months after she retracted her confession Iliana, now a born-again Christian with a coterie of New Christian Rightist friends who were paying her college tuition and living expenses, retracted her retraction, and in doing so, re-demonized Fuster for a society that at this point cared not very much at all. In a letter to the court, she wrote ("Did Daddy Do It?" 2002):

> (I) called some Christians [sic] friends and told them of the pressure the lawyers [representing Fuster] were putting on me and they told me that I was not strong enough emotionally to deal with high power attorneys, to which I agreed. However, the lawyers were able to find me and walk in unannounced into my life. The lawyers told me that they had new evidence to prove that nothing had happened at Country Walk. And they told me that this new evidence will clear my name and criminal record. The more I listened, the more confused I became.... They continued ... talking to me about how the State of Florida brainwashed and even used me for their own purpose 10 years ago. They started asking questions of the past and events, I got into a deep depression and started remembering my horrible past, every time I think about it, it is like living it all over again.... Now that I had time to reflect and not under the pressure of people trying to convince me otherwise, I want my testimony in Court to remain as given 10 years ago. Frank Fuster is guilty, not only of hurting the children but also of hurting me.... Frank Fuster did horrible things to me and I know he did the same to the children. He deserves to be where he is now.

And so he remains, as yet unable to clear the legal hurdles that stand in the way of a new trial. But then, in another startling reversal that has all of the dramatic tension that the film on the Country Walk case never managed to generate, Iliana retracted her retraction and once again de-demonized Fuster. In a PBS *Frontline* documentary titled, "Did Daddy Do it?" (2002) that re-examined the Country Walk case, Iliana faced the camera to insist that she had been pressured to write the letter by her New Christian Right friends, and that the truth is that nothing happened at Country Walk:

> INTERVIEWER: Let me ask you Iliana, now, today, as you sit here with me, these questions. The testimony that you gave in the trial of Frank Fuster—was that truthful testimony?
> ILIANA: It was at the time, because I believed my memory blacked out.

INTERVIEWER: But did those things to which you testified actually occur?

ILIANA: No, they didn't.

INTERVIEWER: Frank Fuster—aside from how you feel about him as a husband or as a man—was he guilty of the things he was accused of and convicted and is serving prison time for?

ILIANA: No, he's not guilty, sir.

INTERVIEWER: Did he do those things? Did you witness any of these acts of which he was accused, those children you all brought into your home?

ILIANA: I never witnessed it.

INTERVIEWER: Did any of this nightmarish scenario that came to be known as the Country Walk child abuse case—did any of this happen?

ILIANA: No, sir. None of that happened.... I never hurt any children specifically or anybody. Country Walk just didn't happen.

But it *had* happened. Iliana's last interview was made public in 2002, nearly two decades after she and Fuster were accused of ritually abusing the young children in their care. That the times had changed, and that new folk devils have emerged—including, ironically, the child-savers, themselves, who over the last twenty years have lost more than a little social honor—is evident in the *Miami Herald's* reaction to the *Frontline* documentary (Garven, 2002, p. 1C):

> Tonight's *Frontline* episode on the Country Walk child-molestation case couldn't be more timely. With the abuse accusations against Catholic priests multiplying seemingly by the hour, "Did Daddy Do It?" is a valuable reminder of how quickly a molestation investigation can devolve into a witch hunt. The Country Walk Babysitting Service case ... was just one of a long string of similar cases around the United States where young children told astoundingly lurid stories of mass sexual abuse and torture at day care centers. The accusations were frightening—but even more frightening was the way many of the cases were prosecuted. The children's allegations were made after hours of shaping and coaching by the therapists who refused to take no for an answer.... In fact, the more extravagant the children's claims, the more credence they were given: "Kids couldn't make that up" was the motto of the age.... Whether Iliana Fuster's recantation in "Did Daddy Do It?" will be enough to win her ex-husband a new trial is unclear; her credibility will certainly be questioned, particularly since she admits she's trying to get out of a jam with U.S. Immigration authorities. But at the very least, "Did Daddy Do It?" should prompt some tough questions to [Janet] Reno from the reporters covering her gubernatorial campaign. She appears briefly on camera, airily announcing she has no time for a 17 year old case. Florida voters may think otherwise.

The Devil Incarnate. If the child-savers had a difficult time discursively linking a convicted child molester to the master symbol of the menacing devil, they had one hell of a time discursively linking an avowed satanist to the master symbols of the vulnerable child and the psychological trauma model. At first blush, the 1986 Presidio case seemed to be an archetypal ritual abuse case, as perfectly as it resonated with the child-savers' Gothic image of ritual abuse. The children, all in care at the Army base's Child Development Center in San Francisco, the city that writer and curmudgeon Ambrose Bierce once called "the moral penal colony of the world," gave accounts of blood-drinking, the forced ingestion of feces and urine, and filmed orgies with costumed adults in a black room with a gold cross painted on the ceiling. While their accounts were not any more or less horrific than those given by children in any of the cases that preceded Presidio, or for that matter any that followed, the person a few of them eventually accused very definitely was.

Michael Aquino has a doctorate in political science and the rank of lieutenant colonel in the Army Reserves. And he is a satanist. Once a devotee of the Church of Satan, founded by impresario Anton LaVey, the same church that psychiatrist Lawrence Pazder just a few years before had speculated was behind the torment of his patient, Michelle, Aquino left in 1975 and established the Temple of Set. According to its slick web page, the Temple of Set "seeks above all to honor and enshrine consciousness ... to apprehend what makes us each individually unique and use this gift to make ourselves stronger in all facets of our being. To do this," it explains, "we preserve and improve the tradition of spiritual distinction from the natural universe, which in the Judeo/Christian West has been called Satanism, but which is generally known as the Left-Hand Path." The introduction to the Temple goes on to describe the antinomianism that is at the heart of its Setian philosophy, and its endorsement of the use of Black Magic to enable its adherents "to influence or change events in ways not understood or anticipated by society" ("Welcome to the Temple of Set").

It was a "Left-Hand Path" of a different sort that led to the ritual abuse allegation against Aquino, and a meander along it affords some interesting insights not only into folk devils and their demonization, but into the ritual abuse moral panic as a form of collective behavior. Like in all of the 22 cases in the sample, the first allegation in the Presidio case was suggestive of sexual abuse, not ritual abuse. It came from a three year old who explained that he was playing with his penis because "Mr. Gary do it," an apparent reference to Gary Hambright, the base's civilian day care provider (Goldston, July 24, 1988). But the specter of ritual abuse loomed over the case from the start, not because of Aquino, who would not find some mischief in it for another year, but because of the priming effect of a series of front page articles on day care ritual abuse that appeared in the *San Francisco Examiner* just a month before the first allegation was made (Ross, 1986).

Although somewhat skeptical in tone, the articles nonetheless lined up the moral panic's usual experts—psychiatrist Roland Summit, cult cop

Sandi Gallant who would later lead the search of Aquino's home, psychologist Catherine Gould whose ritual abuse indicator list was in vogue, and psychiatrist Lawrence Pazder—for credulous commentary on ritual abuse in both community and military base day care centers. Priming is all about awakening expectations, stirring possibilities, and the articles did just that. As more children came forward after the Army sent a letter to parents with children in the Presidio base's care, assuring them this was an isolated incident, the unbelievable started to become believable as primed interviewers beckoned the specter of ritual abuse into the case.

Enter Michael Aquino. The lieutenant colonel, with his arched eyebrows, prominent widow's peak and somewhat supercilious air, was hardly a secret satanist. He had made his beliefs known to the Army, secure that they would be protected under the First Amendment. And they were. He held a secret or top-secret security clearance throughout his military career and was extensively trained in psychological warfare and mind control ("Welcome to the Temple of Set"). But the officer's standing could not protect him from public opprobrium when the three year old stepdaughter of the base's assistant chaplain pointed out him and his wife, Lillith, as the persons who had ritually abused her and other children enrolled in the Presidio Day Care Center (Goldston, October 30, 1987).

Her disclosure prompted interviewers to relentlessly pursue the ritual abuse master narrative in their subsequent interactions with the children, but with disparate results: some of the children remained steadfast that they had not experienced any abuse at the center, some claimed Hambright had sexually abused them there, and others alleged that Hambright had taken them to the Aquino home to be ritually abused. While in the background sexual abuse charges against Hambright were filed and dropped, then re-filed and dropped again, in public discourse the Presidio case was a case of ritual abuse and the prime suspect was Aquino, the satanist. The only discursive task left was to link the two.

The link, however, proved frustratingly elusive. Aquino, accompanied by his wife Lilith, was matriculating at the National Defense University in Washington, D.C., during the months the accusing child was enrolled in the base's day care center. With no corroborating evidence and with a very young child whom any court undoubtedly would find testimonially incompetent, the investigation was closed (Goldston, August 2, 1988). And then, as if taunting child-savers to link him to what they continued to believe was the traumatizing ritual abuse of the Presidio children, Aquino began appearing in living rooms, awakening the expectation and stirring the possibility of day care satanic ritual abuse in communities across the country.

His appearance on, *Oprah* reveals not only how irresistible the temptation was to discursively link him to ritual abuse, but how that temptation was structured in the format of a popular daytime television talk show (Winfrey, 1988). Consider the guests who shared the dais with Aquino and his wife, Lilith, apparently invited to return good for evil. There was Lauren Stratford whose just published autobiography, *Satan's Underground* (1988), details her years as a "breeder" of babies for sacrifice by the satanic cult that held her captive[2]; "Johanna Michaelsen, a New Christian Right writer and lecturer who had converted Stratford and encouraged her to tell her story; and Detective Larry Jones, founder of the Cult Crime Network and editor of the *File 18 Newsletter,* a broadsheet that kept fellow cult cops and clergy current on cult crime and that was the source of the so-called "WICCA Letters," the alleged master plan of satanists to take over the world by, among other methods, infiltrating day care centers, that had so captured the conspiratorial imagination of child-savers."[3]

Prodded by short interrogatives by host Oprah Winfrey, Aquino opened the show with an exegesis on satanism more suitable for a university classroom than a syndicated television talk show. He pontificated on fixed fate and free will, the ontogeny of the soul, the metaphysics of satanism and the mythicization of human agency as evil, to which Winfrey artlessly responded, "Are there human sacrifices, animal sacrifices, at your church?" (p. 3).

If Winfrey was skeptical of Aquino's denial, so was the audience. The first response, more a comment than a question, in fact, more a *cri de coeur* than even a comment, was from an audience member who identified himself as a former satanist and went on to describe his participation in human ritual sacrifice. When interrogated by Aquino as to details, however, he dissembled, claiming he could no longer remember them nor, come to think of it, could he be certain that he participated in the sacrifice as he had just stated, or had merely witnessed it. Aquino dismissed him as a liar. The next audience member who was familiar with the Temple of Set's interest in the occult practices of the Third Reich, accused Aquino of also endorsing the political and social philosophy of Nazism. She was told to read the literature more closely. In the first fifteen minutes of the show, and without comment from the other guests, the scorecard was satanists two, audience nil.

After the commercial break, however, Winfrey evened the score. She nicely segued from an exegesis on satanism to a Gothic wallowing in ritual abuse that began with the introduction of Stratford whose autobiography the host pronounced "very courageous" (p. 8). Stratford offered one of several version of her life story, telling how she had been forcibly impregnated by satanic cultists for the purpose of bearing infants for sacrifice. She explained her failure to protect her children in terms of the brainwashing she had experienced by the satanists who, she went on, "are not the typical people that you think with horns in their head and living on skid row. These are professional people" (p. 9). Winfrey replied with a sly glance at Aquino, "With funny eyebrows?"

The nicely timed *bon mot* made the arched-eyebrowed Aquino central to this emerging focus on ritual abuse. Michaelsen then was called upon to lend some credibility both to the discussion and the inclusion of Aquino as its subject. While she was reluctant to accuse him and his followers of anything, she informed the audience that it is not at all unusual to find the satanic ritual abusers Stratford had described in high places, including the military. "I firmly believe that many in the U.S. Army are deeply involved," she asserted, "and perhaps have gone beyond what he [Aquino] is willing to admit" (p. 10).

The notion of "going beyond" is then linked to day care ritual abuse by Jones who confirmed that young children across the country were reporting it. With only minutes left until the end of the show, the topic had narrowed from satanism, to ritual sacrifice, to day care ritual abuse to which Winfrey then discursively linked Aquino by asking about the accusations that had been levied against him. The exchange between guests on this issue is worth citing verbatim (pp. 11–12):

> WINFREY: You were accused also of child molestation, were you not, Dr. Aquino?
>
> AQUINO: And what he [Jones] refers to is one of the cruelest examples of persecution that extends not just to people who are acknowledged satanists but to a great many innocent people around this country who are being accused wrongfully of ritual abuse of children on virtually no evidence at all. And to dispute what he has said, in case after case after case for years and years, when these have been brought before investigation, where they've been brought into indictments and trials, again and again they've been thrown out because the so-called evidence—
>
> WINFREY: They've been thrown out because nobody believes the children, nobody believes the children. Johanna?
>
> MICHAELSON: Well, that's exactly right. Who's going to believe in a modern civilized society that people are capable of such horrors? Few of us are willing to deal with it. So that when a three year old or a four year or a six year old or even an adult survivor comes up and says, "I have seen children murdered. I have been a part of slaughtering little animals. I've been told my family will be killed if I speak up. I was placed in a coffin. I was forced to drink things that are hideous beyond belief," who's going to believe them?... I can't prove that [Aquino is] sacrificing children. Perhaps he's right. Perhaps he, himself, isn't.

Perhaps, indeed. Now discursively linked, if only by insinuation, to all three master symbols of the decade, the audience hastened to tighten the knot around Aquino. The third audience member Winfrey turned to was a law enforcement officer who confirmed that the bodies of ritual sacrifice victims were being found across the country; the fourth and final was a woman who said her son had witnessed the sacrifice of an infant with its umbilical cord still attached. "I understand that that's a normal satanic ritual," she added (p. 13) before Winfrey went to a commercial break.

The final word went to Stratford who reminded the audience that this was a show about the ritual abuse of children, after all. "The kids are reporting it across the country. They're telling us what the bodies look like, the internal organs, the skull, the color of the skin. Children don't know that. They are being believed.... And there is a way out through the freedom of Jesus Christ" (p. 13). Winfrey closed with "Thank you, I'm all out of time."

She may have been, but Aquino was not. His satanic proselytizing on *Oprah* prompted audience members to write letters to government officials, protesting the Army's tolerance of satanism, and his radio and television show appearances, including on the Geraldo Rivera special, *Devil Worship: Exploring Satan's Underground* (1988), haunted the imagination of child-savers. The temptation to try again to discursively link him to the master symbols of the vulnerable child and the psychological trauma model was irresistible. Just two months after his appearance on the Rivera special, and to the great relief of the frustrated Presidio parents, the Army launched a fresh investigation of Aquino's role in the day care case; six months after that, he was picked out of a video line-up by several children as the master of a "Devil's Club" that had ritually abused them and other children, some of them then enrolled in the Jubilation Day Care Center in Ft. Bragg, California where sisters Barbara and Sharon Orr were accused, but never charged, with ritual abuse three years earlier (Goldston, 1989). No charges were ever filed against Aquino in either case.

While Aquino was using his considerable cultural capital to take on his accusers in court and to defend being titled by the Army (*Aquino v. Stone, 1992*), a journal article and two books were published that merit a closer look. At first blush, psychologist Diane Ehrensaft's (1992) clinical study of five alleged Presidio victims appears to have little in common with former satanist Linda Blood's (1994) exegesis on satanism, or with former state senator John DeCamp's (1992) expose of a credit and loan scandal in Nebraska, except, of course, that Aquino is demonized in all three. But it is the timing of their appearance that is of most interest, because it reveals something about the divergent vapor trails the imploding moral panic left in its wake during the 1990s and into the turn of the new millennium.

One of those vapor trails is a Catherine-wheel cloud of conspiracy. Blood begins her *coupe de langue* with a description of her seduction into satanism by the charismatic Aquino and the "inexorable course to disaster" that followed (p. 9). "Disaster," in her case, not only took the form of a broken marriage and expulsion from the Temple of Set, but a disturbing realization that Aquino and the satanism he espoused were not at all what they seemed to be. What follows is an unmasking of both: what lies beneath the exotic, esoteric trappings of satanism, Blood insists, is a covert criminal movement, an international conspiracy involving "worldwide drug and arms trafficking, prostitution, pornography, and other organized criminal activities" (p. 34); what lies beneath the charming façade of Aquino, she claims, is a master manipulator, fascinated by Nazism and obsessed with power. After vetting various day care ritual abuse cases as obscene examples of the reach of this satanic conspiracy, and confirming the memories adult psychiatric patients were recovering of childhood ritual abuse, Blood goes on to discuss the Presidio case and to put Aquino squarely in the middle of it. Although she acknowledges that the first interviews conducted with the children "obviously employed leading questions" (p. 179), that the medical finding of sodomy for the first complaining child was, in retrospect, inconclusive, and that the evidence of chlamydia for five of the children was based on the use of an inappropriate lab culture, she nonetheless concludes that " something terrible did indeed happen at the Presidio" (p. 189). Like all of the other day care ritual abuse cases that preceded it, the Presidio case, Blood suggests, is evidence of a vast satanic conspiracy of which Aquino is the mastermind.[4]

While Blood's conspiracy theory is inchoate, DeCamp offers a classically Manichaean theory in which the feeble forces of good are pitched against the fierce forces of evil. In his recounting of the 1988 Franklin Community Federal Credit Union scandal, in which manager and Republican Party activist Lawrence King siphoned off $40 million, DeCamp uncovers a tangled conspiratorial web involving international drug smuggling, Iran-Contra money laundering, pornography production, complicity and cover-up at the highest levels of government, and the ritual abuse of children by rich, powerful and, oddly enough, politically conservative satanists. While Aquino is almost reduced to a footnote in this account, it is indeed a note to swell the gale. He is named as an operative in Project Monarch, a joint Central Intelligence Agency/military/satanist secret initiative that ritually brainwashed the children in the Franklin case, as well as children in many other cases, turning them into criminal automatons and sex slaves for political elites.

Trailing the implosion of the day care ritual abuse moral panic, then, are two different conspiracy theories that link fragments of information into "cultural grammars," as folklorist Bill Ellis (2000, p. 124) would refer to them, that are both difficult to comprehend and impossible to prove. In cyberspace, where the current war of words over ritual abuse is being most acrimoniously waged,[5] Aquino, the satanist, is positioned dead center in each. One theory discursively links him to the Presidio case and has an almost nostalgic appeal to child-savers whose salad days have passed; the other discursively links him to a government mind control project and has an almost futuristic appeal to second-wave professionals who are keeping the ritual abuse controversy alive by recovering memories of it from their adult patients.

Those patients, after all, are giving substantively different accounts of childhood ritual abuse than those coaxed out of the children. They are dredging up memories of ritual abuse not in day care centers, which were rare commodities in post–World War II United States society, but within their extended families, communities, and social and political institutions. They are remembering more abusers, more organized and systemic efforts to silence them, more inhumane acts of torture, human sacrifice, baby breeding and cannibalism than the children ever did. And they present with more florid and complex psychological problems like dissociation, multiple personalities, fugues and amnesia (Goodman, 1994). The kind of ritual abuse they are describing seems more sophisticated and purposeful than that described by the children; their abusers more worldly and savvy than the day care providers were ever proved to be. This is ritual abuse for the new millenium, the kind that second wave claims-makers like Bennett Braun and D. Corydon Hammond brought to their eager audiences, and the stuff of what some argue is, in its own right, a burgeoning 21st century moral panic over memory, identity and testimony (Acocella, 1999; Sturken, 1998).

The Ehrensaft article charts the direction of the other vapor trail left by the imploding moral panic. In it, she describes the Presidio Day Care case as one of "sexual abuse with ritualistic features" (p. 234), a revealing turn of phrase that foregrounds the culturally familiar problem of child sexual abuse and not only backgrounds the ritualistic feature of the case, but semantically reduces it to pieces and fragments. In doing so, Ehrensaft signifies the subtle shift in ideology and semantics that child-savers had adopted as the day care ritual abuse moral panic spread across the country.

The logic of that shift is comprised of a set of syllogisms. If the day care cases really were all about sexual abuse, then their ritualistic features were ancillary to the sexual abuse, there to terrify and confuse the children, perhaps, or to heighten the sexual pleasure of the providers. If their ritualistic features are not expressions of the providers' satanic belief system, then they are expressions of their sexual perversity. Therefore, if these are not cases of satanic ritual abuse after all, then they most certainly are cases of sadistic sexual abuse.

Mining Discourse. In his book on the generation of fear in American culture sociologist David Altheide (2002) asserts that how discourse about a particular issue, whether spoken or written, changes over time is often apparent to neither the audience nor the source of the communiqué. Through the method of tracking discourse, that is, "following certain issues, words, themes, and frames over a period of time, across different issues and across different ... media" (p. 34), subtle changes in semantics and ideology become evident.

As a prolix espouser, the discourse of psychiatrist Roland Summit on day care ritual abuse spans the entire course of the moral panic and well beyond. Tracking that discourse, in the way Altheid suggests, proves challenging, but mining it by sampling it at different points in time and in different contexts makes apparent just how much the moral panic's most influential ideologue had changed his tune.

One strain of that tune was about evidence. In the Presidio case, as in all of the day care cases that both preceded and followed it, there simply was none—no evidence that the accused providers were conspiratorial satanists, and none to corroborate the fantastic allegations of the children. Summit, who at the start of the moral panic had urged child-savers to believe that the lack of evidence was really evidence of satanic ritual abuse (1985), said something very different towards its end. In a 1991 interview with the British news magazine, *Social Work Today,* he stated, "In my experience, once the allegations include murdered babies or adults, and if they include elaborate photography, it's usually the beginning of the end of a useful investigation. Those things *should* [italics added] produce material evidence. In no case," he conceded, "has that evidence been found" (Lunn, May 9, 1991, p. 9).

Summit's comment was made all the more ironic by the fact that it was addressed to British social workers who, in 1991, comprised the key interest group in the ritual abuse moral panic that had been exported to their country a few years before by American child-savers. That is why his insistence later that same year that he no longer knows what ritual abuse even is, is so revealing of the sea change in ideology and semantics he and his colleagues were experiencing. "I know it's not a hysterical phenomenon," he said in his address to the British Association for the Study and Prevention of Child Abuse and Neglect (BASPCAN). "It is clearly something terrifying for children which they *cannot explain properly* [italics added]" (cited in Lunn, September 26, 1991, p. 5). The suggestion here that children's inability to follow conversational rules and story-telling conventions is the *sine qua non* of ritual abuse allegations is a change, indeed, from the child-saving orthodoxy of "Believe the Children," as well as from the foundational child sexual abuse accommodation syndrome in which Summit, himself, asserts that the more "illogical and incredible" the child's disclosure, the more likely it is true (1983, p. 183).

There is one more nugget this exercise in mining discourse finds, and that is the finale of Summit's 1991 address to the BASPCAN conference. The psychiatrist who had consistently held belief over empiricism now told his audience, "I wish we could explore [ritual abuse] as a clinical and scientific issue. We need a *moratorium on accusations* [italics added] until the question of ritual abuse can be scientifically clarified" (cited in Lunn, September 26, 1991, p. 5). A moratorium on accusations—not on investigations, or on interviews or trials or civil suits, and certainly not on belief or guilelessness. Summit, who had castigated all of society for not giving children a voice about sexual abuse, now called for their silence about ritual abuse.

The shift in ideology evident from mining the discourse of psychiatrist Roland Summit had semantic and organizational consequences as well. The term "satanic ritual abuse" fell out of use by all but the most strident of child-savers, and the terms "ritual abuse" and "sadistic ritual abuse," the latter an apparent effort to preserve the acronym "SRA," took its place. When ritual abuse slipped its semantic mooring with the master symbol of the menacing devil, the need for a demonology of satanism, replete with lists of satanic holidays, roles and rituals, slipped as well, and those with a strong allegiance to the New Christian Right were marginalized within the child-savers interest group. In fact, the shift in thinking, subtle as it was, assumed a kind of centrifugal force, spinning many of the more shrill child-savers, quite regardless of their religious affiliation, to the margins of the interest group and concentrating the power to define the issue and direct action against it in the hands of a smaller number of professionals with clinical training.

It could be said that this shift in ideology, semantics and organization secularized ritual abuse, and in so doing suggested an origin in sexual perversity, rather than satanic beliefs. It is the discourse of Summit, once again, that reveals this secular turn. It should be remembered that it was he who vetted the Country Walk case as a "true" case of satanic ritual abuse, and who stamped his imprimatur on the leading and suggestive interviews that coaxed, cajoled and coerced the ritual abuse allegations from the children. Yet nearly a decade after the case Summit remembered it as one "*not* burdened with allegations of hooded strangers, satanic ceremonies, birth rituals or human sacrifices." A failure of memory, perhaps, but the completion of the syllogism that underlies the shift in thinking is evident in his conclusion that children really were not talking about satanic ritual abuse, but were describing "the stuff of exorbitant human perversity" (Summit, 1994, p. 399). Frank Fuster, it seems, was a just a garden-variety sexual pervert after all.

It would be unwise to suggest that Fuster or Aquino marks the precise moment that the trajectory of the day care ritual abuse moral panic angled away from satanism and towards perversity. The trajectory, after all, is almost as crooked as a corkscrew and the discourse of the child-savers always overlapped, contradicted and ricocheted around during the entire course of the moral panic. It would be more sensible to suggest that the cumulative weight of the failed attempts to discursively stake accused male providers between all three of the master symbols of the decade teased an alternative trajectory. By the mid–1980s, at the peak of the moral panic, ritual abuse was secularized. Child-savers who took that path always saw the devil dancing around the fringes of the day care cases that followed. But their demonization of the folk devils the accused male providers were now required the tightening of the knot that tied them between the two remaining master symbols—the vulnerable child and the psychological trauma model. More bluntly put, they now had to discursively transform them into predatory sexual perverts.

Secularizing by Sexualizing. The task of perversely sexualizing the accused male providers was made easier through the use of the vocabulary of sexual trauma that enriched language in the decade of the 1980s (Plummer, 1995). The feminist critique of sexual abuse and of the gendered power relations that spawn, sustain and silence it, provided an ample lexicon of terms, ideas and concepts that child-savers could use to follow the path from a spiritual to a secular epistemology of ritual abuse.

This language was not only familiar to the public, but meaningful; it made as much sense, probably even more, of the horrific allegations of the children as satanism and devil-worship ever did. The public pillorying of provider Dale Akiki is a case in point. A naval supply worker, Akiki spent Sunday mornings volunteering in the day care center of Faith Chapel, a 3500 member charismatic church just outside of San Diego, California. From the start, some parents expressed concern that his facial disfigurement might frighten young children. Akiki has Noonan's Syndrome, a genetic disorder that left him with down-slanting eyes and a short-webbed neck; his hydrocephalic head is enlarged, his arms frozen at the elbow joints, and he limps from a clubfoot. The affable Akiki, who is also mildly mentally retarded, soon was asked to leave his volunteer position. A few months later, a three year old who had been in his care told her mother that he had exposed himself to her.

From that point, the Faith Chapel cases took the familiar trajectory. As the allegations expanded in scope as the complaining child named other children as victims and they, in turn, named still others, interviewers who from the start believed this would turn out to be a case of satanism and devil-worship, set about recreating the ritual abuse master narrative in their interactions with them (Okerblom & Sauer, 1993). The public, curiously enough, seemed willing to explore the path less traveled. If the kind of drive-by shouting that passes for discourse in talk radio circles is truly the *vox populi*, then callers who had already judged Akiki guilty were more likely to see him as a monster, a sexual predator, a pedophile, than a devil-worshiper. Akiki, with stigma writ large on his face and body, was in the eyes of the damning public more pervert than true believer.

Even the press tried out this new secular lexicon about ritual abuse. The role of the press in the day care ritual abuse moral panic is complex and inconsistent: it served both as a courier for child-saver orthodoxy and a critic of it, a provocateur of community hysteria and a pacifier, sometimes even playing all of those roles, and others, in response to a single case.

Another exercise in discourse mining reveals this complexity and inconsistency, as well as the use of secular language. The *Miami Herald*, it may be recalled, threw out one rhetorical rope after another in an attempt to lasso Frank Fuster of Country Walk infamy, to the master symbol of the menacing devil. Three years later, though, it took a different tact when James Toward, the director of Glendale Montessori, was accused of sexually abusing some of the children in his care. The case grew from the allegation of a single child into the allegations of 18 children, from a complaint of sexual abuse to complaints of ritual abuse and descriptions of filmed orgies, the forced consumption of blood and feces, and rapes with crucifixes and knives. Yet, in the same way that Ehrensaft (1993) had semantically reduced ritual abuse to just a "feature" of the Presidio case, the *Miami Herald* did the same for this case. The ritualistic allegations were mentioned only in passing and without additional comment. The paper, instead, seemed intent upon revealing Toward as a sexual pervert, a predator who, it alleged by citing information without attribution or proof, paid for sex with prostitutes, drug addicts and a transvestite, and had dalliances with women of all kinds in his neighborhood (*Herald* Staff, 1988). Even the editorial published the day after Toward pled guilty to reduced charges[6] avoided the purple Gothic prose that had been used four years earlier to condemn Frank Fuster to prison for the rest of his "unnatural life." Instead, the editorial affirmed the truthfulness of the children's allegations without reciting them, and then breathed a distracting sigh of relief that all children were finally safe from a sexual predator (*Herald* Staff, 1989, p. 2C):

> Toward, one-time owner of the Glendale Montessori School, posed for months as a man wrongly accused. Parents organized in his defense,

pressuring the Department of Health and Rehabilitative Services to back off. Fortunately, HRS, Stuart police, and the parents of children involved were listening instead to the injured and frightened victims. As the truth unfolded—supported by the children's accounts as well as by physical evidence—the betrayal of a caring community became all too clear.... Many in Stuart and around the state would like to forget Toward and the Glendale School scandal. That is understandable and, perhaps, helpful. The lessons mustn't be forgotten, though. Children need the protection of adults willing to listen and act.

In this search for sexual predators lurking behind masks of civility, the accused male providers' backgrounds came under close scrutiny. Frank Fuster was the only one among them who had a criminal record for child molestation, but in the feminist-inspired consciousness of the 1980s, molestation was only one of a broad range of material consequences of the "rape ideology" of the late 20th century (Brownmiller, 1975). That ideology, socially reinforced and institutionally legitimated, feminists argue, gives men free reign to intimidate, control, exploit and use women and children through a variety of sexual means.

Two contrasting portraits, each published in a large-circulation newspaper, demonstrate how authorial voice, granted or denied, and the selection of biographical material by the press can either construct or deconstruct the image of the sexual predator. The first is of Robert Kelly, one of the accused providers in the Little Rascals case. Kelly's first interview with the press was held just two days after his defense lawyers rested their case in his trial on 100 counts of sexual assault. Despite the article's headline, "Day Care Defendant Reflects on His Life and Troubles" (Durkin, 1992), this is less autobiography than biography. Other than his assertion, "I am not a child molester," that begins the article, it is the reporter, not the provider, who "provides a portrait of a man being watched nationwide" (p. 1A). Relying on his trial testimony and interviews with those who know him, the reporter creates a portrait of a predator, a man who so jealously controlled every aspect of his first wife's life that she considered suicide, was so obsessed with pornography that he humiliated her by demanding she pose for his home movies, who flaunted his sexual interest in another woman, and who angrily smeared food across his son's face when the boy was eating sloppily. The psychologist who counseled Kelly and his first wife before their divorce is quoted in the article: "Mr. Kelly tends to be a rather irresponsible individual who is impulsive and is totally unable to maintain any sort of close emotional relationship with another person" (p. 1A). Despite his assertion of innocence, the "man who is being watched nationwide" but is not allowed to speak in the article, seems very much to be "the kind of man" who would sexually abuse and terrorize young children.

The second portrait is entirely different, although the alleged ritual abuse was just as horrendous. In 1984, the same year that it was vilifying Raymond Buckey as evil incarnate, the *Los Angeles Times* presented an almost angelic portrait of Michael Ruby who was accused of ritually abusing children at the Manhattan Ranch Preschool, just a few short blocks from that dark satanic mill the McMartin Preschool already had become in cultural imagination. The paper offered the 17 year old playground aide a forum not just for denying the 35 criminal charges against him, but for offering a "moral account" of his life, that is, a "moralizing antidote" to mediate the experience of being stigmatized as a sexual predator (Becker, 1997, p. 17). In his own words, Ruby aligns himself with prevailing cultural sentiments and moral values, describing himself as a typical teenager, fascinated with girls, surfing and cars, and thanking his family, friends and God for providing succor at a time of stress and sadness (Feldman & Needham, 1984). The portrait here is dissonant with the charges against him, straining credulity that he is "the kind of man" who would do such horrific things to young children.

As the day care ritual abuse moral panic spread across the country, child-savers grew frustrated by their inability to discursively link the male providers in the sample to all three master symbols of the decade. None of the males, with the notable exception of Aquino, of course, was a satanist, and Aquino never could be linked to the abuse of the children in the Presidio case. What was needed by the mid–1980s was an alternative, more accommodating theory of ritual abuse, one that still would make sense yet save face for child-savers whose reputations hung in the balance. That theory was one of sexual perversity. Ritual abuse, child-savers started saying as if they had meant to all along, is not always an expression of a satanic belief system, but is more often an act of sexual perversity. That alternative explanation resonated well with a culture sensitized to predatory male sexual violence and armed with the language to talk about it. But it, too, was destined to disappoint when the providers in question were women.

A Problem to Puzzle the Devil

Women, a satirist once opined, are a sex by themselves. Indeed, they are, but women always have negotiated their gender roles. The 1980s were testimony to that. The decade's economic, political, social and ideological changes provided the opportunity, incentive and, for some women, the need to negotiate their identities, goals, aspirations, and responsibilities. The choice of so many women to negotiate the gendered roles of wife and mother by combining work with family responsibilities

had wide ranging repercussions. It obligated men to negotiate their reciprocal roles of husband and father; pressured the work place to provide
equal pay and opportunity and family flex-time arrangements; and put
demands on the public sector to offer quality, affordable day care.

In the face of all of the unsettling changes in women's roles during
that decade, it was the role of day care provider that remained constant.
Nostalgically grounded, the role described "women's work," in every
sense of that term—long hours, low pay, low prestige in the care of the
youngest, and most vulnerable, children. Even when the shifting forces
of that decade situated day care centers on the fault line between the family and the market economy, and the role of provider lost some its social
honor, the prospect that any woman in such a traditional role would sexually abuse the children in her care strained credulity.

Feminists, who had such an ideological influence on that decade, had
been saying all along that there was plenty of reason to be incredulous. Pio-
neering feminist Florence Rush (1974) articulated that stance when she
declared, "The sexual abuse of children, who are overwhelmingly female,
by sexual offenders who are overwhelmingly male, is part and parcel of the
male dominated society which overtly and covertly subjugates women" (p.
73–74). By the 1980s there were data to support this dogma. Research
studies consistently found that child sexual abuse by women was a statistical rarity (de Young, 1982; Finkelhor & Russell, 1984; Russell, 1986).

Enter the 27 women who represent just over half of the total of
accused providers in the sample of 22 day care cases. There is nothing
about them, at first look anyway, that would challenge the dogma of
received wisdom or call into question the validity of research findings.
Most of them were intimately involved in the daily care and supervision
of their charges; reading to them, playing with them, escorting them on
outings, wiping runny noses and changing soiled diapers. They were the
ones the parents, usually the mothers, talked to about their children's well-
being, consulted for advice and, every now and then, confided in when
there were problems.

It cannot be argued that the women did not bring to this traditional
role different strengths and weaknesses. Cora Priest, for example, was
like a "sweet old grandmother" to nearly every child she met ("Bizarre
rites," 1986); Fran Keller was both stern and good-hearted, the "undis-
puted boss" of her small day care center (Cartwright, 1994, p. 105); "Mrs.
Janet B." was a soft-spoken professional, well trained and educated in
the care of young children (Rubenstein, 1990, pp. 37–38). Some of the
women in the sample were single, others married, still others widowed;
most had children of their own, some also had grandchildren. Many of
them also volunteered for good causes, regularly went to church, and
attended their children's or grandchildren's recitals and ball games.

They were, both as individuals and a group, if group they can be called, unlikely sexual abusers. And sexual abuse, it bears repeating, is not ritual abuse. To accuse them of that, child-savers had the daunting challenge of fashioning folk devils out of quite ordinary women engaged in traditional women's work, and then persuading the public that evil had lurked unnoticed for so long behind such homely façades.

Sound and Rumor. Over the course of the day care ritual abuse moral panic, the attempts to discursively link the women providers in the sample to the master symbol of the menacing devil took different forms. In the early years of the moral panic, flush with certainty that they had uncovered "a perfectly hidden evil" (Summit, 1994a, p. 339), child-savers boldly stamped the women providers in the day care cases that immediately followed the McMartin Preschool case as satanic ritual abusers and implored everyone to treat them as such.

The Jubilation Day Care case nicely illustrates this point. When suspicions arose that sisters Barbara and Sharon Orr had sexually abused the children in their care, worried parents were encouraged to take their children to a local mental health agency. Social worker Pamela Hudson takes up the story at the epiphanic moment when she realized the children she was assessing had not been sexually abused, not even sadistically abused, but satanic ritually abused: "If anything was going to be done to solve this conundrum, I would have to do it myself" (1994, p. 74). She immersed herself in occult literature, read about brainwashing and shell-shock, talked with colleagues about dissociation, multiple personality disorder and hypnosis, and kept questioning the children, ever mindful that the child sexual abuse accommodation syndrome warns that children will disclose "the least upsetting material first" (p. 79). Once that material was out of the way, Hudson "peeled the onion," as she once referred to her assessment technique, exposing "increasing degrees of horror ending in the bizarre" (1991, p. 60). Once at the bizarre, she proclaimed the Jubilation Day Care case a genuine case of satanic ritual abuse, and the sisters Orr satanic ritual abusers.

The precipitous linking of the providers with satanism in this early case had several consequences that, in retrospect, were sadly predictable. First, it committed those involved in the case to one hypothesis to the exclusion of all others. The Orr sisters had had several complaints levied against them over the years; their license recently had been suspended by the Department of Social Services when it determined there was reason to believe that a six year old in their care had been sexually molested by the young daughter of one of them. In a later hearing on that decision, an administrative law judge revoked their license after determining that the child in question had experienced humiliating punishment and emotional abuse while enrolled in the center. In a subsequent appeal hearing, the same judge suspended the revocation and placed Barbara Orr on three years probation. While social worker Hudson and others were "peeling the onion" to expose the bizarre, they were discarding as irrelevant the outer layers of perfectly credible and pursuable hypotheses—that the Orrs had done nothing untoward; or, that they had emotionally abused one or more of the children in their care; or, that they had sexually abused one or more of the children in their care, or had colluded in that abuse.

Second, the relentless attempt to prove the Orrs were the satanic ritual abusers they boldly were proclaimed to be exhausted resources. The investigation took over a year to complete and produced a report that at 400 pages was 40 times longer than the average investigative report by local police, tying up the resources of the small, rural community. Third, although the district attorney declined to file any criminal charges against the Orrs, citing lack of evidence and the young age of the complaining children, rumors that the devil was afoot in northern California circulated for years. The rumors created deep schisms in the community: some saw them as nothing more than the utterings of mass hysteria, others as the eloquence of truth, a faction that persisted long after the arrests several years later of a number of community people for ritually abusing children in the "Devil's Club" some of the children had once insisted the Orrs had run out of their day care center (Goldston, 1989).

Finally, consider the children. Confident that they indeed had been ritually abused by the satanic Orr sisters, social worker Hudson intervened with a panoply of therapeutic approaches from psychodynamic therapy to deal with their guilt, behavior modification to curb their hyper-aggression, cognitive therapy for undoing the brainwashing, hypnotism for their amnesia, group therapy for the sharing of feelings, play therapy for recalling the details of the ritual abuse, eye movement desensitization to reduce their terror (Hudson 1991). And, after all that, their prognosis is bleak. On that point, social worker Hudson has the last word: "Where I used to think that two or three years of therapy would suffice for ritually abused children, I now believe it might take a lifetime" (Hudson, 1994, p. 75).

In using such bold discourse to link the Orr sisters and other women providers in the early day care ritual abuse cases to the master symbol of the menacing devil, child-savers attempted to shout down the niggling question of why women would ritually abuse children. The answer was simple: belief trumps gender. Women who are satanists do what no other women even imagine. In offering such a definitive answer, though, child-savers had to tiptoe through a minefield of contradictory impressions and evidence. The women providers in the sample were so right-minded, so ordinary, so traditional in their care-giving role that, just as in the case of the males in the sample, a different more gendered theory of their deviance was needed.

Rumor and Science. Soon after the McMartin Preschool case burst into public awareness, raising fears that more devils than hell can hold were lurking in day care centers across the country, the National Center on Child Abuse and Neglect funded a research project proposed by David Finkelhor. No dilettante, Finkelhor is a respected sociologist whose early work on child sexual abuse is credited with bringing this most private of personal woes into the glaring light of public scrutiny (Finkehor, 1979, 1984, 1986).

In this funded project, Finkelhor and his research team proposed to examine sexual abuse in day care between 1983 and 1985. The results were published in a book titled, *Nursery Crimes: Sexual Abuse in Day Care* (1988) that soon became the bible of child-savers both in the United States and abroad. Its elevation to canon had to do with a number of factors. First, as an academic, Finkelhor maintained a distance from the variously skilled and qualified child-savers who had coalesced into an interest group in the wake of the McMartin Preschool case. That distance, coupled with his qualifications as a researcher, vested his book with the kind of scientific rationality that was sorely needed for the legitimization of the burgeoning moral panic. It is important to note that the body of published literature on ritual abuse prior to 1988 was absolutely anorexic, consisting of just a few articles, most of them case studies and none of them based on systematic collection and analysis of data, and very few published in peer-reviewed academic journals (de Young, 2002). The presence of a scientific study, written in the vernacular and therefore accessible to all child-savers, was warmly welcomed.

Second, the book offers a definition of ritual abuse that is as verbose as it is obtuse, thereby giving the subject an aura of validity quite regardless of how it is interpreted or applied in specific cases. Finkelhor and his colleagues define ritual abuse as "abuse that occurs in a context linked to some symbols or group activity that have a religious, magical, or supernatural connotation, and where the invocation of these symbols or activities, repeated over time, is used to frighten and intimidate the children" (p. 59). The very protean idea of satanism lurks around the definition, though, if only because of what passes for common sense excludes from it. Would a devoutly Christian provider who demands enrollees pray to God every morning to avoid an eternity in the fires of hell, ever be accused of *ritual* abuse? Unlikely. Finkelhor and his colleagues may avoid the adjective "satanic" and render ecumenic the context of ritual abuse, but the connotation remains.

Third, in a nice coincidence of timing, *Nursery Crimes* appeared when child-savers were in desperate need of an explanation other than that of satanism to spell out why women providers ritually abused their young charges. Their failure to convincingly discursively link them to the master symbol of the menacing devil was only compounded by their failure to evidentially link them to satanism. The alternative explanation of sexual perversity was working well in regards to the male providers but another explanation, more resonant with gender ideology and sensibilities, was needed to do the same for the women. *Nursery Crimes* provided just that.

Its explanation, though, has no particular fidelity to its data. The 36 ritual abuse cases in the sample of 270 day care sexual abuse cases were considered "substantiated" by Finkelhor if "at least one of the local investigating agencies had decided that abuse had occurred" (p. 13), even if no formal action, such as license suspension or arrest, followed. Given the fact that a plethora of investigating agencies, from children's protective services, to departments of social services, to the police and even the Federal Bureau of Investigation were involved in many of the day care ritual abuse cases, that each has its own threshold of suspicion before it can act, and that the agencies often rancorously disagreed with each other about whether these were even cases to act upon, the criterion for inclusion is liberal, indeed. Once a case of day care ritual abuse was identified, Finkelhor and his colleagues, who were not in a position to conduct independent investigations, collected information from those involved or interested in it. And that means one critical thing given the emotional and ideological climate of the moral panic—they very often got it wrong.

The explanations *Nursery Crimes* provides for ritual abuse by women providers have little fidelity to their own data and their data, in turn, have little fidelity to fact. Yet, Finkelhor and his colleagues theorize on the basis of their data, that there are two motives for the ritual abuse of children in day care. The first is familiar enough in that it points the finger at satanism, thus giving credence to the beliefs that generated the moral panic in the first place. As a motivation, "'identification with evil' ties sexual abuse to ritual abuse in the mind set that may be attracted to so-called satanic practice" (p. 64). The authors go on to conjecture that individuals who are socialized in highly moralistic settings often mature with a dismal view of themselves and after one failed attempt after another to be good and to do good, "they may become prey to a reversal of the whole value system" and will "discover a sense of power and spiritual fulfillment in a doctrine that celebrates participating in intentionally evil acts" (p. 64).

The alternative explanation, "mortification of a child's sexuality," though, is the more interesting in that it has such a nice fit with the sexual politics of the decade. Women providers are not satanists at all, this one suggests, but are acting out of a corrupted sense of sexuality caused by their own "childhood abuse, sexual repression, or some other humiliation" (p. 63) by targeting those of whom they are the most jealous, resentful and hateful—young and innocent children. The woman-as-victim leitmotif, so resonant with feminist-inspired social consciousness of the 1980s, now offers an alternative, and gendered, explanation for why so many women were among the providers in day care ritual abuse cases. Never mind that Finkelhor, himself, had once eloquently argued that gender role socialization precludes the likelihood that women will sexually abuse children; in this new explanation, victimhood trumps socialization.

Finkelhor and his colleagues provide no real data to support either of these explanations and rather than case studies, they use only case snippets to illustrate their points. One of those cases, though, is worth a closer look. It is the "Welcome Child" case in the book, which went to great lengths to change the names of the centers, accused providers and even the geographic locations, but it is much better known as the Wee Care case. And the accused provider Finkelhor and his colleagues use to illustrate their alternative theory of the "mortification of a child's sexuality," is Kelly Michaels. If there is a celebrity of sorts in this moral panic, it is she. No other day care provider in the sample has been the subject of so much journalistic scrutiny, and none has more eloquently protested innocence than has Michaels. The opportunity to compare and contrast Finkelhor's understanding of her with those of several investigative journalists, as well as with her own narrative, is irresistible.

The Faces of Kelly Michaels. In 1985, Michaels was a 23 year old aspiring stage actress who took a $4.00 an hour job as a provider at the Wee Care Day Nursery to make ends meet. A four year old who had been in her care casually commented to a nurse who was taking his temperature rectally during a routine medical exam, "Her takes my temperature." The "her" to whom he was referring was his day care provider, Kelly Michaels.

The child's mother, suspicious that he had been anally abused by Michaels, reported his disclosure to the Department of Youth and Family Services, and then took him to the office of the county prosecutor where he was questioned by the chief of the Child Abuse Unit, Sara McArdle. On an anatomically correct doll, the child demonstrated what Michaels had done to him by putting his finger in the doll's rectum, and then went on to name other children whom she had similarly abused. Those children were then questioned and both confirmed the abuse and when Michaels was brought in by the police for questioning, a fourth child, the son of a Wee Care board member, told his father that she had touched his penis with a spoon. As parents called parents, and word of the accusations spread, the day care center called a meeting where social worker Peg Foster, the co-director of a sexual assault unit at a local hospital, and psychologist Susan Esquilin urged parents to be watchful for the nightmares, biting, spitting, bedwetting and masturbation that are the telltale symptoms of sexual abuse. The next day the local newspaper carried the story that the Wee Care Day Nursery was under investigation.

Having been informed of the initial allegation, Department of Youth and Family Services investigator Lou Fonolleras was eager to be part of the investigation. After Michaels was indicted by a grand jury on six counts of sexual assault involving three children, Fonolleras took on the task of finding more victims. Over 25 days he conducted 82 leading and suggestive interviews with children and 19 with parents (Rosenthal, 1995, p. 251); he identified scores of victims and elicited from them the ritual abuse master narrative with all of its Gothic trappings. Children claimed Michaels inserted knives, swords, spoons and forks into their rectums and vaginas, smeared them with peanut butter and licked it off, forced them to drink her menstrual blood and eat cakes fashioned out of her own excrement. The criminal charges against Michaels kept piling up.

After a 14 month trial, Michaels was convicted on 115 counts of sexual assault and sentenced to 47 years in prison. There is much more to this case study, but it is for a later time. At the moment, the most important question to be addressed is the one that everyone was wondering, What kind of woman is Michaels who ritually abused the young children in her care?

Michaels is severely psychologically disturbed, according to Finkelhor and his colleagues, driven by jealousy, resentment or hatred created by her own childhood abuse to ritualistically mortify the sexuality of the children in her care. The unnamed informants who provided information on Michaels for *Nursery Crimes,* described her as a "very quiet young woman, raised in a highly religious environment, and isolated from heterosexual relations" (p. 46). As in all of the case snippets in the book, Finkelhor passes these impressions of an unbalanced loner along as facts and then uses this synthetic profile to illustrate the alternative explanation for ritual abuse by women day care providers.

That profile was fleshed out in the book *Nap Time* (1990), an account of the Wee Care case. The author, Lisa Manshel, was a recent Harvard graduate who had sat through the trial and interviewed many of those involved in it, with the notable exception of Michaels for whom her antipathy is apparent. That Michaels is psychologically disturbed is obvious to Manshel who hints at the diagnosis of what was then called multiple personality disorder with her descriptions of the provider's "drastic personality shifts" (p. 19), adeptness at the "maneuvers of ingratiation" (p. 49), and lapses of "star[ing] into space" (p. 14).

In the decade of the 1980s, with its master symbol of the psychological trauma model, the inferred diagnosis was more than a little familiar. But unlike other mental disorders that found their way into the 1980 edition of the *Diagnostic and Statistical Manual*, the nosological bible of the mental health professions, the etiology of multiple personality disorder was explicated—its symptoms of dissociation, splitting and amnesia were thought to be caused by severe childhood sexual abuse. The prospect that Michaels was a sexual abuse survivor intrigued Manshel who was deeply suspicious of her mother's stern visage and her father's bonhomie as he touched and hugged his daughter at every opportunity.[7] And what Manshel interpreted as Michael's sexualized persona was even more suspect. Her short skirts and frilly blouses that "strained in a sexual way" (p. 137), her "sultry purr rippled through with an open, girlish inflection" (p. 301) when she testified, and her careful attention to makeup that "all seemed part of making jurors believe that such an attractive woman wouldn't need to molest babies" (p. 153) were to the author the affectations of a personality conditioned by sexual abuse.

Whether psychologically unbalanced, severely mentally ill, a survivor of sexual abuse, or any combination or even all of those things, the portrait of Michaels in *Nap Time* illustrates the alternative explanation for ritual abuse by women providers set out by Finkelhor and his colleagues. That explanation, though, forgives nothing. The woman-as-victim-turned-perpetrator representation it offers is as redolent of the Gothic as the satanist representation ever was. It insinuates a haunting, a harboring of a terrible secret and a contravention of human agency and morality by the unspeakable traumas of childhood. Michaels was, in the public eye, as much a monster as the putative satanic Orr sisters ever were.

But was she? Investigative journalist Debbie Nathan (1988) granted Michaels the right to tell her own story. Her account, given while she was awaiting sentencing, not only humanizes her, but reveals the kind of biographical gerrymandering that really goes on in the construction of ritual abuser profiles. Michael describes a happy childhood in a loquacious family that made religious, social and political issues the topics of daily dinner debates. She talks about her love of the theatre and her starry-eyed ambition to be an actress, her passion for literature and poetry, and her outrage at being falsely accused. So convinced of her innocence was Nathan that she joined forces with journalist Dorothy Rabinowitz and others to form the Kelly Michaels Defense Committee. Over the next several years, the Committee worked tirelessly on her appeal and to keep her name in public discourse. The effect was to turn the Wee Care case into a *cause célèbre* and Michaels into a spokesperson for all of the providers accused in the day care ritual abuse moral panic.

In that role, Michaels drapes herself in the kind of ordinariness that always is an antidote to the Gothic. In an article titled, interestingly enough, "I Am Not a Monster," she describes herself as a trusting, naïve young woman who, until the moment she was convicted, believed that the decent, ordinary people like herself who made up the jury would completely exonerate her. She expresses no animosity towards the children nor for their parents, but reserves her outrage for the interviewers who coaxed and coerced the ritual abuse master narrative from the children, the police and prosecutors who relentlessly pursued her and the justice system, itself, that turned her trial into an inquisition (Michaels, 1993). The article was followed by appearances on nationally syndicated news shows such as *20/20, 48 Hours, Turning Point* and *60 Minutes.* As a defender of innocence, both her own and that of other accused providers, she holds up a mirror so the viewing public is forced to confront the images of its own Gothic imagination. If there were a single thread to her public appearances it would be tied up in a Nietzschean knot: "He who fights monsters might take care lest he become a monster. And if you gaze for long into an abyss, the abyss also gazes into you."

Folk Devils Fight Like Devils

Kelly Michaels's resistance to demonization stands in contrast to how folk devils are portrayed in classic moral panic theory. Usually depicted as hapless dupes, their attempts to oppose their demonization and restore their unspoiled identities often are overlooked, and the impact their resistance has on the trajectory of the moral panic is underestimated. It would be a mistake to repeat those oversights in an analysis of the day care ritual abuse moral panic. The providers, it might be recalled, emerged as folk devils not from the margins of society but from its center when a fault line between the family and the market economy opened up just wide enough for their social honor to take a tumble. That said, though, the providers did not lose all of what sociologist Pierre Bourdieu (1994) refers to as "capital," and it is the various types of capital available to them—moral, social and cultural—that are the currencies of their resistance.

"THE BUBBLE REPUTATION"

Many of the providers had long reputations as nurturers and teachers of young children, and as responsible citizens. By considering reputation as a form of moral capital, illustrations from the sample reveal how it was saved, traded and spent in the protracted process of resisting demonization.

Most of the providers in the sample went to considerable lengths to save their reputations. They not only protested their innocence but held up their reputations as evidence of it and never wavered in that stance for what often were many years of investigation, legal maneuvers, civil suits, trials, imprisonment and appeals. Violet Amirault is a good example. Sixty-one years old when she, her son Gerald, and her daughter Cheryl LeFave were accused of ritually abusing children, she had a great deal to lose. She had built up the Fells Acres Day Care Center from scratch when, years before, her alcoholic and abusive husband had left her penniless with two young children. The center was well-regarded in the community and Amirault staked her reputation on the provision of quality care for young children. Shortly after her son Gerald, better known as Tooky, was arrested and the atmosphere was thick with rumor and innuendo that she and her daughter would be next, the state suspended the center's license. Amirault sued, convinced that her reputation and that of the center would withstand the bizarre charges of children whose words in a license revocation hearing were only paraphrased because they had been deemed too young and traumatized to testify in person. She lost. The license was revoked (Bennett, 1984); soon after, she and her daughter were arrested. Years later, when each was serving 8 to 20 years in prison, Amirault refused to apply for early release, saying that she would rather serve the maximum sentence than tarnish her reputation by admitting to a crime she did not commit (Sennott, 1995).

There is one example of providers in the sample recklessly spending their reputations, leaving them bereft of moral capital and even more vulnerable to the vagaries of demonization. Fran Keller ran a small day care center with the help of her retired husband, Dan, out of their one story fieldstone house in a suburb of Austin, Texas. In the hot summer of 1991 a three year old told her mother and later the therapist who was treating her for behavior problems arising from her parents' acrimonious divorce, that the Kellers had sexually abused her. Her mother immediately contacted the sheriff's department and the prosecuting attorney, and then called a friend whose own son was enrolled in Fran's Day Care and was being treated by the same therapist. Eventually, he too disclosed having been sexually abused, but there was no relief in the disclosure. His behavior deteriorated to such an extent that his mother wondered if he were possessed by the devil. Another friend, who had recently recovered memories of childhood ritual abuse, confirmed the wonderment and declared this a case of satanic ritual abuse. And as horrified parents contacted other parents, a third child accused the Kellers, and a full-scale investigation was launched (Cartwright, 1994).

From that point, the details of the Fran's Day Care case reiterated all of the Gothic themes and tropes of the scores of day care cases that had preceded it. Armed with both the certainty that this was a case of satanic ritual abuse and a list of indicators and symptoms provided by the Believe the Children organization to confirm it, the children were questioned and interrogated by their parents, their therapists, and members of a law enforcement task force specially constituted for the investigation. They were driven to local cemeteries by detectives to identify where the bodies of sacrificed infants and adults had been surreptitiously buried by their providers (Gamino & Ward, 1992), and to homes and businesses around the city where, they alleged, they were filmed as they were ritually abused by strangers dressed as monsters and werewolves (Cartwright, 1994). As the net of suspicion widened and community gossip implicated public officials in the ritual abuse, the children began talking about "bad sheriffs" who joined the providers in their dastardly acts. Suspecting that the "bad sheriffs" were constable Janise White, a friend of the Kellers who sometimes stopped by the day care center, and her partner Raul Quintero, a member of the investigative task force confronted White's ex-husband, Doug Perry, and told him that White and Quintero already had confessed, and had implicated him (Cartwright, 1994).

And this is where the Fran's Day Care, the case that tolled the denouement of the day care ritual abuse moral panic, takes an anomalous turn that finally leads back to the point about squandering moral capital. After taking two polygraph tests and undergoing hours of relentless interrogation, Perry broke down and implicated not only the Kellers, White and Quintero in sexual abuse, but also himself, even though he had never been named by the children. He said not a word, however, about ritual abuse. Although he retracted his confession the next day, warrants were issued for the Kellers who then recklessly squandered their reputations by fleeing the state (Haglund, 1991).

Fran Keller later explained the moral calculus that brought them to that decision. As providers, she and her husband had followed news coverage about the arrests and trials of day care providers across the country and the often draconian sentences that were meted out to them. Frightened they would never make bail if arrested, "scared and humiliated" by the charges, terrified of going to prison, the Kellers left everything behind and fled the state (Cartwright, 1994, p. 152).

In so many ways, this rash expenditure of their reputations left them morally bankrupt. With nothing really left to appeal to, nothing to wrap around themselves that would create just a little quiver of doubt in the minds of the court and the community, everything the Kellers did and said was interpreted as evidence of their imputed identity as ritual abusers. Take, for example, the hand signal—the letter "C" formed by curved thumb and index finger—that Dan Keller flashed to news cameras from the defense table during his trial. What was in reality a greeting to his fellow inmates in the C-Block of the local jail where he had spent nine months awaiting trial, was interpreted by prosecution consultant and expert witness Dr. J. Randy Noblitt[8] as a "cult trigger" satanists use to "stack the deck" with cultists during jury selection, and to "intimidate susceptible witnesses, attorneys and others" during the trial (Noblitt & Perskin, 1995, p. 152).

If the squandering of reputation left no doubt the Kellers were ritual abusers, it *ipso facto* left no doubt that the accusing children were their victims. And if, as the decade's master symbol of the psychological trauma model holds, horrible victimization has horrible consequences, then everything the children did and said became diagnostically relevant. The girl who made the initial complaint was diagnosed with multiple personality disorder; according to her therapist, Karen Hutchins, unless her satanic conditioning is successfully countermanded by therapy, the girl will someday mindlessly return to the satanic cult of which the Kellers were devotees to serve as a "breeder," bearing infants for sacrifice. The two accusing boys in the case also were diagnosed with multiple personality disorder. One is angry and confused; the other is fractured into alter personalities, one of which is Poopsie, a 56 year old man who has bowel movements on command. His mother holds up Poopsie as incontrovertible evidence that her son was ritually abused by the Kellers. "Having a bowel movement at 9 p.m. when your pattern is every other morning," she explains, "you can't fake that" (Cartwright, 1994, p. 156).

Friends and Relations

There is another form of capital that providers in the sample used to resist their demonization. Social capital is the "aggregate of the actual or potential resources which are linked to possession of a durable network of more or less institutionalized relationships of mutual acquaintance and recognition" (Bourdieu, 1994, p. 248). Less eloquently stated, social capital is all about how many friends, supporters and advocates the accused providers had, what kind of resources they could lend to the process of resisting demonization, and how rapidly they could be called into effective actions.

There was not a single provider in the sample who was bereft of social capital. A very few, most notably Deloartic Parks, the Rogers Park Jewish Community Day Care Center janitor who was accused of sticking pins in the genitals of children and filming orgies with them in the basement, seemed to wage a lonely public battle against demonization but, in truth, was quietly supported throughout the investigation and trial by fellow church members (Enstad, October 3, 1985). Bobby Fijnje's family and friends were more vocal in their support. They sought out opportunities to talk to the media and offer insights into the accused 14 year old that repudiated the *monstra lingua* of gossip and rumor about the kind of person he really must be to have ritually abused the children in his care at the night nursery of Old Cutler Presbyterian Church. "He's a great kid," one of his teachers vouched in a press interview. "I bet you won't even find a report that he ever as much sneezed on somebody else. The kid was squeaky clean" (Viglucci & Evans, 1990, p. 1B).

Defenders of the Amirault family raised thousands of dollars for their defense in the Fells Acres case by selling tickets to a "support group and mini-fair" (Taylor, 1986); a decade later, when the vacated convictions of Violet and Cheryl were reinstated and Gerald's appeal was denied, scores of them marched in protest through the streets of Cambridge, Massachusetts to the Governor's mansion where they threaded letters of protest through the iron gate (Duffy, 1997). The steadfastness of supporters through the 20 years of legal maneuverings in what surely must be the most legally complicated day care ritual abuse case in the sample speaks to ideologies stronger than friendship that are the currency of social capital. "I told [Cheryl LeFave] that if we abandon you," one of her loyal supporters told the press, "then we abandon our own humanity" (Duffy, 1997, p. B1).

Humanity, reason and justice, at first, were little more than the incantations of supporters, but as the years went on and the pernicious moral panic spread across the country, the words transformed into the rallying cry of a highly politicized countermovement that eventually would contribute to its denouement. While in the early 1980s the supporters of accused providers like Parks, Fijnje and the Amirault family were holding prayer vigils and bake sales, and rather self-consciously trying to get a word or two of their own into the babble of public discourse about day care ritual abuse, by the early 1990s supporters of accused providers were more politically and socially savvy. Consider, as an example, the supporters of accused provider, Dale Akiki. Developmentally delayed, physically handicapped, incapable in so many ways of comprehending the gravity of the charges against him in the Faith Chapel case, Akiki embodied the risks to humanity, reason and justice posed by the moral panic. His supporters were not content with candlelight vigils and letter-writing campaigns. They held raucous demonstrations at the local jail where Akiki was held for over two years awaiting trial, and they eventually brought down the powerful district attorney who levied the charges that sent him there (Mecoy, 1994).

Journalists and documentarians became part of the durable social network on which some, although certainly not all, of the accused providers could depend. Journalist Dorothy Rabinowitz, who had already assumed the role of outspoken advocate for provider Kelly Michaels in the Wee Care case, wrote a series of scathing articles in defense of the Amirault family in the Fells Acres case for the prestigious *Wall Street Journal.* In it, she put a human face on the monster so many people believed Violet Amirault to be (January 30, 1995), exposed the political machinations that brought a case without corroborative evidence to trial (March 14, 1995), and declared the Amirault family a casualty of the kind of "mass hysteria" that led to the persecution of witches in nearby Salem over three centuries before (May 12, 1995). Documentarian Ofra Bikel, in search of a story about sleepy, small town life, uncovered a viper's nest of rumors and gossip in the bucolic village of Edenton, North Carolina, where providers and others associated with the Little Rascals Day Care Center were accused of the ritual abuse of children. Part one of her three-part *Frontline* documentary, "Innocence Lost," aired on PBS in 1991 and raised the decibel of the national debate over ritual abuse. It was followed in 1993 by part two, "Innocence Lost: The Verdict," examining the trials of Robert Kelly and Dawn Wilson and raising the specter of jury misconduct; and in 1997 by part three, "Innocence Lost: The Plea," focusing on provider Betsy Kelly's decision to plead no contest to charges she denies in return for her release from jail.

The *Frontline* series also had a discursive existence in cyberspace, where anyone interested can download transcripts from Robert Kelly's trial and engage in discussion with other interested parties about this, and other, day care ritual abuse cases. The documentary also prompted Massachusetts Institute of Technology professor Jonathan Harris to create a web site and mailing list for the exchange of information about day care ritual abuse cases.

Over the years of the moral panic, the accused providers' social web spun out from friends and family, to concerned citizens, journalists and documentarians, to eventually ensnare academics. Almost since the beginning of the moral panic, academics in the fields of sociology, anthropology, folklore and cultural studies, sat on the sidelines and watched with something often akin to bemusement. From their vantage point, all of this bold discourse and frenetic activity had nothing at all to do with satanic threats to young children, but with the threats unsettling changes in the social and moral order posed to the civic imagination (Ellis, 1992; Hicks, 1991; Jenkins, 1992; Richardson, Best, & Bromley, 1991; Stevens, 1992; Victor, 1993). It was these academics who offered in defense of accused providers a vocabulary of terms to explain their plight: urban legend, moral crusade, countersubversive narrative, legend ostension, revitalization movement and, of course, moral panic.

Cultural Capital

There is another, more subtle, form of capital that those providers who had it used to resist their demonization. Cultural capital refers, in part, to the ability to understand and use the language, symbols and signs of the culture in meaningful and persuasive ways. It is the kind of capital Kelly Michaels spent in interviews with journalists and in her own personal accounts, both written and spoken, of her arrest and trial. And by the early 1990s, primarily due to the infusion of those new and dissonant concepts and terms into public discourse about day care ritual abuse, it was capital ready to be spent by other accused providers, as well.

A brief exercise in discourse mining illustrates this point. When they were convicted in 1987 of ritually abusing the children at Fells Acres Day Care, Violet Amirault and her daughter Cheryl LeFave were reduced to inarticulateness by the lack of meaningful language to protest their innocence. "I never," Amirault sobbed in front of the news cameras, "I never." As if in counterpoint, LeFave kept gasping, "We didn't. We didn't."

But eight years later, just released from prison, they used the new and expressive language of the new decade to describe their ordeal—and the audience, perhaps not agreeing as one, nonetheless had to consider, perhaps for the first time, an alternative way of interpreting the Fells Acres case. The following excerpt from their appearance on the nationally syndicated tabloid news show, *Rivera Live* (1995), illustrates this point:

> AMIRAULT: We were victims of a media witch-hunt. We find now that papers are writing and retracting everything they had said about us eleven years ago, and they really see now the way they should have researched the cases when they wrote about them.
> LeFAVE: There's been tremendous scientific evidence in place that we can utilize to better educate people as to how these situations arise and how we can better protect ourselves as potential alleged abusers—and fight a defense fairly in the courtroom.

And when offered the opportunity to have the final word, Cheryl LeFave revealed just how much cultural capital, in the form of new terms and ideas, she had accumulated over the decade: "(M)y conviction, let's not forget, happened 10, 11 years ago. And there was a completely different mind set. There was a moral panic happening and ... the view of the children was proposed to be this sterling truthfulness that they held, and that sterling truthfulness that people look at children with empowered the children to have this ... extraordinary moral power.... And we just didn't stand a chance."

The Center Cannot Hold

By way of conclusion, it is important to return from this long and winding discussion to the primary themes of demonization and resistance. In regards to demonization, child-savers were confronted by a dilemma of their own making. While they used the great body of endlessly reproduced and circulated "stuff" on ritual abuse—the satanic calendars, the lists of symbols and rituals, the catalogues of indicators and symptoms, the vast international conspiracy theories—to extract the ritual abuse master narrative from the children in the sample cases, they could not link accused providers to it. None was even convincingly portrayed as, let alone proved to be, a satanist, the Aquino's always the exception here; none was a cultist, a devil-worshipper, a witch, warlock or necromancer.

To redress this gap between rhetoric and reality, child-savers did a couple of things that secularized the concept of ritual abuse and, in doing so, weakened its hold on cultural imagination. First, they either simply dropped the word "satanic" and all references to it in their public discourse, or listed "satanic" as one of any number of contexts in which ritual abuse occurs. The former strategy marginalized some of the more ardent ideologues in the child-savers interest group, particularly the New Christian Rightists whose exegeses on satanism and demonology are the *sine qua non* of the ritual abuse master narrative. Only loosely bound by ideology in the first place, this shunning created discord among child-savers and weakened the power of the interest group. The latter strategy acted as an invitation for the facile appropriation of the term to label the abuse of children in all manner of religious, magical, supernatural, commercial, institutional or organized contexts. By the start of the new decade, the moral currency of the very idea of ritual abuse had been debased.

Second, the child-savers hastily constructed clinical explanations to describe the motivations of the accused providers who kept slipping the knot that tied them to the master symbol of the menacing devil. If the male providers were not satanists after all, they reasoned, then they were sexual predators; if the female providers were not really devil-worshipers, then they were victims-turned-abusers. While these clinical assumptions reproduced the wisdom of the master symbol of the psychological trauma model, and therefore were palatable to the general public, they also invited evidence to the contrary. These assumptions never rose to the level of theory, however, so disconfirming evidence left child-savers bereft of any plausible explanation as to why a provider, male or female, would do such horrific things to young children. By the start of the new decade, the alleged perpetrators of ritual abuse had lost much of their evil luster, and almost all of their Gothic power to terrify.

There is one other theme that requires summary, and that is the providers' resistance to their demonization. In ways that can be appreciated more than measured, their expenditure of moral, social and cultural capital impacted the moral panic. It introduced into the public arena discourse contrary to that of the child-savers and to gossip and rumor, and it replaced the dark and sinister evildoers of Gothic imagination with the faces, biographies and reputations of real people. The expenditure of capital also recruited advocates, some of them powerful, to the cause of the accused providers, and their discourse and material efforts in many ways tolled the denouement of the day care ritual abuse moral panic.

But before it ended, all of this discourse, all of this passion, would be scripted in morality plays performed before judges and juries in courts of law.

6

Morality Plays

On the erratic trajectories of moral panics, one stop common to most is a court of law. For interest groups and those recruited by their inflammatory rhetoric, bringing folk devils to justice in criminal trials has a moral equivalence.

Classic moral panic theory, though, seems more interested in the creation of the laws and policies of social control that bring folk devils *to* trial, rather than with what goes on *in* trial. In his seminal work, Stanley Cohen (1972/2002) models this shortsightedness for future moral panic scholars. He delineates the three sequential reactions to any moral panic by the "control culture" that scholars should be on the lookout for: diffusion, escalation and innovation. Diffusion refers to the ways in which those not intimately involved in the moral panic are drawn to it by the discourse and activities of interest groups; thus recruited, they escalate the reaction by joining the interest groups in calling for tougher laws to regulate the folk devils and stronger penalties to punish them; this reaction, in turn, leads to innovation in the form of newly created laws and methods of social control.

While Cohen and other moral panic scholars go on to speculate, even if they do not always document, that these innovative measures of social control end up bringing folk devils into the hallowed halls of justice to stand trial and suffer punishment, they rarely every elaborate. Historian Philip Jenkins (1998), as an illustration, examines the waves of moral panics about sex offenders, from psychopaths to predators to pedophiles, that washed over 20th century American society, producing inflated statistics, ironclad diagnostic categories, new laws and stiff punishments. But like other theorists before and since, he treats the sometimes spectacular trials of sex offenders as the result of the moral panic, rather than as constituent of it.

And what an opportunity to do just that is afforded by the day care ritual abuse moral panic. Not all of the 22 day care cases in the sample went to trial, but for those that did the criminal trials were fascinating sites of contested discourse. The trials were often the longest and most expensive media events in the respective city's or state's history, treating the nation, indeed even the world, to box seats to long-running morality plays in which innocence was pitted against evil, right against wrong, virtue against venality, and the opportunity for vehemently arguing just which side was really which always presented itself.

"Liberty Plucks Justice by the Nose"

A bit of a digression is required first to take a look at why 19 of the accused providers in the sample comprised of 51 providers from 22 day care ritual abuse cases either were never charged or had their charges dismissed. Table 4 summarizes the legal disposition for each.

Why did liberty pluck justice by the nose in these cases? There certainly is nothing exceptional about these 19 providers, although it should go without saying at this point that the satanic Aquinos are the exception to almost every rule. Demographically, they mirror the providers who did stand trial; among them are women and men in roughly the same proportion, and while one of them is an adolescent, the others reflect the modal age range of the remaining providers. The day care centers with which they were affiliated offer no clue as to why these providers were

---

TABLE 4
Legal Dispositions of 19 Untried Providers

Day Care Case	Accused	Disposition
Georgian Hills	Paul Shell	All charges dismissed
	Betty Stimpson	Charges dismissed during trial; remaining charges later dismissed
Jubilation Day Care	Barbara Orr	No criminal charges filed
	Sharon Orr	No criminal charges filed
Cora's Day Care	Cora Priest	All charges dismissed
	Ralph Priest	All charges dismissed
Craig's Country	Jamal Craig	Charges dismissed during trial; remaining charges later dismissed
Presidio	Gary Hambright	Charges filed twice, dismissed twice
	Michael Aquino	No criminal charges filed
	Lilith Aquino	No criminal charges filed
Gallup Christian	Charlotte Steidl	Charge dismissed
Breezy Point	"Mrs. Janet B."	No criminal charges filed
	"Mrs. Lois S."	No criminal charges filed
Little Rascals	Shelley Stone	All charges dismissed
	Darlene Harris	All charges dismissed
	Robin Byrum	All charges dismissed
Fran's Day Care	Janise White	All charges dismissed
	Raul Quintero	All charges dismissed
	Douglas Perry	Immunity from prosecution

untried. Among the represented centers are church-affiliated, home-based and public centers, ranging in number of enrollees from small to large. There is nothing exceptional about the communities in which the cases occurred. Just like the providers who did stand trial, these providers came from small towns and large cities across the country, and their cases generated as much media attention and rancorous public discourse as any of the other cases. And these providers stand at all points on the historical trajectory of the 1980s day care ritual abuse moral panic, some of them accused at its start, some towards its end, with the others scattered between.

The allegations against these providers are substantively no different than the allegations of ritual abuse levied against the other providers who did stand trial. While in every case there are rogue allegations, too ridiculous for even the most credulous child-saver to believe, they are not over-represented in the cases of these providers. And there is nothing exceptional about the children who accused them; they are of the same tender age as the children in the other cases and, like them, they varied in their intelligence, communicative competence, emotional maturity and truthfulness.

The simple and oft-repeated answer to the question of why charges were never filed or were dismissed against these providers, is that there was not enough evidence to bring the cases to and through trial. Like a lot of simple answers, though, this one is simple only on its face. After all, there was little evidence in *any* of the day care ritual abuse cases, and some of the cases went to trial on even less evidence than was presented in any of these. What this simple answer disguises are complex exercises in judgment, a kind of moral calculus, that figures the costs and benefits of satiating public outrage by proceeding with a trial, against the risks of acquittal and of wrongful conviction.

In regards to a few of these 19 providers, the moral calculus was so simple as to be arithmetic. Deputy Constables Janise White and Raul Quintero were never really serious suspects in the Fran's Day Care case, but as friends of providers Fran and Dan Keller they came under suspicion when one of the accusing children said that uniformed officers sometimes participated in the ritual abuse. Although neither fit the child's description, both were implicated by Douglas Perry in his "confession" that he hastily retracted the following day. On no more evidence than that, and in response to pressure from the accusing children's parents, the two deputy constables were criminally charged (Cartwright, 1994). Moral outrage, just like moral capital, can be rashly used up, and it was on their friends the Kellers whose trial was front page news and the heated topic of over-the-fence gossip for months. When the Kellers were convicted, moral outrage was spent and, after a decent interval, the charges against White and Quintero were quietly dropped. "It's difficult to get a conviction in child abuse cases," Assistant District Attorney Judy Shipway said in defense of the decision.

"On a confession that's been recanted, I still think the jury needs evidence to make a decision.... We don't have any physical evidence. All we have is this recanted confession" (Ward, 1993, p. 5A).

There was no confession in the case of Jamal Craig, but the charges against him in the Craig's Country Day Care case were dismissed during trial when the prosecution's key witness, a seven year old girl, was unable to describe any of the abuse she allegedly experienced and, in fact, was unable to name the day care center or any of the providers (Leff, July 29, 1987). The judge ruled that the child was incompetent to testify and dismissed the six charges against Craig. Although the prosecutor attempted to stoke moral outrage that already had been diminished by the successful prosecution six months before of Jamal's mother, Sandra, by insisting he would pursue a new trial, the remaining charges against the teenager were dismissed without fanfare at a later date.

The analogy of moral outrage to currency is also transparent in the exercises of judgment in the Georgian Hills case where four providers were indicted for ritually abusing children. Betty Stimpson was the first to go to trial in an atmosphere so emotionally charged that precautions had to be taken to protect her life as well as that of her attorney (Berry, 1987). But five days later, the morality play already was played out. The first of the three children to testify against her repeatedly broke down in tears on the witness stand and refused to continue; the second gave a fantastical account none of her many interviewers had ever heard before of saving her baby sister from orgiastic satanists by carrying her on her back over the Mississippi River Bridge. Concerned that the trial was "too injurious" to the accusing children, Assistant Attorney General Tom Henderson asked that the charges against Stimpson be dismissed (Berry, 1987).

Now the economics of moral outrage would suggest that a great deal of it accumulated when Stimpson walked free, and was ready to be spent on the next trial of provider Frances Ballard. Indeed, in a verdict that even puzzled the presiding judge, Ballard was convicted of one of the 16 counts against her (Berry, 1988). Moral outrage now exhausted, provider Jeff Stimpson was acquitted in a trial that never even made it to the front pages of the local newspaper, and the charges against Paul Shell were dismissed for lack of evidence (*Shell, Stimpson and Stimpson v. State of Tennessee*, 1995).

The same economics of moral outrage were evident in the case of Charlotte Steidl who clearly benefited from the trials and convictions of Mary Lou and Edward Gallup and their son, Edward Jr., better known as "Chip," in the Gallup Christian Day Care cases. The cases had been high profile enough to force changes of venue in efforts to find jurors who had not read or heard about the allegations of ritual abuse in the three centers the Gallup family owned. Once convictions had been secured against each family member, the single charge against day care aide Charlotte Steidl, was quietly dismissed.

For almost all of the rest of the cases, the moral calculus is not nearly so transparent. After exhaustive investigations, the "lack of evidence" was cited for dismissing charges against mother and son Cora and Ralph Priest in the Cora's Day Care case, and for dismissing them twice for Gary Hambright in the Presidio case, as well as for declining to bring charges against the Orr sisters in the Jubilation Day Care case, and the Aquinos in the Presidio case. The remaining case of "Mrs. Janet B." and "Mrs. Lois S.," providers at the Breezy Point Day School, however, offers a little insight into the complexity of the moral calculus that underlies the simple explanation that there is "not enough evidence" to proceed with a criminal trial.

Bucks County District Attorney Alan Rubenstein was an experienced prosecutor who followed the day care ritual abuse trials with interest. Well before the allegations against the two Breezy Point providers reached his desk, community rumors and gossip had heralded their arrival. Convinced he was confronting "the crime of the century," Rubenstein took charge of the investigation (Okerblom & Sauer, 1993, p. A1), and was immediately confronted with a dissonant fact: "Mrs. Janet B." had passed a police polygraph test.[1]

Rubenstein explicates his decision-making process from that point. He considered the possibilities that the polygraph test was inaccurate, that "Mrs. Janet B." was a sexual psychopath who could not distinguish lies from truth and who could experience no remorse, or that she was telling the truth and the allegations against her were baseless. He called upon his team to conduct a thorough investigation. "Whatever it costs, whatever it takes," he told them, "do it" (Conroy, 1991, p. 136). Like most of the prosecutors in the day care ritual abuse cases, he was willing to risk prosecution if there was insufficient evidence against the provider and her aide who was later implicated, but unlike most he demanded incontrovertible proof of their innocence if they were not guilty.

After a five month investigation Rubenstein faced down furious parents, dumbfounded interviewers, and a morally outraged community and refused to file charges. His exercise in moral calculus produced results that satisfied him that ritual abuse had never occurred at Breezy Point and that the two providers were innocent of any wrongdoing.

Pleas

A few of the providers traded what capital they had to secure an advantage in the face of moral outrage. Iliana Fuster pled and received a 10 year sentence, served 3 years and was deported to her native Honduras. Although defiantly maintaining their innocence, Betsy Kelly and W. Scott Privott pled no contest in the Little Rascals case to secure their release from jail where they had been awaiting trial for over three years (Thompson, 1994). Sonja Hill pled guilty in the Miss Polly's Day Care case when, in response to public criticism, the charges against her that had been dismissed months before were reinstated by her own attorney when he was elected county prosecutor (*North Carolina v. Figured*, 1994). Brenda Williams, the office manager of the Glendale Montessori Preschool, also negotiated the tension between reputation and expectation of a life sentence by pleading no contest to reduced charges in exchange for a 10 year prison sentence. She, too, obstinately maintained her innocence, and refused to testify against the preschool's director, James Toward (Orr, May 23, 1989). Toward, who was facing a life sentence, accepted the prosecuting attorney's offer of reduced charges and pled guilty the day his trial was to have started. He, too, contumaciously asserted his innocence. When the Judge, in sentencing him to 27 years in prison, declared that the ritual abuse described by the children in the pretrial hearing was so despicable that he "came very close to being physically ill," Toward brusquely replied, "So have I" (Orr, June 15, 1989, p. 26A).

TRIALS AS SITES OF CONTESTED DISCOURSE

Many of the day care ritual abuse trials were spectacles, in every sense of that word, with "the crowds and the cameras; the scandalous revelations of unseemly private behavior, inevitably made into fodder for moralists; the legal maneuvering and posturing and the ensuing public skepticism of law's ability to do justice" (Umphrey, 1999, p. 393). The challenge here is to not be distracted by the spectacle of these show trials, but to concentrate on them as sites of contested discourse in the moral panic.

For discourse to be contested, of course, it must be presented. As in all criminal trials there are players whose role it is to narrate the case. Although what prosecutors, defense attorneys and judges say about a given case is important fodder for analysis, it is the discourse of three sets of witnesses who play roles somewhat unique to the day care ritual abuse trials, that merit the closest look.

"Out of the Mouths of Babes"

For much of the history of American jurisprudence, young children generally were considered testimonially incompetent. In the eyes of the law, they lacked the intelligence, judgment, memory and communicative ability to advance the truth-finding mission of criminal trials. That certainly was the basis of the appeal in the historic *Wheeler v. United States* (1895) case in which the testimony of a five year old witness secured the conviction of the defendant for murder. But in an unexpected decision, the appellate court upheld the conviction, giving credence to the contrary view that under certain conditions children as young as five indeed could be competent witnesses, but at the same time assuring the legal community that "no one would think of calling as a witness an infant only two or three years of age" (p. 524).

Less than a century later, child-savers not only thought about calling "infants" to the witness stand in the day care ritual abuse trials, they actually did. Unlike the five year old in the *Wheeler* case who had given testimony about a murder he had seen, these young children were called to testify about what they had experienced. The fear that testifying in open court would only compound the trauma of their victimization prompted child-savers to demand that innovative procedures be used to protect them from "secondary traumatization" (Berliner & Barbieri, 1984, p. 128), a term that descriptively links two of the master symbols of that decade—the vulnerable child and the psychological trauma model.

In many jurisdictions these innovative courtroom procedures were already in place, albeit infrequently used. By the start of the day care ritual abuse moral panic, some states already had sanctioned the "child-friendly" rearrangement of courtrooms, replacing the judges' raised dais with tables surrounded by pint-sized chairs, and replacing the judges' intimidating back robes with street clothes. Other jurisdictions allowed a support person, such as a parent or a therapists, to stand near the testifying child, or even to provide the comforting lap upon which a testifying child could sit; others still allowed a neutral questioner to either examine the child in the place of the lawyers, or to interpret the child's responses to the lawyers.

While all of these innovations raise issues that pit legal scholars against each other, other innovations specifically put into place to protect testifying children from face-to-face confrontations with their alleged abusers in court raised more serious constitutional issues. In some states, for example, screens can be used to separate children from defendants in the courtroom; in others, children are allowed to testify *in camera*, on videotape, or via closed circuit television.

The constitutional issue raised by these innovations, of course, has to do with defendants' 6th Amendment right to be confronted by the witnesses against them, a right that historically has implied the kind of face-to-face confrontations these very innovations were put into place to prevent. Legal scholar Gary Melton (1981) predicted the constitutional dilemma that many of the day care ritual abuse trials eventually would find themselves in: "[S]ociety's interest in punishing child molesters may come into conflict with its obligation as *parens patriae* to protect dependent minors" (p. 184).

Child-savers balanced the considerable heft of a constitutionally guaranteed right with the ballast of received wisdom that children will be secondarily traumatized by court testimony, and found the latter more weighty. That appraisal was given even more gravidity by the venerable American Psychological Association in an *amicus curiae* brief filed on behalf of the prosecution's appeal in the case of Sandra Craig.

Craig had been convicted in 1987 of sexually abusing children in her care at the Craig's Country Day Care, but her conviction was overturned two years later on the grounds that her 6th Amendment right was violated when the children were allowed to testify via closed circuit television (*Craig v. Maryland*, 1989). Prosecutors immediately appealed the decision to the United States Supreme Court, attaching the brief from the American Psychological Association that asserted that sexually abused children often suffer such emotional trauma as witnesses in courts of law that they cannot give reliable testimony anyway, thus vitiating the very truth-finding intent of the 6th Amendment confrontation clause (Goodman, Levine, Melton, & Ogden, 1991).

In 1990, the United States Supreme Court reviewed the Craig case and decided in a five to four decision that "the confrontation clause does not guarantee criminal defendants an absolute right to face-to-face meeting with the witnesses against them at trial." In language that buoyed the spirits of child-savers and gave a few more years of vitality to the day care ritual abuse moral panic, the Court further opined that "if the State makes an adequate showing of necessity, the state interest in protecting child witnesses from the trauma of testifying in a child abuse case is sufficiently important to justify the use of a special procedure that permits a child witness in such cases to testify at trial against a defendant in the absence of face-to-face confrontation with the defendant" (*Maryland v. Craig*, 1990).[2] The "adequate showing of necessity" for shielding child witnesses with some kind of "special procedure" was largely left to psychologists in the role of expert witnesses who, as the attached brief asserted, could draw on recent scientific findings to make valid and reliable case-by-case determinations of a child witness's need for any kind of limitation of face-to-face confrontation with the accused during a criminal trial.

But can they, really? Legal scholar Jean Montoya (1995) is more than a little doubtful. She examined the transcripts of the trial of Dale Akiki, the provider who was accused of ritually abusing children at the Faith Chapel Day Care Center where he volunteered on Sunday mornings. She compared the testimony of 7 therapists and one parent that predicts how the children would fare if made to testify in the presence of Akiki, with the actual responses and behaviors of the 10 children on the witness stand after the judge denied the prosecution's motion to allow them to testify via closed circuit television. They are strikingly different. Table 5 contrasts the therapists' and the parent's predictions with the children's responses during that part of testimony that child-savers were certain would be the most traumagenic—the cross-examination by defense attorneys.

As Table 5 demonstrates, all of the children were cross-examined for a considerable period of time after they had given direct testimony under questioning by the prosecutor. Although they sometimes asked for a question to be repeated, sometimes answered that they did not understand or could not remember, and sometimes misunderstood the questions asked, none of the children showed any significant distress as a result of the cross-examination, or from testifying in the presence of Akiki, despite their therapists' predictions that they would.

Why were the therapists such poor diviners? Certainly part of the answer lies in their ideological alliance with the children they were assessing and treating, rather than with any body of scientific theory or method. This bias is evident in this exchange between one of Akiki's

---

TABLE 5

Predictions of Testimonial Abilities vs. Actual Performance of Child Witnesses on Cross-Examination in State v. Akiki (adapted from Montoya, 1995, pp. 368–369)

Child/ Time on Cross-Exam	Therapist's testimony	Asks for Repeat	"Don't under-stand"	Mis-under-stands	"Don't know/ remember"	Other
Chad/ 2:55	"severely impact"	2x	2x	3x	9/66	jokes a little
Beau/ 1:40	"virtually impos-sible"	0x	2x	1x	48/90	laughs, smiles, hesi-tant about talking about abuse
Amy/ 2:00	"very com-promised because of fear"	4x	4x	1x	20/198	retracts allegation re: Akiki killing peo-ple
Mich-elle/ 2:11	"probably" would be totally unable	0x	3x	0x	47/113	babyish talk embarrassed to talk about sex games

(TABLE 5 CONTINUED)

Child/ Time on Cross-Exam	Therapist's testimony	Asks for Repeat	"Don't under-stand"	Mis-under-stands	"Don't know/ remember"	Other
Jeremy/ 1:22	will "shut down," "quit talking," "not inter-act"	1x	0x	2x	7/58	mostly yes or no answers
Chris/ 1:53	"signifi-cantly inhibit"	17x	18x	0x	12/48	quiet speech; seems angry; does not want to talk about abuse
Donny/ 1:20	"more likely to be im-paired"	2x	1x	0x	45/34	fairly com-fortable after time
Elyse/ 1:46	"don't know if she will be able to talk"	0x	0x	0x	15/46	squirms; monotone voice
Michael/ 2:13	"impact severely; probably make it im-possible"	0x	11x	0x	10/51	stutters; jokes retracts somewhat re: abuse
Alice/ 2:10	Parent: "might be afraid"	0x	10x	0x	32/220	smiles, giggles; says "I don't remember" a lot to-wards end

defense attorneys and the therapist who predicted that the child, Michelle, would "probably" be totally unable to testify in the presence of the accused provider (Montoya, 1995, p. 356):

> DEFENSE ATTORNEY: Do you feel that it's your obligation to spare Michelle from any trauma that she might experience in testifying, if you can?
> THERAPIST: Yes.
> DEFENSE ATTORNEY: Okay. So it would be fair to say you're not engaged in any balancing act against what Mr. Akiki's rights might be; your only concern is Michelle?
> THERAPIST: That's true.

It is not just the therapists' lack of fidelity to scientific fact and method in determining whether the children's testimony would be enhanced by shielding that is at issue here, but their apparent rejection of both in favor of a more intuitive approach. It should be noted, in all fairness to the intent of the American Psychological Association's *amicus curiae* brief, that the therapists who testified in the Akiki trial were the not doctoral level, licensed clinical psychologists the brief had in mind as scientific experts. They were, instead, social workers and masters level mental health clinicians. That said, though, they are typical of the experts who testified about shielding in the day care ritual abuse trials; indeed, they are typical of the professionals who affiliated and identified with the child-savers interest group. Their non-scientific, intuitive approach is illustrated by this exchange between one of the defense attorneys and the therapist who predicted that the child witness, Beau, would be so frightened by having to testify in the presence of Akiki that it would be "virtually impossible" for him to communicate at all (Montoya, 1995, pp. 358–359):

DEFENSE ATTORNEY: If Beau were in the room, and he were in a room with one support person, a representative of the court, and a non-uniformed bailiff, and there was a two-way closed-circuit television camera operator with the videocam and a monitor, actually three monitors, the monitors would show Mr. Akiki, the attorney doing the questioning, and the judge, do you think under those circumstances Beau would be able to testify?

THERAPIST: I can't say anything definitively, just because I've never had the opportunity to see him in that situation. I would imagine that it would be a highly anxiety producing situation for him, but I would venture a guess that he would be more likely to testify under those circumstances because he would not be in the courtroom, he would be with a support person, there would not be a lot of people around, and he would not be in the same room with Dale Akiki...

DEFENSE ATTORNEY: Would you say that the information that you've given us in your opinions is no more than a guess?

THERAPIST: I'm not merely guessing. I'm giving you my best professional opinion but qualifying that by saying I don't think any professional, even having known a child for the length of time that I've known Beau, could say definitively how a child will perform under that kind of anxiety-producing situation.

It is another brief exchange between defense attorney and therapist that most succinctly captures the intuition versus science approach to assessing the necessity of shielding child witnesses. The therapist is Pamela Badger who, as a member of the San Diego Ritual Abuse Task Force, assumed considerable responsibility for assessing the children in the Faith Chapel case (Sauer, 1993, November 14, p. D-1):

DEFENSE ATTORNEY: Must a diagnosis reached in therapy be based on research verified science?

THERAPIST: That's a different type of science ... I think there's—there are different types of science. There's research science and...

DEFENSE ATTORNEY: What type of science do you practice?

THERAPIST: Artful science.

DEFENSE ATTORNEY: So, you're saying its an art, it's not a science?

THERAPIST: A little of both ... I think there's a lot of counseling theory that has not necessarily been proven in scientific research.

The "artful science" of child-savers acting as experts served as a gatekeeper for the children's testimony in the day care ritual abuse trials, determining whether it was shielded or given in open court. The difference is not just a matter of the legal arabesque that takes place in almost every criminal trial, but raises serious and, as of yet, not consistently answered questions about the quality of testimony given in shielded and unshielded conditions, and the reception of that testimony by jurors who must determine the guilt or innocence of the accused (Eaton, Ball, & O'Callaghan, 2001; Orcutt, Goodman, Tobey, Batterman-Faunce, & Thomas, 2001). As gatekeepers, the testimony of the child-savers had varying results in regards to the conditions under which the children testified in the cases of the accused providers who did go to trial, as Table 6 demonstrates.

Mythic Children

The star witnesses in the day care ritual abuse trials were, without a doubt, the children. Some entered the courtroom or appeared on videotape or closed circuit television adorned in their Sunday best dresses or pressed trousers and clip-on ties, others in whatever was fashionable in casual wear; their hair was brushed to a shine, curls hair-sprayed into place, stubborn cowlicks slicked down. They sat on the floor or on small chairs in their therapists' offices or police interview rooms to answer questions in front of a camera, or they carried teddy bears, dolls or lucky charms to the witness stands where they sat on their knees, pillows, or stacks of law books to reach the microphones. As the hours of their interviews or testimony dragged on, they fidgeted, squirmed, giggled and pouted; some whimpered anxiously, a few cried.

How did these children perform as star witnesses? Well, very much like children. Clutching a stuffed seal named Sammy, a five year old told the prosecutor in the Frank Fuster trial that she likes the color pink, has a younger brother, two dogs, a cat and bird, and refuses to eat squash (Messerschmidt, 1985), a revelation that made the jury snicker. Another five year old, resplendent in a blue baseball cap and jacket and carried

TABLE 6
Open Court v. Shielded Testimony of Children in the Criminal Trials of 26 Providers

Day Care Center	Defendant	Children's Testimony
Manhattan Ranch	Michael Ruby	Open court
Country Walk	Frank Fuster	Closed circuit television
Small World	Richard Barkman	Closed court
Fells Acres	Violet Amirault	Closed court; facing jury, backs to defendant
	Cheryl LeFave	Closed court; facing jury, backs to defendant
	Gerald Amirault	Closed court; facing jury, backs to defendant
Georgian Hills	Frances Ballard	Videotape
	Jeff Stimpson	Videotape
Rogers Park	Deloartic Parks	Open court
Craig's Country	Sandra Craig	Closed circuit television
Wee Care	M. Kelly Michaels	Closed circuit television
Felix's	Martha Felix	Open court; prelim testimony on videotape
	Francisco Ontiveros	Open court; prelim testimony on videotape
Mother Goose	Reginald Huard	Open court
East Valley	Michelle Noble	Videotape
	Gayle Dove	Videotape
Gallup Day Care	Edward Gallup	Open Court
	Mary Lou Gallup	Open Court
	Edward Gallup, Jr.	Open Court
Miss Polly's Day Care	Patrick Figured	Open Court
Old Cutler	Bobby Fijnje	Videotape
Faith Chapel	Dale Akiki	Open court
Little Rascals	Robert Kelly	Open court
	Dawn Wilson	Open court
Fran's Day Care	Fran Keller	1 in open court; 1 on closed circuit television
	Dan Keller	1 in open court; 1 on closed circuit television

into the courtroom on the shoulder of the prosecutor in the Richard Barkman trial, got a laugh out of the judge when he paused in his testimony to offer him a Cert from the sticky roll he clutched in his hand (Jewel, 1985). A six year old made everyone gasp when she suddenly declared from the witness stand that a spectator in the back of the courtroom had witnessed the abuse she had suffered at the hands of her provider, Mary Lou Gallup. And everyone breathed a forgiving sigh of relief when it turned out he had not (Leeson, October 18, 1989). After offering the prosecutor her lollipop, a five year old testifying in the joint trial of Fran and Dan Keller blew into the microphone, intoning like a roadie doing a sound check at a rock concert, "Hello, hello, hello" (Gamino, November 19, 1992). Even jaded journalists whose reportage had inflamed that case into a Southern Gothic were reduced to helpless laughter. Behavior like this that would have earned an adult witness a stern rebuke or even a charge of contempt was tolerated not only because it relieved the tedium of long and complicated trials, but because it affirmed the survival of something that ritual abuse threatened to take away—childhood innocence.

It is important to note that the providers who stood trial had been charged with sexual abuse and, in some cases, additionally with assault, kidnapping or conspiracy, *not* with ritual abuse. The best efforts of child-savers to pass state laws that either specifically criminalized ritual abuse or enhanced sentences if child abuse was committed during the course of rituals, had less than an even modest success. Three states have such laws on the book; all of them passed after 1990, well after most of the day care ritual abuse trials already had ended or already had started. Their symbolic value to the moral panic aside, to date there has never been a charge, trial or conviction under any of these laws.

That necessary digression aside, it was in the best interest of the prosecution that the testifying children not repeat the more fantastical, that is, unproved and uncorroborated, features of their accounts. In other words, they benefited from keeping the devil out of the courtroom. And on direct examination, most of the children did just that. Consider the testimony of a seven year old in the trial of Robert Kelly, the husband of the owner of the Little Rascals Day Care Center ("Innocence Lost," 1998):

> PROSECUTOR: Well, let's first talk about your hiney, then; did Mr. Bob ever touch that part of your body?
> CHILD: Yes, ma'am.
> PROSECUTOR: With what part of his body did he touch your hiney?
> CHILD: He did it with his fingers.
> PROSECUTOR: Where did he put his fingers?
> CHILD: In my hiney.
> PROSECUTOR: How did that feel?
> CHILD: It didn't feel very good...
> PROSECUTOR: All right. Do you remember telling your mom about Mr. Bob putting his penis in your hiney?
> CHILD: Yes ma'am...
> PROSECUTOR: How did that feel when he did that?
> CHILD: Um, it didn't feel very good.

Under cross-examination, though, the child's unembellished testimony about sexual abuse transformed into an elaborate ritual abuse master narrative, as it did for many of the testifying children in the day care trials. The seven year old in this case went on to tell the jury that Kelly had tied him up with a chain, terrorized him with pet sharks and rattlesnakes, locked him in a jail cell, sealed him in a box, hung him by the neck from a tree limb, and prayed to the devil *(North Carolina v. Kelly,* 1994, pp. 6303–6427).

Another child in the same case offers the same kind of bare-bones testimony about sexual abuse after being made to watch pornographic videos by Kelly and his friend, W. Scott Privott, the owner of the only video rental store in the bucolic small town of Edenton, North Carolina ("Innocence Lost," 1998):

> PROSECUTOR: And, um, what kind of movies would you see upstairs?
> CHILD: Ugly movies.
> PROSECUTOR: And what made you say they were ugly movies? Do you remember what you saw?
> CHILD: They had bad things on them...
> PROSECUTOR: And do you remember what, um—what happened or what you saw in the movie that made you think it was bad?
> CHILD: Men and woman had, um, had sex.
> PROSECUTOR: And so did they have clothes on or no clothes on?
> CHILD: No clothes on.
> PROSECUTOR: Now, who brought the movies or who showed you the movies?
> CHILD: Mr. Scott.
> PROSECUTOR: Would Mr. Bob be up there, too?
> CHILD: Yes.
> PROSECUTOR: Did Mr. Bob ever do anything, ah, like you've talked about, ah, just a few minutes ago, to you or your friends during or after those movies?
> CHILD: Yes.
> PROSECUTOR: Any of the things happen to you or was it things that were happening to your friends?
> CHILD: Both.

Like the previous child, and the other 10 who testified against Kelly, this girl also retreated to the well-rehearsed ritual abuse master narrative when persistently prompted by the defense attorney. She went on to describe witnessing and participating in orgiastic sex with all of her providers, watching a mysterious and unnamed black man skin live hamsters and cover the room with blood, and hearing the killing of other animals by her providers in the upstairs room where she and her little friends were forced to watch pornographic films *(North Carolina v. Kelly,* 1994, pp. 11255–11333).

There is a fascinating ambiguity not only about the testimony of these children, but about the children, themselves. They are, in so many ways, emblematic of late-modernity, occupying as they do social spaces— the courtroom and the witness stand—previously occupied by adults, and speaking with an authority once reserved only for adults. So it is not just their ambiguous testimony that must be mediated by direct examination and cross-examination in these trials, but their ambiguous image.

Sociologist Chris Jenks (1996) points out two dominant mythic images of children in Western history. "Competitive to the point of absolute incompatibility" (p. 70), one or the other image tends to have a hold on cultural imagination at any particular point in time. In late modern society, however, they uneasily coexist and, in doing so, stand in moral opposition to each other.

The Appolonian image of children is, at its heart, starry-eyed and romantic. It is an image of unspoiled innocence, natural goodness, and a kind of naïve wisdom that adults can only envy, and over which they wax nostalgic. This image of children evokes from society and its institutions not only admiration and a little awe, but the strongest need to nurture, protect, understand and believe. In contrast, the Dionysian image of children is darkly Dickensian. It is an image of self-gratification, constant demands, and a naïve susceptibility to corruption and evil of which adults should be wary. This image summons from society and its institutions an equally compelling need to monitor, regulate and control. Although Jenks hastens to remind that these are mythic images, not literal descriptions of the way children differ, they are no less evocative for it, since each is morally inscribed.

These two competing mythic images of children were discursively created in the day care ritual abuse trials and then positioned opposite each other along the morally inscribed line between truth and lies, innocence and evil. The questioning of a six year old by defense attorney Michael Spivey and prosecutor Nancy Lamb in the Little Rascals Day Care trial of Robert Kelly illustrates the discursive making, unmaking and remaking of these mythic images (*North Carolina v. Kelly,* 1994, pp. 7715–7718, 7771, 7772–7774):

> SPRIVEY (Cross-Examination): Did you, ah—did you tell Ms. Judy [therapist] that Ms. Betsy hurt four of the babies, that she beat them until blood came out of their eyes?
> CHILD: Yes...
> SPIVEY: Now, did you tell Ms. Judy that she beat their knees and toes and legs, too?
> CHILD: Yes...
> SPIVEY: Okay. Do you remember seeing anybody kill any of the babies at the day care?
> CHILD: No.
> SPIVEY: Well, now, you told Ms. Judy that they killed babies at the day care, didn't you?
> CHILD: Yes.
> SPIVEY: Okay. And where did that happen that you saw babies killed?
> CHILD: I can't remember...
> SPIVEY: After the babies were dead what did they do with them?

CHILD: I can't remember.

SPIVEY: Okay. Now, is that the truth?

CHILD: Yes.

SPIVEY: Are you sure it's the truth?

CHILD: Yes...

SPIVEY: Did they really kill real babies?

CHILD: Sometimes.

SPIVEY: Sometimes. Well, now when you talked to Ms. Judy you didn't tell her that happened at the day care, did you?

CHILD: No.

SPIVEY: You told Ms. Judy it happened in outerspace, didn't you? Isn't that what you told Ms. Judy that Mr. Bob and Ms. Betsy killed the babies in outerspace?

CHILD: Yes.

SPIVEY: And you told her that you went to outerspace with Mr. Bob and Ms. Betsy in a hot air balloon, right?

CHILD: Yes.

SPIVEY: Did you really do that?

CHILD: It was a spaceship...

SPIVEY: Is that the truth?

CHILD: Yes...

SPIVEY: And these are things that Ms. Judy helped you talk about, didn't she?

CHILD: Yes.

LAMB (Redirect Examination): Hi. Now, a little while ago you were asked about babies being killed; were these real babies or were they baby dolls?

CHILD: Baby dolls.

Lamb: And when you talked about going into outerspace and seeing babies killed, was that something that really happened or was it—or what was it?

CHILD: It was a story.

LAMB: Who told you that story?

CHILD: Mr. Bob...

SPIVEY (Recross-Examination): Okay. Now, a little while ago when you told me that, ah, you saw Mr. Bob and Ms. Betsy kill babies, you told me that they were real and that that really happened and you told me that was the truth, didn't you? Didn't you tell me that was the truth?

CHILD: Yes.

SPIVEY: Well, now, when are you telling the truth, when you talk to me or when you talk to Ms. Nancy [Lamb]?

CHILD: When I talk to you.

SPIVEY: Okay. Well, now, which story is true, the one you told her about baby dolls or the one you told me about real babies being killed?

CHILD: Baby dolls.

SPIVEY: Okay. Then why didn't you tell me that before?

CHILD: I don't know...

SPIVEY: Okay. When you talked to me a little while ago you told me that, ah, when you went to outerspace you didn't go in a hot air balloon, you went in a spaceship, right?

CHILD: (Nods head).

SPIVEY: Okay. Why did you tell me that?

CHILD: I don't know.
SPIVEY: Well, now which story is true, the one you tell Ms. Nancy or the one you tell me?
CHILD: Ms. Nancy.
SPIVEY: Okay. Well, why didn't you tell me the truth?
CHILD: I don't know.

And no one else can know, either—at least not for certain. Appolonian or Dionysian, innocent or corrupt, in need of care or control, truthful or deceitful, the image of this child is an ambiguous as that of a shapeshifter. And so, too, is the image of the children who chased Kelly when he was being led away from the courthouse in handcuffs after having been sentenced to 12 consecutive life terms. Public television producer Ofra Bikel was there that day, filming the second of a three-part *Frontline* series on the Little Rascals case, titled "Innocence Lost." Her cameras caught the spectacle of the children, prompted by their parents and news reporters, jeering and taunting the provider even while they mugged and hammed it up in front of the cameras. The image is as disturbing as it is ambiguous or, perhaps, it is disturbing *because* it is ambiguous; regardless, it gives credence to Jenks's (1996) observation that in late-modern society the images of children are being handled, massaged and manipulated "to achieve ends wildly in excess of particular, embodied children" (p. 98).

Passing Judgment

As in any trial, the jury in a day care ritual abuse trial can be treated as what sociologist Wendy Griswold (1994, p. 14) refers to as "cultural receivers," that is, as a group that hears, appreciates, understands, contemplates, remembers and, of course, judges the testimony, evidence and arguments presented in the trial. Far from a passive audience, a jury is an active meaning-maker, interpreting everything presented in the trial against a "horizon of expectations" shaped by the individual juror's previous experiences and current beliefs (p. 83). Each juror interprets the trial, that is, finds its meaning in order to render a judgment, on the basis of how well everything presented in it fits or affronts those expectations. That said, the question remains as to how the juries actually interpreted the evidence and, more specifically, how they interpreted the children's testimony about the ritual features of their abuse.

There are two ways to approach that question, each with its own limitation, unfortunately. Consider first an empirical study on jury decision-making in ritual abuse cases conducted by psychologist Bette Bottoms and her colleagues (1997) using 243 university students as mock jurors. Each was presented with a one page scenario about day care ritual abuse, patterned on the McMartin Preschool case. The scenario described the testimony of seven witnesses—the female alleged victim, her mother, the female and male providers who are the co-defendants, an expert witness for the prosecution and another for the defense, and one of the providers' co-workers at the day care center. Briefly, in the scenario the alleged victim describes sexual abuse by the providers, nude games, the taking of pornographic photographs, and threats to ensure her silence. Her mother recalls that she once questioned her after seeing her posing nude with her playmates but that, although upset, she did not disclose any sexual abuse until she had been in therapy for several months. Both of the providers deny the charges and contend that the psychologist suggested the false allegations during therapy. The prosecution expert, the treating psychologist, asserts that the alleged victim suffered from trauma caused by the abuse, while the defense expert, also a psychologist, claims the treating psychologist had used suggestive therapy techniques. Finally, the co-worker explains that the day care center had a good reputation and had so many employees that it would have been difficult to conceal any abuse.

The mock jurors then were randomly assigned to four different versions of this scenario, based on two dichotomous variables: the nature of the abuse (ritualistic or non-ritualistic) and the age of the victim (5 or 30 years). In the ritualistic version, the abuse is described as taking place as part of ceremonies in which the providers made reference to the devil, wore black robes, and chanted around a circle of candles; in the non-ritualistic version, the abuse is described as taking place in the context of games in which the providers made reference to movie stars, wore movie star clothes, and sang songs. As far as the age variable is concerned, the 5 year is described as having been placed in therapy by her mother, while the 30 year old is described as having entered therapy for depression and then remembering the abuse she had experienced in the day care center as a child.

The methodological limitations of the study are obvious, and acknowledged by the authors. These are mock jurors, not citizens of a community where rumor and innuendo may have been rife for years before a trial even started. They have reviewed a single page summary of testimony rather than testimony offered *in vivo*, and have not been privy to the introduction of material evidence, the arguments between lawyers, the rulings of a judge, or the persuasive opening and closing arguments. And, of course, they did not deliberate so their individual judgment was not influenced by discussion and debate with other mock jurors.

Despite those limitations, the findings are interesting. The study concludes that although the mock jurors were somewhat less likely to believe the ritualistic details than the other case details, with the notable exception of those who had scored high on a previously administered religiosity test, they were just as likely to believe the victim, regardless of her age, in the ritualistic as in the non-ritualistic scenario. This suggests that jurors are willing to suspend their disbelief and render judgment on their perception of the common allegations of the two scenarios: playing naked games, involvement in pornography, secrecy threats and, of course, sexual abuse. As cultural receivers even mock jurors actively evaluate what testimonial evidence they have and they did not let the more bizarre features of the allegation interfere with their assessment of the credibility of the testimony about sexual abuse.

But is that what real jurors did in the very real day care ritual abuse trials? Here, the post-trial comments of jurors who actually decided the cases can be used as the second, admittedly imperfect, source of data on how the children's often ambiguous and contradictory testimony about the ritual features of their abuse really was interpreted.

Jurors in the trial of Michael Ruby in the Manhattan Ranch Preschool case "hopelessly deadlocked" on the 11 charges against him, compelling the presiding judge to declare a mistrial. The children's testimony had baffled them. "It was very difficult to sort out what was true and what was untrue, and what was fact and what was fantasy," one juror told the press. Although none of the jurors really believed the ritual abuse allegations made by the five testifying children, some were willing to suspend that disbelief to conclude that they were "basically telling the truth" about having been sexually abused by the playground aide, but others could not. The closest the jurors got to reaching a verdict was a vote of 10 to 2 on one count; on the remainder of the charges, they were tied 6 to 6 on each count (Waters, 1985, p. 8).

Jurors in the trial of Sandra Craig, in contrast, had little difficulty reaching guilty verdicts on five of the six charges against her in the Craig's Country Day Care case. In a post-trial interview, a juror explained that the six year old, in relation to whom all of the charges had been filed, "seemed to know what she was talking about ... [and] carried herself very well." Yet her knowledge and comportment were not enough to easily convince the jurors in regards to the most serious charge against Craig, that of first degree sexual assault which in the state of Maryland carried a maximum sentence of life imprisonment. That was the charge confounded by ritual abuse. The child had testified that Craig had vaginally penetrated her with a stick, beaten a pet rabbit to death with a hammer and threatened to bury her alive in the woods to secure her silence. It was over that charge that jurors strenuously debated whether all or part of the child's testimony had been unduly influenced by interviewers. In the end, they suspended their skepticism about the ritual abuse features of the testimony and found Craig guilty of the offense. "If we had a murder or rape case it would have been easier," a juror explained to the press, "because you have had more substantial evidence and none of this questioning about the child's credibility" (Leff, April 3, 1987, p. A-6).

The children's credibility was at issue in the trial of Dale Akiki in the Faith Chapel case where the devil was an invited guest. Under cross-examination, the children testified as much about the ritualistic features of the case as they did about the sexual abuse, but jurors were unwilling, or perhaps unable, to suspend their disbelief about the former to render a judgment on the latter. After acquitting Akiki of all charges, a juror speaking for the others said that not only did they not believe the children, but they doubted whether the children even believed themselves (Granberry, June 28, 1993).

Yet doubt can linger after a verdict, suggesting that as cultural receivers jurors take seriously their task of evaluating and then re-evaluating the children's testimony. After the acquittal of Bobby Fijnje in the Old Cutler case, six of the jurors sent the District Attorney a three page letter stating they believed "something happened" to two of the testifying children, but had too many doubts to vote guilty. They urged her to "launch an appropriate investigation and file additional charges as deemed appropriate" (Branch & VanNatta, 1991, p. 1D). After the conviction of Robert Kelly in the Little Rascals Day Care case, a juror told producer Ofra Bikel during the filming of the second installment of the three-part documentary on the case, that he wanted to please fellow jurors by voting guilty but remained unconvinced that the children's testimony was truthful. And in another media *mea culpa,* a juror in the trial of Gerald "Tooky" Amirault in the Fells Acres case told a *48 Hours* interviewer that over the nearly 20 years since he voted guilty he has come to believe that the children's testimony was the product of suggestive and leading questioning by their interviewers, and not truthful after all.

So what does all of this mean? In day care ritual abuse trials, real jurors are more active cultural receivers than the mock jurors in the empirical study. Far from always suspending their skepticism about the ritual features of the children's testimony to focus on the sexual abuse allegations, they variously treat the features as figure and ground—as meaningful to their assessment of the children's credibility or as meaningless. The fact that the verdicts in the day care ritual abuse trials were far from consistent also supports the contention that real jurors exercised a great deal of freedom in meaning-making, sometimes even making what Griswold (1994, p. 90) refers to as "subversive meanings" that flew in the face of public opinion.

Sorrowing Mothers and a Few Fathers

The hi-tech methods for shielding testifying children are little more than whistles and bells compared to the decidedly low-tech method of parental testimony. Under an exception to the hearsay rule, parents were allowed in the day care trials to testify about what their children had disclosed to them about the ritual abuse during those intensely emotional moments that the law variously refers to as "outcries" or "excited utterances" (Marsil, Montoya, Ross, & Graham, 2002).

Excited utterances are considered trustworthy. The law assumes that while under the sway of "exciting events," such as being horrifically abused by day care providers, children have neither the conceit nor the time to prevaricate, the child sexual abuse accommodation syndrome notwithstanding, thus what they tell their parents is generally reliable. So truthful are these utterances considered to be that in theory, at least, the parents would be able to testify in lieu of their children, thus obviating the need for the children to ever be present in the courtroom. In practice, however, that was not the case. Rather, the parents' testimony complemented, augmented and enhanced that of their children, whether their children testified live in the courtroom or via technology.

In this capacity as recipients of excited utterances, mothers took the stand much more often than fathers, a testimony to the constancy or, perhaps, the non-negotiability of "emotion work" as women's work, even in the face of rapidly changing gender roles. The mothers testified not only for their children, but often *as* their children, switching between first and third person pronouns and using puerile language to describe body parts and functions. A mother on the witness stand in the Fran's Day Care case, for example, when asked what her daughter had told her about being abused by Dan Keller, replied, "Danny took his pee-pee and put it in her hole and got glue all inside her and it was yucky" (Ward, November 18, 1992, p. 1A).

If the testifying mothers occasionally wavered in syntax and language, they were remarkably consistent in emotional tone. Riddled with guilt for brokering the care of their young children to others, and for working outside of the home in the first place, they embodied in many ways the conservative sentiment that feminism deludes women into believing they can have it all.

Although the testifying mothers used words like "stunned," "overwhelmed," and "shocked" to describe their reactions to their children's excited utterances about ritual abuse, they never hesitated in believing them. "If my son says it, I have to believe what he says," a mother testified in the trial of Robert Kelly in the Little Rascals case, "no matter how bizarre" (Glass, 1991, p. B1). In the same trial, however, the testimony of the father of a different child illustrates the reluctance fathers often experienced in coming to terms with their children's alleged victimization. Although his daughter had told him that Kelly had "put his privates in her privates," the father testified, he did not believe she had been sexually abused until a pediatrician confirmed evidence of penetration ("Testing at Hospital," 1991, p. B2).

Trial testimony evidence like this of gendered differences in believing the children's excited utterances and in performing the emotion work of listening, talking and nurturing, is supplemented by a few first person accounts written by mothers whose children allegedly were ritually abused in day care centers (Crowley, 1990; Hill, 1996), as well as by a few clinical studies. As an example of the latter, one study funded by the National Center on Child Abuse and Neglect found that mothers whose children allegedly had been ritually abused in southern California cases, including the McMartin Preschool and the Manhattan Ranch cases, were more convinced that the ritual abuse described by their children indeed had occurred, and were more preoccupied and distressed as a result, than were the fathers. This gendered difference was attributed to the fact that the mothers "spent more time with the children or perhaps because [they] in general are more likely to focus on feelings about problems, whereas fathers may be more likely to avoid distressing feelings" (McCord, 1993b, p. 187). A similar finding was reported in a study of parental reactions to the Fells Acres Day Care case (Kelley, 1990). On all measures, the Fells Acres parents experienced more stress than parents whose children had been sexually abused at day care centers; mothers, however, having spent more time talking and listening to their children's accounts, were more likely to believe them and to experience distress and self-blame as a result than were the fathers.

Believing the children indeed may be gendered work, but a whirligig of time passed between the excited utterances of children and parental testimony in the day care ritual abuse trials. That raises an interesting question: just how reliable were the recollections of the excited utterances of their children by mothers who, like the children, were under the sway of an "exciting event?" Social science research would predict that the answer is, not all that reliable. The research indicates that memory of the excited utterance deteriorates somewhat as it passes down the hearsay chain from children, to mother, to jury. In an experiment, young children who had played with a research associate were then interviewed by their mothers on camera about the event several days later. Half of the mothers had been warned that they were participating in an experiment on memory; the other half had not. Three days after interviewing their children, the researchers questioned the mothers as to their recollection of what their children told them, as well as for what kind of questions they had asked. The findings reveal that although the mothers accurately recalled most of the events the children had talked about, they remembered few of the details. They had little accurate recall as to what statements their children made were spontaneously offered, and therefore would meet the legal definition of excited utterances, and what were prompted. And more interesting still, even the mothers who had been warned that this was a test of memory, had even less recall as to who had actually made some of the specific statements—their children, or themselves (Bruck, Ceci, & Francoeur, 1999).

There is testimonial evidence to all of these reliability issues in the day care trials, revealing that even when the "exciting event" is ritual abuse, memory of the excited utterance depreciates over time, even with repeated telling. In the trial of Gerald "Tooky" Amirault in the Fells Acres case, the mother of the boy whose excited utterance had initiated the investigation had trouble on the witness stand remembering the one detail of that disclosure that immediately had raised the suspicions of investigators that this was no ordinary case of sexual abuse (*Commonwealth v. Amirault*, 1989, p. 35):

> ATTORNEY: Do you recall him telling you on that night that he was made to urinate in cups and then drink the urine while his teachers were in the room?
> MOTHER: I remember him telling me about urinating in cups but not about the teachers in the room.
> ATTORNEY: Well, do you remember testifying in the Grand Jury to the effect that he was made to urinate in cups and drink the urine while the teachers were in the room?
> MOTHER: No, I don't remember.
> ATTORNEY: Look at this paragraph right here
> MOTHER: [Witness complies]
> ATTORNEY: [D]oes that refresh your memory with what you testified to in the Grand Jury about what your son had told you on that occasion when he first told you "the whole story?"
> MOTHER: Yes.
> ATTORNEY: Do you recall further your son telling you on that first occasion that when he was being made to drink the urine, Tooky said or did anything?
> MOTHER: Yes.

Some parents who had anxiously listened to rumors and had provided sympathetic ears to friends whose children had disclosed ritual abuse, were determined to get the facts straight if and when their own children did so. But as this segment of testimony from the trial of Robert Kelly in the Little Rascals case illustrates, even taking notes is no guarantee of an accurate record of a child's excited utterance (Ceci & Bruck, 1995, pp. 245–247):

> MOTHER: I wrote down the first conversation with [my son] when he was getting ready to take a nap that day. And I think I wrote down something else, I'm not sure. Because I found it rather hard to do, to go back.

You had a conversation with your child and then you talked to your child about something else, and then the child goes to sleep, to go back in there and sit down and try to remember what you had asked your child and what your child had said, I found it hard to do.

ATTORNEY: Did you turn those notes over to the prosecutor or even to the police?

MOTHER: Yes. [The police officer] called me several times and wanted the notes, and I hadn't written them yet. And this was several weeks afterwards. And I sat down and I wrote down to the best of my recollection what I could remember of just the conversation where he had said that Mr. Bob had stuck his penis in his mouth, and I turned those notes in.

ATTORNEY: [Reads the note in entirety]. Does that accurately reflect the conversation you had with your son on April 28, 1989 that caused you to call Brenda Toppin at the Edenton Police Department?

MOTHER: I don't know. A lot of this I think I put in here from different conversations when I wrote this up. This isn't the exact conversation that was carrying on. Like I said, I was scared.... And I wrote these up several weeks later.... And I tried to get the dates straight when I wrote the date at the top of them.

ATTORNEY: So your testimony is that this not an accurate account of what [your son] told you on April 28.

MOTHER: Sir, I'm sure that I added some to it. I'm sure that I did. I'm sure that I made it out to be a lot worse than it was. Yes, sir, I am...

ATTORNEY: What did you add to it?

MOTHER: Well, I'll tell you what. I didn't put down there everything that I had asked him and all the times that he had denied it. I didn't put all those down there. I didn't put down there that he had been questioned every day. I didn't put down that he had asked to go back to the day care, that he wanted to go back to the day care. I didn't put all of that stuff down there. I didn't put any of it down there.

What certainly had the capacity to compromise parental recollections of excited utterances is what that whirligig of time between that first conversation and court testimony brought with it. Not only did parents continue to question their children after their excited utterances, but they were privy to the interviews their children had with investigators, attorneys and therapists; they talked with other parents of disclosing children in formal meetings and in chance encounters; they confided in their own friends, therapists and spiritual advisors; they read newspaper and magazine articles on the cases, and listened to television and radio news. Given this anxious cacophony, it would be understandable if some of the parents talked themselves right out of accurate memories about those first utterances by their children.

All of that is further complicated by the fact that that whirligig of time also brought with it many distracting and confounding life changes for many of the parents: there were births, deaths, marriages and divorces; moves to new jobs, new homes, new communities, new states; diseases, disorders and cures; savings depleted and, in many cases, later replenished many times over as a result of successful civil suits against the providers.[3] There was much, too, in the lived lives of parents to interfere with their source monitoring, that is, their ability to reliably keep track of the origins of their memories.

Retrospection and Elaboration. Under the exception to the hearsay rule, parents in many of the day care ritual abuse trials also were allowed to testify about their children's behavior—behavior now identified as sequelae of abuse, and therefore corroborative of it. In offering this kind of testimony, parents assumed another new role created by the day care ritual abuse moral panic—that of parent-expert. This is a hybrid role, an uneasy compromise between the role of parent-advocate and that of ritual abuse expert and, as such, it is discursively demanding. It requires that parents testify with the passion of a parent and the equanimity of an expert, with the subjectivity of a mother or a father and the objectivity of an authority. As in all of these newly minted roles, the parents' role performances varied widely, but it is the two approaches to their testimony—retrospective interpretation of behavior and emotions, and elaboration of popular sexual abuse theories—that are of particular interest.

Parent-experts made a specific kind of sense of their children's behaviors and emotions by retrospectively interpreting them as sequelae of day care ritual abuse rather than as reactions to familial stress, the vicissitudes of growing up or, for that matter, the stress of the investigation and the interrogations. In the trial of Robert Kelly in the Little Rascals Day Care case, for example, the parent-experts testified that they never had reason to worry about their children's behavior until they disclosed ritual abuse. Then, to the parent-experts, the temper tantrums, fears and sleep disturbances that once had looked like nothing more than normal growing pains were retrospectively interpreted as sequelae of day care ritual abuse (*North Carolina v. Kelly*, 1992, pp. 5,011, 5,728, 10,010).

Their children's disclosures put time out of joint for some of the testifying parent-experts. One mother, for example, testified that her daughter's urinary problem was a symptom of ritual abuse because it began when she started attending the day care center. Medical records, however, showed that the problem had pre-dated the child's enrollment by more than a year (p. 11,599). Another mother testified that her daughter had broken her clavicle at the day care center, an injury she always had attributed to an accident. Upon hearing rumors that the day care providers threw babies around the room, she retrospectively interpreted the injury as a result of this bizarre ritual, and then questioned her older daughter, also an enrollee at the center, whether she in fact had witnessed this. The child eventually agreed that she had and then named the Little Rascals provider who had thrown her younger sister across the room (p. 7,985).

One more example of parent-expert testimony in Kelly's trial illustrates just how provocatively tautological that testimony could be. From the witness stand, a mother read an early entry from her diary about how her son "tended to stain his pants before going to the bathroom." When the Little Rascals case first was made public, she reasoned that this was not a toileting problem after all, but the sequela of sexual abuse that must have occurred in the bathroom of the center. "If you are abused in the bathroom," she testified, "it makes sense in your mind to think that it's sexual abuse" (pp. 6,740–6,741). Having thus deduced both act and location, she began questioning her son who eventually confirmed what she, at that point, already believed to be true.

Helping parents "make sense" of their children's behaviors and emotions was the vast array of popular literature and the boisterous media talk about sexual abuse that were the artifacts of the psychological trauma model, one of the master symbols of that decade. Abundant with clinical terms and concepts, sparse on empirical data, bereft of theory, this written and spoken discourse was popular with parents who often were encouraged by their children's interviewers and therapists to empower themselves by attending to it.

Once again, the trial of Robert Kelly in the Little Rascals Day Care case is a trove of testimony illustrating how immersion into the popular psychology of sexual abuse gave parent-experts the terms and concepts to retrospectively interpret their children's behaviors and emotions, and to do so with the ring of authority. One father, for example, testified that he had not been at all concerned about his son's behavior until he learned the "psychology of child abuse" and came to realize that the behavior was symptomatic of sexual abuse (p. 10,329). A mother, as another example, testified that once she had learned the psychology of sexual abuse, she realized her child's denial that anything untoward had happened at the day care center actually was a sign that he had been sexually abused (p. 9,592).

That latter example hints at the parent-experts' familiarity with the child sexual abuse accommodation syndrome, that handy set of shibboleths that explains why children do not disclose sexual abuse in a quick, consistent and certain manner. Indeed, the Kelly trial is rife with examples of the naïve elaboration of this, and other, popular theories of sexual abuse by the parent-experts. A mother, for instance, testified that her son's denial that he had been sexually abused was due to the fact that he had repressed memories of it (p. 10,074); another told the jury that her daughter took so long to disclose because she had to "feel safe enough" to do so (p. 8,104). In testimony the parent-experts affirmed the core ideologies of the syndrome that had been synthesized into the rallying cry of the day care ritual abuse moral panic: Believe the Children.

They testified that their children could neither lie nor fantasize about something they had not experienced (pp. 10,307, 10,406); they described their children in Appolonian terms, as too naively wise, too naturally good, to succumb to adult misdirection and suggestion (pp. 6118, 6574).

Popular literature and media talk were not the only sources of the parent-experts' elaborated theories of sexual abuse. The Little Rascals Day Care case, like virtually all of the day care ritual abuse cases in the sample, brought parents and child-savers together in formal and informal fora to talk not only about the progress of the case as it slowly inched towards trial, but about their children's progress as well (Abbott, 1994; Lamb, 1994). These disparate people—parents, police, prosecutors, interviewers, therapists—needed a shared language for meaningful exchanges, and found it in the popular theories of child sexual abuse. And that language, in turn, vested passionate, subjective parents with the aura of equitable, objective expertise.

Learned Opinions

Although parents played the newly minted role of parent-expert in the day care ritual abuse trials, the primary responsibility for educating the triers of facts belonged to unhyphenated experts. Experts always have been used in trials to explain scientific, technological and clinical matters assumed to be beyond the ken of the average juror, but courtrooms became arenas for discursive battles between them during the 1980s when the master symbol of the psychological trauma model brought all types of abuse and injury before the bar.

Expert testimony generally is offered in one of three forms: an opinion, an answer to a hypothetical question, or an exposition on a particular matter (Myers, 1992). Regardless of the form, however, experts usually are not allowed to answer what the law refers to as the "ultimate legal issue," that is, whether the accused indeed is guilty of the alleged abuse. Thus the discursive demand on expert witnesses, whether for the prosecution or the defense, is to identify and interpret the "clues" in the case in such a way that jurors or judges, in the cases of bench trials, can confidently figure out "who done it."

While the day care ritual abuse trials featured a rather wide range of expert testimony, there are two broad types that illustrate just how contested expert discourse really is. The first is medical, the second psychological; one focusing on soma, the other on psyche, but both putting the new "science" of sexual abuse to the test.

Expert Medical Testimony. The day care ritual abuse trials were rife with expert testimony on the medical diagnosis of sexual abuse. Jurors heard about the notched hymen of a child who accused Michelle Noble of digitally penetrating her during secret excursions from the East Valley YMCA Day Care Center to the provider's home (Nathan & Snedeker, 1995); the vaginal scarring of the child who claimed Dale Akiki inserted sharp objects into her vagina while her parents worshipped upstairs in the Faith Chapel Church (Granberry, June 28, 1993); and the seven millimeter opening in the hymenal ring of a child who accused Martha Felix of jabbing a kitchen knife into her vagina while she was in her care at Felix's Day Care Center (*Felix v. State*, 1993). They listened to medical expert testimony about the fresh tears in the vagina of a child who insisted Dan Keller raped her at Fran's Day Care Center (Cartwright, 1994), and about the healed tears in the vaginas of two children who claimed Bobby Fijnje assaulted them with a purple stick in the Old Cutler case (Van Natta, 1991). They heard about the enlarged vaginal area of the child who insisted Deloartic Parks raped her and then forced her and other children at the Rogers Park Jewish Community Day Care Center to eat the flesh of a baby he boiled in the basement (Enstad, September 24, 1985); the vulvitis of three children who said mother and daughter Violet Amirault and Cheryl LeFave fondled them in a magic room at the Fells Acres Day Care Center (*Commonwealth v. Amirault and LeFave*, 1987); and the funneled anus of a child who claimed Patrick Figured assaulted him with a screwdriver at the Miss Polly's Day Care Center (*North Carolina v. Figured*, 1993).

Little of this expert medical opinion was rendered without contradiction by other medical experts who countered that these findings were not indicative of sexual abuse, or at least not of sexual abuse alone. To the triers of fact—the juries and, in the bench trials, the judges—this contested medical discourse probably sounded like nothing more or less than a debate over the medical diagnosis of sexual abuse which, in many ways, of course, it was. But it is the subtext of the debate that informs the analysis of the day care ritual abuse moral panic, for at its core, this is a debate about the distinction between science and advocacy.

The genitals of children, after all, had never been of much interest to physicians who rarely ever had reason to closely examine them, let alone make them the objects of scientific inquiry. That changed in the 1980s when the decade's master symbols of the vulnerable child and the psychological trauma model were discursively linked and child sexual abuse became the typification of all things traumatizing that can happen to innocent children. The cases of sexual abuse that then began flooding into courts of law, though, were not typically the cases of rape and sodomy that left the torn and bleeding vaginas and the bruised and ripped anuses that even to the inexperienced eye made the diagnosis of sexual assault unimpeachable. Rather, they more often were cases of chronic, long-term sexual abuse by fondling, digital penetration or oral-genital contact. The impact of these less violent and intrusive forms of sexual abuse on the genitals of children vexed physicians who often were called upon by courts to render an expert medical opinion as to whether sexual abuse really had occurred, and made the diagnosis, itself, more than little dubitable.

What exacerbated this vexation was the received wisdom, alá the child sexual abuse accommodation syndrome, that children do not disclose sexual abuse, or at least not convincingly. As far as physicians were concerned, then, children's genitals were left to tell the story the children, themselves, were too young, too intimidated, or perhaps simply too naïve to tell.

Imbued with a new diagnostic significance, the genitals of alleged sexual abuse victims were subjected to often repeated medical exams. Physicians saw notched, frayed, bumpy and ringed hymens, skin tags, scar tissues and discolorations, chafe marks, rashes and infections, and dilated anuses that winked when gently touched with cotton swabs. In the absence of comparative medical observations and research on what the genitals of children who had *never* been sexually abused looked like, these unexpected findings had all of the appearances of "micro-traumas" (Woodling & Kossoris, 1981) that spoke volumes about chronic, long-term sexual abuse, even if the embodied children had disclosed nothing.

This advocatory conclusion was quickly reified in the early years of the day care ritual abuse moral panic. Physicians who had joined the cadre of entrepreneurial child-savers in the early years of the moral panic lectured and published widely about the diagnostic significance of these micro-traumas, and even made instructional videos that were marketed to medical schools and handed out to journalists at the end of that tumultuous decade when Peggy McMartin Buckey and her son Raymond, whose case had started it all, finally came to trial (Nathan & Snedeker, 1995, p. 192). The American Medical Association gave its stamp of approval to the notion of micro-traumas by listing such things as lax anal tone, hymenal openings in excess of four millimeters, vaginal discharges and urinary tract infections as diagnostic indicators of sexual abuse (American Medical Association, 1985).

Science, however, was moving but slowly, to paraphrase the poet Tennyson, to catch up with what was trying to pass for it. By the late 1980s, too late for most of the day care ritual abuse trials, well-designed and controlled research began appearing that called into question the diagnostic significance of micro-traumas—indeed, called into question the very notion of micro-traumas in the first place.

Pediatric physician and researcher Jan Paradise (1989), for example, found that physicians were making "a big issue about a little tissue"

(p. 169) when they based their diagnosis of sexual abuse on the hymen alone. Since its appearance varies considerably from one girl to another, quite regardless of any history of victimization, physicians who interpret its anomalies as the micro-traumas of sexual abuse have a 65 percent risk of falsely identifying children as victims in cases in which penile penetration is alleged; that false positive rate increases to 73 percent in cases in which digital penetration is alleged. Pediatric professor and researcher John McCann, as another example, examined the vaginas and anuses of 300 children who had no history of sexual abuse and came across the same topography of bumps, rings, bands, rolls and winks that child-savers were calling micro-traumas. His research found that the sizes and shapes of hymenal orifices depended on the age of the child and the position assumed during medical examination, and that skin tags and discolorations were common in the anuses of children, particularly those of Asian or Hispanic descent, and that after a few minutes in the knees-to-chest medical exam position, most anuses winked when touched with a cotton swab (McCann, 1989, 1990).

By the end of the decade, science finally had overtaken advocacy. In an essay titled, "The More We Learn, the Less We Know 'With Medical Certainty,'" Richard Krugman, editor of one of the leading scholarly journals in the field of child maltreatment, cautioned that "the medical diagnosis of sexual abuse usually cannot be made on the basis of physical findings alone. With the exception of acquired gonorrhea or syphilis, or the presence of forensic evidence of sperm or semen, there are no pathogenic findings for sexual abuse" (1989, pp. 165–166). The American Academy of Pediatrics agrees. Its recent guidelines state, "Physical examination alone is infrequently diagnostic in the absence of a history and/or specific laboratory findings. Physical findings are often absent even when the perpetrator admits to penetration of the child's genitalia. Many types of abuse leave no physical evidence, and mucosal injuries often heal rapidly" (Committee on Child Abuse and Neglect 1999, p. 188).

And, interestingly, some of the day care ritual abuse moral panic's most ferocious child-savers now have changed their tune, and are singing a more scientific song. Pediatric professor Astrid Heger whose findings of sexual abuse in over 300 children in the McMartin Preschool case, and whose 1986 video, "Response—Child Sexual Abuse: A Medical View," taught medical students and journalists the diagnostic significance of bumpy hymens and dilated anuses, now concedes that "decades of research into the medical diagnosis of child sexual abuse indicate that most children remain free of any medical findings diagnostic of penetrating trauma." The finding is supported by a review of 2384 cases of sexual abuse she conducted with colleagues (Heger, Ticson, Velasquez,

& Bernier, 2002, p. 653). Heger, in a personal *Festschrift* to Richard Krugman who had warned a decade earlier that medical advocacy was out-
pacing science, offers what could be read as a *mea culpa* for the advocacy
role she and other child-saving physicians assumed during the "race" that
was the day care ritual abuse moral panic:

> When the race started, we knew that we were responsible for the welfare
> and safety of the child. Once the race was underway, it became easy to
> lose sight of the purpose and become more focused on the process, the
> machine. As we pay tribute to Dick Krugman, let us not forget the cour-
> age it took for him to raise the yellow flag in the midst of a race rife with
> backlash and competition. I hope that we all have the courage to con-
> tinue to drive with the same degree of caution [p. 656].

Expert Psychological Testimony. In their analysis of the sorry state of
the social sciences in academia, Frank Richardson and Blaine Fowers
(1998) find irony in the fact that psychology, the social science that has
achieved the most prominence in American society, and the only one that
"seeks to plumb the most personal and intimate spheres of living or matters of the soul," is also the social science that is "most passionately and
ideologically committed to the canons of dispassionate and objective science" (p. 466). In other words, psychology and the practice of it in psychotherapy, often fail to appreciate the cultural and moral values with
which they are inextricably entwined.

There are, of course, those who disagree with this opinion and others still who insist that if it is true of psychology then it is also true of
the other social sciences as well. But while the debate rages in academia
about the social sciences, and the wisdom of poet W.H. Auden's admo-
nition that thou shalt never commit one, the opinion is in so many ways
well illustrated by both the prosecution and defense expert psychological testimony in the day care ritual abuse trials.

Consider first the testimony on the child sexual abuse accommodation syndrome. It will be recalled that the syndrome, put together by ritual abuse propagandist Roland Summit (1983), describes children's
accommodation to their sexual abusers in terms of secret-keeping,
delayed disclosures, and retracted disclosures. Impressionistic in nature,
recklessly tautological in its insistence that "accusations are always to be
believed, denials never, except when the denial is, as it must be, really an
accusation" (Kincaid, 1998, p. 81), the child sexual abuse accommodation syndrome has no commitment to the tenets of dispassionate and
objective science. But does its passionate and ideological pretence dis-
guise a deeper moral agenda?

To answer that question requires a sociological reading of the syndrome and of the symptom lists that are said to speak for the silent and

inarticulate child. Expert witness Eileen Treacy's testimony in the trial of provider Kelly Michaels for sexually abusing 19 children at the Wee Care Nursery School in bizarre rituals that included drinking urine and blood and licking peanut butter off of genitals, provides the opportunity for just that.

Treacy presented her own version of the child sexual abuse accommodation syndrome. That the syndrome can be so facilely reworked to fit any occasion reveals just how pretentious its claim to objectivity and dispassion really is. That said, over several days of testimony Treacy explained that if the five characteristics common to situations of sexual abuse—engagement, sexual interactions, secrecy, disclosure, and suppression—can be identified in cases where abuse is suspected, abuse indeed had occurred. She then went on to explain that 32 "behavioral symptoms" are indicative of sexual abuse; the presence of 5 to 15 of them speak for the silenced child. The symptoms are: "eating problems (over/under); sleep problems (initial, medial, terminal); needs to sleep with light on; won't sleep alone; comes into others' beds at night; nightmares; cries out in sleep; accident prone; sucks thumb; baby talk; toilet accidents (day or night); clinging behavior; separation problems; won't dress self; won't feed self; excessive bathing/fear of bathing; won't toilet by self; seems to be in a fog; serious temper tantrums; daydreams; aggressive to smaller children/animals; stares blankly; talks about sex a lot; touches self excessively in private spots; postures body sexually; sexually acts out with toys or children/animals; crying spells; hyperactive; withdrawn; changes in school behavior; over-compliant behavior; fear of men" (Rosenthal, 1995, p. 256). Because the parents of all the testifying children used the checklist to determine if their children were sexually abused by Michaels, and all were able to check off at least five symptoms, Treacy concluded that all of the testifying children had been sexually abused.

Why was she so confident that the behavioral symptoms were not due to other stressors in the children's lives, such as problems in the family or starting a new school? Treacy explained that she had conducted a "confounding variable analysis" to determine their influence and found they had none. What exactly that analysis entailed was never explained, perhaps because the very term "confounding variable analysis" was sufficiently jargonistic to pass as scientific method.

Then, by chasing the tail of her own reasoning, the psychologist proved her own theory valid and reliable, thus elevating it to the status of objective and dispassionate science. She told the jury that the children who said they liked Michaels, who stood accused of horrifically abusing them, actually were in the "engagement" phase of the syndrome; those who described sexual abuse, regardless of how and by whom their accounts were solicited, were in the "sexual interaction" phase; those who never disclosed sexual abuse were in the "secrecy" phase; those who had denied having been sexually abused by Michaels were in the "suppression" phase; and those who said anything at all about their interactions with Michaels were in the "disclosure" phase of her version of the child sexual abuse accommodation syndrome (Rosenthal, 1995).

That this is not objective and dispassionate science should go without saying; it has, instead, the hollow ring of pseudoscience.[4] Treacy's version of the child sexual abuse accommodation syndrome begins with an assumption rather than an hypothesis, looks only for instances that confirm the assumption, and then describes by scenario rather than explains by underlying social and psychological processes. It is not empirically tested and not even empirically testable. What it does do, though, and this finally gets to the point about its deeper and well-hidden moral agenda, is rationalize the strongly held beliefs and values that were so disconcertingly threatened by the social strains and stresses of the decade of the 1980s.

It is, after all, the Appolonian child who embodies this syndrome. Naturally good, outrageously vulnerable, exploitatively innocent, the child evokes nurturance, protection and, here is where a deeper sociological reading is revealing, social control. This is a child who must be seen more than heard, reacted to more than interacted with, interpreted more than understood. And for parents who are unable, unwilling or perhaps just uncertain about what they see and how to interpret it, a whole cadre of experts is available to bring its stock of knowledge *sans* science to bear. This is the child whose physical, emotional and spiritual development is dependent on the kind of panopticism[5] that rapidly changing late-modern families cannot guarantee. Thus, the testimony of Treacy and other experts who pass off speculation as science and pathologize normal behavior simply by putting it on a list, can be heard as a call for the restoration of the traditional family, the strengthening of its vigilance and control over the child and, should it fail in its moral imperative, its regulation by the state.

Sociologically heavy-handed? Perhaps. But the "tutelary complex," as Jacques Donzelot (1986) once referred to this exercise in power and control, was voiced in more colloquial terms by the prosecutors upon winning convictions in the day care ritual abuse trials. "I have a message to all parents," prosecutor Debra Kanof exhorted after the conviction of provider Michelle Noble and her sentence to 311 years in prison for ritually abusing children at the East Valley YMCA Day Care Center, "Listen to your children, and love them" (Nathan, 1987, p. 31). Ronnie Earle who successfully prosecuted the Kellers in the Fran's Day Care case, proclaimed, "I think that the jury, on behalf of the community, said to our children, 'we will rock you in our arms and protect you'" (Gamino, November 26, 1992). "This verdict if for *all* the children in America," prosecutor Dennis Wiley exclaimed after the conviction of provider Richard Barkman for ritually abusing a child at the Small World Preschool ("Teacher Convicted," 1985). And from Nancy Lamb upon the conviction of Robert Kelly in the Little Rascals case: "America, this is your wake-up call."

But what exactly was the call all of America was waking up to? For expert witnesses like Treacy, the call was to realize that the Appolonian child is being destroyed by evil and that only vigilance and control will intervene. But for those whose image of the child is Dionysian, the wake-up call takes on a different tone. It is warning that sinister children are undermining hegemonic values and morals.

This image certainly can be mined from the expert testimony of defense psychologist Ralph Underwager in the Kelly Michaels trial. The child of Underwager's testimony is the embodiment of Adamic original sin, an image resonant with the psychologist's education and experience as a Lutheran minister, yet this child seems no more worthy of scientific inquiry than does the idealized child of Treacy's expert testimony. From the stand, Underwager testified to the results of his "Time and Motion Study" that was conducted to determine the range of time it would have taken Michaels to accomplish some of the ritually abusive acts, such as the "nude pile-up" in which she forced naked children to pile on top of sharp utensils. Underwager, however, had never visited the Wee Care Nursery and therefore could only estimate the size and location of the rooms, a detail he dismissed as inconsequential by saying, "We're relatively familiar with buildings and rooms and how to move from one to the other" (Manshel, 1990, p. 279). This insouciant response initiated an angry exchange with prosecutor Glenn Goldberg about the nature of science (*State v. Michaels*, 1993):

> GOLDBERG: Doctor, are you saying that you used subjective experience in terms of how long it takes someone to get undressed?
>
> UNDERWAGER: Sure.
>
> GOLDBERG: And, Doctor, the scientist who relies on subjective experience to make an opinion, has regressed to the level of a witch doctor, isn't it so?
>
> UNDERWAGER: That's a totally different thing.
>
> GOLDBERG: Doctor, isn't that what you wrote in your book, the opinion, "A doctor who bases his opinion on unchecked subjective experience has regressed to the level of a witch doctor"?
>
> UNDERWAGER: That's unchecked
>
> GOLDBERG: Yes.
>
> UNDERWAGER: This is not unchecked.

The psychologist then goes on to explain his method of "intersubjective confrontability" that has as hollow a ring of pseudoscience as does Treacy's method of "confounding variable analysis." The method goes like this: two of his staff independently calculate time estimates, then meet and compare notes; estimates that were similar, although not necessarily identical, then were deemed accurate (Manshel, 1990, p. 280).

From that point, a brief interchange between the residing judge, William Harth, and this defense expert witness brought out the *reductio ad absurdum* of the testimony:

> HARTH: Then if a few witch doctors got together, they could get the same findings you got?
> UNDERWAGER: Yes.

While Underwager's "time and motion study" was offered as evidence that Michaels would not have had the time to ritually abuse the children in her care, it was Underwager's testimonial construction of the Dionysian child that is of most relevance to the morality play that was this criminal trial. In Underwager's view, the child is amoral and asocial, lacking the cognitive ability to think abstractly and thus to experience emotions like embarrassment or shame. Thus the child can lie with impunity or, as Underwager strenuously asserted, can effortlessly be made to lie by overzealous interrogators. To the received wisdom of Treacy's testimony that behavior tells the story the child cannot tell, Underwager predictably disagreed. When asked, for example, what the psychological consequences might be for a child who was forced to drink urine, as some of the children claimed Michaels had made them do, Underwager responded, "Some children, as I've said, could find it attractive, enjoy it, reinforce their fascination" (Manshel, 1990, p. 278).

The Dionysian child of Underwager's expert testimony is a deceiver, and also in need of social control. But it is a different kind of social control—discipline and direction—not just by the family but by all agents of social control. The image assumes a consensual society with little debate over values and morals. The behavior of this kind of child threatens that cohesion and is deserving of punishment.

As sociologist Chris Jenks (1996) reminds, the child is always revealing the grounds of social control. So how children are mythologized in expert psychological testimony affords a glimpse not only at the myth but at the moral gerrymandering underneath. The Appolonian child has to be watched, observed, interpreted by parents and others; the Dionysian child has to be controlled, kept in line, broken down in the battle of socialization. None of the children in any of the day care ritual abuse trials actually embodies these images, but it is the images that make a difference to morality plays.

The Play Play'd Out

The morality plays that were the day care ritual abuse trials were often the longest and most expensive trials in the history of the respective county or state. The trial of Kelly Michaels in the Wee Care case lasted ten months and is estimated to have cost over $3 million; if the pretrial costs of investigations and hearings are added, the sum total for bringing the 25 year old provider to justice is over $7 million (Hass, 1995; p. 40). The price tag on Dale Akiki's 7.5 month trial in the Faith Chapel case is estimated to be $2.3 million (Granberry, November 29, 1993, p. A3). Although the state of North Carolina spent half of that on the trial of Robert Kelly in the Little Rascals case, his was still the most expensive trial in its history and, at 7.5 months duration, the longest (Thompson, 1991, p. 6). Even those trials of shorter duration and less expense took their own tolls. Although Gerald "Tooky" Amirault's trial in the Fells Acres case lasted only three months, the jury deliberated 65 hours before delivering a verdict, the longest deliberation in Superior Court history in the state of Massachusetts (Langner, 1986, p. 1). The trial of Richard Barkman in the Small World case lasted a brief two weeks, but by its end the editor of the local newspaper, the *Niles Daily Star*, declared it two weeks too long—he longed to get back to the homely reportage of rural village life that is the staple of his small circulation paper (Lengel, 1985).

If the purpose of a morality play, quite regardless of its duration or expense, is didactic, that is, to teach a moral, then what lesson can be learned from the verdicts in the day care ritual abuse trials? As Table 7 demonstrates, they are consistent in nothing but their inconsistency.

What Table 7 does not reveal, however, are all of the hot ironies that, were the day care ritual abuse trials the subject of a book or a film, say, would be considered absolutely delicious Take the Kelly Michaels's verdict as an example. One of the counts of sexual abuse on which she was acquitted involved the child whose words during a medical examination—"Her takes my temperature"—brought her as a defendant into a court of law in the first place. Although convicted of 115 counts Michaels, whom reporters covering the trial had nicknamed "The Demon Seed" (Nathan, 1995, p. 86), and whom the trial judge had opined was a threat to civilization (Manshel, 1990, p. 361), was sentenced to an ironically lenient 47 years in prison, with eligibility for parole after 14 years. No such leniency was afforded Michelle Noble. Her trial for sexually abusing and terrorizing children in the East Valley YMCA case was front page news and the talk of the town of El Paso for many months yet, ironically, no sequestration of the jury was ordered and the presiding judge twice let the court out early to watch the University of Texas basketball game on television (Nathan, 1987). Noble eventually was convicted of 18 of t he 19 counts against her and was sentenced to life plus 311 years, the longest prison sentence meted out during the day care ritual abuse moral panic.

There are other hot ironies running unrestrained but invisible through Table 7. Teenager Bobby Fijnje refused a plea bargain, ostensibly offered to spare him the indignity of prison rape and the certainty of acquiring

TABLE 7

Verdicts and Sentences in
Day Care Ritual Abuse Trials

Day Care Center	Defendant	Verdict	Sentence
Manhattan Ranch	Michael Ruby	Mistrial	———————
Country Walk	Frank Fuster	Guilty: 14/14 counts	6 life terms + 65 years
Small World	Richard Barkman	Guilty: 3/3 counts	50–75 years
Fells Acres	Violet Amirault	Guilty: 5/5 counts	8–20 years
	Cheryl LeFave	Guilty: 5/5 counts	8–20 years
	Gerald Amirault	Guilty: 15/15 counts	30–40 years
Georgian Hills	Frances Ballard	Guilty: 1/16 counts	5–35 years
	Jeff Stimpson	Not Guilty	———————
Rogers Park	Deloartic Parks	Not Guilty	———————
Craig's Country	Sandra Craig	Guilty: 5/6 counts	10 years
Wee Care	M. Kelly Michaels	Guilty: 115/131 counts	47 years
Felix's	Martha Felix	Guilty: 3/16 counts	3 life terms
	Francisco Onti-veros	Guilty: 1/4 counts	Life term
Mother Goose	Reginald Huard	Not Guilty	———————
East Valley	Michelle Noble	Guilty: 18/19 counts	Life term + 311 years
	Gayle Dove	Guilty: 6/6 counts	3 life terms + 60 years
		Re-tried after mis-trial declared. Guilty 1/1 count	20 years
Gallup Day Care	Edward Gallup	Guilty: 1/1 count	20 years
	Mary Lou Gallup	Not guilty	———————
		Guilty: 1/3 counts	2 years
	"Chip" Gallup	Guilty: 3/6 counts	10 years
		Not Guilty	———————
		Not Guilty	———————
Miss Polly's Day Care	Patrick Figured	Guilty: 3/3 counts	3 life terms
Old Cutler	Bobby Fijnje	Not Guilty	———————
Faith Chapel	Dale Akiki	Not Guilty	———————
Little Rascals	Robert Kelly	Guilty: 99/100 counts	12 life terms
	Dawn Wilson	Guilty: 5/5 counts	Life term
Fran's Day Care	Fran Keller	Guilty: 1/1 count	48 years
	Dan Keller	Guilty: 1/1 count	48 years

AIDS as a result, put his belief in God, family and justice on the line, and went to trial (Armbrister, 1994). He was acquitted of all charges in the Old Cutler case. Robert Kelly put his reputation on the line, refused a five year prison sentence in exchange for a guilty plea, and went to trial in the Little Rascals case (Sovacool, 1992). Ironically, he was convicted of 99 of the 100 charges against him and was sentenced to 12 consecutive life terms.

In the seventh month of his trial, and after 152 witnesses already had testified, Dale Akiki finally took the witness stand in his own defense in the most notorious case in San Diego history. He was cross-examined by prosecutor John Williams for only 17 minutes, two or three minutes of which were wasted in the prosecutor's theatrical re-enactment of animal sacrifice by repeatedly stabbing a fuzzy toy bunny with a plastic knife. Ironically, only Akiki was upset by the re-enactment; the jury and the spectators laughed (Granberry, October 22, 1993). Fran Keller also took the stand in her own defense. Cocky and confident after the confusing and contradictory testimony of the child she and her husband were alleged to have horrifically ritually abused, she let slip that other children had made similar allegations against them. This crack in her control allowed the prosecutor to call as witnesses two additional children who, ironically, testified with the competence and confidence the well-rehearsed original witness had lacked. Keller and her husband were convicted and sentenced to 48 years (Cartwright, 1994).

The Gallups were tried in multiple jurisdictions, keeping just one venue ahead of the spread of the day care ritual abuse moral panic across the state of Oregon but, ironically, with different results. Edward "Chip" Gallup, Jr. was the first to be accused of ritual abuse but days before his trial was to have begun, the case was dismissed for lack of evidence. Vindicated, he and his parents joined VOCAL (Victims of Child Abuse Laws), an advocacy organization for those falsely accused of sexual abuse.[6] Ironically, their alliance with the organization, and their public assertion of innocence only urged the prosecutor on to find all of them guilty (Gallup, 1989). "Chip" was charged again, tried in a different county, and convicted of three of the six counts against him, but was acquitted in two subsequent trials in two different counties. His father was charged in the same case, convicted and sentenced to 20 years; his mother, Mary Lou, charged in a different case, was acquitted in one trial then tried again in a different county. There she was acquitted of the two most serious charges against her, but convicted of the lesser offense of inappropriately touching the breasts of a six year old girl (Leeson, November 1, 1989).

Anti-Climax

The greatest irony of all is that many of the guilty verdicts, delivered with the certainty that justice was done and all children would now be safe from predatory evil, were themselves unsafe. One after another, and with few exceptions, the convictions of the day care providers were overturned, as Table 8 demonstrates. But by the time they were, the voracious

moral consumerism that had made the day care ritual abuse trials into
morality plays was pretty much sated. There were some objections to
the reversals, of course, some bursts of purgative outrage, and a lot of
scrabbling for higher moral ground by appealing to the "sake of the children" as the reason for letting the reversals stand unchallenged, but the
accused providers already had served their function. They had brought
about a public encounter "between the symbolic order and that which
threatens its stability" (Creed, 1993, p. 11).

To many, the symbolic order had been confirmed *despite* the reversals. The evil done to children had been named; the perpetrators
unmasked and publicly humiliated; the ideological underpinning of the
traditional family strengthened; the institutions of social control buffed
and polished for show; the moral order shored up; the world, despite the
reversals, made better, safer and smarter. "Child sexual abuse has gone
on for centuries, but until ten years ago it almost never was reported. It's
gone from almost no knowledge to a very high awareness in the community," co-prosecutor Henry Williams told a news conference upon dismissing all charges against Frances Ballard in the Georgian Hills case
after the state Supreme Court ordered she either be re-tried or the charges
against her be dismissed. "I think this case had a lot to do with that awareness" (Buser, 1993, p. A1). To hear others talk, the reversals were just so
much legal window dressing—the trial was the thing. Co-prosecutor Mike
Easely said as much when he facilely dismissed the appeal court's reversal of the conviction of Robert Kelly in the Little Rascal's case as "legal
technicalities that are quite insignificant" ("Fundamental fairness," 1995,
p. 16A), never mind that they called into question the morality play that
was the trial and then set free a putative predator of small children.

Legal technicalities, if the term can be used for a moment to indicate
arcane points of law, at least from the public's naïve view, indeed were the
reasons for a few of the reversals, but only a few. Richard Barkman's conviction was overturned because the trial judge had disallowed cross-examination of the child witness about a verifiably false allegation of sexual abuse
he had made against the Small World Preschool provider's wife ("Accused
child molester," 1988). Frances Ballard's conviction was overturned in the
Georgian Hills case because state investigators had improperly destroyed
audiotapes of the early interviews with some of the alleged victims, thus
depriving the defense of evidence it could have used to cross-examine them
at trial (*State v. Ballard,* 1993). After a mistrial was declared when a juror
disclosed that she had voted to convict Gayle Dove only because she did
not want to be perceived as condoning sexual abuse, the East Valley YMCA
Day Care provider was re-tried on a single count of sexual assault and convicted. That conviction was overturned, however, because the trial court
had erred in admitting the statements of children other than the alleged

TABLE 8
Appeal Decisions in Day Care Ritual Abuse Trials

Day Care Center	Defendant	Appeal Decision
Small World	Richard Barkman	Conviction overturned; pled guilty to lesser offense in lieu of re-trial; 5 years probation
Fells Acres	Violet Amirault	Conviction overturned, re-trial ordered. Superior Court overturned re-trial order and reinstated original sentence; that decision overturned by state Supreme Court which overturned conviction and ordered re-trial. All charges posthumously dismissed.
	Cheryl LeFave	Conviction overturned, re-trial ordered. Superior Court overturned re-trial order and reinstated original sentence; that decision overturned by state Supreme Court which overturned conviction and ordered re-trial. In lieu of new trial, credit given for time served, and placed on probation.
Georgian Hills	Frances Ballard	Conviction overturned; all charges dismissed; criminal record expunged
Craig's Country	Sandra Craig	Conviction overturned; all charges dismissed
Wee Care	M. Kelly Michaels	Conviction overturned; all charges dismissed
Felix's	Martha Felix	Conviction overturned; charges dismissed
	Francisco Ontiveros	Conviction overturned; charge dismissed
East Valley	Michelle Noble	Conviction overturned; re-tried; acquitted.
	Gayle Dove	Conviction overturned; all charges dismissed
Gallup Day Care	Mary Lou Gallup	Conviction overturned; re-trial ordered; charge dismissed.
Little Rascals	Robert Kelly	Conviction overturned; re-trial ordered; all charges dismissed; new charges filed, then dismissed
	Dawn Wilson	Conviction overturned; re-trial ordered; all charges dismissed

victim into trial, thus prejudicing the jury (*Dove v. State*, 1989). Mary Lou Gallup's conviction was overturned in the Gallup Christian Day Care case because the trial judge had erred in ruling that some of the materials contained in the prosecutor's file were work products and therefore exempt from discovery by defense (*State v. Gallup*, 1991).

Even high profile convictions, such as those in the Little Rascals Day Care trials, were overturned by small, albeit constitutionally mighty, points of law. Consider the conviction of Dawn Wilson who had given birth to a son six months into her life sentence. It was overturned because the trial judge had erred by allowing prosecutors to introduce unrelated, irrelevant and inadmissible evidence, thus depriving her of her due process rights (*State v. Wilson*, 1995). Robert Kelly, who was "damned to everlasting fame" not just by local media coverage of his trial, but national as well in the form of the three-part *Frontline* series "Innocence Lost," also was set free on what amounted to legal technicalities. The appeals court reversed his conviction on three grounds: the improper admission of testimony as to his guilt by his original defense attorney; the failure of the trial judge to examine the notes of the children's therapists; and the improper admission of testimony by parents in that newly minted role of parent-expert as to the behavioral, emotional and medical sequelae of sexual abuse for their own children.

That latter ground leads nicely into a discussion of how well the innovations in law and procedure—the roles and props of these morality plays—actually fared upon appellate review. The answer, in short, is not all that well. In the clash between the states' interest in protecting accusing children from secondary traumatization by shielding them from the accused, and the 6th Amendment right of the accused to confront their accusers, the latter often prevailed. Michelle Noble's case is illustrative of that point. The East Valley YMCA provider's conviction was overturned when the appellate court ruled that her 6th Amendment right had been violated when the trial court substituted the videotaped testimony of the children for in-person testimony at her trial. She was re-tried, this time with her young accusers testifying from the witness stand, and was acquitted (Nathan, April 26, 1988).

Three Landmark Cases

The Sandra Craig case wended its way through the labyrinthine legal system all the way to the United States Supreme Court, and made legal history on the 6th Amendment point. The highest Court in the land ruled that in some cases, assuring the well-being of victimized children may outweigh a defendant's right to face his or her accusers in court. While childsavers applauded the decision, it was that little three word phrase, "in some cases," that actually set Craig free. The Court ordered the state appellate court, that had earlier overturned her conviction, to re-examine the case to determine if there was indeed sufficient evidence to believe that the children who testified against her on closed circuit television would have suffered such emotional distress from in-court testimony that they would have been unable to reasonably communicate. The appellate court stood by its earlier ruling that there was not. It found that the trial judge had failed to hold pre-trial interviews with the testifying children to determine their emotional state, as was then required in Maryland, overturned Craig's conviction again, and ordered a new trial. Five years after the case that sparked a vigorous debate over shielding young witnesses began, all charges against the owner of Craig's Country Day Care were dismissed.

Kelly Michael's case also made legal history. The Wee Care provider's conviction was overturned on two points: the misuse of closed-circuit testimony, and the abuse of expert testimony. In regards to the first point, the appellate court ruled that the trial judge erred by not making "particularized findings concerning the child's objective manifestations of fear about testifying," as required by the state statute that allows for closed-circuit testimony (*State v. Michaels*, 1993). In fact, the appellate court's own review of the videotapes of the children's testimony led it to conclude that they "manifested virtually no reticence or emotion when speaking of the defendant or the alleged acts of abuse" (*State v. Michaels*, 1993). Interestingly, however, this misuse of closed-circuit television testimony may not have been sufficient for a reversal of Michaels's conviction were it not for something else the appellate court saw in its review of the videotapes: the trial judge playing with the children, holding them on his lap, whispering in their ears, and encouraging and complimenting them during their testimony. In his zeal to put them at ease, trial judge William Harth compromised his judicial role. "For all appearances," the appellate court concluded, "the State's witnesses became the judge's witnesses.... The required atmosphere of the bench's impartiality was lost in this trial" (*State v. Michaels*, 1993).

And so was scientific objectivity. The second point upon which Michaels's conviction was overturned was the abuse of expert testimony. Here the criticism was sharply focused on expert witness Eileen Treacy's rendition of the child sexual abuse accommodation syndrome, behavioral indicators of sexual abuse, and "confounding variable analysis." The appellate court held that her testimony was based on the certain belief that the testifying children indeed had been sexually abused, therefore it was not probative of sexual abuse. "Her testimony constituted nothing less than substantive evidence of [Michaels's] guilt," it concluded, "albeit Treacy's opinion thereof" (*State v. Michaels*, 1993). Unfounded, unreliable and unaccepted by the scientific community, her expert opinion constituted a reversible error.

Although the appellate court did not base its decision on the interviewing techniques used to coax the ritual abuse master narrative from the children, it did devote a significant segment of its opinion to a discussion of them. Citing research conducted by developmental psychologists, it determined that the interviews were sufficiently suggestive to affect the creditability and truthfulness of the children's statements. The appellate court ruled that should the state attempt to retry Michaels, a pre-trial taint hearing would have to be conducted to assess the reliability of the children's testimony.

Prosecutors immediately appealed the reversal of Michael's conviction to the state Supreme Court which refused to hear arguments on either of the critical points. Once prosecutors made it clear that they indeed did intend to retry the provider, the state Supreme Court upheld the requirement of a taint hearing, stating that "competent and reliable evidence remains at the foundation of a fair trial" (*State v. Michaels*, 1994). Armed with the *amicus curiae* brief filed by developmental psychologists Stephen Ceci and Maggie Bruck on behalf of concerned social scientists that provides empirical evidence that the interviewing techniques used in the Wee Care case irreparably undermined the credibility of children's statements, the state Supreme Court ruled:

> The interrogations in this case were improper and there is a substantial likelihood that the evidence derived from them is unreliable. We therefore hold that in the event the State seeks to re-prosecute this defendant, a pretrial hearing must be held in which the State must prove by clear and convincing evidence that the statements and testimony elicited by the improper interview techniques nonetheless retains a sufficient degree of reliability to warrant admission at trial [*State v. Michaels,* 1994].

In late December 1994 prosecutors, citing the best interest of the children in the Wee Care case, decided not to retry Michaels. All charges against her were dismissed. The use of pre-trial taint hearings was the source of debate among legal scholars (Anderson, 1996; Jablonski, 1998; Manshel, 1994), but for child-savers it was the harbinger of a new era of skepticism about the reliability of children as witnesses (Myers, 1994, 1995, 1996). Quite frankly, they should have seen it coming. By December 1994 when Kelly Michaels walked out of prison a free person, a burgeoning body of dubious academic literature on the credibility and reliability of ritual abuse allegations already had been published (de Young, 1994; Jenkins & Maier-Katkin, 1991; Mulhern, 1991; Victor, 1993; Wright, 1994). Reports of official inquiries into controversial ritual abuse cases, all excoriating child-savers for suggestive and coercive interviews, among other sins, already had been filed both in this country (Humphrey, 1985; Lanning, 1992; Rubenstein, 1990; San Diego Grand Jury, 1991/1992; Van de Kamp, 1986) and, as the moral panic spread, in Europe as well (Clyde, 1992; LaFontaine, 1994; Miller 1994; Nottinghamshire County Council, 1990; Werkgroep Ritueel Misbruik, 1994). Organizations like the International

Society for the Prevention of Child Abuse and Neglect and the National Center for the Prosecution of Child Abuse already had warned about the dangers of zealous interviewing and the hasty belief that ritual abuse is real (National Center for the Prosecution of Child Abuse, 1987; Putnam, 1991). The media already had taken a skeptical turn, with reporter David Shaw winning the coveted Pulitzer Prize for lambasting his own newspaper's coverage of the McMartin Preschool case (Shaw, 1990), and Ofra Bikel winning an Emmy for "Innocence Lost," her three-part documentary on the Little Rascals Day Care case. There already had been conversions, of sorts: psychiatrist Roland Summit had called for a moratorium on ritual abuse accusations (Lunn, 1991); and cult-cops Sandi Gallant and Randy Eamon had left the lecture circuit, no longer convinced that ritual abuse even exists outside of their once Gothic imagination.

And by 1994, most of the day care ritual abuse convictions already had been over-turned. Although not going so far as to demand a taint hearing before a re-trial, the Nevada Supreme Court had set the tone for the *Michaels* case by overturning the convictions of providers Martha Felix and Francisco Ontiveros in the Felix's Day Care case a year earlier, citing the leading and suggestive interviews with the accusing children as reason to question the reliability of their testimony.

By 1994, the phrase "taint hearing" had become a floating signifier of all of the controversies that had welled up around day care ritual abuse. It stood for the infirmity of once invincible ideologies, the tarnish on the underside of the gold standard of interview protocols, the clay feet of ideologues and the moon-eyed gullibility of their followers. But if there was any reason for child-savers to protest in 1994, and to persist in their agenda, it was the third legal landmark day care ritual abuse case—the Fells Acres case.

In 1994 the Fells Acres case was almost a decade old. Violet Amirault and her daughter Cheryl LeFave were in the seventh year of their 8 to 20 year prison sentence; Violet's son, Gerald "Tooky" Amirault, was in the eighth year of his 30 to 40 year sentence. The children who were their alleged ritual abuse victims were going on with their lives, the community was going on with its own, and the child-savers who had made it a case in the first place already had moved on to bigger and better things. In 1994 the Fells Acres case was just one year shy of setting off legal machinations that, to this day, leave unanswered the question as to whether they constituted the practice of justice that makes democracy possible, or the predilection for injustice that makes democracy necessary.[8]

In 1995, the Amiraults had exhausted all of their appeals, however, new state legislation mandating that children face the accused in court, gave them the basis for requesting new trials. In both of the Fells Acres trials—Gerald's, and the conjoined trial of Violet and Cheryl—the testifying children had sat at a small table in the front of the court facing the jury, but shielded from the providers by a phalanx of parents and court officers. That year, Superior Court Judge Robert Barton agreed, overturned the convictions of Cheryl and Violet, ordered a new trial, and released the mother and daughter in anticipation of it. Gerald, however, remained in prison, the higher court having determined that he could see the profiles of the children during his trial, and that some of them actually had gone out of their way to make eye contact with him while testifying.

Barton's decision rode the crest of a wave of populist support for the Amirault family that had been swelling ever since *Wall Street Journal* reporter Dorothy Rabinowitz took on the case in a series of stinging editorials, titled "A Darkness in Massachusetts" (Rabinowitz, 1995). No one involved in the case escaped unsullied. From doctoral student Susan Kelley who coaxed the ritual abuse narrative out of the children, to District Attorney Scott Harshbarger who used the case for his own political advantage, to prosecutor Lawrence Hardoon who facilely dismissed the family as "impudent" for maintaining their innocence, to "true believers" everywhere who fell under the sway of the day care ritual abuse moral panic, all were stained with the reporter's untempered ink. In the morality plays that were the Amirault trials, it now was up for debate whether the providers indeed were folk devils worthy of punishment, or folk victims of the legal system. The pitch of the cacophony over the Amirault case became deafening.

The office of the prosecutor appealed the decision. In 1997 the Supreme Judicial Court reversed the lower court. It ruled on the point of the seating arrangements, agreeing that they did violate the Amiraults' 6th Amendment confrontation right, but because their defense team had not objected to it at the time, there were no grounds for a new trial. The court went on to pay lip service to the flaws in the original trial—the suggestive interviewing techniques and the "communicated hysteria" that gripped the parents and the child-savers involved in the case were singled out for criticism—but it nonetheless ruled that the "community's interest in finality" was reason enough for its decision to reinstate the convictions of Violet and Cheryl.

Bringing down the curtain on this morality play did not put an end to the legal curtain calls. Months later, the Supreme Judicial Court refused to review its own decision. Violet, now 70 years old, and Cheryl were preparing to return to prison when their new attorney, James Sultan, seized the local *Zeitgeist* and made a public plea on their behalf. His entreaty coincided with the 300th Anniversary of the "Day of Contrition" on which the entire community of Massachusetts Bay, by proclamation, declared its remorse for "the hardships brought upon innocent persons" during the Salem witch hunt. On that anniversary, two hundred people gathered in Boston to hear playwright Arthur Miller, historian

John Demos, and novelist William Styron talk about the "spectral evidence" that fueled the witch trials. And they heard day care providers Kelly Michaels, Bobby Fijnje, Raymond Buckey, Peggy McMartin Buckey, Violet Amirault and Cheryl LeFave talk about the spectral evidence that fueled their own ritual abuse trials.

Refusing to accept the "finality" imposed by the Supreme Judicial Court, a large part of the social audience to the Fells Acres case demanded an encore. They inundated Governor William Weld's office with pleas for clemency for the Amirault family, and marched to his home to curry his support (Duffy, 1997). Meanwhile, attorney James Sultan requested a new trial. Armed with an affidavit by Violet and Cheryl's original defense attorneys that acknowledged their ineffectiveness as counsel, he secured a hearing before Superior Court Judge Robert Barton, the same judge who two years before had ordered the release of the mother and daughter pending a new trial. The judge once again ruled that Violet and Cheryl had not received a fair trial and that "justice was not done," but recused himself from the hearing because he no longer believed he could be fair and impartial.

The next month, Judge Issac Borenstein overturned the women's convictions and ordered a new trial on the grounds that they had had ineffective assistance of counsel. Any cause for celebration by the Amirault family was short-lived, however. Violet Amirualt, 74 years old, died of stomach cancer several months later.

Prosecutors appealed Borenstein's decision and in December 1997, two months after Violet's death, the Supreme Judicial Court was prepared to hold a hearing on the appeal. When attorney James Sultan told the court that he was prepared to present new evidence, in the form of the empirical studies on children's suggestibility in the face of improper interviewing techniques conducted by developmental psychologist Maggie Bruck who, with colleague Stephen Ceci, had prepared the *amicus curiae* brief that had helped secure the reversal of the conviction of provider Kelly Michaels in the Wee Care case, the court sent the case back to Judge Borenstein for a ruling on its admissibility.

Borenstein presided over a hearing, broadcast to the nation on Court T.V., on that issue in February 1998. He took extensive testimony from Bruck who systematically revealed one error after another in the interview techniques of Susan Kelley, using videotape segments of the interviews to illustrate her points. From the stand, Bruck concluded that the children's testimony in the original trial was "highly suspect" and "unreliable." In a rather remarkable turn of events, prosecutor Lynn Rooney was forced to agree. During closing statements she told the court, "When we look at the interviews by Susan Kelley, the Commonwealth would concede there are throughout the interviews suggestive techniques used by her. Techniques that would not be used today. There's no question about it." But there was more than a little question about her final words to the court. "Justice in this case," she summed up parapraxically, "must come to an end" (Doherty, 1998).

Justice may or may not have come to an end, but the legal proceedings certainly did not. In the summer of 1998, nearly 14 years after the Fells Acres case began, Judge Borenstein posthumously dismissed all charges against Violet Amirault, and ordered a new trial for Cheryl LeFave. His ruling in *Commonwealth v. LeFave* (1998, pp. 6–7) was nothing if not emphatic:

> Overzealous and inadequately trained investigators, perhaps unaware of the grave dangers of using improper interviewing and investigative techniques, questioned these children and parents in a climate of panic, if not hysteria, creating a highly prejudicial and irreparable set of mistakes. These grave errors led to the testimony of the children being forever tainted.

There is that word again—"tainted"—the floating signifier of all that is controversial about the day care ritual abuse trials. Borenstein used it with deliberation, citing the decision in the case of provider Kelly Michaels as precedent and grounding his own in the new science of children's suggestibility. He reversed the conviction of Cheryl Le Fave and once again ordered a new trial, ruling that none of the children who originally testified and who, in his opinion, are "forever tainted," would be allowed to do so again.

Prosecutors immediately appealed. In an attempt to rally support, they enthusiastically re-demomized the Amiraults, reminding the public of the horrific and bizarre ritual abuse crimes for which they were charged. District Attorney Martha Coakley, for example, appeared on a local television talk show with three of the alleged victims in the Fells Acres case, now young adults. One of them, a young woman, is of particular interest because it was her testimony that Borenstein found especially illustrative of the perils of bad interviewing.

"JB," as she is known in his decision, had attended Fells Acres every weekday, from 8:00 in the morning until 3:00 in the afternoon, and until she was interviewed by Susan Kelley, no one ever had any suspicion that she was being abused, let alone ritually abused, by a clown in a magic room at the day care center. JB was not an easy convert to the belief. She initially denied anything amiss had occurred at the center until Kelley, using what Borenstein describes as "every trick in the book" (*Commonwealth v. LeFave*, 1998, p. 44) rehearsed her into repeating the ritual abuse master narrative. Using transcripts from the interviews to illustrate the errors in interviewing, the ruling finds that "the evidence in this motion shows convincingly that JB was subjected to horribly flawed investigatory and interviewing techniques, as well as other influences, including parental pressure, and news media coverage" (*Commonwealth v. LeFave,* 1998, pp. 64–65). Her testimony was dismissed as unreliable.

But her television testimony could not be so easily dismissed. Any first-person narrative of childhood ritual abuse is always emotionally affecting, but it is also sneakily pedantic. If delivered calmly, intelligently and articulately, the narrative reifies the teller's honorific identity of survivor; if not, then it reifies the teller's trauma. Either way, the teller defines the situation and in doing so silences any critique of the narrative by the audience. JB's audience could only listen.

But the prosecutors could act. They immediately appealed Borenstein's ruling, arguing that the empirical evidence for children's unreliability in the face of suggestive interviewing was not new evidence at all; that, in fact, the possibility of tainted testimony had been raised in the original trial and the jury had dismissed it. The Supreme Judicial Court, once again appealing to the need for "finality," agreed. It reinstated LeFave's convictions and, once again, ordered her back to prison.

The maelstrom of criticism this decision generated revealed that the law's finality was not the public's. Although the *Boston Globe,* whose years of reportage on the Fells Acres case ranged in pitch from monotone to one octave below hysteria, applauded the decision as "sensible" ("Fells Acres Finality," 1999), its readers did not. Neither did the venerable *Christian Science Monitor* that decried the decision as "the Commonwealth's worst miscarriage of justice since the Sacco and Vanzetti trial of the 1920s" ("Relapse," 1999). Even the staid *Massachusetts Lawyers Weekly* took the unprecedented stand of criticizing the decision and its whimsical intent to bring finality to the case ("Travesty," 1999), as did the National Association of Criminal Defense Lawyers. Also publicly speaking against the decision were Judge John Paul Sullivan who had resided over the original Amirault/LeFave trial, and Judge Isaac Borenstein who had overturned their convictions. But, not surprisingly, it was *Wall Street Journal* reporter Dorothy Rabinowitz (1999, p. A-20) who had the most astute take on the decision:

> The opinion is a telling document, as much for what the judges left out as for what they put in. Indeed, a reader who came to it knowing nothing about this prosecution would have been hard put to find in this decision any of the reasons this case had won such notoriety; nothing of the frenzied interrogations, the mad pleadings of interviewers exhorting children to tell, of the process by which small children were schooled in details of torments and sexual assaults supposedly inflicted on them in secret rooms, matters—the record of these interviews reveals, that the children clearly knew nothing about [1999, p. A-20].

Fifteen years after the first allegation was made in the Fells Acres case, the country's longest-running morality play looked like it was on the verge of re-opening. But prosecutors, stung by criticism, finally dimmed the house lights and let the principal player, the unrepentant Cheryl LeFave, go home. Her release came at a price. She was to remain on probation for 10 years and drop any and all legal challenges to clear her name; she had to agree not to profit from her notoriety, nor contact her alleged victims, nor have unsupervised contact with any children, nor give interviews on television. She agreed. "I'm grateful," she told the press, "but I just wish it was right" (Rakowsky, 1999, p. A1).

And That Left Tooky. Meanwhile, Cheryl's brother, Gerald "Tooky" Amirault, remained in prison, having exhausted his appeals. In 2000, after having served 15 years of his 30 to 40 year sentence, Amirault came before the Governor's Advisory Board of Pardons, seeking the only judicial redress left to him—a commutation.

The drama that played out on the stage of a small, hot hearing room where Amirault, the parents of some of his alleged victims, and three of those victims, now young adults, sat just ten short feet apart, gives truth to the old maxim that "the stage but echoes back the public voice." The confrontation between the players was but a microcosm of the contentious public debate still waging all these years later over the Fells Acres case.

The parents were ferociously distraught. One testified, "There is not a penalty in existence that could possibly justify having my child's innocence taken at such a young age." Another glared at Amirault and hissed, "You have not *begun* to serve your sentence. And as far as I'm concerned, you never will!" (MacQuarrie, 2000, p. B1). The climax, though, was in the face-to-face confrontation between protagonist and antagonist, although the shifting moral boundaries over the years since the start of the case have rendered it more and more difficult to determine just exactly who was who. On one side was one of Amirault's alleged victims. Now a mother herself, she bitterly recounted the details of her ritual abuse and the ruined life she is enduring because of it. Amirault countered with a tearful avowal of innocence. "I have never hurt a child, and I never could," he insisted (MacQuarrie, 2000, p. B1).

In this hearing, as in other much larger contexts, between the idea of ritual abuse and the reality looms a shadow. The Advisory Board, quite unlike the higher court that in the interest of "finality" rushed to shine light in that dark space, engaged instead in a bit of shadow-play. It was not its responsibility to rule on Amirault's guilt or innocence, only on the fairness of his continued incarceration. The Board, however, lingered in the shadow, concluding that "real and substantial doubt exists concerning the petitioner's conviction.... While executive clemency should never, of course, be simply a response to public clamor, on one side or the other, where, as here, the record of a case raises real and substantial doubt the entire record of the case should be given careful consideration." In an unanimous decision, the Board ruled that the continued incarceration of

Gerald Amirault constitutes "gross unfairness," and recommended the Governor commute his sentence ("Massachusetts Parole Board, 2001).

In February 2002, Governor Jane Swift turned down the recommendation. She never really stated why, and while there are those who speculate that she was swayed by personal meetings with alleged victims, including JB who was publicly speaking out against Amirault's commutation, and others who think she uncovered something in her own investigation of the case that no one else ever had, the decision reeked of politics and coincidence. As an appointed Governor, Swift was fighting an uphill battle for re-election and was loathe to alienate the powerful legal juggernaut that had propelled the Amirault family into prison and then kept them there for so long. But the high arbiter of chance also fell on her side. Just as she was to make the final decision about Amirault's fate, what would turn out to be one of the most shameful scandals of recent history—the sexual abuse of children by priests—was just being uncovered. Clergy abuse has its own rituals, of course, its own embeddedness in dogma, but it was the image of men in trusted positions taking sexual advantage of innocent children that was just analogous enough to the image of day care ritual abuse to justify Swift's decision to deny commutation. In late 2003, Gerald Amirault was granted parole. Upon his anticipated release from prison in the spring of 2004, he will have served 19 years of his 30 to 40 year sentence.

Gerald Amirault is not the only provider in the sample of day care cases still imprisoned all these years after the moral panic ran out of emotive steam. Frank Fuster's appeals in the Country Walk case have been exhausted; he remains incarcerated. So does Patrick Figured who received three life sentences in the Miss Polly's Day Care case, and the Kellers, Fran and Dan, who will have their first parole hearing in 2004. And so does James Toward who pled guilty in the Glendale Montessori case. Although scheduled to have been released several years ago, he remains imprisoned under Florida's Ryce Act that allows the state to continue the incarceration of any prisoner whom psychiatrists deem to be a sexual threat to children. Now elderly, Toward has promised to leave the country and return to his native England, if released. But that scepter'd isle had its own ritual abuse moral panic, as did other European and Australasian countries, stirred up and spread by American child-savers.

7

The Devil Goes Abroad

The ancient mill town of Rochdale is situated in a river valley with the Rossendale Hills to the north and the brooding Pennine Hills to the east. It is the 29th most deprived district in England; the 3rd most deprived in the inchoate sprawl of boroughs and towns that make up Greater Manchester. Despite its deprivation, though, Rochdale has its charms. Its wide esplanade is flanked by a 12th century stone church and a handsome town hall with a 240 foot stone spire. A half a dozen different languages can be heard during a casual stroll through town and, although racial tension sometimes rears its ugly head, the Pakistanis and Bangladeshis who make up most of its minority population peacefully coexist with whites.

A few miles outside of the town center is the Langley Estate. Built in the 1950s, it is the largest overspill estate in England, housing over 12,000 people. Most agree it is a rough place to live. Over one-third of the inhabitants are unemployed, almost every street has boarded up shops and houses, and the spaces meant to be gardens are more times than not just forlorn frazzles of dead greenery (Appleyard, 1990). There are fracases on the estate, drunken brawls, shouting matches between neighbors, and there are crimes, especially against property, but in 1989 the devil came to the Langley Estate. How the devil got to England in the first place and the kind of mischief he found, provides an interesting glimpse into the spread of the ritual abuse moral panic, and the modifying effects of cultural diffusion.

Pink Ghosts, Dead Babies and Spooky Graveyards

In 1989 a 6 year old boy living with his family on the Langley Estate hid in a cupboard in his classroom and refused to come out. The child had a history of problems. He was developmentally delayed, had a speech impediment, and his behavior unpredictably vacillated between withdrawal and unprovoked aggression. But this was something different. He was frightened, prattling away about ghosts and cemeteries and babies being killed. His teacher, already worried that serious emotional problems were behind his outbursts, contacted the headmaster who, in turn, contacted the child's mother and referred her and her son to the local social services.

The social services are part of the Rochdale Metropolitan Borough Council that serves a population of 202,000, just over a quarter of whom are children. Like all social service programs, it had its share of complaints about accessibility, responsiveness and accountability, but the program generally was considered well-run and staffed by competent social workers (Social Services Inspectorate, 1998). But in 1989, both the program and the profession were in crisis. The Rochdale Council had been "charged capped" so that it could neither recruit needed staff nor transfer staff in or out of the social services program. Budget cuts decimated morale; the steady increase in reported child maltreatment cases, especially sexual abuse cases, taxed patience and skill. There was not much pride in being a social worker then, either. The profession was beleaguered by bad press, humiliated by the well-publicized deaths of several children under its care, and by the findings of incompetence by official inquiries into those deaths (Reder, Duncan, & Gray, 1993). It was disgraced by the Cleveland scandal in which more than a hundred children were removed from their families on the suspicion of sodomy that had been diagnosed by the very same and very specious "anal wink" test that had been used by some child-saver physicians to diagnose the ritual abuse of children in the United States day care cases, and then was confirmed by social workers in their repeated interviews with the children. And the profession was overwhelmed by the government regulations and the standards of good social work practice put into place in the wake of the Cleveland scandal (Butler-Sloss, 1988). The Rochdale Council social services program was just one of many local authorities that had not yet implemented the good practice guidelines in 1989; doing so, it estimated, would require the hiring of at least another five social workers at a cost of almost £100,000, and even then would risk opposition from the union because of the additional work the implementation would require (Eaton, 1990).

Despite all that, British social workers carried out their work with a guarded optimism that what they were doing would somehow and at sometime make a difference. It was with that kind of good faith that the two Rochdale social workers assigned to the case of the frightened six year old brought him and his mother to a local child abuse assessment center. Contrary to the good practice guidelines, they did not videotape their first interview with the child, but according to them, the usually inarticulate child was nothing less than eloquent in his description of pink ghosts haunting his bedroom, and midnight visits to cemeteries with his parents to help them bury the babies they had bludgeoned to death with hammers. Concerned for the child's safety, the social workers secured a Place of Safety Order and took him into care. The following day they interviewed the child's older sister who confirmed the presence of ghosts although, she hastened to add, they may have only been in her dreams. She and her two youngest brothers also were removed from the family and taken into care (Bunyan, 1990).

The social workers were convinced the siblings were victims of ritual abuse. Interestingly, none of them had said anything about having been abused, either sexually or physically, but the seductiveness of the diagnosis has never radiated so much from the word "abuse" as from the modifier "ritual," and all of the imaginary evils it conjures up. The social work profession's imagination had been well-primed for just such a diagnosis. By early 1990 when the four siblings had been taken into care, rumors about satanic cults and the ritual abuse of children had spread across Great Britain and social workers had been warned that the devil was afoot.

Investigative reporter Rosie Waterhouse (1990) offers insight into British precursors of the Langley Estate case. The press and television news had quite thoroughly covered the day care ritual abuse cases, especially the McMartin Preschool case, but whatever concerns the reportage created remained inchoate until the Evangelical Alliance, a coalition of fundamentalist churches and groups, set out to find cases of ritual abuse by satanic cults. It was quite successful, finding one adult after another who had recovered, or was in the process of recovering, memories of childhood ritual abuse by satanists. The Alliance's sustained polemic against cults of any and all kinds, and its rather lavish use of the word "satanic" to describe them, had been largely ignored by the British public; now, with its sites sharpened on ritual abuse, the public was beginning to listen. Alliance spokespersons like Maureen Davies of the Reachout Trust, Rev. Kevin Logan, and Dianne Core of ChildWatch, emerged on the scene as the first of the self-anointed experts on ritual abuse.

They soon had secular competition. At the same time that adult "survivors" began telling their stories, social workers uncovered the first case of a ritually abused child. A two year old in Kent who had fits of hysterical laughter and an occasional, albeit irresistible, urge to strip off all of his clothes, came to the attention of social worker Norma Howes. Suspecting that something more wicked than just the terrible two's was behind the child's strange behavior, she contacted her former partner in her sexual abuse consultancy, American therapist Pamela Klein, who immediately diagnosed ritual abuse and sent Howes a symptom list to aid in her assessment.[1]

The symptom list circulated circuitously around Great Britain, passing from one social worker to another, one local council to another, one police department to another.

Its most ignominious use, with a doubt, was in Nottingham[2] where a genuinely horrific case of multi-generational incest in an extended family living on the shabby Broxtowe Estate was worked into a case of satanic ritual abuse by council social workers armed with a symptom list and the conviction that a "vortex of evil" was at work in the case (Dawson, 1990).

By the time the Rochdale social workers took the six year old and his siblings into care in March 1990, there had been three major social work conferences on ritual abuse in Britain, all featuring American experts who distributed their symptom lists, satanic calendars and catalogues of satanic rituals and roles with the kind of wild abandon that only unwavering belief can cause. The Rochdale social workers, in fact, had attended one of those conferences just two weeks before they interviewed the six year old. And by that time, there already had been a sensationalized television documentary on ritual abuse, dozens of only slightly less sensationalized newspapers accounts, and a few incautious articles in the social work press. The Rochdale social workers' conviction that the Langley Estate case was one of ritual abuse, in other words, was hardly formed in a professional and cultural vacuum.

So far in the telling, the Langley Estate case has a distinctive feature: it occurred on a seedy urban housing estate, not a day care center. While this feature reveals something about its cultural affinity, that something was largely lost on the social workers who proceeded to Americanize the case by pressing the children to name other victims, describe more rituals, and finger the satanic perpetrators. When the children complied in naming other children, social workers and police launched dawn raids on the Langley Estate, removing 15 children from five families, all living within a few minutes walking distance from each other (Faux, 1990).

The children were made wards of the court and denied all contact with their parents, including letters and cards. That latter decision was predicated on the warning of American child-savers that even the syrupy sweet verses of greeting cards could contain satanically coded messages that would silence the children from any further disclosures. And then the parents were silenced by a court-ordered injunction that barred them from speaking publicly about the case and from seeking assistance from local counselors, voluntary organizations, the clergy or the press. All of this, for a time at least, assured that social workers had unfettered access to the children, and they took advantage of it. Armed with reams of materials by American child-savers and a bevy of anatomically-detailed dolls, they set about recreating the ritual abuse master narrative with the children.

Even the narrative had a certain cultural affinity that made it distinct from the narrative in the United States day care ritual abuse cases, but that also passed by unnoticed by the social workers. This British version lacked the Gothicism of the American. There were no chanting, orgiastic satanists in this narrative, just ghosts, some of them pink, and one-eyed spirits; there was no cannibalizing of the flesh of dead babies, nor any drinking of their blood; and there were no stupefying drugs, just magical toffees and fizzy drinks that tasted good. And, even more critically, there was no abuse in this narrative—none of the rape, sodomy and torture that rendered the American ritual abuse master narrative so utterly appalling.

But once conjured up, the devil was discursively incarnated. The National Society for the Prevention of Cruelty to Children announced that it was investigating cases similar to the Langley Estate case in seven different areas of Great Britain (Hall, 1990), and the British Association of Social Workers backed its Rochdale colleagues by stating that ritual abuse by satanists was widespread in northern England (Morris, 1990). The secretary of the Association of Directors of Social Services proclaimed that he had no doubt that ritual abuse exists and called for a national inquiry into its extent (O'Sullivan, September 15, 1990). None other than the Bishop of Oxford gave his imprimatur to the claims of the Rochdale social workers by proclaiming on BBC radio that he had it under good authority that by the turn of the new decade, satanists "will be sacrificing one baby per minute" (quoted in Medway, 2001, p. 243).

Not everyone was alarmed. When the press successfully challenged the injunction in court and began reporting on the Langley Estate case, a panoply of persons and groups lined up on the side of the parents and against the social workers. Among them were local labor counselors Peter Thomson who publicly demanded the release of the children, Rita Knight who assailed the social workers for class bias, and Kevin Hunt who likened their dawn raids on the housing estate to Nazi storm trooper tactics (O'Sullivan, September 30, 1990). The advocacy group Parents Against Injustice (PAIN) called for a national inquiry, and Lord Justice Dame Elizabeth Butler-Sloss, whose investigation into the Cleveland debacle resulted in the standards of good practice that so many social service departments still had not implemented, wondered aloud if the Rochdale social workers had learned anything at all from the horrible mistakes their colleagues had made in that case (O'Sullivan, September 20, 1990). And the Chief Constable of Greater Manchester, James Anderton, announced the police had found no evidence of ritual abuse and that criminal charges would not be preferred against any of the parents (Davenport, 1990).

The parents came forward, too. Poor, uneducated and unemployed, they had no real cultural capital to invest in this case, but they could trade on their notoriety as hapless victims of the social work profession and the state machine. That alone vested the Langley Estate parents with a bit of social honor that gave them a discursive credibility that had eluded them until that moment. So when the mother of the six year old whose prattling about ghosts had started the whole case came forward and blamed horror videos and comic books for his outburst, and the father pronounced the social workers' pursuit of the ritual abuse explanation "too ridiculous for words" (Faux, 1990, p. 5), the public began to listen.

The social workers did too, in a way. Although still standing by their belief that this was a ritual abuse case, they admitted they had no evidence that three of the seized children—7, 11 and 16 year old sisters— were abused. They halted wardship proceedings and allowed them to return home (Hunt, 1990). But, as if needing to prove George Bernard Shaw's maxim that all professions are a conspiracy against the laity, they then insisted that even if ritual abuse had never happened on the Langley Estate, they still had evidence that the remaining children had experienced "emotional abuse, degradation, humiliation, the administration of drugs and exposure to acts of violence which would not necessarily result in physical injuries" (O'Sullivan, September 11, 1990). They refused to send the children home, and petitioned the court for their permanent wardship.

Wardship proceedings began in January 1991 against the backdrop of a caustic public debate over ritual abuse and the competence of the profession whose obligation it was to protect children. The debate was fueled by the findings of a Social Services Inspectorate inquiry into operations of the Rochdale Council. Although the inquiry did not look in to the Langley Estate case, it did sample 30 child protection cases and found the services sorely inadequate. The final report made 40 recommendations for improving social services in Rochdale, almost every one of which could be applied to the Langley Estate case (Brindle & Sharratt, 1990). By the time wardship proceedings began, in this putative "conspiracy" of professionals against lay people, the latter was the hands-on favorite to come out on top.

After hearing 47 days of testimony, Mr. Justice Douglas Brown delivered a nearly three hour long oral judgment. He castigated the parents of the child who had started the case for providing him and his siblings a "rich diet" of violent videos, and ruled that they should remain in care. All of the other children he returned to their families, finding no evidence of maltreatment. Then he turned to the social workers. He chided them for their baseless belief in ritual abuse and for the improper interviewing techniques and procedures that had elicited from the children disclosures that, in the end, were "valueless and unreliable." He criticized them for swearing out "inaccurate and misleading" affidavits that had led to the deplorable dawn raids on the Langley Estate, and expressed "grave doubts" about the reliability of the evidence they had presented in the wardship proceedings. Although he thought them well-intentioned, he found the quality of their training "suspect," and reprimanded them for failing to seek to expert consultation before they acted in a manner that he described as an expression of "an unhealthy degree of professional single-mindedness" (Green, 1991). With a kind of righteous indignation, he banged the gavel and declared the Langley Estate case closed.

From the court's point of view, it was. But the case that had cost over £2 million to bring to its legal finality already had been discursively constructed into a cultural object, a "shared significance embodied in form" (Griswold, 1994, p. 1). Like all cultural objects, this much discussed case told a story; like most stories, it had multiple meanings. For some, the case was all about the incompetence of the social work profession and the concomitant danger of granting it unfettered power to meddle in family life; for others, many of them social workers, it was all about the futility of caring for the deprived and vulnerable in a political climate that denied their need and treated their powerlessness as subversion (Pringle, 1998). For others still, the case really was about ritual abuse, unproved perhaps, but a threat real enough to be vigorously pursued over the next few years in places like Hull, Epping Forest, Bishop Auckland, Ayshire and Orkney Islands in Scotland, and Pembroke, Wales.

And for others, the Langley Estate case was all about a moral panic that had washed over the shores of Britain in what the poet William Morris would have described as "an eventide of fear."

Common to all of those interpretations is the recognition of the role that United States child-savers played in the British experience. Cultural anthropologist J.S. LaFontaine (1994) was one of the first to document that role. Commissioned by the British Department of Health to look into the nature and extent of ritual abuse in Britain, she found little evidence of abuse associated with rituals of any kind, and none of abuse associated with the ritual worship of Satan, such as was alleged in the Langley Estate case. She attributes the spread of the idea that satanists are everywhere, everywhere, and that no British child should be considered safe from their malevolence, to the preachings of British evangelical Christian groups, and the persuasive rhetoric of United States child-savers who, at the peak of the day care ritual abuse moral panic, disseminated reams of materials on ritual abuse, conducted workshops, lectured at conferences, and consulted on British cases.

The International Spread of the Ritual Abuse Moral Panic

Like LaFontaine, other indigenous commentators point to the influence of United States child-savers on the pursuit of ritual abuse around the world (Table 9). Investigative reporter Richard Guilliatt (1996), for example, traces the onset of what he refers to as the "ritual abuse hysteria" that swept across Australia to the alarmist presentations of United States child-savers at the International Society for the Prevention of Child Abuse and Neglect conference in Sydney in 1986. Sociologist Mike Hill (1998), investigative reporter David McLoughlin (1996), and writer Lynley Hood (2001) all credit the invited workshops and speeches of those child-savers for stirring up the ritual abuse fears in New Zealand that culminated in the notorious Christchurch Civic Creche case that sent provider Peter Ellis to prison for a decade.

At the turn into the new millennium, global communications made it possible for child-savers to extend their influence to foreign shores without ever leaving the United States. Reporter David Lees (1994), for example, concludes that it was inevitable that an "American-style" day care ritual abuse case would occur in Martensville, Canada, because of the extent to which the purveyors of American popular culture—television, magazines and videos—had saturated regions of Canada contiguous with the United States. A workgroup commissioned by the Ministry of Justice cites the thorough news coverage of the McMartin Preschool case and the reams of materials on ritual abuse sent to Dutch professionals by child-savers for creating what it describes as the "mass hysteria" over ritual abuse that seized the Netherlands (Werkgroep Ritueel Misbruik, 1994). Folklorist and religious historian Asbjørn Dyrendal (1998) finds no reference to ritual abuse in Norway until the claims made by child-savers on the 1988 *Geraldo* special, "Devil Worship: Exposing Satan's Underground," were extensively reported by the Scandinavian media. In the wake of the reportage, ritual abuse cases began cropping up across Norway, the most infamous of which was the Botngård case in which an assistant kindergarten teacher was accused of sexually abusing 50 children in rituals that included cannibalism and human sacrifice. His acquittal on all charges ripped apart the idyllic community, pitting testifying children against retracting children, the court against the social services, much of the public against the police, and led to national legislation on the use of child witnesses in courts of law (Kringstad, 1997).

The same is said of Sweden where psychology professor Lennart Sjoberg (1997), writer and activist Per Lindegberg (1999), and forensic

TABLE 9

Sample of European and Australasian Child Ritual Abuse Cases

Location Familiar Case Name	Year	Accused	Legal Outcome
Hamilton, Canada Cannibal Case	1985	Parents	2 children into care; no arrests
Oude Pekela, Netherlands	1987	Foreign strangers	No arrests
Nottingham, England Broxtowe Estate Case	1987	Parents, relatives	18 children into care 10 adults convicted, total sentence 48 years
Sydney, Australia Mr. Bubbles Case	1988	Day care providers	Charges dismissed
Stockholm, Sweden Cutting-Up Case	1988	Parent, family friend	Mistrial; acquitted at 2nd trial
Prescott, Canada	1989	Community members	65 charged; 1 convicted
Rochdale, England Langley Estate Case	1989	Parents, strangers	19 children into care, 15 returned; no arrests
Trafford, England	1989	Parents, neighbors, strangers	13 children removed, all returned; no arrests
Salford, England	1990	Parents, neighbors	13 children into care, 8 returned; no arrests
Liverpool, England	1990	Parents, neighbors	8 children into care, all returned; no arrests
Ayshire, Scotland	1990	Parent, relatives	8 children into care, 7 returned; no arrests
Epping Forest, England Black Magic Case	1990	Parents, godparents	Directed verdict: acquittal
Orkney Islands, Scotland	1990	Minister, community members	9 children into care, 7 returned; no arrests
Saskatoon, Canada Klassen Foster Care Case	1990	Foster parents, extended foster family members, parents	Charges dismissed in return for guilty plea by one family member; 4 year sentence
Nar Nar Goon, Australia	1990	Neighbors, strangers	No arrests
Mornington, Australia Mornington Child Care Centre Case	1991	Day care providers	No arrests

(TABLE 9 CONTINUED)

Location *Familiar Case Name*	Year	Accused	Legal Outcome
Martensville, Canada *Sterling Babysitter Case*	1991	Day care providers, police officers	2 acquitted; 1 convicted 5 counts, 4 over turned, 5 year prison term; 1 convicted 7 counts, overturned; charges dismissed during trial for 1; all charges against others dismissed
Christchurch, New Zealand Christ- church *Civic Creche Case*	1991	Day care providers	1 convicted, 10 year prison term; charges against others dismissed
Münster, Germany *Montessorri Case*	1991	Teacher	Acquitted
Worms, Germany	1992	Teachers, community members	Acquitted
Pembroke, Wales	1992	Neighbors	6 convicted, sentences range 5–15 years; 1 acquitted; charges against 5 dismissed
Bjugn, Norway *Botngàrd Kinder- garten Case*	1992	Teacher	Acquitted
Bishop Auckland, England	1993	Neighbors	Charges dismissed during trial
Newcastle-upon- Tyne, England *Shieldfield Case*	1993	Day care providers	Acquitted

psychologists Astrid Holgerson and Birgit Hellborn (1997) all trace the ritual abuse scare to the extensive coverage of the United States day care cases by the Swedish media. And psychologist Gunter Kohnken's (1995) court-commissioned report on the Münster Montessori case in which provider Rainer Möllers was acquitted of ritually abusing 63 children, finds that the suggestive and leading style used by German interviewers had been strongly influenced by the teachings and writings of child-savers from the United States.

A quick perusal of Table 9 reveals that the international diffusion of the influence of American child-savers was aided by a common language. It is in those countries in which English either is the native language or is widely spoken and understood that the discourse, both spoken and written, of the child-savers was most influential. Simply put, nothing was lost in the translation.

What is not so obvious from a perusal of Table 9, however, is that the diffusion of influence also was facilitated by professional networks that not only provided United States child-savers platforms from which to present their beliefs, but large and appreciative international audiences. The International Society for the Prevention of Child Abuse and Neglect (ISPCAN) conference in Sydney, Australia, for example, had over 1600 conferees representing nearly every country on the globe. Although ISPCAN's prestigious journal, *Child Abuse & Neglect,* was still silent on the topic of ritual abuse in 1986, the year of the conference, the child-savers who were invited to speak certainly were not. Psychiatrist Roland Summit, social worker Kee MacFarlane, and pediatrician Astrid Heger were featured speakers; each made the McMartin Preschool case which in 1986, it should be remembered, was still very much draped in Gothic frippery, the focal point of his or her presentation. Sociologist David Finkelhor vetted the expressed belief that the accused McMartin Preschool providers were part of an international cabal of satanists by presenting data he had collected on other American day care ritual abuse cases for his soon to be published book, *Nursery Crimes.*

Three-Pronged Argument Against Cultural Colonialism

The discourse of the United States child-savers was as compelling as it was authoritative. Yet its influence in precipitating ritual abuse cases in other countries should not be understood as a simple product of cultural colonialism for several reasons.

Cross-Fertilization of Ritual Abuse Beliefs. First, as international child-savers learned about ritual abuse and even discovered cases of it in their own countries, they came to the United States to learn more and to share their experiences. A couple of examples of this cross-fertilization of ritual abuse beliefs are in order.

Dianne Core, founder of the independent child welfare agency, Childwatch, had acquired an interest in ritual abuse when she came across a series of videotapes on the subject put together by cult-cop Sandi Gallant. Soon after, Core stumbled upon her first case of ritual abuse right in her own backyard in Hull, England—a stumble, by the way, that set off a six year, £3 million investigation that failed to find evidence of the ritual abuse Core was insisting was epidemic in Hull, and that exonerated the 22 police officers whom she had accused of being in consort with satanists (Wainwright, 1997). In 1988 Core addressed a conference in the

United States; her speech, "We are in the Middle of Spiritual Warfare," included her own ritual abuse symptom list: "Crying for no apparent reason. Inordinate fear of adults. Nightmares. Appetite changes. Conversation about bizarre foods. Acting out behavior which is not common. Strange language forms or content." She concluded by stating that she had reason to believe that St. John the Divine Cathedral in New York City was the center of satanic activity on the east coast. The speech was printed in its entirety in the *New Federalist* (Medway, 2001).

Maureen Davies, director of the Reachout Trust, an anti-cult/occult ministry in Great Britain, came across her first cases of ritual abuse in 1988. She traveled to the United States the following year to learn more. While there, she was a guest on a Christian television show and was interviewed by cult-cop Larry Jones, who crowed in his *File-18 Newsletter,* the cult-cop guide to all things satanic, that her discovery of British cases put a lie on the lips of anyone skeptical that a satanic conspiracy was afoot in the world. Davies also met cult-cop Jerry Simandl and invited him to speak at a conference in Reading, England where he told an audience of 250 aghast social workers that ritual abusers prepare infants for cannibalistic consumption by cooking them in microwave ovens—an allegation, by the way, that had never been made in an American day care case. Yet just one short week later, conferees who were involved in the Broxtowe Estate ritual abuse case in Nottingham, solicited just such an anomalous account from one of the children they interviewed (Medway, 2001).

The Devil in the Details. The second factor that argues against cultural colonialism is that the details of many of the international cases differ significantly from those of the United States day care cases. Part of that difference is found in the "local color" that hues the allegations, themselves. Rochdale, Trafford, Salford and Liverpool are in Lancashire, a region of north England steeped in ancient lore about witches, goblins, malevolent spirits and ghosts. The region has more haunted buildings than in all of England, and rumors of devil worship have vexed it from 1612 when a score of local citizens were convicted of witchcraft on the word of a child and executed, and on through the 1960s when the bodies of the children they murdered were buried on the moors by Ian Brady and Myra Hindley, the star-crossed lovers who, it was rumored, had entered into a pact with the devil. Ghosts, spirits and witches hardly ever materialize in the allegations of children in the United States day care ritual abuse cases, but they haunt the allegations of the children in the Lancashire cases.[3]

Rumor vested allegations with local color in other cases. It had long been rumored throughout the western world that the Netherlands was the center of an international child pornography cartel. Although government investigations failed to find evidence to support the rumor, it seemed to be confirmed in the Oude Pekela ritual abuse case where children described in detail to their interviewers the production of child pornography by strangers with foreign accents (Jonker & Jonker-Bakker, 1991). A rumor of a different kind had been circulating through Christchurch, New Zealand for several years before the Civic Creche case. This one implicated the high and the mighty in local circles in a Masonic sexual abuse ring. Indeed, the rumor found some confirmation in the interviews with the children in the Civic Creche case. They named not only their providers as their ritual abusers, but prominent local citizens, and claimed the abuse took place not just in the day care center, but in the local Masonic Lodge (Hood, 2001).

If the allegations in some of the European and Australasian cases differ from those in the American day care cases, the difference really is more interesting than significant. The ritual abuse master narrative, after all, was nothing if not elastic, expanding and contracting on a case-by-case basis to let in and out all kinds of anomalous and unusual allegations, some of which had a distinctly local hue, such as the allegation made by some of the children in the Little Rascals case that they were used as shark bait in the coastal waters off of North Carolina. What really distinguish many of these international cases from the United States day care cases are some interesting sociological variables that, in the long run, modified the nature of the ritual abuse moral panic as it spread abroad, as well as the international reaction to it.

Consider the sociological variable of age. In many, although not all, of the international cases, the alleged victims were older, in fact often much older, than the three, four and five year olds of the United States day care cases. Their age vested them with credibility: it is quite one thing, after all, to immediately find credible an horrific description of ritual abuse by a four year still trapped in the iron cage of preoperational thinking, and quite another to find immediately credible the same description by a twelve year old. Assumed credibility, in turn, hastened the pace of the ensuing investigations. While the United States day care cases dragged on for years before coming to any kind of conclusion, let alone resolution, many of the international cases were closed in a matter of months. This abbreviated time made it difficult for the kind of improvised news that romped around in the shadows of the day care cases, muddling and mystifying them, from getting a running start. This is not to suggest that the European and Australasian cases were free from shadow play, or that rumor did not surround them long after they were closed, but it is to suggest that time can be the devourer of critical thinking, so the less there is of it from the start of a ritual abuse case to its end, the less likely time will be sated.

Also consider the sociological variable of identity. While in the United States day care cases providers and other employees were fingered as ritual abusers, in many of the international cases parents and relatives were the usual suspects. Their identities had significant procedural implications.

TABLE 10

Examples of Public Inquiries into International Ritual Abuse Cases

Case	Inquiry Author (Date)	Commissioner: Conclusions
Oude Pekela	Werkgroep Ritueel Misbruik (1994)	Ministry of Justice: "The fact that no provable cases [including Oude Pekela] have been demonstrated, does not mean that it has been incontrovertibly proved that ritual abuse does not occur. [There] are very serious cases of sexual child abuse but whether these are ritual abuse cases remains unclear" (p. 54).
Broxtowe Estate	Nottinghamshire County Council (1990)	County Council: "(T)here is no evidence of satanic ritual abuse in [this] case.... (I)t is doubtful whether the practice and type of satanic ritual abuse being promulgated by [social workers] actually exists. It has never been substantiated by empirical evidence" (p. 30).
Shieldfield	Barker, Jones, Saradjian & Wardell (1998)	Newcastle City Council: "As well as (the charged providers) ... others outside the nursery were involved in abusing children ... and probably also for the production of pornographic material" (p. 1).
Prescott	Children's Services Advisory (1995)	Health Canada: The children's statements are reliable; the case is not unique in Canada.
Mr. Bubbles	Wood (1996)	Royal Commissioner: An inquiry into pedophilia investigations includes an inquiry into the Mr. Bubbles case. The Commission makes no finding of guilt or innocence because the "trail is too old, the evidence of the children too contaminated, and there was nothing the Commission could find to independently corroborate or disprove the matters raised" (Volume 4, Chapter 7).

(TABLE 10 CONTINUED)

Case	Inquiry Author (Date)	Commissioner: Conclusions
Ayshire	Miller (1994) Leslie & Kearney (1995, unpublished)	Court of Session: "(I)t is possible that this has been a case of child sexual abuse but any evidence of it has been so ineptly collected and so contaminated" (p. 425). Strathclyde Regional Council Social Work Committee: Social workers involved in the case were "naïve and gullible" in pursuing the ritual abuse hypothesis, yet they acted in good faith and without collusion, and did not exceed their authority ("Naive," 1995, p. 13).
Orkney Islands	Clyde (1992)	Secretary of State for Scotland: "Whether the beliefs (about ritual abuse) were true or not had to be left as a distinct and unresolved question" (p. 4). Although precipitate, the return of the children was justified.
Christchurch Civic Creche	Eichelbaum (2001, unpublished) Thorp (2001, unpublished)	Ministry of Justice: The children's statements are reliable; convicted provider Peter Ellis should be denied pardon. Ministry of Justice (upon 2nd application for Royal Prerogative of Mercy): "It would in my view be difficult to argue against the existence of a serious doubt about the safety of (Ellis's) convictions" (McLoughlin, 2001, p. 1).
Münster Montessori	Kohnken (1995)	Court: The interviewing styles were so suggestive and leading in this case that the reliability of the children's statements is in doubt.
Bishop Auckland	Thompson (1995, unpublished) Durham Area Child Protection Committee (1995, unpublished)	Defense Lawyers: "A systematic review procedure would never have allowed this case to progress as far as it did" (Marsh, 1995, p. 1). County Council: "(P)rofessionals worked to a high standard of practice. Their actions were neither precipitate nor draconian but in the best interests of the children and families" (Marsh, 1995, p. 1).

Unlike the children in the day care cases who found succor in the bosoms of their protective and supportive families, children in many of the international cases were removed from their families and placed into care, thus adding on-going wardship hearings to the tangled skein of legal proceedings in these cases. More importantly, though, this relationship of accuser to accused was adversarial, with children pitted against their own kith and kin. While in the day care cases parents formed or joined advocacy groups to support their children, in many of these international cases parents formed or joined advocacy groups to protect them *from* their children.

Finally, consider the sociological variable of organizational response. The United States day care cases, perhaps because they occurred in the public sphere and were subject to what so many believed were the self-correcting mechanisms of a democratic justice system, never prompted official inquiries, but many of the European and Australasian cases did, as Table 10 demonstrates.

The inquiry reports are as different as night and day, not only in their brief, but in the wattage of light they shine on the cases in particular, and on ritual abuse in general.

The Prescott inquiry report, as an example, offers an uncritical summary of this complicated case yet treats it as a harbinger of ritual abuse cases yet to come in Canada. The Broxtowe Estate inquiry report, in contrast, critically analyzes the case from its beginning to end, and then sets out specific guidelines for social worker-police cooperation in complicated cases. While the report acknowledges that this indeed was a convoluted case, it concludes that this was not a ritual abuse case, and it casts doubt on the received wisdom that ritual abuse is a real and exigent threat to children throughout Great Britain.

It was not the brief of the Orkney Islands inquiry report to even address the question of whether this was indeed a ritual abuse case. Yet, it does treat the case as a complex and controversial one that reveals more about the weaknesses and flaws of the child protection system than it does about any ritual abuse threat to children. The report sets out 194 recommendations for what would amount to a complete overhaul of the Scottish child protection system. The Mr. Bubbles inquiry report comprised one chapter of one volume of a comprehensive investigation into police corruption and pedophilia investigations in New South Wales, Australia. It rips apart the police handling of this case, but makes no findings of the accused providers' guilt or innocence, nor offers any assessment of the claims that ritual abuse is widespread in Australasia.

The inquiry into the Shieldfield case merits attention. Funded by the local city council, the inquiry team was composed of a university professor, a child protection consultant who, as a lead social worker, had been the first to label the Broxtowe Estate case a ritual abuse case, a clinical psychologist, and a retired social service department manager. Although the two accused providers already had been exonerated in court when the trial judge ruled that the evidence was so weak against them that he would not submit the case to jury, the inquiry team found otherwise. It concluded that the providers indeed were ritual abusers and that they had procured almost 400 children for a diabolical ring of pedophile pornographers.

What went on after the inquiry report was published in 1998 offers insight into the commodification of fear in a moral panic. Newspapers and the tabloid press vied for readers by reporting rumor as news, fancy as fact. Television show host Esther Rantzen boosted her ratings when she challenged the two accused providers to come out of hiding and prove their innocence (McKay, 1999). A pediatrician who achieved almost heroic status in the case boosted her reputation by diagnosing sexual abuse for each and every child she examined. Parents who convincingly communicated their fears that their ritually abused children would never enjoy satisfying and successful lives were awarded large settlements by the city council that had administrative oversight of the Shieldfield nursery, tucked away in a corner of a drab tower block in a dicey neighborhood in Newcastle-upon-Tyne.

The two providers, Dawn Reed and Christopher Lillie, commodified their own fear. For nearly a decade each had traveled from one city to another, sometimes under an assumed name and always with a hastily constructed and well-rehearsed autobiography in mind just in case there were questions. Reed's marriage fell apart, Lillie lost all contact with his family, each at one time or another considered suicide. Together, they sued the authors of the inquiry report and the local council that had commissioned it for libel, and won. In a stunning judgment by British standards, each was awarded £200,000 for having been maliciously pilloried as ritual abusers by the inquiry report authors and the commissioning council (*Lillie and Reed v. Newcastle City Council, Barker, Jones, Saradjian, and Wardell,* 2002).

Just months after the judgment, two other reports—inquiries of the inquiries—were made public. The first, drawn up by the Law Commission, recommends extending the statutory qualified privilege that protects reports discussed in public council meetings from libel claims, to any local authority inquiry report as long as both the proceedings and the publication are fair (Batty, 2002). The second, put together by an organization of local council executives, sets out the guidelines councils should follow in planning and conducting fair and unbiased *ad hoc* inquiries (SOLACE, 2002).

Official inquiries, let alone inquiries-of-inquiries, often are time-consuming and expensive to conduct. Sir Thomas Eichelbaum spent over 400 hours assessing the quality of the videotaped interviews of the children in the Christchurch Civic Creche case for his inquiry report. The Broxtowe Estate inquiry report is over 600 pages in length. The inquiry into the Ayshire ritual abuse case took 155 days to complete; the inquiry into the Orkney Islands ritual abuse case took 210 days and came with a price tag of £6 million.

Setting aside time and money for a moment, the inquiries also are oh, so political. The concept of governmentality is helpful in explaining why. In its truest form, governmentality describes the processes of regulation and social control that bring individual and group conduct into line with state mandated policies, statutes and regulations (Foucault, 1986). It has long been theorized that the "truth regimes," that is, the "knowledges" created by these processes, often are internalized by individuals and groups who, in treating these subjective realities as truth, use them to regulate themselves. As self-regulatory, they require less surveillance and control by the state but, having been co-opted into this process, they end up paradoxically reinforcing the power of the government or of official institutions and regulatory bodies to control their behavior.

The inquiries commissioned by the government offer a neat example of governmentality and an insight into how it actually tolled the denouement of the ritual abuse moral panic in Europe and Australasia. The Orkney Islands ritual abuse case inquiry is particularly illustrative. It concludes with 194 recommendations for improving child protection in Scotland, almost every single one of which is directed towards regulating the provocateurs of the moral panic. A sample of recommendations will illustrate this point (Clyde, 1992):

Recommendation 2: In regards to terminology, "it is recommended that in the investigation and practical management of cases of child sexual abuse care should be taken to avoid the use of labels without a common understanding of the definition and the purpose of the label" (p. 353);

Recommendation 8: "Where allegations are made by a child regarding sexual abuse those allegations should be treated seriously, should not necessarily be accepted as true but should be examined and tested by whatever means are available before they are used as the basis for action" (p. 353);

Recommendation 30: National guidelines should "include guidance on all forms of sexual abuse including multiple abuse, and should recognize the difference between operational and managerial guidance in cases of multiple sexual abuse" (pp. 354–355);

Recommendation 40: "Removal of a child should be recognized as a course to be considered where no alternative exists and the urgency of the risk requires it. Caution must be exercised. The gravity of the threat has to be considered and the applicant must be satisfied that the situations calls for immediate removal of the child" (p. 355);

Recommendation 55: "The child and his or her parent or guardian should have an immediate opportunity to have the [Child Protection] Order varied or cancelled by the Sheriff [Judge]" (p. 356);

Recommendation 62: "At least in complex cases those involved in the removal of the child should be given full written instructions" (p. 356);

Recommendation 104: "The Sheriff [Judge] should be empowered to authorize a child to be taken for a medical examination, although the carrying out of examination should not proceed if the child refuses to be examined" (p. 357);

Recommendation 113: "The importance of full training in the art of interviewing and the techniques of recording should be fully recognized" (p. 357);

Recommendation 155: "The press should be encouraged to enable a greater understanding by the public of child sexual abuse and of child protection work" (p. 361);

Recommendation 173: "It should be recognized that the area of child abuse in general and child sexual abuse in particular is an area of expertise into which not all members of the [social work] profession should necessarily enter" (p. 362);

Recommendation 190: "Steps should be taken to improve the public understanding of and encourage a debate about the work of child care and child protection" (p. 363).

A self-serving sample of recommendations, perhaps? Not at all. Any random sample would reveal how the recommendations are attempts to resolve the problems of state-family relations by using legal and scientific knowledge to both delimit and justify state intervention into the private sphere of the family when abuse of any kind is suspected. And in the kind of complex abuse cases, such as the Orkney Islands ritual abuse case about which the inquiry report was written, the recommendations also are attempts to regulate the discourse, actions, emotions and accountability of all those professions and interest groups that by mandate or vested interest become involved.

For governmentality to have occurred, however, these regulations must be incorporated into the discourse and practices of those involved in ritual abuse cases, and there is evidence that for the social work profession, that indeed did occur. Upon publication of the Clyde Report (1992), leaders in the social work profession called upon their colleagues to make the "truths" of the inquiry their own. "The criticisms and comments were all made with the advantage of hindsight," a social work district manager wrote in *Child Abuse Review,* the official journal of the British Association for the Study and Prevention of Child Abuse and Neglect (BASP-CAN), "but it is important that agencies consider their practice, for few of us could withstand the detailed scrutiny of a public inquiry without revealing some flaws" (Black, 1993, p. 50). The director of ChildLine, a national crisis line for maltreated children, encouraged her colleagues to learn three valuable lessons from the Clyde Report: stop, think, and plan before acting (Cohen, 1992). With a touch of chagrin, the chairperson of the Committee on Child Abuse Network urged his colleagues to "re-analyze the position, assess what has gone wrong, and come forth with a constructive way forward. We need to consider why it is, time after time, we appear to get it wrong" (Bibby, 1991, p. 17).

There was some resistance, of course, to any insinuation that social workers were getting it wrong. At the annual meetings of the British Association of Social Workers, one social worker after another took to the podium to lambaste the Clyde inquiry. "The amazing fact is not that we sometimes get it wrong," said one of them, "but that so much is done so well" (Brindle, 1991). Despite the sentiment, conferees unanimously passed an emergency resolution calling for greater resources and more mandatory training in protecting children in ways commensurate with the recommendations set out in the Clyde Report.

The peer and self-regulation that is part and parcel of governmentality slowed the spread of the ritual abuse moral panic across Great Britain as it did in other European and Australasian countries that conducted public inquiries. But the inquiries, themselves, acted in other ways to impede the spread of the moral panic and contain its volatility. By calling into question the epistemological adequacy of social work knowledge and the legitimacy of its power to intervene in family life, the inquiries left the social workers involved in these ritual abuse cases, as well as their supervisors, in a vulnerable position. Not only were they the objects of public opprobrium, which led to the resignations of the disgraced directors of social services in Nottingham, Rochdale and the Orkney Islands, but they sometimes were the subjects of legal actions. There were law suits, of course, as well as cash settlements that almost bankrupted local social services departments, but in the Ayrshire ritual abuse case, the Crown Prosecutor seriously considered, but later decided against, filing criminal charges against the social workers for colluding in the presentation of contaminated and false evidence to the court (Arlidge, 1995).

All of this ratcheted up the risk of continuing to pursue the discredited ritual abuse hypothesis across Europe and Australasia, and then marginalized those who persisted in taking that risk. It is a truism that any moral panic builds up more and more emotive steam as the interest groups promoting it move to the center of public discourse and, more importantly for this discussion, dispels more and more steam as the interest groups move, or are moved to, the margins. Their trailing social honor creates a credibility vacuum that skepticism and criticism rush to fill.

Since much of this discussion has centered on Great Britain, consider it as an example. The official inquiries in the major ritual abuse cases discredited the belief that these indeed were cases of ritual abuse, thus marginalizing and disuniting those interest groups that insisted they were, or at least acted as if they were. At the margins, the remnants of these interest groups re-grouped and attempted to regain the ground at the center of public discourse by reopening the debate that had started a decade before in places like the depressingly rundown Langley Estate and the breathtakingly beautiful Orkney Islands.

None of those attempts, to date, has been successful; many, in fact, have been stunningly unsuccessful. Promising to offer proof—the potent antidote to skepticism—psychotherapists Valerie Sinason and Rob Hale secured a £22,000 grant to write the definitive report proving that "within satanism is a small group dedicated to abuse as part of a belief system involving every perversion known to man [sic] (Perthen, 1997, p. 2). When finally delivered, the Ministry of Health deemed it inadequate and wholly unconvincing. It was never published. Neither was the book that authors Beatrix Campbell and Judith Jones, the latter the social worker at the center of both the Broxtowe Estate and the Shieldfield cases, promised would be a scathing expose of the organized attempts of various professionals and interest groups to silence children in ritual abuse and other controversial abuse cases. *Stolen Voices* was withdrawn by the publisher in the midst of a blaze of publicity when lawyers representing those named in the book as "advocates of sex with children" threatened suit (Barton, 1999). As late as 2002 a small interest group that almost looked like a nostalgic recreation of the original child-savers interest group that had fired up the day care ritual abuse moral panic in the United States two decades before, publicly warned that satanists were redoubling their threat to British children. At a private meeting at Westminster, this coalition of psychotherapists, lay advocates and evangelical Christians pleaded for new laws that would specifically criminalize ritual abuse. What they got instead was a barrage of bad press that ridiculed their claims and reminded them that their liminal status does not afford them begging rights (Thomson, 2002).

Points of Resonance. Finally, the third factor that argues against cultural colonialism is the attitudinal and institutional obstacles in European and Australasian countries to the diffusion of a United States moral panic. Sociologist Joel Best (2001) explains that international audiences are only receptive and reactive to American moral panic discourse if they perceive their own societies to be similar to that of the United States.

When similarities are hard to recognize and even harder to imagine, international audiences are not responsive, and the diffusion of the moral panic is slowed or even stopped completely. In a similar vein, sociologist Keith Pringle (1998) asserts that the structural and ideological differences between the child protection systems of some European and Australasian countries and that of the United States act to slow the diffusion of any moral panic that has to do with the protection of children.[4]

It is quite reasonable to think that some attitudinal and structural constraints exist in the very European and Australasian countries to which the ritual abuse moral panic had spread. And if that is true, then the discourse of the United States child-savers who were responsible for spreading it must have been very persuasive indeed, because it not only overcame those constraints, but it recruited others into believing the discourse was true and into acting as if it were.

On this issue of the cross-national recruitment of participants into a moral panic, sociologist Colin Hay (1995) offers some insight. In an analysis of the youth crime moral panic that welled up after the abduction and murder of toddler Jamie Bulger by a pair of ten year old boys in Liverpool, England, he conjectures that participants are recruited into a moral panic when panic discourse finds or creates what he refers to as "points of resonance" with their sensitivities, sensibilities and lived experiences. When so appropriated, panic discourse has both ideological and material effects—it causes recruits to think and to act in ways consistent with the discourse, thus spreading the moral panic through their own countries.

Now consider the fact that the discovery of child sexual abuse in all of the countries to which the ritual abuse moral panic eventually spread, problematized public sentiments and child-saving efforts. It did so in ways that raised three very sensitive, stinging points of resonance.

First, sexual abuse introduced ambiguity into child-saving. Quite unlike physical abuse where "the bones tell the story the child is too young or too frightened to tell" (Kempe, Silverman, Steele, Droegmueller, & Silver, 1962: 20), sexual abuse cannot be medically or otherwise corroborated with confidence unless penetration of some kind has taken place (Kerns 1998). Only a minority of sexual abuse cases involves penetration, however; for the majority the proof of sexual abuse rests not in medical evidence but in the kind of uncertain, inconsistent and delayed disclosures of young children that were normalized in the child sexual abuse accommodation syndrome. This shift in the standard of proof from hard evidence to ephemeral words raised the cultural profile of young children and vested them with dubious moral power. It is little wonder that no matter how much their hesitant disclosures were lionized, questions about their credibility and veracity, and about the gullibility of child-savers who believed them and acted on their allegations, dominated both child-saving and public discourse in the early 1980s both in the United States and many other countries (Beckett 1996; Franklin & Parton 1991; Van Montfoort 1993).

Second, sexual abuse politicized child-saving by infusing sexual politics into practice (Armstrong, 1994). Unlike physical abuse, most of its abusers are males, most of its victims female, and this startling gender asymmetry begged analysis of, and action in relation to, the oppressive power relations underlying it. That demand served as an entrée for feminist scholars and clinicians whose critique of these power relations both inside and outside of the family, and attempts to redress them, influenced the child-saving movement. According to sociologist Chris Jenks (1996, p. 95):

> The patriarchy thesis burgeoned. It was argued that there exists within modern Western society a dominant ideology of male supremacy and that the organization of families, accepted patterns of socialization, the occupational structure and the very formation of identity are regulated in relation to it.... Rather than seeking to conserve the family, such feminist arguments were far more radical in terms of recommending a dissolution of the existing order, as well as the protection of victims and the criminalization of abusers.

Despite the fact that child-saving historically has been a female-dominated activity, the movement always has been rooted in the preservation of the status quo and has been devoid of any real critique of the power and gender relations that sustain it (Parton, 1985). But contemporary child-savers could not avoid the critique, the disconcertingly radical social consequences of it, or the polarized public sentiments all of this created. The vitriolic public discourse on sexual abuse in the United States fueled a "backlash" against child-savers, depicting them as anti-male, anti-family and dangerously out of control (Myers, 1994). And in Britain, feminists called for child-savers to challenge male dominance and the patriarchal family which breed sexual abuse (Dominelli 1987), and the conservative press responded by caricaturizing them as intrusive busybodies with faddish notions about men and families (Franklin & Parton 1991).

With the discovery of sexual abuse, then, males and their institutions were being incriminated not just of a social ill, but of "the supreme evil of our age" (Webster 1998, p. 39), by children and women. This reversal of the epistemic gaze not only polarized public sentiments, but politicized child-saving.

Third, sexual abuse disenchanted child-saving. Unlike physical abuse that at least appeared amenable to a family support and preservation initiative, sexual abuse only revealed its weaknesses. The darling of both pro-family conservatives and pro-social services liberals, family preservation had become the goal of the child-saving movement, but it did not stand up well against the ambiguity of sexual abuse, the feminist critique of the family, or the vast army of variously qualified and trained child-savers in place to deal with it. Highly publicized scandals of sexually abused children not believed while falsely accusing ones are, of children returned to their families only to be sexually abused again, of innocent fathers carted off to jail and guilty ones using their cultural capital to resist legal consequences, rocked the child-saving movement.

Pro-family and anti-child-saving pressure groups coalesced in response to the scandals and exerted increasing influence over public perception and public policy. As a result, child-saving was forced to become more procedural and bureaucratic, more formally rational in a way sociologist Max Weber would have appreciated (1904/1958), and therefore more constraining of individual initiative, intuitive judgment, and independent action. By the early 1980s the image of the child-saver as a good-hearted rescuer was being replaced with an image of the child-saver as uninspired technocrat.

If that was true in the United States, it was just as true in much of Europe and Australasia. Child-saving was becoming increasingly proceduralized in Great Britain in the mid–1980s, for example, as a means of protecting agencies and individual child-savers who found themselves working in an atmosphere of debilitating fear in the face of highly publicized sexual abuse scandals (Parton, 1985). Criticisms of child-savers for "adhering too long to [bureaucratic] principles even when it has become clear they have failed" were being voiced all over Germany and the Netherlands (Wustendorfer 1995: 243). Increasing concern about the proliferation of rules and procedures that were replacing the judgment of child-savers in individual cases of sexual abuse were being expressed in those countries in Western Europe, Scandinavia and Australasia, that shared with the United States a "significant degree of similarity in the ways they explain why [sexual] abuse happens and in the principles that underpin the various forms of intervention" (Pringle, 1998, p. 160).

Child-savers in the countries to which the ritual abuse moral panic spread, then, had three points of resonance through which the panic discourse of United States child-savers could be appropriated—the image of the child as more victimizer than victim, the image of the abuser as male, and the image of the rescuer as technocrat (de Young, 1999). It mattered not one bit that the discourse they were listening to had little fidelity to fact or to established scientific proof. But it did matter, and matter a great deal, that the discourse they were listening to was palliative, that is, it restored the images of the child, the abuser and the rescuer to what they familiarly were before the discovery of sexual abuse had so disconcertingly problematized them.

There is no need repeat that discourse here; more than enough attention already has been paid to it. But there is a need to tear away its elaborate Gothic façade to reveal the simple, familiar and oh so persuasive fairy tale about innocence, evil and the rescue of innocence that hides behind it.

Discourse to Restore the Image of the Child as Innocent Victim. If, indeed, "myth and childhood belong together" (Rose 1985, p. 88), then the image of the ritually abused child in the discourse of the United States child-savers is as contrary to that of the sexually abused child as myth allows. Innocent, pure, guileless and naturally good, this child shares no characteristics with the adult and is, in fact, an ontology in his or her own right, eminently believable and deserving of protection and care.

This image of the child as innocent victim is prismatic in the discourse of United States child-savers. It is their innocence, they say, that makes children perfect victims of ritual abuse; it is their innocence that ritual abusers, by some diabolic mandate, must defile to achieve power; it is their innocence that is swapped for a panoply of horrific symptoms and sequelae.

The imagined child of child-saver discourse is the embodiment of the age-old struggle of good against evil, innocence against unworldliness. This is a nostalgic, Appolonian image of the child that pleads for adult vigilance and control, and when tarnished by the unspeakable evil of ritual abuse, about which the child-savers in fact had more than a little to say, provokes adult outrage and reprisal.

Indeed, all of these reactions are the material effects of the ritual abuse moral panic as it spread across Europe and Australasia. International child-savers who were recruited into the moral panic placed allegedly ritually abused children under therapeutic control and in some countries, most notably England and Scotland, under state control through orders of care that removed them from their homes when their parents and family members were the suspected abusers.

Discourse to Occlude the Image of the Abuser as Male. If, as feminist Florence Rush asserts, "the sexual abuse of children, who are overwhelmingly female, by sexual offenders who are overwhelmingly male, is part and parcel of the male dominated society which overtly and covertly subjugates women" (cited in Armstrong, 1994, p. 75), then the image of the ritual abuser in the discourse of United States child-savers is as contrary to the image of the sexual abuser as imagination allows. Ritual abusers, they say, are as likely, if not more likely, to be women as men. As women, they are exempt from the privilege of male-domination and are unprotected by patriarchal ideologies and institutions, thus their evil is all the more sinister for it.

This discourse created a new criminal type: the insatiable female sex fiend lurking behind the homely façades of socially accepted gender roles such as mother, day care provider, preschool teacher, community volunteer. In conjuring up an image of a female ritual abuser, United states child-savers distracted their international colleagues' attention from the on-going and unsettling critique of patriarchal ideology and the structure of male privilege that the discovery of sexual abuse had introduced. Their discourse created a straw woman, engendered by the sexual revolution and the rise of feminism, that could be flailed at, pathologized, vilified and demonized, but whose subduing does not first require sweeping ideological and social change.

Discourse to Re-Enchant the Image of the Rescuer. Finally, if the public perception of rescuers is that they are uninspired and beleaguered technocrats, then the image of rescuers in the discourse of United States child-savers is its mirror-opposite. The child-savers of this discourse are thoroughly enchanted. They believe that ritual abuse is real in the absence of compelling evidence that it is, and in the presence of scathing criticism that the belief, itself, is even believable. They risk their reputations by doing what they believe is right, and their health and well-being by confronting what they believe is evil. In elevating belief over empiricism, the discourse of the child-savers celebrates intuition and risk, embraces the unusual and the unexpected, and vests recruited international child-savers with a charismatic authority they had never before enjoyed in their work.

In summary, the discourse of the United States child-savers was appropriated by international child-savers through three sensitive points of resonance created by the controversies that had risen up around sexual abuse. The persuasiveness of that discourse, that is, its ability to ideologically and materially recruit international child-savers into the ritual abuse moral panic, has nothing to do with the often contradictory facts and figures and the always unsettling horror stories that comprise its Gothic façade, but everything to do with the simple and nostalgically familiar morality tale it tells by creating an image of the innocent child, the demonic abuser, and the valorous rescuer.

8

When All Is Said and Done

By the early 1990s, the day care ritual abuse moral panic had run its course. Any temptation to celebrate its end as proof that the forces of innocence and good had finally and forever triumphed over the force of evil is best resisted. Its denouement was less dramatic than that, unless drama can be found in what the poet T.S. Eliot once described as "the intolerable wrestle with words and meaning." Less poetically put, by the turn into the new decade, day care ritual abuse had lost much of its denotative dignity and no longer boldly inscribed the moral contours of late-modern American society.

How did that happen? As the object of the moral panic, day care ritual abuse stood for the deep and unsettling concerns in 1980s America signified by the master symbols of that decade: the vulnerable child, the menacing devil, and the psychological trauma model. The child-savers' discursive linking of those master symbols resonated with social audiences, and although not everyone shared its meaning, enough did to believe the claims, interpret and repeat them, and react to them as if they were indisputably true. Hence the moral panic.

Inevitably, meanings shift as time slips by, particularly if they are complex meanings that are not neatly tied to a single referent. A red traffic light may always and forever have meant "Stop," but day care ritual abuse took on new and different meanings over that decade. It came to stand for the creation and purgation of intimate enemies in times of moral uncertainty; it suggested a reworking of ancient myths and legends about evil and innocence to fit contemporary times; it pointed to the irresistible inclination for extravagant irrationality. New terms started being bandied about to capture these new meanings: countersubversion ideology (Bromley, 1991; Hicks, 1991), contemporary legend (Victor, 1993), folk mythology (Stevens, 1992; Woodman, 1997), legend ostension (Ellis, 2000), rumor panic (Victor, 1991), witch hunt (Brion, 1993; LaFontaine, 1998; Nathan & Snedeker, 1995), and, of course, moral panic (de Young, 1998; Jenkins, 1992).

These new, semantically freighted terms both labeled and heralded the slow transmogrification of the meaning of day care ritual abuse over the decade of the 1980s. The alternative meanings they suggest certainly tolled the end of the day care ritual abuse moral panic, but there were other forces at work to bring it to its end.

When All Is Said, Meaning Matters

Ironically, one of these forces was the child-saver interest group, itself. As the years wore on, its cohesion wore out. While anyone pledging allegiance to the interest group could faithfully recite the ritual abuse master narrative, it was a rare child-saver who could keep track of, let alone make sense of, the flotsam and jetsam of unpublished and endlessly photocopied symptom and indicator lists, satanic calendars, catalogs of cult and occult symbols, rosters of brainwashing triggers, fragments of case studies, inventories of conspiracy theories, epistles, marginalia and *obiter dicta* that circulated through the convoluted rumor and communication networks that connect child-savers around the world.

So child-savers made choices as to which embellishments of the ritual abuse master narrative they believed true, and their choices came to position them within the interest group. By the 1990s, some of the "hard apologists" (Greaves, 1992, p. 47) who had espoused any or all of the satanic conspiracy theories and brooked no challenges to their beliefs, had changed their minds completely. Cult Cop Sandi Gallant, for example, had spent a decade chasing ritual abusers but finally gave up and renounced her belief in an international satanic conspiracy targeting young children; so did cult cop Randy Eamon who closed shop at the Christian Occult Investigators Network (COIN) he had formed at the start of the moral panic to link cult cops around the country. And so did Geraldo Rivera, the mass media's chief propagandist of day care ritual abuse. In a December 1995 segment of his talk show titled, "Wrongly Accused and Convicted of Child Molest," he apologized to his audience: "I want to announce publicly that as a firm believer of the Believe the Children movement of the 1980s, that started with the McMartin trials in California, I am now convinced that I was terribly wrong ... and many innocent people were convicted and sent to prison as a result. And I am equally positive [that the] repressed memory therapy movement is also a bunch of crap." Thus spake Geraldo.

Other hard apologists found themselves spun off to the margins of the child-saver interest group, their beliefs too extreme for the changing times. Among them were many of the New Christian Rightists, cult cops, parent-advocates, and social workers who had played instrumental roles in dealing with and proselytizing about the day care cases. Their move to the margins concentrated the power to explicate the meaning of ritual abuse in the hands of a smaller number of "soft apologists" who ardently believed children had been horrifically abused in day care centers, but were willing to concede that at least some of what they had described to their eager interrogators was not literally true.

Capitulation, though, further weakened the child-saver interest group. After all, if the children's accounts of ghastly abuse by robed and hooded day care providers in the ceremonial worship of the devil were, perhaps, more metaphorically than literally true, then exactly what *is* ritual abuse? By the end of the decade the very term, let alone its meaning, was up for grabs (Gallagher, 2000).

In that "intolerable wrestle with words and meaning," alternative terms entered the ring, each changing to some extent the meaning of ritual abuse. The new term "sadistic ritual abuse," favored by some of the child-savers (Goodman, 1992), nicely preserved the acronym "SRA" even as it sidestepped the controversy around the original "S"—satanic— but it was inadequate to the task of denoting the stylized, repetitive, ceremonial nature of the alleged abuse the day care children described. "Cultic abuse" at least inferred that the alleged abuse was in service to some overweening belief system (Noblitt & Perskin, 1995), but left the ecumenical impression that any old belief system—from voodoo, to Freemasonry, to fundamentalist Christianity—could have been at work in the day care cases. "Multidimensional sex rings" nicely chased the devil out of the ritual abuse controversy (Lanning, 1992), as did the terms "organized abuse" and "network abuse" that were favored by European child-savers (LaFontaine, 1996). Their clinical sterility, though, deprived them of denotative power, thus they never were able to capture the horror, the sheer bizarreness, of the allegations that fueled the moral panic, and left them vulnerable to facile appropriation by those in search of a term for the abuse of children by other organized groups, such as pedophiles, pornographers, propagandists and even priests.

Also entering the ring were the second wave claims-makers, the psychologists and psychiatrists who in mid-decade began assisting often extremely disturbed adult patients in recovering memories of childhood ritual abuse, alá the pseudonymous Michelle of *Michelle Remembers*. And what memories they were: under clinical sway these patients recalled the breeding of babies for infant sacrifices, unspeakable acts of physical torture, Manchurian candidate-like brainwashing sessions, and highly stylized satanic ceremonies (Goodman, Qin, Bottoms, & Shaver, 1994), all of which raised the Gothic ante against anything the children in the day care cases had ever reported. While the child-savers had grafted all of these rooted sorrows plucked from the memories of adult mental patients onto their own symptom and indicator lists, the second wave claims-makers rarely reciprocated. By the early 1990s two versions of ritual abuse—one for children in day care, the other for adults in psychiatric care—uneasily co-existed, with nothing more than an elaborate skein of conspiratorial musings to connect them.[1]

The Media: A Nation Talks to Itself

While child-savers bickered amongst themselves about the definition, indeed the very meaning, of ritual abuse (Frude, 1996; Jones, 1991; Lloyd, 1992; McFayden, Hanks, & James, 1993), the mass media began attacking as false what it so often had guilelessly presented as true just a few years before. Television news format shows like *60 Minutes, Dateline, Primetime Live* and *48 Hours* featured segments critical of day care ritual abuse cases and of the child-savers involved in them.

Consider, as an example, the *60 Minutes* segment aired just two weeks after Raymond Buckey and Peggy McMartin Buckey were acquitted in the McMartin preschool trial ("McMartin Child Molestation Case," 1990). In his introduction to the segment, anchor Mike Wallace strips the term "ritual abuse" of its denotative power:

> After six years of lurid accusations and interminable court proceedings, the most expensive criminal trial in US history came to an end two weeks ago. A Los Angeles jury in the McMartin preschool child molestation case acquitted 62-year-old Peggy Buckey and her 31-year-old son Ray on 52 counts of sodomy, rape, oral copulation and conspiracy. They did, however, deadlock on 13 charges against Raymond Buckey, and he's scheduled to be retried next month. How could things have turned out this way? Why did the jury find so little credible evidence in a case that seemed all but airtight when it exploded in the national press? Well, as we said three years ago on this broadcast, there were big problems with the McMartin case, not the least of which were allegations of satanism and animal mutilations.

By rhetorically positioning ritual abuse as the primary "big problem" in the case, Wallace has *carte blanche* to offer an opportunity for the Buckeys to elevate their status from folk devils to folk heroes who prevailed in the end against all those who refused to see the "problem" of ritual abuse. After describing the crusade that brought him to trial as a "witch hunt, plain and simple," Raymond Buckey tries on the new status of folk hero when asked what he will do if the 13 deadlocked charges are re-filed and he once more has to stand trial:

> I don't want to go through another McMartin trial, but I will because I know I'm innocent. I'll fight to my last breath to get vindicated in the

system in some way, because there's—there's no end to what they've done to me. I can't just put this behind me. So if they want to go with 13 charges, I'll—I'll fight them because I have no other way to go. I'm not going to roll over for something I never did.

Television talk shows like *Geraldo, Sally Jesse Raphäel* and *Montel Williams* also elevated the accused providers' status, but usually with neither the intelligence nor the integrity of the primetime news shows. A stunning example of the gracelessness of daytime talk shows is a segment on the *Montel Williams* show. Small World Preschool provider Richard Barkman, recently released from prison upon successful appeal, appeared on the dais with the mothers of a few of his alleged victims. They screamed at him like harridans and one lunged at him in an apparent attempt to do grievous bodily harm (Jones, 1993). In confrontational television like this it is often difficult to discern the good guest from the evil one, but in the balance of things, the calm, articulate Barkman came off very much the better, having accrued over the years more moral capital as a victim of the moral panic than the aggrieved women had saved as mothers of his alleged victims.

The press, too, began treating the accused providers as more sinned against than sinning. Only a few journalists had dared to speak out early in the moral panic against a rush to judgment in the day care cases (Charlier & Downing, 1988; Fischer, 1988; Nathan, 1987), but by its end it was *de rigueur.* In the moral economy of the mass media, the transformation of folk devils into folk victims requires the creation of new folk devils, so with some enthusiasm the press went after the child-savers, casting them in this complementary role (Hentoff, 1993; McGrory, 1999; Ritter, 1994; Sauer, 1993; Sennot, 1995). The more prominent child-savers seemed at times to actually aspire to the role. Kee MacFarlane, who had set the gold standard for interviewing children in day care ritual abuse cases, walked off the set of *48 Hours* when asked how her interviewing style had changed after the McMartin Preschool debacle. In defending her interviewing style in the Fells Acres case as necessary for determining if the children would make suitable witnesses, Susan Kelley seemed to dismiss the groundbreaking empirical research of developmental psychologists Stephen Ceci and Maggie Bruck that proved otherwise ("Persistent Interviews," 1995). And prosecutor Nancy Lamb did more than just dismiss it. Her elation short-lived when Robert Kelly's convictions were overturned, she angrily dismissed the corpus of research that specifically calls into question the credibility of the children's statements in the Little Rascals case, as nothing more than "garbage" (Helms, 1995, p. A1).

Lamb and the other child-savers involved in the Little Rascals case had to defend themselves against more than empirical research. Documentarian Ofra Bikel, in search of a good story on child sexual abuse, had meandered into the idyllic small town of Edenton, North Carolina in 1990, just in time to get whiff of the rumors and gossip about ritual abuse at the Little Rascals Day Care Center. For the next eight years the case would consume her. She produced a trilogy of documentaries for public television's *Frontline* series on the case, beginning in 1991 with the segment, "Innocence Lost." Bikel explains, "My interest [was] to take a very complicated subject, understand it very well, and find a way to really tell people what I see and how to look at it" (Bedford, 1997). But the documentary series, which details how the case unfolded and introduces those who were to become its key players, resonated with the changing *Zeitgeist*. Appalled that another McMartin Preschool-like case was brewing in the South just months after the one that had started it all had been closed in the West, viewers inundated Edenton officials with incensed letters and telegrams. The parents of the children in the case were so deluged with angry missives that they faxed statements to 13 newspapers and television stations in the surrounding area pleading with them to remind viewers of the "limitations of the documentary" (Durkin, May 15, 1991, p. 3B).

Awards were heaped upon Bikel, including the prestigious duPont-Columbia Silver Baton Award, but she remained ambivalent about the case. Uncertain as to whether the Little Rascals children indeed had been ritually abused, yet certain there was no evidence against the seven accused providers, she returned to Edenton to a less than enthusiastic welcome. When Bikel made her intentions known to interview video store owner Willard Scott Privott who was in jail awaiting trial, she was denied access to him. Furious, she had a lawyer take out a court order granting her access to Privott, but before she ever stepped foot in the jail the bail of the video store owner, rumored to be the child pornography kingpin of the South, was quietly reduced from $1 million to $50,000 (Bedford, 1997). The Edenton justice system did not want to look bad in another documentary.

But it did, anyway. "Innocence Lost: The Verdict" was aired in 1993. The four hour documentary focused on the trials of Robert Kelly and Dawn Wilson, the day care center cook, and in the case of the former, it exposed serious jury misconduct. Three Kelly trial jurors—Roswell Streeter, Mary Nichols, Marvin Schakelford—faced the camera to say they believed Kelly innocent but were pressured by other jurors to vote for conviction. Streeter went on to describe how a *Redbook Magazine* had been smuggled into the deliberation room by one of the jurors so that its article on child molesters could be used to diagnose Kelly as a pedophile (Thompson, 1993). Two years after the first, this installment

of the trilogy did not so much resonate with the *Zeitgeist* as resound with
it. Now state officials as well as local were blasted with letters and telephone calls condemning the prosecution of the providers. Viewers not
only spewed outrage, but harnessed it into action: some boycotted products manufactured or grown in the state; a few terminated business con-
tracts with state companies or found other venues for conferences and
meetings; many contributed money for the legal defense of the providers;
and a handful created the Committee for the Support of the Edenton
Seven that, among other things, gave the Little Rascals case a discursive
existence on internet web pages and cyberspace chat rooms ("TV Show,"
1993).

If the first two installments of the trilogy called into question the
very meaning of ritual abuse, the final documentary delivered the *coup
de grâce*. "Innocence Lost: The Plea" aired in 1997. It details day care
owner Betsy Kelly's anguished decision to plead no contest to 30 felony
charges in return for a 7 year sentence with credit for two years served
awaiting trial, and Willard Scott Privott's decision to plead no contest in
return for a 10 year suspended sentence and probation. It also reveals
the raw emotion of the remaining providers—Shelley Stone, Robin
Byrum and Darlene Harris—when their charges were serendipitously
dismissed the year before.

No child-saver or parent would talk to Bikel for this segment of the
documentary; none demanded a televised follow-up session to present a
contrary point of view like the sessions that had been set up by UNC-
TV after the first two installments (Bedford, 1997). It was as if the micro-
physics of outrage over ritual abuse had been spent, as if ritual abuse
had lost all meaning for them, as well. Soon after the airing, all charges
were dismissed against Kelly and Wilson who were awaiting new trials
after their original convictions were overturned on appeal.

Organizations: Professionals Talk Quietly to Themselves

Over the decade of the moral panic, the very idea of ritual abuse
had become institutionalized as prominent child-savers were elected to
advisory boards of the many state and national organizations put into
place to deal with child abuse. Kee MacFarlane, for example, served on
the advisory board of the National Center for the Prosecution of Child
Abuse, and in that capacity co-authored its 1987 forensic interviewing
protocol. Psychiatrist Roland Summit served as a policy advisor to the
National Office of Victim Assistance and as a member of the advisory

board on missing children for the Office of the United States Attorney General (Nathan & Snedeker, 1995).

MacFarlane and Summit also were on the board of the American Professional Society on the Abuse of Children (APSAC). Formed in 1987 in response to increasing social consciousness about child sexual abuse, the organization's roster of members reads like a veritable who's who of hard and soft apologists for day care ritual abuse. Its quarterly newsletter, *The APSAC Advisor,* occasionally featured articles credulous of ritual abuse, and the editorial board and consultants of its journal, *The Journal of Interpersonal Violence,* was comprised of some of the moral panic's most prominent child-savers—Kee MacFarlane of McMartin Preschool fame; David Finkelhor, author of *Nursery Crimes*; Ann Burgess, supervisor of Susan Kelley's dissertation on the Fells Acres case; Jon Conte, consultant on the Rogers Park Jewish Community Day Care Center case—among others.

APSAC, though, offers an interesting case study of how a child-saver organization scrabbles for neutral ground on the contentious issue of ritual abuse and, in doing so, reworks its own organizational history. To its credit, the organization was never so ideologically hidebound as to make an unwavering belief in ritual abuse a requirement for membership, but its goals of providing professional education, and promoting research to inform practice and policy brought in many new members over the years. It would be fair to conjecture that all were passionately committed to protecting children from abuse, but some were skeptical, others completely dismissive, of the idea of ritual abuse.

And that makes APSAC's 1995 fact sheet on ritual abuse all the more interesting (APSAC, 1995). It begins with an acknowledgement of the argument over whether ritual abuse even exists:

> "Ritual abuse" is one of the most talked about, rarest, and least understood forms of alleged child maltreatment. Experts disagree about whether or not "ritual abuse" exists, the range of situations to include in the category, and the extent and significance of these situations. Some argue that the term "ritual abuse" should be abandoned because it confuses more than it clarifies. Many more questions than answers exist around this highly controversial topic.

"Ritual abuse," so suppositional that the very term is enclosed in quotation marks, nonetheless is then described in the fact sheet in the kind of Gothic language that resonates with the day care ritual abuse master narrative that many of APSAC's founders and most prominent members had a role in creating and recreating in their interactions with children:

> Most allegations of what comes to be called "ritual abuse" involve one
> or more of the following elements: terrorizing acts (e.g., threats to kill
> parents, pets, or loved ones if the abuse is disclosed); acts involving
> supernatural symbolism or ritual (e.g., the use of masks or robes, the
> use of crosses or pentagrams); acts involving real or simulated killing of
> animals and sometimes human infants (these acts can serve both ritual
> and terrorizing ends); acts involving real or simulated ingestion of urine,
> feces, blood, and "magic potions" which might include mind-altering
> substances; severe sexual abuse, often including penetration with
> objects. Experts have proposed that allegations often classified as "ritual
> abuse" might reflect three very different situations: cult-based ritual
> abuse ... pseudoritualistic abuse ... [or] psychopathological ritualism.

The fact sheet then retreats from this reification of ritual abuse by
calling into question its own description and classification scheme by
insisting some allegations of ritual abuse may be false, the result of fantasy, delusion, persuasion by the mass media, or, in an intriguingly
unelaborated clause, of "misinterpretation or suggestions by interven-
ers." And then it chases its own tail, trying to maintain its pretence of
neutrality. It goes on to assert that investigators have never found evidence of a widespread satanic conspiracy, then to insist that David
Finkelhor and his colleagues actually had in 13 percent of the day care
cases they had examined for their book *Nursery Crimes,* and finally to
add that Finkelhor and his colleagues could not be certain that the ritual abuse allegations in these cases were even true.

What is "fact" in this fact sheet is baffling. And so is its conclusion.
As if neutrality requires the dismissal of all facts, the fact sheet ends with
a plangent plea for a definition agreeable to all differently-minded child-
savers, of this "rarest" and "least understood" form of "alleged" child
abuse that may not even exist at all.

> Professionals are divided over whether or not "ritual abuse" occurs.
> Much of the controversy in the professional community would likely
> disappear with the introduction of a coherent, widely accepted definition
> of "ritual abuse."

APSAC may assume a position of neutrality on the issue of ritual
abuse, but it is an armed neutrality with which the organization can attack
any argument without ever revealing its own history or ideological under-
pinnings. That certainly is evident in the review of *Satan's Silence* by
APSAC President, Theresa Reid (Reid, 1996). Written by investigative
journalist Debbie Nathan, whose articles turned the Wee Care ritual abuse
into a *cause célèbre,* and attorney Michael Snedeker who successfully
appealed the convictions of many of the community members imprisoned in the Kern County ritual abuse case, the book is a no-holds-barred

exposé of the ritual abuse "witch hunt," as the authors refer to it, and a sustained polemic against its injustice. Written for general readership, the book was favorably reviewed by just about everyone except Reid.

Reid begins the review by positioning APSAC in the reasoned middle of the extreme beliefs that characterized the beginning and the end of the decade of the 1980s:

> *Satan's Silence* is important primarily for the opportunity it provides to examine the strangely parallel rhetoric of extremists on both sides of the "ritual abuse" controversy. Publication of this book also invites us to consider the forces at work in the media and in the culture that have focused on these extreme voices to the exclusion of those that are rational, tempered, and serious, making the extreme appear to represent the whole discourse.

Once again, the quotation marks around "ritual abuse" apparently are used to semaphore the organization's neutrality. Yet Reid treats ritual abuse as if it is very real indeed, and therefore unworthy of the quotation marks, by criticizing the authors for not defining the term, despite APSAC's failure to do so in its own fact sheet:

> Nathan and Snedeker never even attempt a definition of "ritual abuse," a term that elicits so many conflicting interpretations and strong emotions that many experts recommend that it be abandoned.... This failure to define the term bedevils the entire book, so that when the authors use the phrase "ritual abuse allegations" the reader has no clear idea what they really mean.

Much of the remainder of the review is devoted to highlighting the "striking parallels" between the "zealous believers" who acted as if ritual abuse were real, and the critical authors who insist it is not. Yet, to indict both positions on this issue is to suggest that there is a factual and empirical middle ground—that *some* cases of ritual abuse are real in fact, or can be proven real by science. If indeed that is APSAC's position, the organization fails its members by not explicating the support for that middle ground, an explication, by the way, that despite abrogating the organization's neutrality, would go a long way towards resolving the controversy over ritual abuse and correcting any injustices.

Instead, Reid ends the review with a striking statement that, on its face, indicts APSAC's founders for their unprofessionalism and the organization, itself, for its self-conscious neutrality:

> The most important fuel for *Satan's Silence* and other work purportedly exposing the "ritual abuse hoax" is the indefensible professional practice associated with beliefs in a widespread satanic conspiracy. Evidence has

been available for at least a decade that some professionals motivated by such beliefs have engaged in "professional" practice that, at the very least, is not supported in the empirical research literature and, at the worst, is highly destructive. The failure of licensing boards, professional peers, professional society ethic committees, insurance companies, and the courts to protect individuals from extreme instances of bad professional practice has opened the door for critics from outside the field. There is a glaring need for reforms that effectively protect consumers, particularly of mental health services; if those reforms do not come from within the professions, they will be imposed from without.

On this point, Reid certainly is correct. None of the licensed or registered child-savers involved in the day care ritual abuse cases in the sample had a license suspended; none has been censured by a state or organizational ethics committee, despite often egregious violations of professional ethics codes (Fisher, 1995); none has ever been successfully sued.[2] On the other hand, no professional organization in the United States or abroad, including the prestigious International Society for the Prevention of Child Abuse and Neglect (ISPCAN), has ever published a position statement on ritual abuse, or insisted upon opening inquiries into the cases of those convicted of it who remain in prison.

But new organizations have. One certain sign that even a virulent moral panic is about to burn itself out is the emergence of new organizations that have as their mission the adding of fuel for the burning. First on the scene were the grassroots advocacy organizations, Victims of Child Abuse Laws (VOCAL) and the False Memory Syndrome Foundation (FMSF). Although neither was formed to address ritual abuse alone, or the day care cases in specific, each takes a critical stance on both. And each is none too delicate in its trouncing of child-savers who brought idea and place together to set off the moral panic.

Other organizations followed, each tossing more skeptical, even dismissive, interpretations of ritual abuse into the discursive ring. Among them, the recently created National Center for Reason and Justice (NCRJ) deserves mention. Although the organization does not have a position statement on day care ritual abuse, its roster reads like a who's who of ritual abuse critics: Michael Snedeker serves as President, Debbie Nathan as an advisor. Created to educate the public about false accusations of sexual abuse and to provide legal and financial assistance to the falsely accused and the wrongfully convicted, the organization sponsors three of the day care providers who remain in prison: Fran and Dan Keller who were convicted in the Fran's Day Care case, and Gerald "Tooky" Amirault, convicted over 17 years ago in the Fells Acres case, and finally scheduled for parole in 2004.

These, and other, organizations raise the decibel of the disagreement over what ritual abuse is and what it means. They prick holes in the over-inflated beliefs that set off the moral panic, the over-wrought emotions that fueled it, and the over-confident actions that were its material consequences. But hole-pricking is, itself, advocatory, and therefore subject to the same criticisms about beliefs, emotions and actions it levies at the child-savers. When scientific inquiry entered into the debate over ritual abuse, that was quite another thing.

Research: Science Shouts at Professionals

Although professional organizations declined to take a position on day care ritual abuse, they did publish working papers and best practice standards that tolled the end of the moral panic. As statements based on the findings of empirical research and controlled clinical observations, these missives also can be read as criticisms of the unexamined and untested beliefs that were the incendiary ideological fuel of the day care ritual abuse moral panic.

A pastiche of organizational statements will illustrate this point. The American Academy of Pediatrics (1991), following the example set a few years earlier by the American Medical Association (1985), set out guidelines for the medical evaluation of child sexual abuse that reminded its members that in the absence of a documented history and specific laboratory results, physical examination findings alone are only infrequently diagnostic of sexual abuse. In working papers, the American Psychiatric Association (1993) cautioned that there is no psychiatric profile that accurately distinguishes those who sexually abuse children from those who do not; the American Psychological Association (1995) stated that without corroborative evidence, there is nothing at all that distinguishes a true memory of sexual abuse from a false one; and the International Society for Traumatic Stress Studies concluded that there is no scientific consensus for the belief that traumatic memories are any different than ordinary memories (Roth & Friedman, 1998). In those countries to which the moral panic had spread, professional organizations also published statements to check the execrable excesses of the previous decade. The Canadian Psychological Association (1996) warned that there is no constellation of symptoms that is diagnostic of sexual abuse alone, a conclusion echoed by Great Britain's Royal College of Psychiatrists (Brandon, Boakes, Glaser, & Green, 1998).

It was the paradigm-shifting research on children's suggestibility that prompted the most emphatic warnings from professional organizations about zealous interviewing and moon-eyed gullibility. Although the interview protocols vary somewhat across organizations, all are predicated on the empirically verified principle that the most reliable and credible information is solicited from children in unbiased, developmentally sensitive interactions by trained and qualified professionals. To that end, such organizations as the American Academy of Child and Adolescent Psychiatry (1990/1998), the American Professional Society on the Abuse of Children (1990/1998), and the American Prosecutors Research Institute (1990), published guidelines and/or posted them on their internet web pages where they easily could be accessed by non-members. Other organizations, most notably the National Children's Advocacy Center, sponsors forensic interviewing training sessions around the country for professionals from those fields with a stake in child sexual abuse.

This new research on children's suggestibility was incorporated into both investigative and judicial protocols as well. The Justice Department's Office of Juvenile Justice and Delinquency Prevention's series of portable guides discusses the implications of the research for law enforcement officers investigating cases of child sexual abuse (Cage & Pence, 1994; Sawitz & Faller, 1994). The American Bar Association's Center on Children and the Law, as another example, published judicial training manuals on child sexual abuse that discuss research findings on zealous interviewing (Bulkley, *et al.*, 1994; Walker, 1999), as well as an assortment of booklets on the topic aimed at both judges and attorneys (Baker *et al*, 1997; Berliner, Saywitz, Schudson, Sandt, & Horowitz, 1994; Smith & Elstein, 1994).

Not all child-savers belong to these, or any other, professional organizations; many, in fact, have no organizational affiliation at all. And the very fact they do not means that within the child-saver interest group the guidelines function to separate professionals from laypersons, informed practitioners from advocates, scientists from dabblers. While at the frenzied peak of the day care ritual abuse moral panic those distinctions were made irrelevant by a shared ideology, at its end, with the ideology bested by science, these distinctions began to matter a great deal.

By the start of the 1990s, intervention into child sexual abuse was becoming increasingly professionalized. It was licensed clinicians who were doing most of the interviewing of children; trained law enforcement officers who were investigating most of the cases; medical specialists who were conducting most of the physical examinations; expert prosecutors who were trying most of the cases in courts. Whatever tendency there remained to the excesses of the 1980s was being held in check by best practice standards, ethical guidelines, currency in the field and peer regulations. The professionalization of child-saving may carry its own price—the creation of social and prestige hierarchies within and between professions with a stake in child-saving,[3] bureaucratization, formal rationality—but it also helped write *finis* to the day care ritual abuse moral panic.

When All Is Done

The 1980s day care ritual abuse moral panic may have ended with that decade, but as the poet T.S. Eliot reminds, "the end is where we start from." What remains to be scrutinized is its legacy and the scrutiny, itself, must begin with the wisdom of moral panic theorist Stanley Cohen, who started it all.

In Cohen's (1972/2002) considered opinion, most moral panics are tendentious in that they are slanted in the favor of dominant ideologies and values, that is, the status quo. By directing outrage towards socially dishonored folk devils, most moral panics distract attention, time and resources from what Cohen somewhat glibly refers to as "the real problems." They leave in their wake moral landscapes littered with new experts, programs, laws and hardened attitudes—so much stage scenery that makes it look *as if* threats have been contained, *as if* moral boundaries have been defended, *as if* dominant values and ideologies had been right all along. That may be true of most moral panics, but the question remains, is it also true of the day care ritual abuse moral panic? The deliciously ambiguous answer is yes ... and no.

Like most other moral panics, this one distracted attention from "real problems" that were its cultural crucible by focusing on the constructed threat posed by the day care providers who were its folk devils. Its beguiling Gothicism lured the public, professionals and policy-makers into a make-believe world of devil worship, secret tunnels, live burials, infant sacrifices, *Doppelgängers,* and mind control, and away from the real world of changing families, weakening moral authority and increasing ontological uncertainty that had fomented it in the first place. The distraction protected the status quo, even shored it up. After all, what was needed in this illusory battle with evil was *more* of everything—more policies and laws, more control and punishment, more consensus, courage and conviction.

That said, unlike most moral panics, this one on rare occasions also revealed its own origins and in doing so became a courier for ideologies and values contrary to the ones it protected and preserved. Thus the delicious irony: the day care ritual abuse moral panic acted as a courier *both* of the status quo and its challengers, sometimes even concurrently. Like all ironies, delicious or not, this one deserves a closer look through the prisms of the master symbols of the 1980s.

The Vulnerable Child

Cohen's observation that moral panics are slanted in favor of dom-inant values and ideologies would be nicely supported if this moral panic had put a halt to the steady evolution of the family and, in doing so, had reduced the vulnerability to children brought by change that outpaces old ideas and infrastructures. That, however, did not happen. The fam-ily, that foundational social institution, kept right on changing over the 1980s, keeping questions and concerns about the vulnerability of chil-dren very much in the forefront. The divorce rate more than doubled over that decade, the single mother birth rate almost did, and the num-ber of female-headed households with young children rose 3 percent. The average age of first marriage crept up a couple of years, as did the average age of first birth for married women (Rawlings, 1993). At the decade's start 45 percent of all women with children under the age of 5 years worked outside of the home; at its end, that figure increased to 54 percent (Hofferth & Phillips, 1991). Those working women earned 62¢ for every $1.00 made by men in 1980; a decade later they made a dime more than that, but those with young children spent that raise, and more, on increased child care costs. The moral panic did not keep families from enrolling their children in day care. In 1985 at the peak of the day care ritual abuse moral panic, in fact, with one center after another being investigated and one provider after another being led off in handcuffs, 22 percent of all preschoolers with working mothers were enrolled in licensed day care centers; by 1990 that figured increased to 28 percent (Health Resource and Human Service Administration, 2002).

While the day care ritual abuse moral panic neither slowed the evo-lution of the family, as if there were only one prototype, nor decreased the vulnerability of children to the vagaries of family change, it did act tendentiously by concealing the "real problems" of that decade—the unsettling social, economic, political and ideological strains to which the family always has been exquisitely sensitive, and the almost desperate need for day care those strains created. How did it do that? By trans-forming the providers who were the folk devils into objects of suspicion, scrutiny and surveillance, the moral panic directed attention away from those "real problems." It is in regards to providers and the day care cen-ters that were the *loci delecti* of ritual abuse that the moral panic's capac-ity for legerdemain is starkly apparent.

Treat the state of Florida as a case study. Rocked by three stun-ningly Gothic day care ritual abuse cases in five years—Country Walk, Glendale Montessori and Old Cutler—it aggressively set out to prevent another by focusing attention, discourse and action on the folk devils providers had become. The state's House and Senate cooperated on a massive piece of legislation that, in part, required fingerprinting and background checks of all applicants for day care employment, and mandated annual training for all providers. In a self-congratulatory moment, state officials shook hands, embraced, and nudged each other out of the way to take credit for a piece of legislation they promised would protect children from abuse in day care. "I'm claiming victory!" exclaimed Senator Roberta Fox, pumping her fist in the air. "This legislation puts us right out in front as far as what states are doing to protect children," declared David Pringee, secretary of the state's Department of Health and Rehabilitative Services (Bivins, 1985, p. 1A).

By the turn into the new decade, 47 states had joined Florida in passing legislation requiring background, that is, criminal record and child abuse registry, checks of all applicants for day care employment. In another five years, those states would find themselves in the same quandary Florida found itself in: fingerprint checks did little more than create a "false sense of security" that applicants with a propensity for child abuse, let alone ritual abuse, would be found out; background checks screened out applicants with felony records, but overlooked those with misdemeanor records as well as those against whom felony charges had been filed but not yet adjudicated (Fernandez, 1990).

Just how safe these methods kept children from predatory providers is not known (Burkhardt, Golden, Karolak, & Stoney, 2003). But what is known is that of the 7 accused McMartin Preschool providers and the 51 others in the sample of 22 day care ritual abuse cases, background checks would have flagged none for prior child abuse, and only one with prior felony convictions: Frank Fuster of Country Walk infamy had been convicted of murder and of child sexual abuse. As the spouse of the provider and not responsible for the daily care of children, however, even under that groundbreaking Florida law he would have been exempt from the mandated background check.

Well-intentioned though they are, laws like these are little more than stage scenery, hastily strewn across the moral landscape in response to the hue and cry, "there ought to be a law." But hues and cries are the cerebral versions of visceral screams: they are soon soothed by succor. Again, the state of Florida is illustrative. Five years after the fingerprint/background check law was passed to great hurrah, over 40 pieces of companion legislation passed to protect the state's youngest children from all forms of maltreatment had not yet been funded (Fernandez, 1990).

Lurking in the shadows of this stage scenery were the "real problems" that these hastily constructed laws and policies never acknowledged, let alone touched: the availability of affordable, quality day care for parents in all economic strata; the ideological battle over the definition of the family; the clash between women's rights and children's interests; the disagreement over whether child care is a family or a societal responsibility (Howes & Droege, 1994; Michel, 1999). Ironically, though, the day care ritual abuse moral panic occasionally revealed these real problems and provided opportunities, not always taken, for these "real problems" to be redressed.

The state of Florida once again provides an interesting case study. After the notorious Country Walk case, The Governor's Constituency for Children held public hearings to discuss the day care crisis. Although these fora were intended to be platforms for parents, in their newly minted role of parent-advocate, to voice outrage and grief over the ritual abuse their children were alleged to have suffered while in the care of Iliana and Frank Fuster, other parents with children enrolled in other centers weighed in as well, not about ritual abuse, but about the sorry state of day care in the Sunshine State.

Their testimony about their difficulty, even desperation, in finding affordable, quality day care illustrates the irony that the day care ritual abuse moral panic did not always distract from the "real problems" that were its cause, but sometimes revealed them, creating the potential for real social change. The parents' testimony, often hesitant and tearful, was self-referential and therefore particularly revealing about the effects of larger social forces, those "real problems" Cohen refers to, on individual lives. They talked about economic strains on their families, the jeopardy uncertain day care arrangements posed for their jobs, relationships and marriages, the concerns they had about their children's welfare and safety in day care, and their guilt in leaving them to the care of others (Ynclan, September 16, 1984).

The hearings concluded with a promise that the state of Florida would create its own "child-centered society" in which the needs of all families would be met (Bivins, 1985). By necessity, such a society would be built on the detritus of the "real problems" that had stood in its way; more directly put, it would be built upon real social change. Neither change nor child-centeredness happened in Florida, though, despite the best of intentions, nor did it in any other state. Rather, the "real problems" that strained families ran rampant through the rest of the decade, deepening the day care crisis and, another irony here, increasing the vulnerability of children (Gordon & Chase-Lansdale, 2001; Hofferth & Collins, 2000; Winic, 2000).

Parents were not the only ones feeling these strains. So were providers, but their folk devil status concealed their plight as casualties of the "real problems" that had fomented the moral panic in the first place. Between the start of the day care ritual abuse moral panic, marked by the McMartin Preschool case in 1983, and its end, marked by the

Fran's Day Care case in 1992, the average salary of providers employed in licensed day care centers decreased almost 20 percent; that of home-based providers, who more often than not were unlicensed and unregulated, increased 100 percent, but on a per hour basis never exceeded minimum wage (Hofferth, 1996; Schulman, 2000). Providers were leaving day care centers in droves and, in doing so, leaving their young charges to a rapid succession of new and often inexperienced providers who tried their hands at child care before moving on to more lucrative jobs (Whitebook, Phillips, & Bowes, 1993).

Leading the pack were male providers. Although there are no reliable data on the number of men who cared for young children during the 1980s, the best guesstimate is that they constituted 5 percent of all providers employed in licensed day care centers (Weinbach, 1987). In a decade that witnessed increases in divorce and in single-parent families, men who embraced the emerging ideology of gender role equality and took low paying, low prestige jobs as day care providers were welcomed, at first, as father-figures and role models for children in need of them. The day care ritual abuse moral panic tarnished that welcome by raising suspicions about the motivations and proclivities of the "new males" who wanted careers in child care, and about the new gender ideology, so threatening to the status quo, they embraced. Sociological research consistently shows that when men enter a woman-dominated profession, pay and prestige increase (Cassidy, 1990); when they began exiting this one, day care was re-feminized. The care of young children fell once again on the stooped shoulders of underpaid, overworked, and underappreciated women.

It was not just low pay that pushed so many providers out of the profession during the 1980s, but the high cost of doing business. As the scene of the crime of the moral panic, day care centers often had to be cosmetically altered to rise above suspicion. Windows were placed into walls for easy viewing of classroom interactions, doors were taken off of bathrooms and closets, cameras were mounted in room corners to provide video records of all activities (Bordin, 1996). Any day care center that aspired to be above suspicion had to be transformed from a warm and cozy home-away-from-home into a veritable panopticon that "embodied an ideal for maximizing scrutiny and control while minimizing the response and intervention of those being controlled" (Jenks, 1996, p. 78).

Policies were altered too, but with different costs to both providers and their young charges. In many licensed centers, new "hands-off" policies warned against hugging, holding, touching and being alone with enrollees. Consider the irony here: the very child-savers who were coaxing the ritual abuse master narrative out of young children were also the first to decry these new policies, pointing out that the withdrawal of tactile stimulation only increases children's need for it, thus increasing their vulnerability to sexual victimization (Timnick & McGraw, 1990).

Adding to the high cost of business were skyrocketing insurance rates. Although even *Nursery Crimes* (Finkelhor & Williams, 1988), the witch-hunting manual of the day care ritual abuse moral panic, conceded that children were at much more risk for abuse of any kind within their own families than they were in day care, the sensational day care ritual abuse cases suggested otherwise. In the words of one insurer who, perhaps wisely, preferred anonymity, "One pervert can cost you $10 million" (Pave, 1985, p. 114). Faced with rates that increased 1500 percent or more over the decade, day care directors were faced with a choice: cut back on staff and services, continue to provide child care without insurance, or pass the costs on to parents. Each alternative was unpleasant in its consequences. Cutting back on staff and services disadvantaged day care centers in the competitive marketplace; operating without insurance was not just reckless, but in many states illegal; and passing the costs on to parents was a certain way to lose their business.

Insurers defended the increases by pointing to the spectacular day care ritual abuse cases and to the cultural climate that rendered the claims made in them not only believable, but actionable, and winnable in civil suits. In an astute essay titled, "Good-Bye Day Care," journalist Dorothy Wickenden (1985) reveals the rough magic behind the day care liability crisis. She asserts that the crisis had little, if anything, to do with the day care ritual abuse cases, and everything to do with forcing a confrontation with clever lawyers who in *every* personal injury civil case were "stretch[ing] the definition of harm beyond recognition, and [with] sympathetic juries increasingly willing to assign responsibility for what once would have been construed as unfortunate accidents" (p. 14). Wickenden lays bare the ironies that are the heart of this liability crisis:

> Whatever the cause [of the day care liability crisis], the result is that insurance and litigation—social institutions intended to produce economic stability and social justice—are producing instability and chaos instead. In day care the ironies are particularly apparent. A crucial industry is discouraged from expanding, or even continuing at a time of unprecedented demand. As a consequence, the risks that so worry insurers and parents— those that result from inadequate supervision of children—are made more likely. Thanks to exaggerated concerns about virtually nonexistent liabilities, many of the real liabilities of day care—high cost; insufficient supply; and widely inconsistent standards of care, licensing procedures, and regulation from state to state—are probably going to get worse [p. 14].

Indeed, they *did* get worse, but the point here is that when examined through the lens of the master symbol of the vulnerable child, the day care ritual abuse moral panic acted tendentiously and concealed the "real problems" that were battering families during the 1980s and increasing the vulnerability of their children. The frenetic activity it set off assured that reasoned, responsive policy and funding initiatives that could have addressed these underlying problems would be set aside in favor of legislative quick-fixes. The moon-eyed beliefs it forged silenced civic discourse about the care of children by changing families and orchestrated instead a high-pitched wail about perverts posing as providers. The fear it stoked boarded up day care centers, jacked up the price of enrollment, and sometimes left children in the care of providers afraid to touch them. If an irony can be brutal it is this: young children were left no less vulnerable for all of this fuss and bother.

But there is another irony here, more delicious than brutal. While the day care ritual abuse moral panic distracted attention from the "real problems" that were its cause, it also sometimes revealed them, producing opportunities, not always taken at the moment, for real social change. Stanley Cohen (2002), somewhat tongue-in-cheek, suggested that a moral panic can be bad or good—it can distract attention from the "real problems" that are its cause, thus preserving and protecting the status quo, or more rarely, it can be all about the "real problems," thus prefiguring social change. The day care ritual abuse moral panic was, in these terms, a whole lot more bad than good, but the fact that it was *both* at the same time affords a different, slightly more optimistic, reading of how moral panics actually work.

Menacing Devil

On the slow, inexorable march towards to millennium, the devil continued to mischievously meddle in human, social and political affairs. The devil's Svengali-like hold over America's cultural elite was evident to those who believed it in the National Endowment for the Arts' funding of "anti–Christian" art (Lalonde, 1991); the feminist movement's flip dismissal of theologian Karl Barth's dictum that "women are ontologically inferior to men" (cited in Fuller, 1995, p. 176); the scientists who separate the quest for knowledge from divine revelation by inventing the microchip and the computer (Webber & Hutchings, 1986); the secular humanists who promote the devil's playground of globalism, peace and tolerance (Hunt, 1990).

At least that was what the New Christian Rightists were saying. Their apocalyptic message was more shrill at the end of the decade than the start, but the difference at the end was that fewer child-savers were listening. These ideologues who had reified the "satanic" in ritual abuse with their exegeses, and then said and did nothing while exegeses were made extraordinary to suit the size of the fear the moral panic was stirring up, had been pushed to the margins of the child-savers interest group. The distracting devil, however, had not accompanied them.

Although, as previously discussed, the *term* "satanic ritual abuse" fell out of favor with child-savers before the day care ritual abuse moral panic had run its course, and with it the chimerical concepts of cults and conspiracies, the *idea* of satanic ritual abuse had colonized the imagination of both child-savers and social audiences. A brief compare and contrast of the cases that started and ended the day care ritual abuse moral panic bolsters this point. The most Gothic allegations coaxed out of the children in the McMartin Preschool case were repeated a decade later by the children in the Fran's Day Care case. Both sets of children described infant and animal sacrifices, blood-drinking and cannibalism, magic elixirs, and ritual invocations of the devil. Hard core apologists will insist this proves the concepts of cults and conspiracies are not so chimerical after all, but in the absence of evidence of either, the reiteration of the ritual abuse master narrative is grander proof of its hold on imagination, even after the term "satanic ritual abuse" fell out of favor. Indeed, the lexical marginality of the term towards the end of the moral panic is evident in the fact that it was the defense, not the prosecution, that entered it in to the Fran's Day Care trial in an effort to discredit the children's testimony.

All of this is offered in aide of the point that throughout the moral panic, even as ideologues were being marginalized and terms being replaced by other terms, ritual abuse was *always* associated with the devil, *always* connoted with malevolence. And that conferred upon it a special status. As the "ultimate evil" it came to be situated at the pinnacle of a hierarchy of child maltreatment, relegating more commonplace forms of child abuse—incest, battering and neglect—to the lower rungs. Here the tendentious tendency of the day care ritual abuse moral panic is evident: by discursively situating ritual abuse on the pinnacle of the hierarchy, it served as a distraction from more prosaic forms of child abuse, committed not by robed and hooded providers in secret rooms and tunnels, but by parents in the context of the inviolable family.

Feminist writer Louise Armstrong (1994) makes this same point, only with panache. To her, the day care ritual abuse moral panic was a distraction from one particular type of child maltreatment—incest—and from one particular type of perpetrator—males. Since males enjoy power and privilege, the tendentious tendency of the moral panic is not just evident to her, but glaringly so:

> Actually, bad as a word didn't even begin to cut it. Neither, really, did wickedness and sin. Evil was the only word you could assign to the

specter [of ritual abuse] conjured up by the gruesome, gross, comic-book monstrousness being related and ascribed the proportions of a scourge. It was a truly epic distraction from the humdrum business of ordinary men allowed to molest children in the normal, everyday, routine course of events. In fact, as dialogues, speculation, and passion zoomed over what was variously called satanic, cult, or ritual (or ritualized or ritualistic) abuse, incest plain and simple was left behind to eat the dust [p. 244].

Armstrong goes on to reveal the sleights-of-hand that distracted attention from incest and to ritual abuse. She mentions the trainings and seminars that were the bully pulpits from which child-savers consecrated the belief of believers and converted skeptics; the task forces that cloaked belief in technical jargon and passed it off as science; the talk shows, made-for-television movies, and documentaries that incautiously mixed folklore, occultism, paganism and end-time eschatology with pure non-sense and called it information and news.

To that list could be added the ritual abuse bills that came before the legislatures of several states. The testimony heard by Texas legislators from cult-cops about confiscated satanic calendars that marked the days for human sacrifices prompted the crafting of the "Diabolic Cult Acts" as an addition to the state penal code. The bill, had it been passed into law, would have criminalized a variety of so-called "ritualistic" acts, including the consumption of human or animal blood, mutilation and dismemberment, as well as the "ritualistic" physical or psychological abuse of any person. House Bill 1693, proposed but not passed in Pennsylvania, would have prohibited the "ritualistic physical or psychological abuse of a child when undertaken as a part of a ceremony, rite, initiation or observance." The language of House Bill 928 crafted by Louisiana legislators was nearly identical save for the use of the adjective "deviant" to describe the ritualistic acts, thus assuring that a Christian parent, say, who initiates his or her own child into a version of the Christian faith by verbal abuse would never be accused, let alone charged, with ritual abuse (Hicks, 1991).

None of those bills was passed into law, but that was not the case in Idaho, Illinois and California, although the law in the latter state has since been annulled. Despite the fact that, to date, no one has ever been charged, tried or convicted under these laws—or, perhaps, *because* of that fact—they are worth a closer look (Table 11).

The laws are prime examples of panic legislation, hastily cobbled together in response to the cry, "there ought to be a law," passed by legislators unwilling to take a stance critical of the *Zeitgeist*, and then offered as evidence by child-savers that ritual abuse must be real after all, otherwise there would not be a law against it. Lauren Stratford, whose completely

TABLE 11

Brief Summary of Three Ritual Abuse Laws

State (Year)	Intent	Prohibited Acts
Idaho (1990)	"To provide a felony offense for specified abuse of a child as part of a ritual."	Simulation or torture, mutilation, sacrifice of any warm-blooded animal or human; forces injection or ingestion of drugs to dull sensitivity, cognition, recollection, or resistance to any criminal activity; forces ingestion or external application, of human or animal urine, feces, flesh, blood, bones, body secretions, non-prescribed drugs; involves child in mock marriage ceremony with person or representation of any force or deity, followed by sexual contact with child; places child in coffin or open grave containing human corpse or remains; threatens death or serious harm to child, parents, friends or pets; dissects, mutilates, or incinerates human corpse.
Illinois (1993)	A person is guilty of a felony when he or she commits any of the following acts with, upon, or in the presence of a child as part of a ceremony, rite, or similar observance	Simulates or tortures, mutilates, sacrifices any warm-blooded animal or human being; ingestion, injection or application of any narcotic drug, hallucinogen or anesthetic to dull sensitivity, cognition, recollection, or resistance to any criminal activity; forces ingestion or external application of human or animal urine, feces, flesh, blood, bones, body secretions, non-prescribed drugs or chemical compounds; involves child in mock marriage ceremony with person or representation of any force or deity, followed by sexual contact with child; places child into coffin or open grave containing human corpse or remains.

(TABLE 11 CONTINUED)

State (Year)	Intent	Prohibited Acts
California (1995)	3 year sentence enhancement if "offense was committed as part of ceremony, rite, or any similar, observance."	Simulates or tortures, mutilates, or sacrifices any mammal; forces ingestion, or external application of human or animal urine, feces, flesh, blood, or bones; places child in coffin, open grave, or other confined area containing animal remains or a human corpse or remains.

bogus account of breeding babies for satanic sacrifices elevated her for a moment or two during the moral panic to the lofty status of ritual abuse expert, illustrates just how easy it is to get hoisted by the petard of that tautology: "If there is no evidence of ritual abuse or sacrifices, then why in the world would intelligent, successful and clear-thinking politicians ... work so tirelessly to get bills passed through the legislature making the ritualized abuse of a child a felony?" (1993, p. 53).

Why, indeed? The answer, of course, lies in the persuasive power of panic discourse to ideologically and materially recruit participants into the moral panic, so that they believe and act as if ritual abuse *is* the ultimate evil and as if the identification, control and punishment of its perpetrators *is* a matter of urgent concern. The untangling of the tautology, though, reveals another interesting thing about these laws: they have the potential to overreach. The control culture pumped up by the moral panic, with its new laws like these, its policies, institutions and regulations, its censors, vigilantes and moral arbiters, has the potential to ensnare not just the moral panic's folk devils, but others who seem in the heat of the moment to share their propensity for threatening the social and moral order and, ironically, even those who do not.

On its web site, the Ontario Consultants for Religious Tolerance provide a splendid analysis of these three ritual abuse laws (Robinson, 2001), revealing the unconstitutionality of some of the clauses, the ethnocentricity of others, as well as the potential of others still to criminalize the behavior of those who are not the moral panic's folk devils. The laws in all three states, for example, expressly prohibit the sacrifice of animals, a practice integral to the Santeria religion which boasts 35,000 adherents in the United States, and is constitutionally protected according to United States Supreme Court rulings. The Idaho and Illinois laws, as another example, also prohibit the external application of drugs to the body of a child, a practice common not only in Native American folk medicine but in mainstream American home remedies, as any child whose chest cold was treated by a vigorous application of Vicks VapoRub will attest.

The term "satanic" is not found in the letter of any of these three laws, but it certainly is in the spirit of all three. The ceremonies, rites and rituals they prohibit are lifted from the ritual abuse master narrative; they imply, without stating, that the overweening belief system of ritual abusers is demonological. In doing that, they reify ritual abuse as the ultimate evil and secure its place at the pinnacle of the child maltreatment hierarchy.

Battling the ultimate evil is also expensive. A brief exercise in number-crunching makes that point. It is estimated that the combined direct and indirect costs of child maltreatment in the United States totals a staggering $94 billion annually (Fromm, 2001). If the $15 million it cost to investigate and prosecute the McMartin Preschool case were available as cash-in-hand, it would pay the medical bills of 1,364 battered children with limb fractures, or the mental health counseling bills of 5,245 sexually abused children. If just slightly less than half of that $15 million were available, the $7 million it cost to bring Kelly Michaels to justice in the Wee Care case, for example, it would pay for the special education costs of 10,687 abused and neglected children who develop learning disorders. Or, say that a mere $2 million, the cost of bringing Bobby Fijnje to justice in the Old Cutler case, were available for spending. In 1989 dollars, it would have funded the salaries of 150 new state day care inspectors, paid the increased insurance liability costs of 1,500 day care centers, or subsidized day care expenses for over 2,000 children from low income families.

From its pinnacle high atop the child maltreatment hierarchy, ritual abuse attracted attention and diverted resources, but it also did something much more insidious: it added one more master narrative to a culture already rife with narratives of incest, molestation, pornography, child-snatching and sexual exploitation. Critic James Kincaid (1998) concedes that the preoccupation with sexual abuse during the 1980s certainly benefited those who were abused by legitimizing their accounts and enabling their search for healing and justice. But that preoccupation also had an unintended consequence: it eroticized children by taking as axiomatic that "adults by the millions find children so enticing that they will risk anything to have sex with them" (p. 14). All that talk about sexual abuse, says Kincaid, made children sexy; all that certainty that most adults were potential predators rendered those adults who were not, powerless to do anything about it.

Kincaid's argument brings into sharp focus the observation that bringing sexual trauma narratives into the realm of cultural discourse "is not always or even generally a progressive or liberatory strategy" (Alcoff & Gray, 1993, p. 260). Some narratives do challenge the dominant discourse about sex and the power relations that support it, but others sustain the status quo by merely reiterating, without critique, the dominant cultural discourse. The ritual abuse master narrative, in Kincaid's view, does the latter, but in Grand Guignol style. All of its Gothic conventions—sinister perpetrators passing as ordinary folk, innocent victims and valorous rescuers, unspeakable horror in homely places, silence and secrecy, signs misread and clues missed—distract from the fact that it is little more than a cautionary tale about the inevitability of sexual abuse.

As Kincaid reminds, "(T)he Gothic is not a promising form for casting social problems. Instead of offering solutions, such tales tend to paralyze; they do not move forward but circle back to one more hopeless encounter with the demon" (pp. 10–11). Not promising, indeed. With a touch of insouciance Kincaid makes the same points Louise Armstrong makes with panache: the ritual abuse master narrative draws attention both to isolated acts of Gothic horror and away from acts of ordinary child maltreatment, including any that actually may have occurred in the day care cases, and to personal and psychological explanations and away from the moral uncertainty, apocalyptic fears, loss of faith and trust that were its own structural and ideological causes. As a master narrative it can be listened to with revulsion, outrage, horror and, if Kincaid is right, even titillation, but it cannot really be acted upon.

Through the prism of the master symbol of the menacing devil, the meta-narrative, that is, the moral of the day care ritual abuse moral panic is revealed. It is this: the most evil sexual predators lurk behind the most banal facades, and no child can be considered safe from them. This is an oft-told moral with a fairy tale-like familiarity. And it is, ironically, a comforting moral. It requires of those who believe it no critical thinking about the "real problems" that are its origin, no critique of its Gothic trappings, no analysis of its underlying assumptions, and no concerted action that might bring about real social change.

Psychological Trauma Model

In late-modern society, psychological trauma is both a clinical syndrome and a trope, that is, an injury and an interpretation (Farrell, 1998). Throughout the decade of the 1980s behaviors once seen as offensive, attitudes once dismissed as insulting, natural disasters once deemed caprices of nature, social problems once thought of as enfeebling, policies once perceived as pitiless, increasingly were interpreted as traumagenic, and those affected by any or all of these increasingly diagnosed as traumatized.[4] Certainly one of the mechanisms that was both a cause and an effect of this gestalt switch was the reification of psychological trauma in the form of the official diagnosis of Post-Traumatic Stress Disorder (PTSD). Included for the first time in the 1980 version of the *Diagnostic and Statistical Manual of Mental Disorders-III*, the nosological bible of the mental health profession, the diagnosis and all of the misery and misfortune it implies, swiftly garnered the attention of clinicians and researchers throughout the Western world. The eagerness with which they set out to identify traumatic stressors, and to theorize about the nuances of the experience and the memory of trauma, is measured by the growth and the professionalization of the specialty. It is also measured by treatment innovations—phase-oriented therapy, eye movement desensitization and reprocessing, exposure therapy, anxiety management training, cognitive-behavioral therapy, and psychopharmacological intervention and more were being used to help traumatized adults and children "move from being haunted by the past and interpreting arousing stimuli as a return of the trauma, to being present in the here and now, capable of responding to current exigencies to the fullest potential" (van der Kolk, McFarlane, & Weisaeth, 1996, p. xiv).

What did the day care ritual abuse moral panic contribute to the burgeoning science of psychological trauma? Bluntly answered: hardly a single thing. A decade's worth of cases breathlessly described as "filled with atrocities comparable to and greater than some of the concentration camp stories we have heard of" (Lempinen, 1987, p. 1), so uniquely horrific as to be evidence of a "new clinical syndrome" (Young, Sachs, Braun, & Watkins, 1991, p. 182), so epidemic "that it is growing faster than AIDS" (Raschke, 1990, p. 56), so menacing to the moral and social order that ritual abuse constituted the "most serious threat to children and to society that we must face in our lifetime" (Summit, 1990, p. 39), produced a paucity of empirical studies,[5] contributed nothing to the refinement of psychological trauma theory, and left no legacy of innovations in the treatment of psychological trauma.

Despite that, the day care ritual abuse moral panic serves as a bridge to a more social/cultural understanding of psychological trauma in late-modern culture. Claims about trauma confer to claimants the status of victim; that status, in turn, grants them a moral right to demand attention, protection, compensation, justice and belief. When victims are young children, and the trauma is not just ordinary child abuse but the "ultimate evil" of ritual abuse, it is not just their moral right to make these demands, but the moral imperative of adults and social institutions to meet them.

The gravity of this moral imperative is evident in the discourse of child-savers who, during the day care ritual abuse moral panic, said things like this: "If there is even a small chance that one ritual abuse claim is true, we owe it to all potential victims to explore the problem of ritual abuse in greater depth" (Smith, 1993, p. vii), and "even if 10 percent of this stuff is true, then we're in big trouble" (Braun, 1988). Only in the presence of a moral imperative would paltry results of moral calculi such as these serve as both inspiration and incentive to keep pursuing day care ritual abuse in the absence of substantive evidence. Only in the presence of a moral imperative would subversively empirical questions like, what if only 5 percent of "this stuff" is true, or only 1 percent, or none of it all, be silenced by the damnation of *any* critical interrogative as traumagenic, in and of itself.

And only in the presence of a moral imperative would cocamamie conspiracy theories pass for fact, and egregious errors in sound reasoning be so generously forgiven. A brief exercise in the logic of late-modern therapeutic culture will illustrate this point. In this cultural milieu, the status of victim not only confers a moral right for redress, but affirms the presence of the stressor. In other words, to be a victim is to have been traumatized by *something*. That is why "trauma talk" is inherently political—it always reveals the causes of the victimization (Herman, 1992).[6] No victim of a concentration camp, say, can meaningfully tell his story without reference to the virulent anti–Semitism that dotted Europe with concentration camps to carry out the "Final Solution"; no victim of spouse abuse can give an account of her ordeal without some description of the dynamic of male privilege, even if it is contextualized no further than her own marital relationship. To fail, or to refuse for some reason, to talk about the cause of the victimization, the "stressor" as psychological trauma theory would refer to it, is to invite questions like, Why did that happen, and, more specifically, Why did that happen to you?

Child-savers were more than prepared to describe in Gothic detail *what* happened to children in the day care ritual abuse cases, *how* it happened, to *what* effect, and *who* was to blame, but that pressing question *why* demanded a wherefore. So they put into discursive circulation a cluster of haphazardly constructed conspiracy theories about satanic cults, WICCAN Letters, international child pornography rings, Freemasonry, occultism, paganism, demonic Nazis and CIA mind control experiments, to answer the niggling question, *why.* On their face, the conspiracy theories have little in common, but a more analytical reading of them reveals their close conformity to the culturally familiar classic conspiracy narrative.

Whether the stuff of comic books or political theories, mystery novels or popular eschatology, suspense films or cyberspace assassination theories, there are three invariant features of the classic conspiracy narrative, according to legal and communications scholar Mark Fenster (1999): an emphasis on individual agency, narrative velocity, and resistance to closure. All three are features of the ritual abuse conspiracy theories that, like other theories of their ilk, are discursive attempts to bind social anxiety into a populist answer to the question, *why*.

In all of the ritual abuse conspiracy theories, the child-savers as protagonists insert themselves into the historical moment with their description of their own confrontation with day care ritual abuse. Like a conversion experience, the encounters changes their world view, thus every conspiracy theory is peopled with demonic perpetrators and vulnerable children, and suffused with evil. In the words of psychiatrist Roland Summit (1994b): "The [discovery of ritual abuse] comes in little pieces. And when you see what you think is the picture, you see it everywhere."

Indeed, it is the "everywhereness" of the evil machinations that is a feature of the conspiracy theories. Whether in the iambic pentameter of Hallmark greeting cards, casual hand signals, silly nursery rhymes, or tote board figures of national telethons; in behind-closed-doors doings of the World Bank, AT&T, or the Federal Bureau of Investigation; in the person of international drug smugglers, morticians, politicians, or day care providers, evidence of the conspiracy is everywhere, everywhere. No wonder it is the moral imperative of child-savers to act, that is, to ferret it out of all of the cracks and crevices where it hides, and to warn others about it.

The theories describe the conspiracy as having penetrated the social and moral order, or at least as on the verge of doing so, and that urgency vests them with a narrative velocity measured in the effulgent flow of speculation, insinuation, rumination and imagination that is passed off as information. There is little logical coherence in this "information" or between the various ritual abuse conspiracy theories, but the apocalyptic ante always could be raised by little more than off-the-cuff remarks. Consider the comments of Ted Gunderson, the retired Federal Bureau of Investigation agent who led parents on the hunt for tunnels and secret rooms under the McMartin Preschool: "I can state without hesitation that there is indeed a national cult network, including satanic, witchcraft, and pedophilic groups, which is operating at full throttle in our society. The activities of these groups (it is in reality one group which operates on many levels) include the kidnapping and molestation of children, as well as the torture and murder of human beings" (cited in Earl, 1995, p. 131). In a single off-hand comment, he intertwines strands and wisps of disparate conspiracy theories—"satanic, witchcraft and pedophilic groups"—into something bigger—"*one* group"—more Gothically sinister—"operat[ing] on many levels"—and then vests it with the imprimatur of truth—"in reality." That is as good an example as there is of narrative velocity.

The ritual abuse conspiracy theories seductively flirt with closure, but never achieve it, that is, they never satisfactorily answer the question, *why*. The sheer volume of their narrative production precludes resolution; it simply is impossible to tie up all the loose ends, connect all the collusive dots, expose all the trickery and chicanery. The theories supped on the emotions generated by the day care ritual abuse moral panic; the emotions, in turn, supped on them. So as the moral panic dried up, the question *why* lost much of its urgency, and the conspiracy theories fell out of discursive existence. They left behind, though, what Fenster (1999, p. 130) would refer to as an "affective residue" of fear and suspicion that, at some time in the future when the *Zeitgeist* is favorable, can be discursively scraped up into another version of a classic conspiracy narrative.[7]

There is one last point about the ritual abuse conspiracy theories, and an important one at that: they are, when all is said and done, disempowering theories. Those who put them together waste their time pursuing, collecting and interpreting "stuff," flailing at spectral windmills, and weaving tangled webs of conspiratorial evil out of so much nonsense. An intricate web may bind conspiracy theorists and believers together, and keep others out, but it also binds them so tightly that they can neither think critically nor act effectively. Even Roland Summit (1994b), a decade after his involvement in the McMartin Preschool case, recognized this disempowerment:

> If everyone who disagrees with us is someone we see as the enemy, and if the next stage is if they disagree with us it's because they're one of them and they're out there to be agents of disinformation; and so, that person who disagrees with me is obviously my enemy; and if I'm not careful, he'll kill me. [If] we get into that kind of struggle, then in our attempts to attack or immobilize all those enemies, *we are paralyzed ourselves* [italics added].

Paralysis, as Summit refers to it, is yet another of the many ironies of the day care ritual abuse moral panic. In a phenomenological sense, paralysis is very much like the numbing and emotional anesthesia, loss of interest in activities, difficulty in concentration and experience of intrusive imagery that are the hallmark symptoms of psychological trauma. Their similarity blurs the line between healer and victim. Although they treat this finding as a virtue, psychologist Jill Waterman and social worker Mary Kay Oliveri (1993) reveal just how hazy that line really is. In their sample of 21 mental health clinicians who were treating alleged victims of day care ritual abuse, 78 percent described having symptoms that meet the diagnostic criteria for Post-Traumatic Stress Disorder.[8] Troubled by recurrent memories of their young patients' disclosures, hypervigilant to danger in their own lives, detached from those they loved as well as from their colleagues, whatever satisfaction these mental health clinicians felt about helping traumatized children was overshadowed by the dissatisfaction that they could not help themselves.

The psychological trauma literature is rife with personal narratives from and about "wounded healers"; indeed, the syndrome, if syndrome it is, even has its own diagnostic label: vicarious traumatization (McCann & Pearlman, 1990). But nowhere is the wound described as deeper, more painful, and more disabling than in the personal narratives of child-savers involved in the day care ritual abuse cases. The psychological trauma model emerged as one of the master symbols of the decade in the 1980s precisely because those confronting real traumatic stressors—rape, spouse abuse, war, torture, political oppression—refused to be disempowered. Ironic, is it not, that child-savers who created an unreal traumatic stressor in the form of day care ritual abuse, should be so disabled by their own creation?

Perhaps that is too strongly put. Child-savers undoubtedly would counter that they were far from paralyzed and would offer as proof the material consequences of their beliefs and interventions: the testimonial innovations that gave all victimized children their day in court; the increased enforcement of licensing standards that raised the quality of care for all children enrolled in day care; the creation of specialized units to investigate and to prosecute all cases of child abuse. They also might point out that their adamancy that ritual abuse is an exigent threat to children helped to increase awareness about child abuse in general, and about sexual abuse in particular, and that that awareness had both cultural and systemic consequences that benefited all children.

And in all of those assertions, they not only would be correct, but would be offering good examples of the irony of the day care ritual abuse moral panic. On the one hand, it distracted attention, time and resources from "real problems," such as ordinary child sexual abuse and the arrangements of patriarchal power and privilege that underlie it, while on the other hand, it created opportunities for those "real problems" to be heard and their underlying causes exposed and even redressed. But if child-savers were also to counter that the benefits of their actions against the traumatic stressor they created outweigh the costs, there would be more than good reason to beg to differ.

Consider, for example, the hidden costs racked up by something as simple as the ritual abuse symptom lists they assembled. The lists effectively convert the ups and downs of normal child development and the bumps and grinds of everyday family life into symptoms of trauma. Bad dreams that otherwise would have been seen as the simple residue of bad days, toileting accidents that would have been dismissed as just one of those things, temper tantrums that would have been patiently, or impatiently, dealt with, are seen as symptoms when looked at through the distorting carnival glass of the lists. Trauma becomes the contextual reference for child development, and family life becomes organized around it.

With what cost? In the absence of long-term follow-up or life course studies of the children involved in the day care ritual abuse cases—an absence that gives weight to the impression that children were used in this moral panic to achieve ends that had little to do with them—cost can only be measured in anecdotes. Perhaps the good stories are just not being told, because the anecdotes speak more of lingering pain and shame than of happiness and healing. There is the young woman who raged at Gerald "Tooky" Amirault's commutation hearing that her entire life had been ruined by ritual abuse at Fells Acres (Kurtz, 2001); the young man who, over a decade after the start of the McMartin Preschool case, still finds himself publicly defending the accuracy of his memories (Cerone, 1995); the 25 year old who posted an anonymous e-mail to PBS *Frontline's* web page to confess she had caved into pressure and had falsely accused the Small World Preschool providers of ritual abuse almost twenty years ago ("Did Daddy Do It?" 2002).

When family life is organized around the trauma of day care ritual abuse, then the family system also incurs the cost. The empirical studies conducted by Susan Kelley (1990, 1992) on the parents of the children involved in the Fells Acres case reveal the emotional toll the case had on them. When compared to the parents of children who had been sexually, not ritually, abused at other day care centers, the Fells Acres parents were significantly more psychologically distressed. The same can be said of the parents of the children in the McMartin Preschool case. Not only was their overall level of distress remarkably higher than that of parents whose children were sexually abused in other day care cases, but their frequent contacts and interactions with the media, the legal system, medical and mental health professionals decreased their trust in, and increased their disillusionment with, professionals and the organizations they represent (McCord, 1993a).

The erosion of trust in the marital relationship of parents in the McMartin Preschool case also is noted in empirical studies. Wives and husbands reported significant changes in communication and in intimacy, especially for the first year following their children's disclosures of ritual abuse. They disagreed on how to interact with their children, with wives tending to show more physical affection to them after disclosure, while husbands physically withdrawing, perhaps out of fear that displays of affection might be misinterpreted as sexual in intent by their traumatized children. Both wives and husbands tended towards leniency in disciplining their traumatized children, although that same tendency was often not extended to siblings (Waterman, 1993). Husbands often increased their consumption of alcohol and outbursts of aggression to cope with the stress; wives often battled depression, blaming themselves for sending their children to day care in the first place and for not seeing the symptoms that could have told the story of ritual abuse their children were too traumatized to tell (McCord, 1993b).

And what of communities and their institutions? Roland Summit had predicted it would take 20 years for Manhattan Beach to "reconstitute a comfortable sense of trust" after the McMartin Preschool and Manhattan Ranch ritual abuse cases ("Brink of Disaster?" 1984, p. 1). In defiance of his augury, the seaside community rebounded more quickly than that. By 1996 it was being described as a "prosperous enclave ... with a prestigious address" and the McMartin Preschool case was relegated to the same footnote that mentioned that decades before rattlesnakes used to sun on the boardwalk (Rasmussen, 1996).

Yet to say that all was well in Manhattan Beach in the late 1990s is to gloss over the costs incurred by that community and others to which to the day care ritual abuse moral panic had spread during the 1980s. Some of those costs were financial and easy enough to calculate: the drop in property values in the Country Walk subdivision when the infamous day care ritual abuse case by the same name was front page news (Adams, 1996); the loss of new business when a group of investors changed its mind about building a textile factory in North Carolina after watching PBS *Frontline's* documentary, "Innocence Lost" ("TV Show," 1993); the loss of old business when rumors and fears shut down day care centers in the wake of notorious local cases, and shot up insurance premiums to unaffordable rates; the exorbitant costs of the investigations and the trials of the accused providers.

If feelings and sentiments had price tags, the costs incurred by communities very well might be incalculable. Rumors, suspicions and fears took their toll in friendships, neighborliness, and daily commerce. In Edenton, North Carolina, a hamlet of 18th century houses fringing the choppy waters of Albemarle Sound local merchants, as if in defiance of the town's history as the intellectual center of Revolutionary resistance, refused to discuss the Little Rascals case with their customers because it was just plain bad for business (Leonnig, 1995). In Niles, Michigan, a rural community that proudly boasts 46 churches representing 24 different denominations, hardly a single religious leader sermonized about the Small World Preschool case because it was just too hard on faith. Antipathies led to discomfiting outbreaks of civil disorder. The McMartin Preschool was repeatedly vandalized with ominous graffito that read,

"Ray Will Die" (Citron, 1989); a vacant house, mistakenly believed to be owned by the Gallup family in Roseburg, Oregon was set afire (Lesson, October 18, 1989); shots were fired through the living room window of Gerald Amirault's home, not once but twice, the last time narrowly missing his wife and child (Taylor, 1986). It is in places like these, and the others overrun by the day care ritual abuse moral panic, that the activities of child-savers racked up considerable costs to such intangibles as sense of safety, community cohesion, interpersonal trust, and social ties.

There are institutional costs as well, also incurred in the currency of distrust, cynicism and outright hostility. When communities, indeed the entire nation, are as deeply divided as they are over the day care ritual abuse cases, institutions and those who represent them are blasted with equipotent vehemence for acting, and for not acting. The San Diego Grand Jury, convened to investigate child abuse in the county, ripped apart every systemic response to alleged cases of ritual abuse, from the media, to the local ritual abuse task force, to the Department of Social Services, to the San Diego Commission on Children and Youth, to the Children's Hospital Center for Child Protection, to the office of District Attorney Ed Miller, the state's longest serving prosecutor, who was roundly defeated for re-election just months after provider Dale Akiki was acquitted of all charges in the Faith Chapel case (San Diego Grand Jury, 1991/1992). The Utah State Task Force on Ritual Abuse (1992), on the other hand, criticized mental health clinicians, law enforcement officers, and district attorneys for failing to respond effectively to alleged cases of ritual abuse, and demanded more state funds for training, investigation and prosecution. In opposition to the commutation of Gerald "Tooky" Amirault in the Fells Acres case, angry parents, children and supporters marched through the streets of Boston where just a few years before, hundreds had met to commemorate the Day of Contrition. On that day, like the public officials 300 years before who had bowed their heads in shame for their roles in the Salem witch trials, the group asked for public apologies for the "plague of injustice" that had swept the country in the form of the day care ritual abuse moral panic. A touch of irony was added to that solemn day when a columnist for the very newspaper that would call for an end to the two decade-long "persecution" of the Amirault family, insisted that "even when the prosecution is overzealous, (e)ven when it is flawed, (e)ven when it is flat-out wrong," it is never persecutory to pursue alleged abusers of children (McNamara, 1997, p. B-1).

While the phrase "damned if you do, damned if you don't" comes easily to mind, it is the "real problems" stirring beneath the tranquility of this axiom that need attention because they are the ledger on which the social costs of child-saver activity is marked. It was these "real problems"—the loss of trust in traditional institutions, pervasive fears about the future, ontological insecurity, and an aching nostalgia for an earlier better and safer time—that were signified by the master symbol of the psychological trauma model, and that were constituent of the cause of the day care ritual abuse moral panic in the first place. So the question must be asked: did the activities of child-savers do anything at all to reveal these "real problems" beneath the master symbol, or to allay them? The answer is an unequivocal, *no*.

By discursively constructing an imaginary traumatic stressor out of remnants of folklore, occultism, paganism, New Christian Rightist images of premillennarian evil, and utter inanity, child-savers only reified those underlying "real problems." By discursively creating disempowering conspiracy theories that implicate the organizations, traditions, and symbols of contemporary culture, and then identifying that most innocuous of social institutions, the local day care center, as the scene of the crime of the "ultimate evil" of ritual abuse, they empowered these underlying "real problems" to affect everyday life. On this moral ledger, the costs of child-saver activities far outweigh any benefits.

And So...?

Through the lens of the master symbols of the 1980s, the tendentious nature of the day care ritual abuse moral panic is evident. Although, with a touch of irony, it did provide glimpses of insight about "real problems" and quick opportunities for their expression and redress, in the end it served the status quo, and impeded real social change.

It littered the moral landscape with new experts, programs, laws and hardened attitudes that made it seem, for a decade, that a demonic threat to the social and moral order was heroically being battled. But stripped of all of its distracting Gothic frippery, its conservative and preservative nature is revealed. The day care ritual abuse moral panic was little more than a late-modern version of a very old, and very familiar morality play about innocent children, demonic threats, heroic rescuers, and the inevitability of sexual violence. When all is said and done, society was no safer or better for having experienced it—and neither were its children.

BEYOND CLACTON-ON-SEA

In the anniversary edition of his groundbreaking study, *Folk Devils and Moral Panics* (1972/2002), Stanley Cohen looks back on 30 years and concludes that the objects of moral panics have proved quite predictable: working class violence, school violence, drugs, welfare cheats and single mothers, media sex and violence, and sexual threats to children. He illustrates the latter with brief discussions about the contemporary moral panics over missing and abducted children, pedophile networks, and recovered memories of sexual abuse, and uses all to support a larger point that in these moral panics real threats to children are massaged and manipulated to serve larger ideological and material ends. But, as Cohen points out, the day care ritual abuse moral panic is different in that the threat to children is fictitious, thus it constitutes in his considered opinion, "One of the purest cases of moral panic" (p. xv).

That an imaginary threat is given a discursive reality is, in fact, only one feature of the day care ritual abuse moral panic that distinguishes it from most others. It is also a multi-mediated panic, represented not just in the steady stream of words from the mouths and pens of child-savers who constituted its interest group, but in films, television talk shows, documentaries, religious and secular fiction, cyberspace chat rooms, internet web sites, trial transcripts, and daily discourse.

Through these media, the moral panic crossed community, state, national and international boundaries with ease, and with each crossing it took on local color. Unlike most moral panics, this one is not culture-bound. It is, instead, protean. Its migration across North America, Western Europe and Australasia assured its variability by attaching new culturally resonant claims, different interest groups, and fresh policy responses to it as it spread.

In the United States, where the day care ritual abuse moral panic began and from which it spread internationally, the folk devils are quite unlike those of other moral panics. The demonized day care providers were well-regarded by their communities and well-integrated into them. Far from sinister, far from marginalized, they had become vulnerable to the vagaries of panic discourse by an entirely unique route: the loss of social honor attached to their role as surrogate parents to the country's youngest children. The loss of social honor, though, did not deprive them of cultural capital. Far from the defenseless, ineffectual folk devils of other moral panics, the providers fought back. They asserted their innocence and actively resisted their demonization, and in doing so, they impacted the course of the day care ritual abuse moral panic over time, shaped public discourse, and challenged efforts at social control. And so did those who resisted recruitment into the ideology of this moral panic. Its persuasive rhetoric not withstanding, not everyone was convinced that the accused providers were guilty of anything, let alone ritual abuse. Their contrary and advocatory discourse and actions also influenced the course and content of the day care ritual abuse moral panic.

Finally, the end results of the day care ritual abuse moral panic are different than those of most moral panics as well. While it did act tendentiously by distracting and concealing its own causes and thwarting any meaningful social change, it also provided glimpses into the "real problems" that caused it, as well as opportunities, albeit fleeting, to redress them. It was, in effect, a courier for both dominant interests and values, and their challengers for hegemony, simultaneously serving contradictory social ends.

All of these unique qualities make certain demands of moral panic theory. Still clad in its Clacton-on-Sea mod clothes and winkle-picker shoes, the theory is in need of a makeover if it is to retain its explanatory and analytical power in a complexly differentiated, multi-mediated, late-modern world.

After all, when all is *finally* said and done, the day care ritual abuse moral panic may not resemble most other moral panics, but it is more than a little likely that it looks an awful lot like those yet to come.

Notes

Chapter 1

1. The term "child-savers" is used to indicate the wide array of variously qualified, differently motivated, professionals, advocates and lay-persons who constituted the loosely organized interest group that advanced the day care ritual abuse moral panic.

2. All statistics cited are the result of a search of the Odum Institute Public Opinion Question Data Base which can be found on the World Wide Web at <http://www.irss.unc.edu/data_archive/pollsearch.html>.

3. The most notable of those cases involved the British heavy metal group Judas Priest. The parents of two teenage boys who attempted suicide, one successfully and the other not, after listening to hours of music, sued the heavy metal group, claiming that subliminal messages embedded in the music of its album "Stained Glass" encouraged suicide. Pretrial hearings featured expert testimony on subliminal messages, including that of a salesman with a Ph.D. from a mail-order degree mill who opined that subliminal messages have supernatural power; a probation officer who had published a manual on "depunking" fans of heavy metal music; Dr. Wilson Key, author of *Subliminal Seduction*, who pointed out subliminal sexual messages in Rembrandt paintings, Ritz Cracker boxes and Abraham Lincoln's beard on $5 bills; and Professor Howard Shevrin, a University of Michigan psychoanalytically trained psychologist who testified that subliminal messages prove the existence of the subconscious mind. Only Shevrin's testimony was allowed in trial. The Judge ruled against the parents in

1990, stating that although there were subliminal messages in the music, there was no evidence they had been intentionally placed there, and only questionable evidence that they exert any influence on behavior. For a more detailed discussion of the case, see Medway (2001) and Richardson (1991).

4. The parent was Pat Pulling whose teenage son, a devoted Dungeons and Dragons player, had committed suicide rather than kill his family, which he had been "cursed" to do by the Dungeon Master. Pulling started the group BADD (Bothered about Dungeons and Dragons) and became a high-profile critic of all fantasy role-playing games, appearing often on Christian radio and television talk shows, and lecturing to cult-cops and mental health professionals who work with adolescents. Pulling, a fundamentalist Christian, believed these games taught the demonologies of witchcraft and devil worship. Five years after her son's 1982 suicide, Pulling was advertising herself as an "occult investigator" and was offering seminars on satanism and consulting on "occult-related" cases throughout the country. For a critical review of Pulling's role as a moral entrepreneur, see Stackpole (1989).

5. In Michelle's account, "Malachi" was the leader of the coven of satanists who were ritually abusing her. Folklorist Bill Ellis (2000) suggests that while the name "Malachi" seems a bit unusual for a satanist, given that it is the name of both a minor prophet and a book of the Old Testament, it is the first name of former priest Malachi Martin whose book, *Hostage to the Devil* (1976), is credited with renewing interest in the ancient rite of exorcism by Catholics. For an extended discussion of

Martin's role in contemporary demon-mongering, see Cuneo (2001).

6. In a 1990 interview with the British press, Pazder claimed that he had consulted on 1,000 alleged cases of ritual abuse in North America and Europe (Allen & Midwinter, 1990, September 30).

7. For example, Rebecca Brown's, *He came to Set the Captives Free* (1986) is the story of how she rescued one of her patients, Elaine, a former high priestess of an international satanic cult bent on world domination and a ritual abuser herself, and "detoxified" her of her satanic belief system. Her account, meant to be a testimony to the redeeming power of the Christian faith, can only be taken as such if the reader is blissfully ignorant of the fact that the pseudonymous "Elaine" has a suspicious history of lying and fantasizing, and the pseudonymous author had lost her license to practice medicine for abusing controlled substances, falsifying patient records, and diagnosing demon possession as the cause of her patients' various ailments (Fisher, Blizard, & Goedelman, 1989).

Chapter 2

1. The "Naked Movie Star" game, according to some children, was introduced by a song that went like this: "What you say is what you are/You're a naked movie star." To folklorists, the song is reminiscent of other rhymed schoolyard taunts, such as "I am rubber/ You are Glue/Everything bad you say/Bounces off me/And sticks on you" (Nathan & Snedeker, 1995, p. 74).

2. Child-savers were convinced that pornography was the primary motive in the McMartin Preschool case. In a *Los Angeles Times* interview, Deputy District Attorney Eleanor Barrett estimated that the providers could have produced and sold "millions of child pornography photographs and films" (Rohrlich & Welkosp, 1984, p. II–1). Despite an intensive investigation conducted by local and state police and the Federal Bureau of Investigation, and the offer of a $10,000 reward for any photograph or film featuring a McMartin Preschool child, no evidence of pornography was discovered in this, or any other, day care ritual abuse case.

3. In March 1985, the same month Judy Johnson was hospitalized for a psychotic

episode, a cadre of parents and their children descended on the McMartin Preschool property to search for tunnels and a subterranean chamber that some of the children had described in their interviews. None was found by them, nor by the archaeological firm hired by the District Attorney's office.

The "dark tunnels of McMartin," as Roland Summit (1994a) refers to them, would consume that group of parents for many years, and would become part of the folklore of the day care ritual abuse moral panic. In a case where the only evidence was the often uncertain and implausible disclosures of young children, the discovery of tunnels certainly would resolve any lingering skepticism about the truth of their disclosures. The parents hired their own archaeologist, Gary Stickle, to excavate the property. His 185-page report, an executive summary of which can be found on the World Wide Web at <http://www. tesserae.org/tess/prose/tunnels2.html>, that cites finding two filled in tunnels, four feet high and three to nine feet wide, leading to a nine foot chamber, is heralded by Summit as offering "unprecedented dimensions of truth" to the allegations of the children.

"Dimensions" of truth often are taken *as* truth in a moral panic. But this truth has tarnished dimensions that too frequently go unnoticed. For example, the report remains unpublished and therefore not subject to peer review by scientists, nor critical evaluation by other interested readers; its author's expertise and ethics have been questioned by his colleagues in other archeological projects; its findings were not confirmed by either the archeological firm hired by the District Attorney, or a geologist hired by the parents; and its description of the location of the tunnels does not correspond with descriptions offered by the children. In addition, there is evidence that the parents planted some of the more incriminating "artifacts" at the site (Earl, 1995; Nathan & Snedeker, 1995). Yet the sheer repetition of the finding of the "dark tunnels of McMartin" made a "truth" of what was fated to remain only a "dimension" of truth when the preschool was leveled to make way for a three-story office building in 1990.

4. Bob Currie, a mortgage banker and real estate investor, quit working in order

to investigate the alleged satanic angle in the McMartin Preschool case. In addition to appearing on local and national television news and talk shows, Currie held a press conference in 1985 with seven alleged victims, hidden behind a backlighted screen. In it, Currie announced an initiative to "show that ritualistic abuse is happening all across this country." To further that initiative, he started a ritual abuse hotline and offered a $10,000 reward for any of the pornographic photographs or films allegedly taken at the McMartin Preschool (Sharpe, 1986, p. A-6).

5. In 1984, Johnson's allegations, made on behalf of her son, became bizarre and incomprehensible. She claimed that her son had been taken to an armory where he was ritually abused in the presence of a "goatman"; that Peggy McMartin Buckey drilled a hole in a child's armpit; that Raymond Buckey flew in the air and that the other providers were dressed in witch costumes; that Betty Raidor had buried him in a coffin and Babette Spitler had put scissors in his eyes; that her son had been hurt by a lion, witnessed the decapitation of a baby, was forced to drink blood, and had his eyes, nipples and tongue stapled (cited in Nathan & Snedeker, 1995, pp. 84–85). She also told prosecuting attorneys that her son had been sexually abused his father, and AWOL Marine, employees of a local gym, and members of the Los Angeles School Board, and that someone had broken into her home and sodomized her dog.

Johnson had become reclusive, and when her brother attempted to make contact, she greeting him with a shotgun. Police and hostage negotiators were called to the scene and Johnson was taken to a psychiatric facility where she was diagnosed with paranoid schizophrenia.

Johnson's disclosures to the prosecutors and her threatening behavior led to an interesting twist in the McMartin Preschool case. Former Deputy District Attorney, Glenn Stevens, who was removed from the prosecution team when he expressed doubts over the guilt of the providers, testified in the trial of Raymond Buckey and Peggy McMartin Buckey that he had complied with the order of lead prosecutor Lael Rubin and had withheld evidence from the defense about Johnson's bizarre allegations and subsequent hospitalization. Although Stevens originally had recommended that charges be filed only against Raymond Buckey in this case, he testified that he no longer believed that Buckey was guilty (Timnick, January 21, 1987).

The role of Stevens in the McMartin Preschool case is Gothically ambiguous. To the supporters of the McMartin providers, he was a man of conscience; to his colleagues and superiors, he was an opportunist who colored the facts to his own advantage; to child-savers, he was a pariah who lied and then tried to profit from his deceit by offering to sell inside information about the case to screenwriter Abby Mann. Regardless of his image, there is no doubt that his testimony, and the sudden introduction into evidence of the audiotaped diary of his involvement in the case which he claimed he had lost, provided some riveting moments in the trial. So did the subsequent cross-examination in which Stevens admitted that he had never really concluded that Johnson was mentally ill, although he considered it a real possibility; that he had attempted to set up a meeting with Johnson to solicit her assistance in writing a screenplay about the case in partnership with Abby Mann; and that it was Mann who had suggested to him that Johnson may have tainted the case by calling other McMartin Preschool parents (Timnick, January 24, 1987).

Chapter 3

1. At the 8th National Conference on Child Abuse and Neglect, for example, Summit began his presentation on ritual abuse with the exhortation, "Down with doubt!" (cited in The National Resource Center on Child Sexual Abuse, 1989, p. 81).

2. This was the Bakersfield/Kern County case that began in 1982 when a 5 year old, upon being questioned and genitally examined by her grandmother, said that she and her sister had been sexually abused by their parents and others during orgies in the family home. Her parents, Debbie and Alvin McCuan, and their friends Brenda and Scott Kniffen, were arrested. Under intense interrogation, the Kniffen's young sons, named as victims by the McCuan girls, agreed they, too, had been abused, and agreed to testify against their parents. The two couples were convicted in 1984; their sentences were overturned on appeal in 1996.

The McCuan/Kniffen case led to a wide-spread search for other children victimized in the orgies the McCuan girls described. Three young brothers were among those questioned, and after repeated interviews with the police and social workers who were influenced by the satanic trappings being reported about the nearby McMartin preschool case, the oldest described orgies directed by his father, Rick Pitts, in a "Satanic Church." In the ensuing investigation, 75 local people were arrested, scores were convicted and sentenced to some of the longest prison sentences in state history.

In 1985 a grand jury convened to look into the case. Its report, sharply critical of the investigation and the interrogation of the children, many of whom had been taken from their homes and placed in psychiatric facilities where they were drugged and interviewed on a daily basis, called for a full inquiry. Published in 1986, the $500,000 inquiry found 23 procedural errors that called into question the credibility of the children's allegations and the security of the subsequent convictions (Van de Kamp, 1986). Although the inquiry helped secure the releases of many of those convicted in the Bakersfield/Kern County case, as late as 2003 two defendants, Grant Self and John Stoll, remain in prison. For an expose of the case against them, see<http://users.erols.com/mpeters5/kstoll1.htm>

3. In their study of persuasion in everyday life, Pratkanis and Aronson (1992) define a factoid as an "assertion of fact that is not backed up by evidence, usually because the fact is false or because evidence in support of the assertion cannot be obtained" (p. 71).

4. A sample of videos produced on the subject of ritual abuse reveals the intimate alliance between the mental health community and New Christian Rightists. Cultivate Ministry, for example, produced "Revival of Evil"; Passport Ministry produced "America's Best Kept Secret"; Followers of Jesus Christ Ministry produced "Satanic Ritual Abuse and Secret Societies"; and Cephas Ministry produced "Satanic Ritual Abuse."

Other videos widely disseminated among child-savers include, "An Overview of Ritual Abuse, Mind Control and Dissociation," and "Trauma-Mediated Learning and Altered States of Consciousness," produced by the Freedom of Thought Forum in Tucson, Arizona, that features psychologist J. Randy Noblitt who was an expert witness in the Fran's Day Care case and is a founding member of the International Council on Cultism and Ritual Trauma; "Satanism and the CIA," produced by Preferred Network in Edmonton, Canada, in which retired FBI agent Ted Gunderson explicates the link between the McMartin Preschool case and the CIA's illicit trafficking of drugs and pornography.

Cavalcade Productions in Nevada City, California, produced and distributed "Children at Risk in America—Satanic Ritual Abuse, the Cover-up of the Century," an expose of the "international satanic conspiracy" that had infiltrated day care centers; "Sessions and Sand Trays," that features psychologist Roberta Sachs who with colleague psychiatrist Bennett Braun specialized in treating ritual abuse cases; and "Treatment of Ritually Abused Children: Identification of the Ritually Abused Child," that gives psychologist Catherine Gould a platform for presenting her ritual abuse symptom and indicator list.

Audiotapes of conference presentations on ritual abuse also were sold by distributors and even marketed on Christian radio and television talk shows, and in the newsletters of such conservative Christian groups as the "pro-family, anti-feminism" Eagle Forum, under the leadership of Phyllis Schafley; Exodus, an organization dedicated to "freedom from homosexuality through the power of Jesus Christ"; and the Cult Crime Network, an organization of Christian cult-cops formed by Larry Jones.

5. Braun's ignominious fall from grace began in 1986 when he started treating Patricia Burgus for depression. Within a year, he had diagnosed the hospitalized Burgus as suffering from multiple personality disorder and through recovered memory therapy, stiff doses of mind-altering drugs, and day-long hypnosis sessions, he determined that she had been ritually abused as a child and programmed by the cult to be the high priestess of a Midwestern satanic cult. After Burgus's two sons were also diagnosed as ritual abuse victims and hospitalized for three years, and her medication level was reduced when her $3 million insurance policy dried up, she filed

a suit against Braun, alleging gross negligence; dishonorable, unethical and unprofessional conduct; making false or misleading statements; and improper prescription of controlled substances, including Inderal, a blood pressure drug, administered at a dosage level that had not been tested on animals, let alone humans. Braun settled the suit in October 1997 for $10.6 million. In 1999, after having settled yet another multi-million dollar suit by another adult patient, Mary Shanley, whom he also had diagnosed with multiple personality disorder brought on by childhood ritual abuse, and facing multiple charges of professional misconduct, Braun surrendered his medical license for two years, and agreed to an additional 5 years probation. Braun was expelled permanently from the Illinois Psychiatric Society and the American Psychiatric Association. For a compilation of information and a summary of court actions in the cases against Braun, see the False Memory Syndrome Foundation (1995). The case against Braun was documented by film-maker Ofra Bikel for the PBS *Frontline* series, titled "The Search for Satan," aired in November 1995.

Hammond did not so much fall from grace, as step away from it. His much touted "Dr. Greenbaum" account became the subject of considerable skepticism as the moral panic progressed, and as some mental health professionals who took his notion of satanic programming literally and subjected their patients to months, even years, of stressful "deprogramming," lost their licenses to practice.

6. A sample of television talk shows that featured the topic of ritual abuse includes: "Satanism" (1988), "Sex in the Name of Satan" (1991), and "A Satanic Cult Survivor" (1991) on *Larry King Live;* "Witchcraft" (1986), "Satanic Worship" (1988), "Preschool Ritual Abuse" (1990) on *Oprah;* "Satanism" (1988), "Baby-Breeders, Parts 1 and 2" (1989), "Devil Babies" (1991), "I was Raised in a Satanic Cult" (1992), and "They Told Me I Have the Devil Inside Me" (1992) on *Sally Jesse Raphael;* "Witchcraft" (1986), "Satanic Cults and Children" (1987), "Teen Satanism" (1988), "Satanic Breeders" (1988), "Drugs, Death and the Devil" (1989), "Satan's Black Market" (1989), and "Recovered Memories" (1991) on *Geraldo.*

7. Although the Believe the Children

organization no longer exists, its egregiously out-of-date list of ritual abuse convictions is alive and well on the internet. Among other URL's, it can be retrieved on the World Wide Web at <http://www.healingroads.org/ra_cases.html>

Chapter 4

1. In the Breezy Point case, however, a parent did videotape her own interrogation of her daughter and turned the tape over to the police (Rubenstein, 1990).

2. One of the things that child-savers believe distinguishes the Country Walk case from most of the other day care ritual abuse cases is that the children's allegations are backed up by "hard evidence" in the form of positive findings for gonorrhea. Fuster's son, Noël, had been tested along with the children in his father and stepmother's care; his were the only results that came back positive. Although the Braga's got the 6 year old to admit that his father had forced him to fellate him, he retracted the allegation a month later. For Noël's recollection of this interview with the Braga's, see<http://www.pbs.org/wgbh/ pages/frontline/shows/fuster/interviews/goodman.html > It is interesting to note that four years after the test was administered to Noël, the Centers for Disease Control warned that it was highly unreliable and prone to false positive findings (Whittington, Rice, Biddle, & Knaff (1988). Fuster's pretrial test for gonorrhea was negative.

Chapter 5

1. Fuster was convicted in 1982 of sexually fondling the 9 year old daughter of a family friend. He had vigorously denied the charge, and had passed two polygraph tests (Nathan & Snedeker, 1995).

2. Lauren Stratford's autobiography, *Satan's Underground* (1988), describes years of ghastly ritual abuse culminating in forced impregnations so that the satanic cult that was holding her captive could sacrifice the babies she bore. The book was the inspiration for the "satanic breeder" tales told by scores of women who were recovering memories of childhood ritual abuse. Despite the book's influence, and Stratford's popularity on the radio and tele-

vision talk show circuit, her account has been disproved on even the most banal of details by investigative journalists (Passantino, Passantino, & Trott, 1990); the book was withdrawn by her publisher, Harvest House, in 1990. Stratford, who had attempted to insinuate herself into the McMartin Preschool investigation by claiming that she had had a lesbian affair with Virginia McMartin who had confided in her about ritually abusing the children in her care, now remembers that it was not really a satanic cult that had held her captive as a child, but a cadre of Nazis. She now is claiming that she is one of only a handful of survivors of the deadly medical experiments conducted by Dr. Joseph Mengele during World War II on Jewish children in Auschwitz concentration camp (Passantino, Passantino, & Trott, 1999).

3. The WICCA Letters, widely circulated among child-savers, are the product of the fertile imagination of San Diego County Deputy Sheriff Dave Gaerin who said he had discovered them in an issue of an obscure Christian fundamentalist newsletter, and then had "translated" them for reproduction and dissemination. Reminiscent of the notorious "Protocols of the Learned Elders of Zion," a fabricated document alleging a Jewish conspiracy to take over the world, and used as justification for the Holocaust, the Letters are the supposed plan for world domination put together by international satanists who convened in Mexico City in 1981. The seven-point plan, with point 5-b focusing on day care centers, is as follows (cited in Carlson & O'Sullivan, 1989, p. 102):

1. Bring about covens, both black and white magic, into one and have the actress to govern all—ACCOMPLISHED

2. Bring about personal debts causing discord and disharmony within families—ACCOMPLISHED

3. Remove or educate the "new age youth" by:
   a. infiltrating boys/girls' clubs and big sister/brother programs
   b. infiltrating schools, having prayers removed, having teachers teach about drugs, sex, freedoms
   c. instigating and promoting rebellion against parents and all authority
   d. promoting equal rights for youth—ACCOMPLISHED

4. Gain access to all people's backgrounds and vital information by:
   a. use of computers
   b. convenience
   c. infiltration—ACCOMPLISHED

5. Have laws changed to benefit our ways, such as:
   a. removing children from the home environment and placing them in foster homes
   b. mandatory placement of children in our day care centers
   c. increased taxes
   d. open drugs and pornography market to everyone—ACCOMPLISHED

6. Destroy government agencies by:
   a. overspending
   b. public opinion
   c. being on the offensive always, opposing, demonstrating, demoralizing—NOT YET ACCOMPLISHED

7. Not to be revealed until all else has been accomplished. Target date for revelation—June 21, 1986—the beginning of the Summer Solstice and great feast on the Satanic Calendar.

4. When Aquino filed a libel suit against Blood, Warner Books withdrew *The New Satanists* (Hughes, 1994).

5. The Presidio case has a lively discursive existence on the Internet, largely due to the postings by "Curio Jones" whose mission it was to unmask all those involved in a vast satanic conspiracy targeting young children. Although "Curio Jones" took on those accused in the day care ritual abuse cases and the critics of the very notion of ritual abuse with equal fervor, Aquino appeared to be her favorite target.

In 2000, a couple of cybersleuths set out to unmask "Curio Jones." They discovered that she was actually Diana Napolis, a 44 year old former child protection investigator from La Mesa, California (Sauer, 2000). From that point, the mystery becomes a tragedy. In the months following her unmasking, Napolis came to believe that she was "being used to field-test some unusual new technology which included cybertronics and the implantation of a device behind the optic nerve which allows others to monitor one on a computer terminal from a distance" (Napolis, 2002). One of the "others" in this case was filmmaker Steven Spielberg who took out a restraining order against Napolis when she harangued him via telephone (*Spielberg v. Napolis*, 2002); another was singer/actress Jennifer Love Hewitt. Napolis's stalking of Hewitt, her physical altercations with her, and the death threats she made against her resulted in six felony charges. In late 2002 a hearing was held to determine if Napolis, who was being detained in the county jail, was competent to stand trial on those chargs. The court determined that she was not, and she was committed to Patton State Hospital (Sauer, 2002).

6. Florida's Alfred Rule allows a defendant to maintain innocence yet enter a guilty plea if he or she believes the plea is in his or her best interest.

7. Rumors, allegedly leaked from the prosecutor's office, circulated among reporters and Wee Care parents that Kelly Michaels indeed had been sexually abused as a child. One version of the rumor blamed her mother, another her father, and still another both parents acting in concert. The rumors were given substance by the testimony of a corrections officer who swore on the stand that she had witnessed Michaels's father fondling her during a visit. Rumors also spread that her mother sent her nude photographs of herself, her 81 year old grandmother sent her cocaine, and that her incestuous father would call her daily while she was working at Wee Care to find out how she was doing in indoctrinating the children into pederasty. The press took to calling her "The Demon Seed" amongst themselves (Nathan, 1995; Rabinowitz, 1990).

8. Psychologist J. Randy Noblitt Ph.D. founded the Society for the Investigation, Treatment and Prevention of Cult Ritual Abuse in 1993, renamed the International Council on Cultism and Ritual Trauma in 1995, the same year that its annual conference was the subject of a participant-observation study conducted by Temple University social psychology graduate student, Evan Harrington (1996). The 200 or so professionals and lay-persons attending the Dallas, Texas conference listened to a veritable who's-who of child-savers, conspiracy theorists and converted cultists whose talks showed just how slippery the very notion of ritual abuse had become at the end of the moral panic. Among those speaking were author Walter Browart who claimed the False Memory Syndrome Foundation which, among other things, dismisses recovered memories of childhood ritual abuse as fallacious, is actually a Central Intelligence Agency project to discredit mental health professionals who specialize in recovered memory cases; Doc Marqui, a self-proclaimed former witch, who told his audience that former President Bill Clinton is the Anti-Christ; former Federal Bureau of Investigation agent Ted Gunderson who presented even more "new" evidence, this in the form of photographs of a burned-out house, to substantiate accounts by some of the McMartin Preschool children that they had been taken there to be ritually abused by robed and hooded strangers; former Nebraska State Senator John DeCamp, author of *The Franklin Cover-up* (1992), who claimed that some of the country's elite political conservatives were involved in a ritual abuse ring; Michigan native Cathy O'Brien who described how she was brainwashed by a secret government mind control project into having sex with then First Lady, now Senator, Hillary Clinton, former Presidents Ronald Reagan, George Bush, Jimmy Carter, and Gerald Ford, the latter of whom, a fellow Michiganian, she referred to as the "neighborhood porn king"; and psychologist Catherine Gould who, in an advanced workshop on mind control, conceded that she simply does not understand why satanists, who engage in the high risk behaviors of blood-drinking and "unsafe cult sex," are not "dropping like flies" from AIDS. The conference offered continuing education credits through the Texas State Board of Licensed Professional Counselors.

Chapter 6

1. It is not known with certainty how many accused providers were given polygraph tests, or if any failed the test. What is known, though, is that in addition to "Mrs. Janet B.," Kelly Michaels in the Wee Care case, Richard Barkman in the Small World Preschool case, and Dale Akiki in the Faith Chapel case all took and passed polygraphs.

2. Justice Scalia wrote the stinging dissent to the majority decision: "Seldom has this Court failed so conspicuously to sustain a categorical guarantee of the Consti-

tution against the tide of prevailing current opinion... It is not within our charge to speculate that 'where face-to-face confrontation causes significant emotional distress in a child witness,' confrontation might 'in fact disserve the confrontation clause's truth-seeking goal.' If so, that is a defect in the Constitution—which should be amended by the procedures provided for such an eventuality, but cannot be corrected by judicial pronouncement that it is archaic, contrary to 'widespread belief' and thus null and void. For good or bad, the Sixth Amendment requires confrontation, and we are not at liberty to ignore it" (*Maryland v. Craig*, 1990).

3. Non-disclosure agreements between insurance companies, providers and litigious parents makes it difficult to assess just how much money traded hands in the flurry of law suits following each of the day care ritual abuse cases in the sample, but a conservative estimate would $50 million.

4. Roland Summit (1992) describes his child sexual abuse accommodation syndrome as a "clinical observation that has become both elevated as gospel and denounced as dangerous pseudoscience" (p. 153). He blames the denunciation on his unfortunate choice of the word "syndrome," which he intended to be synonymous with "description," but was understood by others, particularly the courts, as being more akin to "diagnosis." Said Summit, "Had I known the legal consequences at the time, I might have chosen a name like the Child Sexual Abuse Accommodation *Pattern* to avoid any pathological or diagnostic implications" (p. 157).

5. The panopticon was the sinister invention of the 18th century British moral philosopher and jurist, Jeremy Bentham. It was a circular prison with cells arranged in a layer of rings around a central observation tower. A single inmate occupied each cell, subject to the constant gaze of the guards in the tower who looked through slots so the inmate does not know when he is being watched—only that he *is* being watched. In sociologist Michel Foucault's (1981) assessment, the panopticon represents the very essence of power.

6. VOCAL (Victims of Child Abuse Laws) was formed in the mid–1980s by parents who were falsely accused in the Jordan, Minnesota case. The case began when a woman reported her live-in boyfriend and convicted child molester, James Rud, had sexually abused her daughter. Rud confessed, but implicated the child's mother and other adults in the abuse. As the investigation proceeded, scores of local children in the small town were identified as victims of a ritual abuse ring involving dozens of adults. A total of 24 people were arrested. The case culminated in the conjoint trial of Robert and Lois Bentz who were acquitted of all charges when their two youngest children retracted their allegations while on the witness stand. The charges against the remaining adults were dismissed; Rud, in exchange for his cooperation, received a 40 year sentence (de Young, 2002, pp. 60–64).

VOCAL has branch offices in every state and many foreign countries. It is dedicated to protecting children from what it calls the abusive behavior of the very agencies that are in place to protect children (Wimberley, 1994).

7. Chris Bean was Kelly's original defense attorney. When he came to believe his own son was ritually abused by Kelly at Little Rascals, he resigned, and then testified against him at his trial.

8. This is a paraphrase of Reinhold Niebuhr's (1944) statement that "Man's capacity for justice makes democracy possible, but man's inclination to injustice makes democracy necessary."

Chapter 7

1. Waterhouse does not mention it, but when the case went before a hearing, the judge dismissed the ritual abuse allegation as fanciful and declared that the boy's mother, who was divorced from his father, had put him up to the satanic symptoms. For a brief discussion of the case, and more elaborate discussion of the British precursors to the panic, see Medway (2001).

2. In the Broxtowe Estate case, 18 children from related families were taken into care for sexual abuse; 10 family members were arrested on 53 counts of incest and child cruelty, and were sentenced to a total of 48 years. The ritual abuse allegations emerged when the children were in foster care and being interviewed frequently by social workers. An intensive police investigation, labeled Project Gollom, failed to

find evidence to substantiate the children's allegations. The rift that developed between social workers and the police led to the formation of a joint inquiry into the case that was completed in late 1989. Although the 650-page report is confidential, a summary of its findings has been published in written form, and posted on the internet (Nottinghamshire County Council, 1990).

3. A little aside: the family of the Rochdale boy who had made the initial allegation in the Langley Estate case had had their previous flat exorcised when they suspected it was haunted by ghosts, and one of the accused parents in the Liverpool case was a practicing WICCAN.

4. In support of this statement, it is interesting to note that the ritual abuse moral panic has not been documented in Asian, Mediterranean, Middle Eastern or Eastern European countries which have distinct and different philosophies about child protection, and different practices (Pringle, 1998).

Chapter 8

1. Second-wave claims-makers who were helping adults recover childhood memories of ritual abuse also formed their own organization: The International Society for the Study of Dissociation and Multiple Personality (ISSDMP), now named the International Society for the Study of Dissociation (ISSD). Past presidents include ritual abuse aficionados Bennett Braun and Colin Ross.

2. The same cannot be said of recovered memory cases. There have been dozens of suits against mental health professionals for the implantation of false memories of childhood ritual abuse, and many have resulted in the suspension or the forfeiture of professional licenses.

3. This steady progression seems to have reached its apogee by the turn into the new millennium when, in the time-honored fashion of professions and bureaucracies everywhere, ruckuses began breaking out over ownership of the problem of child sexual abuse. By 2002, law professor and child advocate John E.B. Myers was urging the interdisciplinary membership of the International Society for the Prevention of Child Abuse and Neglect to pull together with "each discipline coordinating its

efforts with the others" (p. 566). The times had definitely changed.

4. Examples of the wide net cast by the notion of psychological trauma can be found in a simple survey of the contents of the *Journal of Traumatic Stress,* published by the International Society for Traumatic Stress Studies. Volume 15 of the journal covers 2002 and features articles on the prevalence of PTSD for international peacekeepers and human rights workers; victims of sexual harassment, rape, childhood sexual abuse, and family violence; political prisoners, torture victims and refugees; earthquake and hurricane survivors; AIDS and breast cancer patients; car crash victims; firefighters and rescue workers; combat soldiers and veterans; care providers and mental health professionals.

5. Empirical studies on the children involved in the day care ritual abuse cases are few and far between. Of note are the studies of the children in the Fells Acres case (Kelley, 1989, 1990, 1992, 1993), and the National Center on Child Abuse and Neglect funded study that included some of the children in both the McMartin Preschool and the Manhattan Ranch cases (Waterman, Kelly, Oliveri, & McCord, 1993). A stunning omission from the literature on ritual abuse is any study that examines the long-term effects or the life course trajectory of children involved in the day care ritual abuse cases.

6. To follow this logic a little further, consider what happens when the link between victim and stressor, or the personal and the political, is effaced by false claims of victim status. Binjamin Wilkomirski is a case in point. In his critically acclaimed autobiography, *Fragments* (1995), he describes in heart-rendering detail a childhood incarcerated in a Nazi death camp during World War II. Wilkomirski, who garnered numerous awards and was feted throughout Europe and the United States, especially by Holocaust survivors, was exposed as a fraud by a Swiss journalist. Wilkomirski, it turns out, was never in a concentration camp, and is not a Polish Jew as he claims. He actually spent his childhood in the relatively safe and loving confines of a well-to-do adoptive family in his native Switzerland. For a discussion of this controversial case and the moral outrage that greeted Wilkomirski's unmasking, see Gouveritch (1999).

But what of the other side of this moral equation? What if the stressor is illusory? If it is, then any claims to victim status are, *ipso facto*, bogus and are likely to be met with disdain, dismissal and derision. That was the case when Harvard psychiatrist John Mack (1994) supported his trauma-tized patients' stories of having been abducted by aliens. For a critical read on these claims, see Bryan (1995) and Sagan (1997).

It is probably not at all surprising that any number of ritual abuse "skeptics" find analogies between ritual abuse and alien abduction claims (Baumeister & Sommer, 1997; Musgrave & Houran, 2000; Paley 1997; Spanos, Burgess, & Burgess, 1994).

7. For interesting examinations of the recycling folklore and conspiracy theories about the devil and innocent children, see Ellis (2000) and LaFontaine (1998).

8. In a British study, 71 helping profes-sionals are members of RAINS (Ritual Abuse Information Network and Support) were surveyed as to the stress they experi-ence in their work with child and adult rit-ual abuse victims: 97 percent reported nightmares, loss of appetite, psychosomatic symptoms, depression or anxiety; 86 per-cent reported increased concerns about their own personal safety; 54 percent reported decreases in social activities (Youngson, 1993).

Bibliography

Abbott, J.S. (1994). Little Rascals Day Care Center case: The bitter lesson, a healthy reminder. *Journal of Child Sexual Abuse, 3*, 125–131.

Accused child molester granted new trial. (1988, September 14). *United Press International Newswire.*

Acocella, J. (1999). *Creating hysteria: Women and multiple personality disorder.* San Francisco, CA: Jossey-Bass.

Adams, D. (1996, May 25). On rebound: Neighborhoods overcome tarnished images. *Sun-Sentinel*, p. 1A.

Adler, J.S. (1996). The making of a moral panic in 19th century America: The Boston garroting hysteria of 1865. *Deviant Behavior, 17*, 259–278.

Alcoff, L., and L. Gray (1993). Survivor discourse: Transgression or recuperation: *Signs, 18*, 260–290.

Allen, C.V. (1980). *Daddy's girl.* NY: Wyndham.

Allen, D., and J. Midwinter (1990, September 30). *Michelle remembers:* The debunking of a myth. *Mail on Sunday*, p. 41.

Almond, S. (1993, December 15). Who's abusing who? *Miami New Times*, p. A2.

Altheid, D. (2002). *Creating fear.* Hawthorne, NY: Aldine deGruyter.

American Academy of Child and Adolescent Psychiatry (1990/1998). *Guidelines for the clinical evaluation of child and adolescent sexual abuse.* Retrieved from the World Wide Web at <http://www.aacap.org/publications/policy/Ps22.htm>.

American Academy of Pediatrics Committee on Child Abuse and Neglect (1991). Guidelines for the evaluation of sexual abuse of children. *Pediatrics, 87*, 254–259.

American Medical Association (1985). AMA diagnosis and treatment guidelines concerning abuse and neglect. *Journal of the American Medical Association, 254*, 796–798.

American Professional Society on the Abuse of Children (1995). *Fact sheet: Ritual abuse.* Chicago, IL: Author.

_____. (1990/1998). *Psychosocial evaluation of suspected sexual abuse in children.* Chicago, IL: Author.

American Prosecutors Research Institute (1990). *Children's Justice Act: Training on investigation and prosecution of child sexual abuse.* Alexandra, VA: Author.

American Psychiatric Association (1993). *Memories of sexual abuse.* Retrieved from the World Wide Web at <http://www.psych.org/public_info/memori~1.cfm>

American Psychological Association (1995). *Questions and answers about memories of childhood abuse.* Washington, D.C.: Author.

Anderson, D.D. (1996). Assessing the reliability of children's testimony in sexual abuse cases. *Southern California Law Review, 69*, 2117–2161.

Appleyard, B. (1990, September 30). Children speared on the horns of a demonic dilemma. *London Sunday Times*, p. A3.

Aquino v. Stone 957 F.2d 139, 142 (4th Cir. 1992).

Aranza, J. (1983). *Backward masking unmasked.* Shreveport, LA: Huntington House.

Arlidge, J. (1995, March 23). Sex abuse case social workers may be charged. *Independent*, p. 5.

Armbrister, T. (1994, January). Justice gone crazy. *Readers Digest*, pp. 33–40.

Armstrong, L. (1978). *Kiss daddy goodnight.* NY: Pocket Books.

_____. (1994). *Rocking the cradle of sexual politics.* Reading, MA: Addison-Wesley.

Arnold, R., and C. Decker (1984, April 29). McMartin case: A community divided. *Los Angeles Times*, pp. I–1, I–3, I17–I18.

Baker, D.R., J. Chiancone, N.S. Davis, J. Feller, S.S. Imada, Y. Samerson, and C. Sandt (1997). *What I wish I'd learned in law school: Social science research for children's attorneys.* Chicago, IL: American Bar Association.

Balmaseda, L. (1984, August 17). Tearful parents demand abuse probe. *Miami Herald*, p, 1C.

Barker, R., J. Jones, J. Saradjian, and R. Wardell (1998). *Abuse in early years.* Newcastle, England: Newcastle County Council.

Barton, F. (1999, October 17). Controversial book on child abuse withdrawn. *Mail on Sunday*, p. 2.

Bass, E., and L. Thornton (eds.) (1983). *I never told anyone.* NY: Harper and Row.

Batty, D. (2002, August 1). Councils advised on averting abuse libels. *Guardian*, p. 5.

Baumeister, R.F., and K.L. Sommer (1997). Patterns in the bizarre: Common themes in satanic ritual abuse, sexual masochism, UFO abductions, factitious illness, and extreme love. *Journal of Social and Clinical Psychology, 16*, 213–223.

Beck, U. (1992). *Risk society.* London: Sage.

Becker, G. (1997). *Disrupted lives.* Berkeley, CA: University of California Press.

Beckett, K. (1996). Culture and the politics of signification: The case of child sexual abuse. *Social Problems, 43*, 57–76.

Bedford, K.E. (1997, June 23). "Something was very wrong." *Current.* Retrieved from the World Wide Web at <http://www.current.org/prog/prog711b.html>

Believe the Children (n.d.). Symptoms of ritualistic and sexual abuse. Manhattan Beach, CA: Author.

Belsky, J. (1980). Future directions for day care research. *Child Care Quarterly, 9*, 82–99.

Bennett, P. (1984, September 14). Judge denies request to re-open day care center. *Boston Globe*, pp. 17, 24.

Ben-Yehuda, N. (1980). The European witch craze of the 14th and 17 centuries: A sociological perspective. *American Journal of Sociology, 86*, 1–31.

Berliner, L., and M.K. Barbieri (1984). The testimony of the child victim of sexual assault. *Journal of Social Issues, 40*, 125–137.

_____, K. Saywitz, C. Schudson, C. Sandt, and M. Horwitz (1994). *A judicial primer on child sexual abuse cases.* Chicago, IL: American Bar Association.

Berry, M. (1987, April 24). Charges dropped in sex abuse trial. *United Press International Newswire.*

_____. (1988, January 22). Judge calls Ballard verdict "strange." *United Press International Newswire.*

Best, J. (2001). The diffusion of social problems. In J. Best (ed.), *How claims spread* (pp. 1–18). Hawthorne, NY: Aldine deGruyter.

_____. (1990). *Threatened children: Rhetoric and concern about child-victims.* Chicago: University of Chicago Press.

Bibby, P. (1991, October 3). Breaking the web. *Social Work Today*, pp. 17–19.

Bikel, O. (Executive Producer). (1991, May 7). *Innocence Lost.* Boston, MA: WGBH.

Bivins, L. (1985, May 25). House eases court rules in sex cases. *Miami Herald*, p. 1-A.

Bizarre rites at day-care center alleged. (1986, September 15). *Seattle Post-Intelligencer*, p. D1.

Black, A. (1993). The Orkney inquiry: A summary of some key comments and recommendations. *Child Abuse Review, 2,* 47–50.

Blaikie, A. (1995). Motivation and motherhood: Past and present attributions in the reconstruction of illegitimacy. *Sociological Review, 43,* 641–657.

Blood, L. (1994). *The new satanists.* NY: Warner Books.

Bordin, J.A. (1996). The aftermath of nonsubstantiated child abuse allegations in childcare centers. *Child and Youth Care Forum, 25,* 73–87.

Bottoms, B.L., K.R. Diviak, and S.L. Davis (1997). Jurors' reactions to satanic ritual abuse allegations. *Child Abuse & Neglect: The International Journal, 21,* 845–859.

Bourdieu, P. (1994). *Distinction: A social critique of the judgment of taste.* (R. Nice, Trans.). Cambridge, MA: Harvard University Press.

Brady, K. (1979). *Father's days.* NY: Seaview Books.

Branch, K., and D. Van Natta (1991, May 17). Sitter's jury urges review. *Miami Herald,* p. 1D.

Brandon, S., J. Boakes, D. Glaser, and R. Green (1998). Recovered memories of childhood sexual abuse. *British Journal of Psychiatry, 172,* 296–307.

Braun, B.G. (1992). Cult and ritual abuse. Paper presented to the Midwestern Conference on Child Sexual Abuse and Incest. Madison, WI.

_____. (1988). Recognition of possible cult involvement in MPD patients. Paper presented to the 5th International Conference on Multiple Personality/Dissociative States. Chicago, IL.

_____, and G. Gray (1987). Report on the 1986 MPD questionnaire—MPD and cult involvement. Paper presented to the 4th International Conference on Multiple Personality/Dissociative States. Chicago, IL.

Brennan, J. (1989). *The kingdom of darkness.* Lafayette, LA: Acadiania House.

Brindle, D. (1991, April 12). Remarks by judge "outrageous." *Guardian,* p.12.

_____, and T. Sharratt (1990, November 30). Checks sought on child abuse procedures. *Guardian,* p. 24.

"Brink of Disaster?" (1984, November 1). *Daily Breeze,* p. 1.

Brion, D. (1993). The hidden persistence of witchcraft. *Law and Critique, 4,* 227–252.

Bromley, D. (1991). Satanism: The new cult scare. In J.T. Richardson, J. Best, and D.G. Bromley (eds.), *The satanism scare* (pp. 49–72). Hawthorne, NY: Aldine de Gruyter.

_____, and B.C. Busching (1989). Understanding the structure of contractual and covenantal social relations. *Sociological Analysis, 49,* 15–32.

Brown, K. (1985, April). Do working mothers cheat their kids? *Redbook,* pp. 75–77.

Brown, R. (1986). *He came to set the captives free.* Chino, CA: Jack Chick Ministries.

Browne, A., and D. Finklehor (1986). Impact of child sexual abuse: A review of the research. *Psychological Bulletin, 49,* 66–77.

Brownmiller, S. (1975). *Against our will: Men, women and rape.* NY: Simon and Schuster.

Bruck, M., and S.J. Ceci (1995). Brief on behalf of *amicus* developmental, social and psychological researchers, social scientists, and scholars. *Psychology, Public Policy, and the Law, 1,* 1–51.

_____, _____, and E. Francoeur (1999). The accuracy of mothers' memories of conversations with their preschool children. *Journal of Experimental Psychology, 5,* 89–106.

Bucky, S., and C. Dalenberg (1992). The relationship between training of mental health professionals and the reporting of ritual abuse and multiple personality disorder symptomatology. *Journal of Psychology and Theology, 20,* 233–238.

Bulkley, J., C. Sandt, J. Feller, S. Kaplan, K. Olson, and D. Whitcomb (1994). *Child sexual abuse judicial education manual.* Chicago, IL: American Bar Association.

Bunyan, N. (1990, September 8). Satanic claims split children from families. *Daily Telegraph,* p. 3.

Burkhardt, S., O. Golden, E. Karolak, and L. Stoney (2003). Child care and development fund report of state plans FY 2002–2003. National Child Care Information Center. Retrieved on the World Wide Web at <http://nccic.orgpubs/stateplan/index.html>.

Buser, L. (1993, September 10). State won't retry Ballard; ends epic child abuse case. *Commercial Appeal*, p. A1.

Butler-Sloss, E. (1988). *Report of the inquiry into child abuse in Cleveland, 1987.* London: HMSO.

Bryan, C.D.B. (1995). *Close encounters of the fourth kind.* NY: Knopf.

Cage, R.L., and D.M. Pence (1994). *Criminal investigation of child sexual abuse.* Washington, D.C.: Office of Juvenile Justice Delinquency Prevention.

Canadian Psychological Association (1996). *Guidelines for psychologists addressing recovered memories.* Retrieved from the World Wide Web at <http://www.cpa.ca/recmem.pdf>.

Carlson, P. (1984, April 16). A therapist uses puppets to help crack California's horrifying nursery school child abuse case. *People Weekly*, pp. 78–81.

Carlson, S., and G. O'Sullivan (1989). *Satanism in America.* El Cerrito, CA: Gaia Press.

Cartwright, G. (1994, April). The innocent and the damned. *Texas Monthly*, pp. 100–105, 145–156.

Cassidy, M.L. (1990). Gender difference in work-related status within selected female- and male-dominated occupations. *Current Research on Occupations and Professions, 5,* 111–129.

Cates, G. (Director). (1989). *Do you know the muffin man?* (Made for television film).

Cavalcade Productions (1989). Ritual Abuse: A Professional Overview. [Video]. (Available from Cavalcade Productions, PO Box 2480 Nevada City, CA 95959).

Ceci, S.J., and M. Bruck (1995). *Jeopardy in the courtroom: A scientific analysis of children's testimony.* Washington, D.C.: American Psychological Association Press.

Cerone, D.H. (1995, May 22). HBO film on McMartins stirs feelings. *Los Angeles Times*, p. 1.

Chambers, M. (1987, January 6). Prosecutors on sex abuse disclose witness's complaints to the police. *Los Angeles Times*, p. A-15.

Champagne, R. (1998). Oprah Winfrey's scared silent and the spectatorship of incest. In A.C. Hall (ed.), *Delights, desires and dilemmas: Essays on women and the media* (pp. 123–136). Westport, CT: Praeger.

Charlier, T., and S. Downing (1988, January). Justice abused: A 1980s witch-hunt. (Series). *Memphis Commercial Appeal.*

Children's Services Advisory (1995). *From crisis to coordination—An integrated community response to a multi-victim child abuse crisis.* Toronto: Health Canada.

Christensen, P.H. (2000). Childhood and the cultural constitution of vulnerable bodies. In A. Prout (ed.), *The body, childhood and society* (pp. 38–59). NY: St. Martin's Press.

Citron, J. (1989, November 19). McMartin remains a festering, open sore in Manhattan Beach. *Los Angeles Times*, pp. A-1, A-34–35.

Clyde, J.J. (1992). *The report of the inquiry into the removal of children from Orkney in February 1991.* Edinburgh, Scotland: HMSO.

Cockburn, A. (2000, October 2). The Gores' culture wars. *The Nation*, p. 10.

Cohen, P. (1992, November 26). Lines of defence: Val Howarth, director of Child-Line, draws a controversial conclusion from the Orkney experience. *Social Work Today*, p. 10.

Cohen, S. (1972/2002). *Folk devils and moral panics: The creation of the Mods and Rockers.* London: Macgibbon & Kee.

Commonwealth v. LeFave (1998).

Committee on Child Abuse and Neglect (1999). Guidelines for the evaluation of sexual abuse of children: Subject review (RE9819). *Pediatrics, 103,* 186–191.

Commonwealth v. Amirault. (1989). 535 N.E. 2d 193, 404 Mass. 221.

Commonwealth v. Amirault and LeFave. (1987).

Cuneo, M.W. (2001). *American exorcism: Expelling demons in the Land of Plenty.* NY: Doubleday.

Conroy, T. (1991, April). The devil in Bucks County. *Philadelphia*, pp. 81–83, 136–137, 139–140.

Cozolino, L.J. (1989). The ritual abuse of children: Implications for clinical practice and research. *Journal of Sex Research, 26,* 131–138.

Craig v. Maryland (1988) 76Md. App. 250, 544 A.2d 1120.

Creed, B. (1993). *The Monstrous-feminine.* London: Routledge.

Crewes, F. (1995). *The memory wars.* NY: New York Review of Books.

Cross, R.J. (1998). The Teddy Boy as scapegoat. *Doshisha Studies in Language and Culture, 1,* 263–291.

Crowley, P. (1990). *Not my child.* NY: Doubleday.

Cullen, B.T., and M. Pretes (2000). The meaning of marginality: Interpretations and perceptions in social science. *Social Science Journal, 37,* 215–229.

Daugherty, J. (1985, June 8). Babysitter's sexual abuse trial is delayed. *Miami Herald*, p. 3B.

_____. (1984, December 21). Day care videotapes released: Kids describe sex at Country Walk. *Miami Herald*, p. 1A.

_____. (1985, July 17). Judge may limit kids' questioning. *Miami Herald*, p. 3B.

Davenport, P. (1990, September 14). No evidence for charges in ritual abuse enquiry. *Times*, p. 6.

Dawson, J. (1990, October 5). Vortex of evil. *New Statesman and Society*, pp. 12–14.

DeCamp, J.W. (1992). *The Franklin cover-up.* Omaha, NE: A.W.T. Publishers.

Delbanco, A. (1995). *The death of Satan: How Americans have lost the sense of evil.* NY: Farrar, Straus and Giroux.

DeMause, L. (1994). Why cults terrorize and kill children. *Journal of Psychohistory, 21,* 501–518.

Demos, J. (1982). *Entertaining Satan: Witchcraft and the culture of early New England.* NY: Oxford University Press.

Dewar, H. (1994, August 20). Fuster asks for new child sex abuse trial. *Miami Herald*, p. 1B.

de Young, M. (1998). Another look at moral panics. *Deviant Behavior, 19,* 257–278.

_____. (1996c). Breeders for Satan: Toward a sociology of sexual trauma tales. *Journal of American Culture, 19,* 111–117.

_____. (2000b). The devil goes abroad: The export of the ritual abuse moral panic. *British Criminology Conferences Selected Proceedings, 3.* Retrieved from the World Wide Web at <http://www.lboro.ac.uk/departments/ss/bsc/bccsp/vol03/deyoung. html>.

_____. (1997). The devil goes to day care: McMartin and the making of a moral panic. *Journal of American Culture, 20,* 19–25.

_____. (2000a). Folk devils, stigma contests and the uses of power. Paper presented to the British Society of Criminology Conference, Leicester, England.

_____. (1994). One face of the devil: The satanic ritual abuse moral crusade and the law. *Behavioral Sciences and the Law, 12, 389–407.*

_____. (1996b). A painted devil: Constructing the satanic ritual abuse of children problem. *Aggression and Violent Behavior, 1,* 235–248.

_____. (2002). *The ritual abuse controversy: An annotated bibliography.* Jefferson, NC: McFarland.

_____. (1982). *The sexual victimization of children.* Jefferson, NC: McFarland.

_____. (1996a). Speak of the devil: Rhetoric in claims-making about the satanic ritual abuse problem. *Journal of Sociology and Social Welfare, 23,* 55–74.

Did daddy do it? (2002, April). *Frontline*. Retrieved from the World Wide Web at <http://www.pbs.org/wgbh/pages/frontline/shows/fuster/talk>.

Doherty, W.F. (1998, April 15). Fells case technique wrong, says prosecutor. *Boston Globe*, p. A1.

Dominelli, L. (1987). Father-daughter incest. *Critical Social Policy, 16*, 8–22.

Dove v. State (1989) 768 S.W. 2d 465; 1989 Tex. App. Lexis 733.

Ducassi, J. (1985, August 14). Fuster gets 15 years for probation breach. *Miami Herald*, p. 1B.

Duffy, J.A. (1997, April 7). Pro-Amirault rally directed at Governor. *Boston Globe*, p. B1.

Durkheim, E. (1938). *The rules of sociological method.* (S. Solovay and J.H. Mueller, Trans.). Chicago: University of Chicago.

Durkin, M. (1992, March 8). Day-care defendant reflects on his life and troubles. *Charlotte Observer*, p. 1A.

_____. (1991, May 15). Parents in day care case say program is misleading. *Charlotte Observer*, p. 3-B.

_____. (1991, September 29). Wild tales at trial test children's credibility: What to believe in day-care sex case? *Charlotte Observer*, p. 1-A.

Duyvendak, J.W. (1995). The Dutch approach to an epidemic: Why ACT UP! did not succeed in the Netherlands. *Acta Politica, 30*, 187–214.

Dyrendal, A. (1998). Media constructions of satanism in Norway. *FOAFTale News, 43*, 2–5.

Earl, J. (1995). The dark truth about the "dark tunnels of McMartin." *Issues in Child Abuse Allegations, 7*, 76–131.

Eaton, L. (1990, November 15). Going by the book. *Social Work Today*, p. 1.

Eaton, T.E., P.J. Ball, and M.G. O'Callaghan (2001). Child-witness and defendant credibility: Child evidence presentation mode and judicial instructions. *Journal of Applied Social Psychology, 31*, 1845–1858.

Eberle, P., and S. Eberle (1993). *The abuse of innocence: The McMartin Preschool trial.* Buffalo, NY: Prometheus Books.

Edmondson, B. (1988, August). Bringing in the sheaves. *American Demographics, 10*, pp. 28–32, 57–58.

Ehrensaft, D. (1992). Preschool child sex abuse: The aftermath of the Presidio case. *American Journal of Orthopsychiatry, 62*, 234–244.

Ellis, B. (2000). *Raising the devil: Satanism, new religions, and the media.* Lexington, KY: University of Kentucky Press.

_____. (1992). Satanic ritual abuse and legend ostension. *Journal of Psychology and Theology, 20*, 274–277.

Emmerman, L., and M. Taylor (1985, April 19). Expert in day-care probe can't back up his resume. *Chicago Tribune*, p. 1.

_____, and _____. (1985, April 21). Sex-abuse probe rife with errors. *Chicago Tribune*, p. 1.

Enstad, R. (1985, September 24). Doctor saw 'possible abuse' of pupil. *Chicago Tribune*, p. 4.

_____. (1985, October 3). Janitor cleared of 1 sex charge. "I have no choice," Judge says. *Chicago Tribune*, p. 1.

Epstein, J. (1995). *Altered conditions.* NY: Routledge.

Etaugh, C. (1981). Effects of non-maternal care on children. *Annual Progress in Child Psychiatry and Child Development, 1981*, 392–411.

Faller, K.C. (1990). *Understanding child sexual maltreatment.* Newbury Park, CA: Sage.

Fallows, D. (1985, October). "Mommy, don't leave me here!": The day care parents don't see. *Redbook*, pp. 160–162.

False Memory Syndrome Foundation (1995). Compilation on Dr. Bennett Braun. Retrieved from the World Wide Web at <http://www.fmsonline.org/braun.html>.

Farrell, K. (1998). *Post-traumatic culture*. Baltimore, MD: Johns Hopkins University Press.

Faux, R. (1990, September 8). Parents fight for return of children after satanic tales. *Times*, p. 5.

Feldman, G.C. (1995). Satanic ritual abuse: A chapter in the history of human cruelty. *Journal of Psychohistory, 22,* 340–357.

Feldman, P. (1984, November 29). Child resumes testimony in molestation case. *Los Angeles Times*, pp. 2, 3.

_____, and J. Needham (1984, November 30). "Victim of witch-hunt," accused molester says. *Los Angeles Times,* pp. 2, 8.

Felix v. State 109 Nev. 151; 849 P. 2d 220; 1993 Nev. LEXIS 27.

Fells Acres finality. (1999, August 19). *Boston Globe*, p. A-18.

Fenster, M. (1999). *Conspiracy theories: Secrecy and power in American culture*. Minneapolis, MN: University of Minnesota Press.

Fernandez, L. (1990, March 11). '80s reforms didn't end abuse cases. *Miami Herald*, p. 3B.

Finkelhor, D. (1984). *Child sexual abuse: New theory and research*. NY: Basic Books.

_____. (1979). *Sexually victimized children*. NY: Free Press.

_____. (1986). *A sourcebook on child sexual abuse*. Beverly Hills, CA: Sage.

_____, and D.E.H. Russell (1984). Women as perpetrators: Review of the evidence. In D. Finkelhor (ed.), *Child sexual abuse: New theory and research* (pp. 171–187). Beverly Hills, CA: Sage.

_____, and L. Williams (1988). *Nursery crimes: Sexual abuse in day care*. Newbury Park, CA: Sage.

Fischer, M.A. (1988, May). In search of justice. *Life Magazine*, pp. 164–167.

Fisher, C.B. (1995). American Psychological Association's (1992) Ethics code and the validation of sexual abuse in day care settings. *Psychology, Public Policy, and Law, 1,* 461–478.

Fisher, R., P. Blizard, and K. Goedelman (1989). *Drugs, demons and delusions*. St. Louis, MS: Personal Freedom Outreach.

Foucault, M. (1977). *Discipline and punish*. London: Allen Lane.

_____. (1986). Governmentality. *Ideology and Consciousness, 6,* 5–21.

_____. (1981). *Power/knowledge*. NY: Pantheon Books.

Franklin, B., and N. Parton (1991). *Social work, the media, and public relations*. London: Routledge.

Fromm, S. (2001). Total estimated cost of child abuse and neglect in the United States. Retrieved from the World Wide Web at <http://www.preventchildabuse.org/learn_more/research_docs/cost_analysis.pdf>.

Frude, N. (1996). Ritual abuse: Conceptions and reality. *Clinical Child Psychology and Psychiatry, 1,* 59–77.

Fukurai, H., E.W. Butler, and R. Krooth (1994). Sociologists in action: The McMartin sexual abuse case, litigation, justice and mass hysteria. *American Sociologist, 25,* 2–44.

Fuller, R. (1995). *Naming the Antichrist: The history of an American obsession*. NY: Oxford University Press.

Fundamental fairness: The Court of Appeals is right (Editorial) (1995, May 10). *Charlotte Observer*, p. 16A.

Fuster v. Singletary (1997). Case number 97-1369-Civ-Lenard. Deposition of Maggie Bruck, Ph.D.

Gallagher, B. (2000). Ritual, and child sexual abuse, but not ritual child sexual abuse. *Child Abuse Review, 9,* 321–327.

Gallup, M.L. (1989, December 4). Letter.

Gamino, D. (1992, November 19). 5 year old testifies in day car abuse case: Girl gives contradictory account at trial. *Austin American-Statesman*, p. 1A.

_____. (1992, November 26). Kellers found guilty of sexual assault. *Austin American-Statesman*, p. 1A.

_____, and P. Ward (1992, December 13). Speaking the unspeakable: Nightmares of Fran's Day Care stalk families. *Austin American- Statesman*, p. 1A.

Garven, S., J.M. Wood, R.S. Malpass, and J.S. Shaw (1998). More than suggestion: The effects of interviewing techniques from the McMartin Preschool case. *Journal of Applied Psychology, 83,* 347–359.

Garvin, G. (2002, April 25). Child abuse probe of 80s questioned. *Miami Herald,* p. 1C.

Gerth, H.H., and C.W. Mills (1958). *From Max Weber.* NY: Oxford University Press.

Giddens, A. (1991). *Modernity and self-identity.* Cambridge, England: Polity Press.

Glass, J. (1991, August 28). Mother says she believes son's story; defense paints child's tale of abuse as fabrication. *Greensboro News and Record,* p. B1.

Goldston, L. (1987, October 30). Abuse investigation turns to Army officer. *San Jose Mercury News,* p. 1G.

_____. (1988, July 24). Army of the night: Were the children really being sexually abused at Presidio? *San Jose Mercury News,* p. 14.

_____. (1988, August 2). D.A. won't charge officer in day care case. *San Jose Mercury News,* p. 8B.

_____. (1989, May 17). Mendocino county cops, parents, seek help in child abuse probe. *San Jose Mercury News,* p. 4B.

Goode, E. (1990). The American drug panic of the 1980s: Social construction or objective threat? *International Journal of the Addictions 25,* 1083–1098.

_____, and N. Ben-Yehuda (1994). *Moral panics.* Cambridge, MA: Blackwell.

Goodman, G.S., J. Qin, B.L. Bottoms, and P.R. Shaver (1994). Characteristics and sources of allegations of ritualistic abuse. (Final Report to the National Center on Child Abuse and Neglect. Grant No. 90CA1405). Chicago, IL: National Center on Child Abuse and Neglect.

_____, M. Levine, G.B. Melton, and D.W. Ogden (1991). Child witnesses and the confrontation clause: The American Psychological Association's brief in *Maryland v. Craig. Law and Human Behavior, 15,* 13–29.

Goodwin, J.M. (1992). Sadistic abuse: Definition, recognition and treatment. *Dissociation, 6,* 181–187.

Gordon, R.A., and P.L. Chase-Lansdale (2001). Availability of child care in the United States. *Demography, 38,* 299–316.

Gorney, C. (1988, May 18). The community of fear. *Washington Post,* p. D1.

_____. (1988, May 17). The terrible puzzle of the McMartin Preschool. *Washington Post,* p. D1.

Gould, A. (1994). Sweden syringe exchange debate: Moral panic in a rational society. *Journal of Social Policy, 23,* 195–217.

Gould, C. (1995). Denying the ritual abuse of children. *Journal of Psychohistory, 22,* 329–339.

_____. (1992). Diagnosis and treatment of ritually abused children. In D.K. Sakheim and S.E. Devine (eds.), *Out of darkness: Exploring satanism and ritual abuse* (pp. 207–248). NY: Lexington Books.

_____. (1988). Signs and symptoms of ritualistic abuse in children. Encino, CA: Author.

_____, and V. Graham-Costain (1994). Play therapy with ritually abused children, part I. *Treating Abuse Today, 4,* 4–10.

Gouveritch, P. (1999, June 14). The memory thief. *New Yorker,* pp. 48–68.

Granberry, M. (1993, November 29). Case illustrates flaws in child abuse trials. *Los Angeles Times,* p. A-3.

_____. (1993, October 22). Former preschool worker cries on the stand in denying molestation. *Los Angeles Times,* p. A3.

_____. (1993, June 28). Is trial of church volunteer accused of abusing children a witch hunt? *Lost Angeles Times*, p. A3.

Greaves, G.B. (1992). Alternative hypothesis regarding claims of satanic cult activity: A critical analysis. In D.K. Sakheim and S.E. Devine (eds.), *Out of darkness: Exploring satanism and ritual abuse* (pp. 45–72). NY: Lexington Books.

Greek, C.E., and W. Thompson (1992). Anti-pornography campaigns: Saving the family in America and England. *International Journal of Politics, Culture and Society, 5*, 601–616.

Green, M. (1984, May 21). The McMartins: The "model family" down the block that ran California's nightmare nursery. *People Weekly*, pp. 109–115.

_____. (1991, March). Rochdale—The lessons. *Solicitors Journal*, p. 317.

Grescoe, P. (1980, October 27). Things that go bump in the night in Victoria. *Maclean's*, pp. 30–31.

Griswold, W. (1994). *Cultures and societies in a changing world.* Thousand Oaks, CA: Pine Forge Press.

Gulliatt, R. (1996). *Talk of the devil.* Melbourne, Australia: Text Publishing.

Hadden, J.K., and A. Shupe (1981). *Televangelism: Power and politics on God's frontier.* Reading, MA: Addison-Wesley.

Haglund, K. (1991, December 7). Police find Jeep, weapon belonging to couple wanted on assault charges. *Austin American-Statesman*, p. 2A.

Hall, A. (1990, September 17). Focus on Rochdale. *Daily Telegraph*, p. 13.

Hall, S., C. Critcher, T. Jefferson, J. Clarke, and B. Roberts (1978). *Policing the crisis: Mugging, the state, and law and order.* London: Macmillan.

Hammond, D.C. (1990). *Handbook of hypnotic suggestions and metaphors.* NY: W.W. Norton.

_____. (1992). Satanic ritual abuse and multiple personality. Paper presented to the 4th Annual Regional Conference on Abuse and Multiple Personality. Philadelphia, PA.

Harrington, E. (1996, September/October). Conspiracy theories and paranoia: Notes from a mind control conference. *Skeptical Inquirer*, pp. 32–36.

Hass, N. (1995, September 10). Margaret Kelly Michaels wants her innocence back. *New York Times Magazine*, pp. 37–41.

Hawdon, J.E. (2001). The role of presidential rhetoric in the creation of a moral panic: Reagan and Bush and the war on drugs. *Deviant Behavior, 22*, 419–450.

Hay, C. (1995). Mobilisation through interpellation: James Bulger, juvenile crime and the construction of a moral panic. *Social and Legal Studies, 4*, 197–223.

Health Resource and Services Administration (2002). *America's children.* Retrieved from the World Wide Web at <http://www.childstats.gov/americaschildren>.

Heger, A., L. Ticson, O. Velasquez, and R. Bernier (2002). Children referred for possible sexual abuse: Medical findings in 2384 children. *Child Abuse & Neglect:The International Journal, 26*, 645–659.

Helms, A. (1995, November 4). When should we believe children? *Charlotte Observer*, p. 1A

Hentoff, N. (1992, June 9). Cotton Mather in Maplewood New Jersey. *Village Voice*, pp. 22–23.

Herald Staff (1985, October 4). The Fuster trial. *Miami Herald*, p. 22A.

_____. (1989, June 18). Heed the children. *Miami Herald*, p. 2C.

_____. (1988, July 2). Statements: Prior owner solicited sex. *Miami Herald*, p. 1B.

Herman, J.L. (1992). *Trauma and recovery: The aftermath of violence—from domestic abuse to political terror.* NY: Basic Books.

Hertenstein, M., and J. Trott (1993). *Selling Satan:The tragic history of Mike Warnke.* Chicago, IL: Cornerstone Press.

Hicks, R.D. (1991). *The pursuit of Satan: The police and the occult.* Buffalo, NY: Prometheus Books.

Hill, J. (1996). Believing Rachel. *Journal of Psychohistory, 24,* 132–146.

Hill, M. (1998). Satan's excellent adventure in the Antipodes. *Issues in Child Abuse Accusations, 10.* Retrieved from the World Wide Web <http//www.ipt-forensics. com/journal/volume10/j10_9.htm>.

Hill, S., and J.M. Goodwin (1989). Satanism: Similarities between patient account and pre–Inquisition historical sources. *Dissociation, 2,* 39–44.

Hiltrand, D. (1990, January 15). Unspeakable acts (Review of the made-for-television film, *Unspeakable Acts*). *People Weekly,* pp. 8–9.

Hofferth, S. (1996). Child care in the United States today. *The Future of Children.* Retrieved from the World Wide Web at <http://www.futureofchildren.org/information2826/information_show.htm?doc_id=73628>.

Hofferth, S.L., and N. Collins (2000). Child care and employment turnover. *Population Research and Policy Review, 19,* 357–395.

_____, and D.A. Phillips (1991). Child care policy research. *Journal of Social Issues, 47,* 1–13.

Holgerson, A., and B. Hellborn (1997). *Facts or fictions as evidence in court.* Stockholm, Sweden: Almquist Wiksell International.

Holland, J., C. Ramazanoglu, and S. Scott (1990). AIDS: From panic station to power relations. *Sociology, 24,* 499–518.

Hollingsworth, J. (1986). *Unspeakable acts.* NY: Congdon and Weed.

Hood, L. (2001). *A city possessed: The Christchurch Civic Creche case.* Dunedin, New Zealand: Longacre.

Howes, C., and K. Droege (1994). Child care in the United States and industrialized nations. *Pediatrics, 94,* 1081–1084.

Hubler, S. (1990, January 19). At last, shadow has been lifted from Manhattan Beach. *Los Angeles Times,* p. A-18.

Hudson, P.S. (1994). The clinician's experience. In V. Sinason (ed.), *Treating survivors of satanist abuse* (pp. 71–81). London: Routledge.

_____. (1991). *Ritual child abuse: Discovery, diagnosis and treatment.* Saratoga, CA: R & E Publishers.

Hughes, B. (1994, November 16). Books on satanists draws libel charge. *Oakland Post,* p. 3.

Humphrey, H.H. III (1985). *Report on Scott County investigations.* St. Paul, MN: Office of the Attorney General. 100 protest decision in child sexual abuse case. (1997, April 7) *Standard-Times,* p.1.

Hunt, A. (1999). Anxiety and social explanation: Some anxieties about anxiety. *Journal of Social History, 32,* 509–528.

_____. (1998). The great masturbation panic and the discourses of moral regulation in 19th and early 20th century Britain. *Journal of the History of Sexuality, 8,* 575–615.

Hunt, D. (1991). *Global peace and the rise of the Anti-Christ.* Eugene, OR: Harvest House.

Hunt, L. (1990). Council stands by ritual abuse claims. *Independent,* p. 3.

Hutchison, E.D. (1992). Child welfare as a woman's issue. *Families in Society, 73,* 67–77.

Ingebretsen, E.J. (2001). *At stake: Monsters and the rhetoric of fear in public culture.* Chicago, IL: University of Chicago Press.

Innocence lost: The plea. (1998) *Frontline.* Retrieved from the World Wide Web at <http://www.pbs.org/wgbh/pages/frontlineshows/innocence>.

Jablonski, J.A. (1998). Where has *Michaels* taken us? Assessing the future of taint hearings. *Suffolk Journal of Trial and Appellate Advocacy, 3,* 49–63.

Jenkins, P. (1992). *Intimate enemies: Moral panics in contemporary Great Britain.* Hawthorne, NY: Aldine deGruyter.

_____. (1998). *Moral panics: Changing concepts of the child molester in modern America*. New Haven, CT: Yale University Press.

_____, and D. Maier-Katkin (1991). Occult survivors: The making of a myth. In J.T. Richardson, J. Best, and D.G. Bromley (eds.), *The satanism scare* (pp. 127–144). Hawthorne, NY: Aldine deGruyter.

Jenks, C. (1996). *Childhood*. London: Routledge.

Jewel, S. (1985, March 22). Mother says son, 4, "almost begged" her to avoid preschool. *Herald-Palladium*, p. 1.

Jones, D.P.H. (1991). Ritualism and child sexual abuse. *Child Abuse & Neglect, 15*, 163–170.

Jones, F. (1993, October 11). TV talk show made me feel a bit chicken. *Toronto Star*, p. E1.

Jonker, F., and I. Jonker-Bakker (1991). Experiences with ritualistic child sexual abuse: A case study from the Netherlands. *Child Abuse & Neglect: The International Journal, 15*, 191–196.

Jorstad, E. (1990). *The New Christian Right, 1981–1988*. Lewiston, NY: Edwin Mellen Press.

Kahaner, L. (1988). *Cults that kill*. NY: Warner, 1988.

Kelley, S.J. (1990). Parental stress response to sexual abuse and ritualistic abuse of children in day-care centers. *Nursing Research, 39*, 25–29.

_____. (1993). Ritualistic abuse of children in day care centers. In M.D. Langone (ed.), *Recovery from cults: Help for victims of psychological and spiritual abuse* (pp. 343–355). NY: W.W. Norton.

_____. (1992). Stress responses of children and parents to sexual abuse and ritualistic abuse in day care settings. In A.W. Burgess (ed.), *Child trauma I: Issues and research* (pp. 231–257). NY: Garland.

_____. (1989). Stress responses of children to sexual abuse and ritualistic abuse in day care. *Journal of Interpersonal Violence, 4*, 505–513.

Kelly, R.J., and S. Ben-Mier (1993). Emotional effects. In J. Waterman, R.J. Kelly, M.K. Oliveri, and J. McCord (eds.), *Behind the playground walls: Sexual abuse in pre-schools* (pp.106–119). NY: Guilford Press.

Kempe, C.H., F.N. Silverman, B.F. Steele, W. Droegmueller, and H.K. Silver (1962). The battered child syndrome. *Journal of the American Medical Association, 181*, 17–24.

Kent, S.A. (1993). Deviant scripturalism and ritual satanic abuse, part two: Possible Masonic, Mormon, magick, and pagan influences. *Religion, 23*, 355–367.

Kerns, D.L. (1998). Triage and referrals for child sexual abuse medical examinations: Which children are likely to have positive medical findings? *Child Abuse & Neglect, 22*, 515–518.

Kincaid, J.R. (1998). *Erotic innocence: The culture of child molesting*. Durham, NC: Duke University Press.

Kohnken, G. (1995). Wissenschaftliches gutachen [Scientific expert opinion]. Münster, Germany: Penalty Court.

Kringstand, H. (1997). *Bjugnformelen* [The Bjugn formula]. Oslo, Norway: Tiden Norsk Forlag.

Krugman, R. (1989). The more we learn, the less we know "with medical certainty." *Child Abuse & Neglect: The International Journal, 13*, 165–166.

Kurtz, M. (2001, August 3). Victims speak out against Amirault going public; they oppose commutation. *Boston Globe*, p. B1.

LaFontaine, J.S. (1994). *Extent and nature of organised and ritual abuse: Research findings*. London: HMSO.

_____. (1996). Organized and ritual abuse. *Medicine, Science and the Law, 36*, 109–117.

_____. (1998). *Speak of the Devil*. Cambridge, England: Cambridge University Press.

Lalonde, P. (1991). *One world under the Anti-Christ.* Eugene, OR: Harvest House.

Lamb, N.B. (1994). The Little Rascals Day Care Center case: The ingredients of two successful prosecutions. *Journal of Child Sexual Abuse, 3,* 107–116.

Langner, P. (1986, July 21). Verdict not end of trauma for families. *Boston Globe,* p. 1.

Lanning, K.V. (1992). *Investigators' guide to allegations of "ritual" child abuse.* Quantico, VA: Federal Bureau of Investigation.

_____. Lanning, K.V. (1991) Ritual abuse: A law enforcement view or perspective. *Child Abuse & Neglect: The International Journal, 15,* 171–173.

Larson, B. (1989). *Satanism: The seduction of America's youth.* Nashville, TN: Thomas Nelson.

Lees, D. (1994, May). Martensville. *Saturday Night,* pp. 15–18, 20, 22, 26 81–83.

Leeson, F. (1989, October 27). Gallup testifies in sex abuse trial. *Oregonian,* p. D10.

_____. (1989, November 1). Jury finds guilt on sexual abuse. *Oregonian,* p. D10.

_____. (1989, October 18). Sexual misconduct trial begins for Roseburg preschool operator. *Oregonian,* p. B5.

Leff, L. (1987, July 29). Abuse charges dropped. *Washington Post,* p. A-7.

_____. (1987, April 3). Child, experts cited in Craig conviction; day care owner blames pretrial publicity. *Washington Post,* p. A-6.

Lembcke, J. (1998). The "right stuff" gone wrong: Vietnam vets and the social construction of Post-traumatic Stress Disorder. *Critical Sociology, 1–2,* 37–64.

Lempinen, E.W. (1987, November 5). Satanism linked to scores of child abuse cases. *San Francisco Chronicle,* p. 1.

Lengel, A. (1985, May 19). A nightmare in Niles. *Michigan,* pp. 13–14, 16, 18, 20, 22–23.

Leonnig, C.D. (1995, September 10). Talk of new trial makes Edenton shudder. *Charlotte Observer,* p. 1B.

Lester, E. (1992). The AIDS story and moral panic: How the Euro-African press constructs AIDS. *Howard Journal of Communications, 3,* 230–241.

Lillie and Reed v. Newcastle City Council, Richard Barker, Judith Jones, Jacqui Saradjian and Roy Wardell. Case No. HQ9903605, HQ9903606. High Court of Justice, Queens Bench Division. London, England.

Lindegberg, P. (1999). *Doden är en man* [Death is a man]. Stockholm, Sweden: Fischer and Company.

Lloyd, D.W. (1992). Ritual child abuse: Definitions and assumptions. *Journal of Child Sexual Abuse, 1,* 1–4.

Lorentzen, L.J. (1980). Evangelical life style concerns expressed in political action. *Sociological Analysis, 41,* 144–154.

Lundberg-Love, J. (1988). Update on cults, part I: Satanic cults. *Family Violence Bulletin, 5,* 9–10.

Lunn, T. (1991, May 9). Confronting disbelief. *Social Work Today,* p. 18.

_____. (1991, September 26). Court stifles research. *Social Work Today,* p. 5.

Mack, J. (1994). *Abduction: Human encounters with aliens.* NY: Scribner.

Mackenzie, R. (1987, August 3). The good news of evangelism. *Insight, 3,* 8–13.

MacQuarrie, B. (2000, September 21). Victims' families oppose Amirault commutation. *Boston Globe,* p. B1.

Manshel, L. (1994). The child witness and the presumption of authenticity after *State v. Michaels. Seton Hall Law Review, 26.* 685–763.

_____. (1990). *Nap time.* NY: William Morrow.

Marsella, A.J., M.J. Friedman, and E.H. Spain (1996). Ethnocultural aspects of PTSD. In A.J. Marsella, M.J. Friedman, E.T. Gerrity, and R.M. Scurfield (eds.), *Ethnocultural aspects of Post-traumatic Stress Disorder: Issues, research, and clinical applications* (pp. 105–129). Washington, D.C.: American Psychological Association.

Marsh, B. (1995, May 17). Cleared parents brand child abuse report as "whitewash." *Northern Echo,* p. 1.

Marsil, D.F., J. Montoya, D. Ross, and L. Graham (2002). Child witness policy: Law interfacing with social science. *Law and Contemporary Problems, 65,* 209–242.

Martin, D., and G.A. Fine (1991). Satanic cults, satanic play: Is "Dungeons and Dragons" a breeding ground for the devil? In J.T. Richardson, J. Best, and D.G. Bromley (eds.), *The satanism scare* (pp. 107–123). Hawthorne, NY: Aldine deGruyter.

Martin, M. (1976). *Hostage to the Devil.* NY: Readers Digest Press.

Maryland v. Craig, 110 S. Ct. 3160 (1990).

Massachusetts Parole Board Majority Opinion on Amirault case (2001, July 6). Retrieved from the World Wide Web at <http://cltg.org/cltg/amirault/01-07-06-Parole%20Board.htm>.

Masson, J.M. (1984). *The assault on truth: Freud's suppression of the seduction theory.* NY: Farrar, Straus and Giroux.

Mattoesian, G.M. (1999). The grammaticalization of participant roles in the constitution of expert identity. *Language in Society, 28,* 491–521.

McCann, I.L., and L.A. Pearlman (1990). Vicarious traumatization: A framework for understanding the psychological effects of working with victims. *Journal of Traumatic Stress, 3,* 131–149.

McCann, J. (1990). Genital findings in prepubertal girls selected for non-abuse: A descriptive study. *Pediatrics, 86,* 428–439.

_____. (1989). Perianal findings in prepubertal children selected for non-abuse: A descriptive study. *Child Abuse & Neglect: The International Journal, 13,* 179–193.

McCord, J. (1993a). Impact on parents. In J. Waterman, R.J. Kelly, M.K. Oliveri, and J. McCord (eds.), *Behind the playground walls: Sexual abuse in preschools* (pp. 169–176). NY: Guilford Press.

_____. (1993b). Parental reactions and coping patterns. In J. Waterman, R.J. Kelly,

McFadyen, A., H. Hanks, and C. James (1993). Ritual abuse: A definition. *Child Abuse Review, 2,* 35–41.

McGough, L.S. (1994). *Fragile voices: The child witness in American courts.* New Haven, CT: Yale University Press.

McGraw, C. (1991, May 8). McMartin figure wins $1 in civil trial. *Los Angeles Times,* p. B-1.

_____. (1990, January 20). McMartin lawsuits may go on for years. *Los Angeles Times,* p. A-30.

McGrory, B. (1999, October 22). Just who is guilty here? *Boston Globe,* p. B1.

McKay, N. (1999, May 11). Rantzen plea to abuse case duo. *Journal,* p. 1.

McLoughlin, D. (1996, August). Second thoughts on the Christchurch Civic Creche case: Has justice failed Peter Ellis? *North and South,* pp. 54–59, 61–63, 65–66, 68–69.

_____. (2001, March 16). Secret report: Ellis guilt in doubt. *The Dominion,* p. 1.

McMartin child molestation case. (1990, February 4). *60 Minutes.* NY: Burrelle's Transcripts.

McMurran, K. (1980, January 1). A Canadian woman's bizarre childhood memories of Satan shock shrinks and priests. *People Weekly,* pp. 28–30.

McNamara, E. (1997, January 15). Hardly a case of persecution. *Boston Globe,* p. B-1.

Mecoy, L. (1994, June 13). Backlash builds over abuse claims. *San Jose Mercury News,* p. 3B.

Medway, G.J (2001). *The lure of the sinister.* NY: New York University Press.

Melton, G. (1981). Procedural reforms to protect child victim/witnesses in sex offense proceedings. In J. Bulkley (ed.), *Child sexual abuse and the law* (pp. 184–198). Washington, DC: American Bar Association.

Messerschmidt, A. (1985, September 5). Girl, 5, says Fuster played knife game. *Miami Herald,* p. 1D.

Miceli, V. (1981). *The Antichrist.* West Hanover, MA: Christopher Publishing.

Michaels, M.K. (1993, November). I am not a monster. *Mademoiselle*, pp. 126–133.

Michaelson, J. (1989). *Like lambs to the slaughter*. Eugene, OR: Harvest House.

Michel, S. (1999). *Children's interests/Mothers' rights*. New Haven, CT: Yale University Press.

Millegan, K. (2000, July 3). Twenty-two questions answered. *The Konformist*. Retrieved from the World Wide Web at <http:www.konformist.com/2000/alex-constantine.htm>.

Miller, C.B. (1994). *In the Sheriffdom of South Strathclyde, Dumfries and Ayr: Report*. South Strathclyde, Scotland: Author.

Mittenthal, S. (1985, August). Can you work and have a happy, health child? *Glamour, 83*, pp. 130, 132–133.

Montoya, J. (1995). Lessons from *Akiki* and *Michaels* on shielding child witnesses. *Psychology, Public Policy, and Law, 1*, 340–369.

Moriarty, A.R. (1990). Psychological dynamics of adolescent satanism. *Journal of Mental Health Counseling, 12*, 186–198.

Morris, M. (1990, September 12). Move to end Satan case secrecy. *Guardian*, p. 6.

Mulhern, S.A. (1991). Patients reporting ritual abuse in childhood: A clinical response. *Child Abuse & Neglect, 15*, 609–611.

_____. (1992). Ritual abuse: Defining a syndrome versus defending a belief. *Journal of Psychology and Theology, 20*, 230–232.

Murphy, S. (2001, July 7). Victims' parents decry decision on Amirault. *Boston Globe*, p. A8.

Musgrave, J.B., and J. Houran (2000). Flight and abduction in witchcraft and UFO lore. *Psychological Reports, 86*, 669–688.

Myers, J. E. B. (1994b). *The backlash: Child protection under fire*. Thousand Oaks, CA: Sage.

_____. (2002). Keep the lifeboat afloat. *Child Abuse & Neglect, 26*, 561–567.

_____. (1992). *Legal issues in child abuse and neglect*. Newbury Park: Sage.

_____. (1995). New era of skepticism regarding children's credibility. *Psychology, Public Policy, and Law, 1*, 387–398.

_____. (1994a). Taint hearings for child witnesses? A step in the wrong direction. *Baylor Law Review, 46*, 873–946.

_____. (1996). Taint hearings to attack investigative interviews: A further assault on children's credibility. *Child Maltreatment, 1*, 213–222.

Naïve, inept and gullible: Report brands social workers in the Ayshire sex abuse case. (1995, March 23). *Daily Mail*, p. 13.

Napolis, D.L. (2002). Corrections to Description of Conduct and Declaration of Diana Napolis, Defendant. Retrieved from the World Wide Web at <http://mind-controlforums.com/napolis.htm>.

Nathan, D. (1988, April 26). Day-care witch trials. *Village Voice*, p. 17.

_____. (1987, September 29). The making of a modern witch trial. *Village Voice*, pp. 19–22, 27–32.

_____. (1993). Revisiting Country Walk. *Issues in Child Abuse Accusations, 5*, 1–11.

_____. (1995, June). Sweet justice: My fight to free Kelly Michaels. *Redbook*, pp. 84–87, 122, 124.

_____. (1988, August 2). Victimizer or victim? *Village Voice*, pp. 31–39.

_____, and M. Snedeker (1995). *Satan' silence: Ritual abuse and the making of a modern American witch hunt*. NY: Basic Books.

National Center for the Prosecution of Child Abuse (1987). *Manual of the National Center for the Prosecution Of Child Abuse*. Washington, D.C.: Author.

National Resource Center on Child Sexual Abuse (1989). *Think tank report: Investigation of ritualistic abuse allegations*. Huntsville, AL: Author.

Niebuhr, R. (1944). *The children of light and the children of darkness*. NY: Prentice Hall.

Noblitt, J.R., and P.S. Perskin (1995). *Cult and ritual abuse: Its history, anthropology, and recent discovery in contemporary America.* Westport, CT: Praeger.

North Carolina v. Figured No. 9315SC539 Fifteen-B District, North Carolina Court of Appeals (1993).

North Carolina v Kelly, Defendant-Appellant's Brief. (1994, April 21).

North Carolina v. Kathryn Dawn Wilson (1995). 118 N.C. App. 616; 456 S.E.2d 870; 1995 N.C. App. LEXIS 334.

Nottinghamshire County Council (1990). *The revised joint enquiry (JET) report.* Nottingham, England: Author.

O'Donnell, K. (1999). Poisonous women: Sexual danger, illicit violence and domestic work in Southern Africa, 1904–1915. *Journal of Women's History, 11,* 31–54.

Okerblom, J., and M. Sauer (1993, November 22). Was Akiki inquiry rush to judgment? *San Diego Union-Tribune,* p. A-1.

Oliveri, M.K. and J. McCord (eds.), *Behind the playground walls: Sexual abuse in preschools* (pp.205–221). NY: Guilford Press.

_____, and J. Waterman (1993). Impact on therapists. In J. Waterman, R.J. Kelly, M.K. Oliveri, and J. McCord (eds.), *Behind the playground walls: Sexual abuse in preschools* (pp. 190–202). NY: Guilford.

Orcutt, H.K., G.S. Goodman, A.E. Tobey, J.M. Batterman-Faunce, and S. Thomas (2001). Detecting deception in children's testimony: Factfinders' abilities to reach the truth in open court and closed-circuit trials. *Law & Human Behavior, 25,* 339–372.

Orr, R. (1989, June 15). Ex-owner of school guilty of sex abuse. *Miami Herald,* p. 26A.

_____. (1989, May 23). Woman takes plea bargain in abuse case. *Miami Herald,* p. 1B.

O'Sullivan, J. (1990, September 30). Abuse case parents "left in dark." *Independent,* p. 2.

_____. (1990, September 15). National inquiry urged into "ritual child abuse." *Independent,* p. 2.

_____. (1990, September 11). Release children in Satan case. *Independent,* p. 3.

_____. (1990, September 20). Rochdale abuse case transferred. *Independent,* p. 5.

Paley, J. (1997). Satanist abuse and alien abduction. *British Journal of Social Work, 27,* 43–70.

Paradise, J. (1989). Predictive accuracy and the diagnosis of sexual abuse. *Child Abuse & Neglect: The International Journal, 13,* 169–176.

Parton, N. (1985). *The politics of child abuse.* London: Macmillan.

Passantino, B., and G. Passantino (1992). Satanic ritual abuse in popular Christian literature: Why Christians fall for a lie searching for the truth. *Journal of Psychology and Theology, 20,* 299–305.

_____, _____, and J. Trott (1999). Lauren Stratford: From satanic ritual abuse to Jewish Holocaust survivor. *Cornerstone, 28,* 12–16.

_____, _____, and _____. (1989). Satan's sideshow. *Cornerstone, 18,* 23–28.

Pave, I. (1985, June 17). The insurance crisis that could cripple day care. *Business Week,* p. 114.

Persistent interviews (1995, March 19). *Boston Globe,* p. 17.

Perthen, A. (1997, January 26). Satanic child abuse soaring, say docs. *The People,* p. 2.

Phillips, D.A., C. Howes, and M. Whitbook (1991). Child care as an adult work environment. *Journal of Social Issues, 47,* 49–70.

Plummer, K. (1995). *Telling sexual stories: Power, change and social worlds.* London: Routledge.

Pratkanis, A., and E. Aronson (1992). *Age of propaganda: The everyday use and abuse of persuasion.* NY: W.H. Freeman.

Preschool investigated (1984, March 28). *Los Angeles Times,* p. A-1.

Pringle, K. (1998). *Children and social welfare in Europe.* Buckingham, England: Open University Press.

Putnam, F.W. (1991). Commentary: The satanic ritual abuse controversy. *Child Abuse & Neglect, 15,* 175–180.

Rabinowitz, D. (1995, January 30). A darkness in Massachusetts, Part I. *Wall Street Journal,* p. A-20.

_____. (1995, March 14). A darkness in Massachusetts, Part II. *Wall Street Journal,* p. A-14.

_____. (1995, May 12). A darkness in Massachusetts, Part III. *Wall Street Journal,* p. A-12.

_____. (1999, August 24). Judgment in Massachusetts. *Wall Street Journal,* p. A-20.

_____. (1990, May). From the mouth of babes to a jail cell. *Harper's Magazine,* pp. 52–64.

Rakowsky, J. (1999, October 22). LeFave granted freedom; striking deal, she drops bid. *Boston Globe,* p. A1.

Raschke, C. (1990). *Painted black: Satanic crime in America.* San Francisco, CA: Harper and Row.

Rasmussen, C. (1996, November 29). City smart. *Los Angeles Times,* p. B-2.

Rawlings, S.W. (1993). *Household and family characteristics.* Washington, D.C.: U.S. Department of Commerce.

Reder, P., S. Duncan, and M. Gray (1993). *Beyond blame: Child abuse tragedies revisited.* London: Routledge.

Reid, T. (1996). Satan's silence [Review of the book *Satan's Silence*]. *The APSAC Advisor, 9.* Retrieved from the World Wide Web at <http://www.apsac.org/pasatan.html>.

Relapse in Fells Acres case (1999, August 23). *Christian Science Monitor,* p. 8.

Richardson, F.C., and B.J. Fowers (1998). Interpretive social science. *American Behavioral Scientist, 41,* 465–495.

Richardson, J.T. (1991). Satanism in the courts: From murder to heavy metal. In J.T. Richardson, J. Best, and D.G. Bromley, *The satanism scare* (pp. 205–217). Hawthorne, NY: Aldine deGruyter.

_____, J. Best, and D.G. Bromley (eds.) (1991) *The satanism scare.* Hawthorne NY: Aldine deGruyter.

Riddle, L. (1988, January 31). Maine couple pick up lives after nightmare. *New York Times,* p. 43.

Ritter, J. (1994, November 3). Molestation cases walk thin line—child abuse charges get second look. *USA Today,* p. 8.

Rivera, G. (Executive Producer). (1988, October 22). Devil worship: Exploring Satan's underground. NY: Investigative News Group.

_____. (Executive Producer. (1995, December 27). *Rivera live.* NY: CNBC News Transcripts.

Robie, J.H. (1991). *Reverse the curse in your life.* Lancaster, PA: Starburst.

Robinson, B.A. (2001). Ritual abuse legislation passed by U.S. state legislatures. Retrieved from the World Wide Web at <http://www.religioustolerance.org/ra_law.htm>.

Robison, J. (1980). *Attack on the family.* Wheaton, IL: Tyndale House.

Rohrlich, T., and R. Welkos (1984, March 28). Pornography was the main aim of pre-school, D.A. charges. *Los Angeles Times,* pp. II–1, II–4.

Rose, J. (1985). State and language. In: C. Steedman, C. Urwin and V. Walkerdine (eds.). *Language, gender and childhood* (pp. 85–95). London: Routledge & Kegan Paul.

Rosenthal, R. (1995). *State of New Jersey v. Margaret Kelly Michaels:* An overview. *Psychology, Public Policy, and Law, 1,* 246–271.

Ross, A.S. (1986, September 29). Child abuse cults: How real? *San Francisco Chronicle,* pp. A1, A7.

_____. (1986, September 28). Satanism or mass hysteria? *San Francisco Chronicle*, p. A-8.

Roth, S., and M.J. Friedman (1998). Childhood trauma remembered. Retrieved from the World Wide Web at <http://www.istss.org/publications/CTR. htm# anchor1308873>.

Rubenstein, A. (1990). *Investigation into the Breezy Point Day School.* Doylestown, PA: Office of the District Attorney, Bucks County.

Rush, F. (1974). The sexual abuse of children: A feminist point of view. In N. Connell and C. Wilson (eds.), *Rape: The first sourcebook for women* (pp. 73–78). NY: American Library.

Russell, D.E.H. (1986). *The secret trauma: Incest in the lives of girls and women.* NY: Basic Books.

Ryder, D. (1992). *Breaking the cycle of satanic ritual abuse.* Minneapolis, MN: Compcare.

Sachs, R.G. (1990). The role of sex and pregnancy in satanic cults. *Pre- and Peri-Natal Psychology Journal*, 5, 105–113.

Sagan, C. (1997). *The demon-haunted world: Science as a candle in the dark.* NY: Ballantine.

San Diego Grand Jury (1991/1992). *Child sexual abuse, assault and molest issues.* San Diego, CA: Author.

Satanism growing worry for police (1987, October 8). *Chicago Tribune*, p. 45.

Sauer, M. (1993, August 29). Believe the children? *San Diego Union Tribune*, p. D-1.

_____. (1993, November 14). Psychology on trial: Akiki case raises questions on reliability of psychotherapy. *San Diego Union Tribune*, p. D-1.

_____. (2002, December 31). Stalking suspect to undergo more psychological tests. *San Diego Union Tribune*, p. E-2.

_____. (2000, September 24). A web of intrigue: The search for Curio leads cyber-sleuths down a twisted path. *San Diego Union Tribune*, p. E-1.

Savage, D.G. (1990, March 27). High court refuses to hear McMartin suit on civil rights. *Los Angeles Times*, p. B-3.

Saywitz, K., and K.C. Faller (1994). *Interviewing child witnesses and victims of sexual abuse.* Washington, D.C.: Office of Juvenile Justice Delinquency Prevention.

Schulman, K. (2000). The high cost of child care puts quality care out of reach for many families. Retrieved from the World Wide Web at <http://www.childrens defense.org/pdf/highcost/pdf>.

Schumacher, R.B., and R.S. Carlson (1999). Variables and risk factors associated with child abuse in daycare settings. *Child Abuse & Neglect*, 23, 891–898.

Schur, E. (1980). *The politics of deviance.* Englewood Cliffs, NJ: Prentice Hall.

Schwarz, T., and D. Empey (1988). *Satanism: Is your family safe?* Grand Rapids, MI: Zondervan.

Sennott, C.M. (1995, March 19). Questions prompt reexamination of Fells Acres sexual abuse case. *Boston Globe*, p. 1.

Shalit, R. (1995, June 19). Witch hunt. *New Republic*, pp. 14–16.

Sharpe, I. (1986, September 29). How the specter of satanism led to LA uproar in childcare. *San Francisco Examiner*, p. A-6.

Shaw, D. (1990, January 20). Reporter's early exclusives triggered a media frenzy. *Los Angeles Times*, p. A-1.

_____. (1990, January 22). *Times* McMartin coverage was biased, critics charge. *Los Angeles Times*, pp. A-1, A-20.

_____. (1990, January 19). Where was skepticism in the media? Pack journalism and hysteria marked early coverage of the McMartin case. *Los Angeles Times*, pp. A1, A20-A21.

Shell, Stimpson and Stimpson v. State of Tennessee (1995). 893 S.W. 2d 416; 1995 Tenn. LEXIS 14.

Shuker, R. (1986). Video nasties: Censorship and the politics of popular culture. *New Zealand Sociology, 1,* 64–73.

Simandl, R.J. (1997). Teen involvement in the occult. In G.A. Fraser (ed.), *The dilemma of ritual abuse* (pp. 215–230). Washington, D.C.: American Psychiatric Press.

Sjoberg, L. (1998). A case of alleged cutting-up murder in Sweden. Retrieved from the World Wide Web at <http://www.mediemordet.com/sjoberg.html>.

Smith, B., and S.G. Elstein (1994). *The prosecution of child sexual and physical abuse cases.* Chicago, IL: American Bar Association.

Smith, M. (1993). *Ritual abuse: What it is, why it happens, and how to help.* San Francisco, CA: Harper Collins.

_____, and L. Pazder (1980). *Michelle remembers.* NY: Congdon & Lattes.

Social Services Inspectorate (1998). *Rochdale: A report of the review of social services in Rochdale Metropolitan Borough Council.* London: Department of Health.

Sokolov, R.A. (1978, August 6). Nonfiction in brief. *New York Times Book Review,* pp. 16, 20.

SOLACE (Society of Local Authority Chief Executives and Senior Managers) (2002). *Getting it right: Guidance on the conduct of effective and fair ad hoc inquiries.* London: Author.

Sovacool, J. (1992, April 10). Abuse defendant says he rejected plea bargain. *Charlotte Observer,* p. 6C.

Spanos, N.P., C.A. Burgess, and M.F. Burgess (1994). Past-life identities, UFO abductions, and satanic ritual abuse: The social construction of memories. *International Journal of Clinical and Experimental Hypnosis, 42,* 433–446.

Speaker, S.L. (2001). 'The struggle of mankind against its deadliest foe': Themes of countersubversion in anti-narcotic campaigns, 1920–1940. *Social History, 34,* 591–610.

Spielberg v. Napolis (2002). Petition for Injunction Prohibiting Harassment. Retrieved from the World Wide Web at <http://mindcontrolforums.com/napolis.htm>.

Stackpole, M. (1989). The truth about role-playing games. In S. Carlson and G. O'Sullivan (eds.), *Satanism in America* (pp. 231–283). El Cerrito, CA: Gaia Press.

State v. Ballard (1993). 855 S.W. 2d 557; 1993 Tenn.

State v. Fuster Escalona (1985). Case No. 84-10728 in the Circuit Court of the Judicial Circuit, Dade County, Florida, Criminal Division.

State v. Gallup (1991). 108 Ore. App. 508; 816 P.2d 6691 Ore. App.

State v. Kelly (1991–1992). 116 N.C. App. 1; 446 S.E. 2d 838.

State v. Michaels (1993). 625 A.2d 489, 513 (N.J. Super, 1993)

State v. Michaels (1994). 642 A 2d 1372; 1994 N.J. LEXIS 504.

State v. Wilson (1995). Superior Criminal Court, Perquimans County, North Carolina, #92-CRS-4296-4306; 92-CRS-4309-4312.

Statement of Iliana Flores Regarding Florida v. Fuster. (1994, October 15). Case number 84-10728.

Stevens, P. (1992). Universal cultural elements in the satanic demonology. *Journal of Psychology and Theology, 20,* 240–244.

Stickle, E.G. (1993). *Archaeological investigations of the McMartin Preschool site, Manhattan Beach, California: Executive summary.* Retrieved from the World Wide Web at <http://www.tesserae.org/tess/prose/tunnels2.html>.

Stone, D.A. (1993). Clinical authority in the construction of citizenship. In H. Ingram and S. Smith (eds.), *Public policy for democracy* (pp. 45–66). Washington, DC: Brookings Institute.

Stratford, L. (1988). *Satan's underground.* Eugene, OR: Harvest House.

_____. (1993). *Stripped naked.* Gretna, LA: Pelican.

Sturken, M. (1998). The remembering of forgetting: Recovered memory and the question of experience. *Social Text, 16,* 103–125.

Summit, R.C. (1992). Abuse of the child sexual abuse accommodation syndrome. *Journal of Child Sexual Abuse, 1,* 153–159.

_____. (1983). The child sexual abuse accommodation syndrome. *Child Abuse & Neglect: The International Journal, 7,* 177–193.

_____. (1994a). The dark tunnels of McMartin. *Journal of Psychohistory, 21,* 397–416.

_____. (1987). Recognition of cult phenomena in MPD. Paper presented to the 4th International Conference on Multiple Personality/Dissociative States. Alexandria, VA: Audio Transcript Vlb-383.

_____. (1994b). Ritual abuse: Disclosure in the 80s, backlash in the 90s. Speech to the 2nd Annual National Believe the Children's Conference. Chicago, IL.

_____. (1990). Satanic ritual abuse. In Office of Criminal Justice Planning (ed.), *Occult crime: A law enforcement primer* (pp. 39–41). Sacramento, CA: Office of Criminal Justice Planning.

_____. (1985). Too terrible to hear: Barriers to perception of child sexual abuse. Testimony before the U.S. Attorney General's Commission on Pornography. Miami, FL.

_____. (1989). Untitled lecture. 2nd Annual Conference on Multiple Personality and Dissociation. Costa Mesa, CA.

Taylor, J. (1986, September 14). The many trials of Gerald Amirault. *Boston Globe,* pp. A13, A16.

Teacher convicted in preschool abuse case (1985, April 3). *United Press International Newswire*

Testing at hospital found child abuse, father testifies in Little Rascals trial (1991, October 29). *Greensboro News and Record,* p. B2.

Thompson, E. (1991, December 7). Day care case costs $1 million. *Charlotte Observer,* p. 6.

_____. (1994, June 17). Privott pleads no contest in Little Rascals case. *Virginian Pilot,* p. 1.

_____. (1993, July 18). TV updates Little Rascals saga. *Charlotte Observer,* p. 2-C.

Thompson, K. (1998). *Moral panics.* London: Routledge.

Thomson, D. (2002, March 22). The people who believe that satanists might eat your baby. *Daily Telegraph,* p. 5.

Timnick, L. (1989, July 29). Angry Buckey is grilled on his behavior. *Los Angeles Times,* p. B-3.

_____. (1990, June 26). Buckey takes the stand, denies abusing children. *Los Angeles Times,* p. B-1.

_____. (1987, January 24). "Lost" McMartin tape surfaces, court thrown into pandemonium. *Los Angeles Times,* p. I–30.

_____. (1989, May 17). Never molested child, say Peggy McMartin Buckey. *Los Angeles Times,* pp. I–1, I–22.

_____. (1990, July 29). Trial may be over—but McMartin will never end. *Los Angeles Times,* p. A-1.

_____. (1987, January 21). Withheld facts in McMartin case—Ex-prosecutor. *Los Angeles Times,* pp. II–1, II–6.

_____, McGraw, C. (1990, January 19). Initial hysteria provoked positive changes in day care. *Los Angeles Times,* p. A-18.

Travener, J. (2000). Media, morality and madness: The case against sleaze t.v. *Critical Studies in Media Communication, 17,* 63–85.

Travesty of justice (1999, September 13). *Massachusetts Lawyer Weekly,* p. 1.

TV show on day care abuse draws letters blasting state (1993, August 22). *Charlotte Observer,* p. 8-C.

Umphrey, M.M. (1999). The dialogics of legal meaning: spectacular trials, the unwritten law, and narratives of criminal responsibility. *Law and Society Review, 33,* 393–423.

U.S. Department of Justice (1986). *Attorney General's commission on pornography: Final Report.* Washington, D.C.: Author.

U.S. House of Representatives (1984). *Joint hearing before the subcommittee on oversight of the Committee on Children, Youth and Families.* Washington, DC: Author.

Utah State Task Force on Ritual Abuse (1992). *Final report.* Salt Lake City, UT: Author.

Valente, S.M. (1992). The challenge of ritualistic child abuse. *Journal of Child and Adolescent Psychiatric and Mental Health Nursing, 5,* 37–46.

Van de Kamp, J. (1986). *Report of the Attorney General on the Kern County child abuse investigations.* Sacramento, CA: Office of the Attorney General.

van der Kolk, B.A., A.C. McFarlane, and L. Weisarth (1996). *Traumatic stress: The effects of overwhelming experience on mind, body and society.* NY: Guilford Press.

Van Montfoort, A. (1993). The protection of children in the Netherlands. In H. Ferguson, R. Gilligan, and R. Torode (eds.). *Surviving childhood adversity* (pp. 53–67). Dublin, Ireland: Social Studies Press.

Van Natta, D. (1991, March 26). Doctor doubts medical proof in sexual abuse case. *Miami Herald,* p. 1.

Victor, J.S. (1991). The dynamics of rumor-panics about satanic cults. In J.T. Richardson, J. Best, and D.G. Bromley, *The satanism scare* (pp. 221–236). Hawthorne, NY: Aldine de Gruyter.

_____. (1993). *Satanic panic: The creation of a contemporary legend.* Chicago, IL: Open Court.

Viglucci, A., and C. Evans (1990, March 4). Regular kid accused of unthinkable. *Miami Herald,* p. 1B.

Voboril, M. (1986, December 29). Country Walk revisited. *Miami Herald,* p. 1C.

VOICES in Action (1991). *Ritualized abuse, battered women and child sexual abuse: Fear or fact?* Chicago, IL: Author.

_____. (n.d.). Untitled handout. Chicago, IL: Author.

Wainwright, M. (1997, July 12). Police cleared of failures in child sex case. *Guardian,* p. 11.

Waite, L.J. (2000). The family as a social organization: Key issue for the 21st century. *Contemporary Sociology, 29,* 463–469.

Walker, A.G. (1999). *Handbook on questioning children: A linguistics perspective.* Chicago, IL: American Bar Association.

Ward, P. (1993, December 4). Charges dropped in child abuse case. *Austin American-Statesman,* p. 5A.

_____. (1992, November 18). Mother says girl revealed sex assault by couple. *Austin American-Statesman,* p. 1A.

Waterhouse, R. (1990, September 16). Satanic cults: How the hysteria swept Britain. *Independent,* p. 3.

Waterman, J. (1993). Impact on family relationships. In J Waterman, R.J. Kelly, M.K. Oliveri, and J. McCord (eds.), *Behind the playground walls* (pp. 169–189). NY: Guilford.

_____, and M.K. Oliveri (1993). Impact on therapists. In J Waterman, R.J. Kelly, M.K. Oliveri, and J. McCord (eds.), *Behind the playground walls* (pp. 190–202). NY: Guilford.

_____, R.J. Kelly, M.K. Oliveri, and J. McCord (1993). *Behind the playground walls.* NY: Guilford.

Waters, T. (1985, November 24). Girls' testimony blamed in mistrial. *Los Angeles Times,* pp. 2, 8.

_____, and L. Timnick (1985, March 23). Baby-sitting service under probe: Parents had been referred there by McMartin teachers. *Los Angeles Times,* p. 1.

Webber, D., and N. Hutchings (1986). *Computers and the Beast of the Revelation.* Shreveport, LA: Huntington House.

Weber, M. (1904/1958). *The Protestant Ethic and the spirit of capitalism.* NY: Scribners.

Webster, R. (1998). *The great children's home panic.* Oxford, England: Orwell Press.

Weinbach, R.W. (1987). Refeminization of day care: Causation, cost and cures. *Journal of Sociology and Social Welfare, 14,* 31–40.

Welcome to the Temple of Set (n.d.) Retrieved from the World Wide Web at <http://www.xeper.org>.

Werkgroep Ritueel Misbruik (1994). *Report of the ritual abuse workgroup.* The Hague:Netherlands: Ministerie van Justitie.

Wexler, R. (1990). *Wounded innocents: The real victims of the war against child abuse.* Buffalo, NY: Prometheus Books.

Wheeler v. United States, 159 U.S. 523 (1895).

Wheeler, B.R., S. Wood, and R.J. Hatch (1988). Assessment and intervention with adolescents involved in satanism. *Social Work, 33,* 547–550.

Whitebook, M., D. Phillips, and C. Bowes (1993). *National child care setting study revisited.* Oakland, CA: Child Care Employee Project.

Whittington, W.L., P.J. Rice, J.W. Biddle, and J.S. Knaff (1988). Incorrect identification of Neisserian gonorrhoeae from infants and children. *Pediatric Infectious Disease Journal, 7,* 3–10.

Wickenden, D. (1985, December 9). Good-bye day care: The insurance crisis hits pre-school. *New Republic,* p. 14.

Wilcox, C., M. DeBell, and L. Sigelman (1999). The second coming of the New Christian Right. *Social Science Quarterly, 80,* 181–192

Wilkomirski, B. (1995). *Fragments: Memories of a wartime childhood.* NY: Schocken.

Williams, B. (1988, May 12). Abuse cases ebb, leaving closed preschools behind. *Los Angeles Times,* p. 10.

_____. (1993). Bail bandits: The construction of moral panics. *Critical Social Policy, 13,* 104–112.

Wimberly, L. (1994). The perspective from Victims of Child Abuse Laws. In J.E.B. Myers (ed.), *The backlash: Child protection under fire* (pp. 47–59). Thousand Oaks, CA: Sage.

Winfrey, O. (Executive Producer). (1988, February 17). The Oprah Winfrey show. Transcript #W373: Satanic worship. Chicago, IL: WLS-TV.

Winic, L.W. (2000). The demise of child-rearing. *The Public Interest, 141,* 41–54.

Wood, J.R.T. (1996). *Royal Commission into the New South Wales Police Service.* Sydney, Australia: Royal Commissioner.

Woodling, B., and P. Kossoris (1981). Sexual misuse, rape, molestation and incest. *Pediatric Clinics of North America, 28,* 481–499.

Woodman, J. (1997). Psychologising Satan: Contemporary satanism, satanic-abuse allegations, and the secularisation of evil. *Scottish Journal of Religious Studies, 18,*129–145.

Wright, L. (1994). *Remembering Satan.* NY: Alfred A. Knopf.

Ynclan, N. (1984, September 16). Legislature may convene on child abuse. *Miami Herald,* p. 1B.

_____. (1984, September 12). Parents sue Fusters. *Miami Herald,* p. 2D.

Young, A. (1995). *The harmony of illusions: Inventing Post-Traumatic Stress Disorder.* Princeton, NJ: Princeton University Press.

Young, W.C. (1992). Recognition and treatment of survivors reporting ritual abuse. In D.K. Sakheim and S.E. Devine (eds.), *Out of darkness: Exploring satanism and ritual abuse* (pp. 249–278). NY: Lexington Books.

_____, R.G Sachs, B.G. Braun, and R.T. Watkins (1991). Patients reporting ritual abuse in childhood: Report of 37 cases. *Child Abuse & Neglect: The International Journal, 15,* 181–190.

Youngson, S.C. (1993). Ritual abuse: Consequences for professionals. *Child Abuse Review, 2,* 251–262.

Zaslow, M.J. (1991). Variation in child care quality and its implications for children. *Journal of Social Issues, 47*, 125–138.

Zatz, M.S. (1987). Chicano youth gangs and crime: The creation of a moral panic. *Contemporary Crises, 11*, 129–158.

Index